*The Three Estates
in Medieval
and Renaissance Literature*

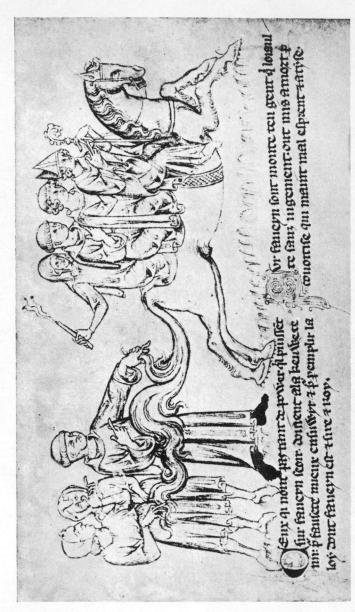

THE CURRYING OF FAUVEL

From *L'Histoire de Fauvain*

THE
THREE ESTATES
IN MEDIEVAL
AND RENAISSANCE
LITERATURE

RUTH MOHL

28107

FREDERICK UNGAR PUBLISHING CO.
NEW YORK

TO THE MEMORY OF

FRED MOHL

AND OF

ANNA PAULSON MOHL

PREFACE

E VERY age has its *états du monde,* its "estates" or classes of society; but no age, probably, has had more distinct class lines than the later Middle Ages and the Renaissance— the days of feudalism and its conflict with the growing power of monarchy. Nobility, clergy, and commons provided medieval French moralists and their imitators with ample subject matter as well as a precise literary form in which to lament the short-comings of those estates and to try to find adequate remedies. The present work, begun in 1924 at Columbia University, at the suggestion and under the direction of Professor Ayres, aims to set forth the distinguishing traits of that literary form, and the political theories and social changes that it reveals.

As a contribution to the study of French forms in England and of the persistence of medieval themes among those of the Ren-aissance, this volume should be of some service. The reader may logically question why so much attention has been devoted to English literature of estates in the sixteenth century and so little to that of France in the same period. Limits of time and space have made it necessary to leave certain aspects of the subject still untouched. Further evidence of the use of the form may still be found. The outlines are even now definite and distinct, however; and its history may be amplified without being considerably changed.

It gives me pleasure to record here my gratitude to those who have helped to bring this book to its present form. I am indebted to the Early English Text Society and the Carnegie Institution of Washington for their generous permission to reproduce the wood-cuts of Fortune's Wheel and the Dance of Death from Lydgate's *Fall of Princes.* To M. Paul Geuthner, of the Librairie Geuthner, Paris, I am also grateful for permission to use the illustration of Fauvel. Professor Lawrence and Professor Krapp have read my manuscript and made valuable suggestions for revision. To the staffs of Columbia University Library, the New York Public Library, and the John Pierpont Morgan Library I feel much indebted for their many courtesies during the years over which the research has extended. My great obligation to such critics and editors as C. V. Langlois, Paul Meyer, G. C. Macaulay, Thomas Wright, F. J. Furnivall, and others too numerous to mention, is evident throughout the book. I am grateful to all of them for the results of their earlier interest in this form.

To Professor Ayres my greatest debt is due. To him I owe more than I can ever express. It was only with his encouragement and farsighted counsel that I have been able to complete the work. For the innumerable benefits of his criticism and for the inspiration of his interest and confidence I am deeply grateful.

R. M.

Garden City, New York
March, 1933

CONTENTS

ILLUSTRATIONS

CHAPTER I

INTRODUCTION

MOST of the important literary patterns of the Middle Ages and early Renaissance have been carefully defined and described for us. We are familiar with such forms as the love allegory, the metrical romance, the pastoral, the fabliau, or the beast epic. A pattern no less characteristic, widely employed, and itself reflecting the very structure of medieval society, has hitherto escaped thorough treatment. One may search the card catalogues in vain for any reference to the Literature of the Estates of the World. The frequent occurrence of the word *estate* in Old French and in English before the seventeenth century has, to be sure, secured recognition for it in the dictionaries: the Century gives ten different meanings and the Oxford thirteen. But the part the *états du monde* play in literature, particularly in English literature, has received scant attention. It was at the suggestion of Professor Ayres that I undertook the collection and analysis of the material. I was working at the time on the different versions of the *Ship of Fools*, and I was at once struck with the extent to which Barclay had availed himself of the literature of estates in his additions to his Latin original. It appeared also in the changes made in the Latin and French versions of the German by Brant. As my investigations widened, much of the Anglo-Latin, the Anglo-Norman, the Middle English, and the sixteenth-century literature of England took on for me new meanings and a fuller significance.

The literature of estates has naturally received most extended treatment in France, where it originated. C. V. Langlois in *La Vie en France au moyen âge* (Paris, 1908, and new edition, 1925) discusses the work of several medieval French moralists, most of whom introduce the *états du monde* as a matter of course. His analysis of each is so full as to give a very clear idea of the *genre* in France in the Middle Ages. Paul Meyer, in his article in *Romania,* IV:385 (1875), indicates further use of the type in shorter pieces, especially one Anglo-Norman poem of the first half of the thirteenth century. Some medieval and modern instances are cited by H. Gaidoz in *Melusine,* VI:49, 97 (1892-93), and VII:147, 190, 222 (1894-95). But French treatment for the most part concerns French literature of estates and says little or nothing about adaptations in other countries. Studies like Lenient's *La Satire en France au moyen âge* are naturally concerned with formal satire and not with the literature of estates alone.

In German there are dissertations on estates in French literature, like that of Paul Grabein, *Die altfranzösischen Gedichte über die verschiedenen Stände der Gesellschaft* (Halle, n.d.-ca. 1894), or that of Fritz Meyer, *Die Stände, ihr Leben und Treiben, dargestellt nach den altfranzösischen Artus- und Abenteuerromanen* (Marburg, 1888), or G. Feger's *Rutebeuf's Kritik an den Zuständen seiner Zeit* (Freiburg, 1920). Gröber's *Grundriss* and Paul's *Grundriss* list the German, French, Italian, English works relating to classes of society, along with the numerous other didactic pieces of the time. Professor Ewald Flügel, in *Anglia,* XXIV:437 (1901), compares Gower's *Mirour de l'omme* and Chaucer's Prologue to the *Canterbury Tales* to show that Chaucer, too, followed the fashion of estates literature. But there is no general treatment in German of the literature of estates.

In English, similarly, the subject has been touched upon, in some one or other of its phases, but with no attempt to treat the type as a whole. Professor H. S. V. Jones, in *Modern Philology,* XIII:45 (1915), finds the influence of the three-fold division of society in Chaucer's plan of the *Canterbury Tales.* Professor Tupper's monograph on *Types of Society in Medieval Literature* (New York, 1926) indicates certain pieces that treat of estates without aiming at exhaustive consideration of the type. R. M. Alden's *Rise of Formal Satire in England* (Philadelphia, 1899), and S. M. Tucker's *Verse-Satire in England before the Renaissance* (New York, 1908), analyze English class satire, but without discussion of the literature of the estates of the world. It is not surprising, perhaps, that no study of the type has been made in English, since its first forms in England are Anglo-Latin and Anglo-Norman, and since even Gower treats it at greatest length, not in English, but in Latin and French. However, the more or less voluminous contributions of Gower, Caxton, Lydgate, Lyndsay, Barclay, Starkey, Gascoigne, Hake, Breton, and Dekker, not to mention numerous others, make such a study both interesting and profitable.

It is the purpose of this study, therefore, to define the literature of the estates of the world, to indicate its scope and origins and development on the continent in the Middle Ages, and then to show how it was adopted in England and persisted there into the late sixteenth and early seventeenth centuries. Many well-known works contain estates material that goes unnoticed unless the reader's attention is called to it. It must not be thought, however, that the present study claims to be exhaustive, and occasional reflections of the theme in romances and in documents devoted to the discussion of one estate, rather than all three, are passed by. Nor can this study include the literature of political theory in the Middle Ages. Excellent analysis of medieval argument about the organization of society is to be found in Otto von Gierke's *Political Theories of the Middle Ages* and in W. A. Dunning's *Political Theories Ancient and Medieval*, and similar analysis of sixteenth-century political theory is provided in J. W. Allen's *A History of Political Thought in the Sixteenth Century* (London, 1928). If in the following pages the *genre* has been made somewhat more distinct and if the main facts in its development as a literary device have been in a measure determined, this study will have accomplished its purpose.

At the outset, it seemed desirable to omit such chronological, bibliographical material as is contained in chapters three, four, and five. However, as the work progressed, the necessity of including it became obvious. The reader who is not concerned with the texts in which this material is found may omit those chapters and still secure a fairly good idea of the chief traits of the form.

CHAPTER II

THE DEFINITION OF THE FORM

1. PROBLEMS INVOLVED IN ANALYSIS OF THE TYPE

THE attempt to analyze the literature of the estates of the world, like that of analyzing any similar literary phenomenon, quickly raises several insistent problems. The first concerns its nature and form. What was it? What form did it take? Was it literature in the more restricted sense of the term? Was it a form of *belles lettres* or was it rather a species of encyclopedic sermon with the sole purpose of improving the reader? Was it recognized in its own day as a distinct literary form or device? Did the writers who employed it do so consciously? Did they deliberately follow the rules of the game or only chance to write in a vein similar to that of numerous predecessors and contemporaries? The second problem is involved in the questions of origin and duration. Where did this phenomenon flourish? How did it originate and what led to its disappearance? Much of the evidence essential to any very satisfactory answers to these questions has so far been ignored or treated only incidentally. In the following chapters, as a kind of historical survey of the *genre,* I have compiled and summarized a long line of Latin, French, German, and English specimens, dating from the late twelfth to the early seventeenth centuries. They present fairly convincing evidence for certain definite conclusions about the form. Some of these conclusions may profitably be stated here, though the evidence follows later.

2. THE FIRST PROBLEM: ITS NATURE AND FORM

In the first place, after a careful examination of the works extant, there is no doubt that the medieval verse or prose catalogues of the classes of society and their "defections," that is, their shortcomings, which we shall call the Literature of the Estates of the World, were regarded in their own time as a distinct literary form. Written in the days when literature gave much attention to ordering, cataloguing, or classifying, a literature that would classify medieval humanity was felt to be both fitting and necessary. While "encyclopedias," "treasuries," "bibles," and "mirrors" catalogued the beasts and birds upon the earth, the fish in the waters under the earth, the hierarchies of angels in heaven above, the seven deadly sins, the Ten Commandments, the seven gifts of the Holy Spirit, the seven ages of the world, the four monarchies, plants, planets, stones, and anything else that submitted to classification, it was not likely that mankind would be omitted. In an age of feudalism, class distinctions and class consciousness were matters of first importance. There were clearly defined classes or "estates" to be catalogued. As a result, the literature of the estates reproduced feudal society, from over-lord to chief vassal and villein and serf, from pope and cardinal to archbishop, bishop, archdeacon, dean, parish priest, monk, and mendicant friar. It reproduced all their loves and hates, their fears and faiths, their nobility and pettiness, as well as the elusive but ever-present political philosophy and economic necessity that kept them in their appointed places, and the moral fervor that exhorted them to the performance of their class duties.

The chief evidence for regarding the literature of estates as a distinct literary form seems to me to lie in certain well-defined traits that persisted throughout the series of adaptations. Not every one of these reworkings has all the distinguishing traits, but all works have at least some of the traits, and not a few have all of them. The first, that of enumerating or cataloguing the estates of the world, has already been mentioned. The aim of the classification seems to have been completeness. No rank of which the writer has definite information must be omitted. Another distinguishing trait is its lament over the shortcomings of these various estates. Here is no doctrinaire generalizing about vices and virtues, but an outspoken account of specific faults.

Each estate fails in its duty to the rest. The writer's own experience is usually his source of information in his enumeration of the defections of the estates, and here he tries to show the breadth of his knowledge and observation by giving details not mentioned by his models. Along with the enumeration of the shortcomings of the estates goes a philosophy of the divine ordination of the three estates, of the dependence of the state upon all three, and of the necessity of remaining content each with his station lest the structure of the whole government be destroyed. This philosophy is also elaborated as the *genre* develops; its almost constant presence serves an an earmark of the form. The last outstanding characteristic of the type is its attempt to find remedies for the defections of the estates. Sometimes the remedy is a religious one: an appeal to each class to perform its God-appointed duty. Sometimes it is a bit of medieval politics: the reminder that the organization of society is based on love and that each class must love and serve the others. Sometimes the remedies have a more modern tone: resort to law or to some new form of government may be the only way to secure obedience on the part of all estates. Whatever the remedy suggested, most of the writers feel the need of finding a way out. Only the earlier ones lament without hope. These four distinguishing traits constitute the chief "rules of the *genre*," and few writers ignore any of them.

Further evidence for concluding that the literature of estates was very generally regarded in its own day as a definite literary form is found in the fact that it keeps its identity even when combined with other literary devices and adornments or when incorporated in other forms. The wheel of fortune, the dance of death, the currying of Fauvel, the game of chess, the devil's net, or the ship of fools served admirably as an introduction for the ensuing sermon on estates. Many other devices or adornments were similarly used, as will be pointed out in Chapter V. Sometimes, apparently, the introductory device proved so alluring as to invite development for its own sake, and the estates, when the writer finally reached them, became more like an appendage than the theme of primary consideration. But even then it is apparent that the writer is exercising his skill in an ingeniously varied approach to his real theme, and seeking to add to his own literary fame by a novel recommendation of familiar and important doctrine.

3. THE SECOND PROBLEM: ITS DURATION AND SCOPE

The second problem that meets the student of this literature of estates, as I have said, is that of its origin, scope, and duration. Was it a purely medieval or feudal fashion? Was it not rather a part of the very wide-spread tendency of all times and all peoples to enumerate their political ranks? Was it not simply a continuation of the Latin class satire of Horace, Juvenal, and Persius? Or was it not a result of the philosophy of classes of Plato and Aristotle? Perhaps, flourishing among the Franks, it was akin to the Anglo-Saxon and Scandinavian catalogues of classes? Some critics, in discussing the literature of estates, have pointed out parallels between it and other classifications. The natural assumption from these parallels seems to be that the literature of estates was not a new phenomenon but a continuation of a fashion in existence before the days of feudalism.

In the general sense that there is nothing new under the sun and that the stream of human thought and experience is continuous, the kinship between these older social registers and philosophies and the literature of estates may, of course, be demonstrated. As will be seen later, some of these older forms undoubtedly did influence the literature of estates once it was under way. But there are reasons, it seems to me, why the literature of estates may be said to originate in the Middle Ages and to be a distinctly medieval form, a literature of feudalism. The classes that it enumerates are feudal classes. To compare it with other classifications is to compare two distinct political régimes.

The three estates of feudalism are not those of Plato, Aristotle, Horace, Juvenal, Persius; and the strictly developed philosophy of estates is not that of Alfred or Ælfric, the *Rig-Veda* or the *Rígsþula*. In the second place, the literature of estates rises and falls with feudalism. Where feudalism made its way, and as long as feudalism survived, the literature reflecting the feudal organization of society flourished. Where feudalism did not penetrate, the literature, with its characteristic French name and the distinctive traits described above, did not go. With the decline of feudalism came the decline of the literature also, a decline protracted into the early seventeenth century.

4. Types Not Included

A survey of the literary treatments of the classification of society beyond the limits of feudal Europe and its tradition would take us far afield and would merely confirm the opinion that the characteristics of the literature of estates are nowhere else fully reproduced. While the theme of the classification of society is widespread, the three-fold division, the insistence upon the shortcomings of each group, the obligation of maintaining the structure, and the need of amendment according to specific proposals, all of these traits remain peculiar to the literature of estates. A very brief examination of a few non-feudal classifications will suffice here to indicate the differences.

Plato's *Republic* finds four kinds of citizens essential to the state: husbandmen, builders, weavers, and shoemakers.[1] But since each worker should do one job only, several kinds of workers are necessary within those groups: carpenters, smiths, merchants, shopkeepers, hired laborers, sportsmen, artists, contractors, manufacturers of trinkets, nurses, tutors, hair-dressers, barbers, confectioners, cooks, swine-herds, physicians, state-guardians (soldiers). Though Plato's classification is different from the three-fold division of the Middle Ages, his philosophy of

[1] *Works,* ed. Henry Davis, London, 1861, II, 49.

classes is somewhat similar to that of the literature of estates. The different classes must work together, he says, for there can be no harmony in the state if one group fails. If one group fails, then "neither will the husbandman be really a husbandman, nor the potter a potter; nor will any one else be really of any of those professions of which the state is composed."[2] Harmonious working together produces happiness for all, to that degree which they are capable of enjoying. Certain things corrupt the various classes of the state, especially riches and poverty. If a member of one class shows himself superior, he should be promoted to the class of guardian; if a guardian proves unworthy of his class, he should be dismissed to another class. Justice results when everyone attends to his own business. Injustice results from undeserved promotion or from one person's doing many things, not the work of his own class. Such lack of attention to one's own business means the destruction of the state. The influence of Plato's philosophy of classes on the literature of estates is evident and will be noted later.

The classes of Aristotle in his *Politics* are also distinctly not those of the literature of estates. His philosophy, however, is like that of his master, with some few additions.[3]

For a state is not a mere aggregate of persons [he says], but a union of them sufficing for the purposes of life; and if any of these things (the indispensables) be wanting, it is as we maintain impossible that the community can be absolutely self-sufficing. A state then should be framed with a view to the fulfilment of these functions. There must be husbandmen to procure food, and artisans, and a warlike and a wealthy class, and priests, and judges to decide what is necessary and expedient.

The good of the state (the end of all Aristotle's political philosophy) demands that certain individuals should be assigned to these classes. The affairs of state should be in the hands of the "citizens," who must not lead the life of mechanics or trades-

---

[2] *Ibid.*, p. 103.

[3] *Politica*, ed. Benjamin Jowett, Oxford, 1921, Book VII, Secs. 8 and 9.

men, "for such a life is ignoble and inimical to virtue. Neither must they be husbandmen, since leisure is necessary both for the development of virtue and the performance of political duties." The citizens, then, must form the classes of warriors, councillors, and priests. To the duties of priesthood, the old men among the warriors and councillors should be assigned. The husbandmen "will of necessity be slaves or barbarian Perioeci. ... It is no new or recent discovery of political philosophers that the state ought to be divided into classes," he adds, "and that the warriors should be separated from the husbandmen. The system has continued in Egypt and in Crete to this day." Aristotle approves of slavery, as do Greek political theorists generally, and he gives as his reason that some people are of servile disposition by nature. The state, then, for Aristotle, is composed of warriors, councillors, and priests—the citizens, the oligarchy. But this state must rest on the husbandmen, craftsmen, and laborers of all kinds. Even in his own day, of course, Athens was more democratic than Aristotle's philosophy of government, and he was already considerably behind the times. What the writers of the Middle Ages did to reconcile the government they then found themselves subject to with what they read in Aristotle will be treated later.

Even more remote from the feudal treatment of the theme and certainly less likely to have exerted any influence upon it are the lamentations over the vices of society, particularly avarice, in the *Rig-Veda*,[4] though here, as in the Scandinavian *Rígsþula*,[5] there is a three-fold division drawn of nobles and priests, freemen, and servile laborers. Still further afield, the

[4] Ed. Max Müller, *The Hymns of the Rig-Veda*, 2 vols., London, 1877. Trans. by Ralph T. H. Griffith, 2d ed., 2 vols., Benares, 1897. See especially trans. Book IX, Hymn 113, II, 380, and Book X, Hymn 90, II, 519. See p. 263 below, note 5.

[5] Ed. Karl Hildebrand and Hugo Gering, *Die Lieder der Älteren Edda*, Paderborn, 1904, pp. 166-78. Trans. by Henry Adams Bellows, *Edda Sœmundar*, New York, 1923, pp. 203-16.

Popol Vuh,[6] epic of the Mexican Indians, classifies the members of those early tribes as priest-rulers, warriors, freemen, tributaries, and slaves in a manner not at all suggestive of feudal orders.

In the domain of Old English, King Alfred's version of Boethius[7] adds to the original an account of the kingly office supported by *gebedmen, fyrdmen,* and *weorcmen,* priests, warriors, and laborers; and the *Proverbs of Alfred*[8] (probably composed in the twelfth century) describe the duties of each of these classes. Ælfric, in a manuscript dating from the tenth century,[9] mentions the three classes with a brief exhortation to well-doing and the support of the throne. Ælfric Bata in a colloquy[10] reproduces the Platonic doctrine of sticking to the last. These references, however, are all to non-feudal classes and only serve to emphasize further the differences between this earlier literature and the literature of estates.

5. A Survey of Feudal Classes

It is unnecessary here to review the institution of feudalism in detail. It was such a hierarchy of classes of society as has never existed before or since. Each class had its duty to those above and below. In return for a benefice (the term used at first also for a fief), the vassal must do "homage," or become his lord's man, and swear fealty. He must render military service and attend feudal court and on certain occasions pay certain fees. The subvassal must, in turn, render his homage by tilling

[6] Ed. Étienne Charles L'Abbé Brasseur de Bourbourg, Paris, 1861, pp. cxxiv, 199 f., 341-42.

[7] Ed. W. J. Sedgefield, Oxford, 1899, pp. 40-41, ll. 12 f.

[8] Ed. Helen Pennock South, New York Univ. Press, 1931, pp. 105-6.

[9] See Thomas Wright's *The Political Songs of England from the Reign of John to that of Edward II,* Camden Society Collections, London, 1839, VI, notes, pp. 365 ff.

[10] In Benjamin Thorpe's *Analecta Anglo-Saxonica,* London, 1846, pp. 18-36.

the particular strip of land allotted to him, by yielding up to his lord the stipulated rentals in produce, and by presenting himself for military service when called. From the tenth century on, the Church likewise became more and more feudal. The parish priest carefully farmed his parish and usually sent so much of the revenues to those above him that he was poor himself. The bishop rendered up the tithes of his church; the archbishop, of his diocese; and in Rome were the college of cardinals and the great chancellory of secretaries constituting the papal *curia*, to take care of the vast financial and legal business of the greatest landholder in the medieval world.

This agricultural and military society was characterized by further complexities after the rise of the towns in the late eleventh and twelfth centuries. The towns were a disturbing element, since they swore no fealty in the feudal sense and produced none of the feudal revenues. They were independent units, composed often of ex-serfs but existing on a basis of equality with feudal lords and clergy. They were increasingly prosperous and consequently more and more to be reckoned with. To clergy and feudal lords alike they were a source of irritation. With the development of monarchy in the later Middle Ages, the monarch usually encouraged them, since they served as a check on powerful over-lords on whose lands they were. The industrial town produced new classes: the merchants, the professions, and the artisans. At times the number of trades and crafts and professions seems countless. Into the three-fold division of society, these new classes made their way, and their entry is duly recorded in the literature of estates.

Originally, of course, no feudal over-lord sought the legislative assistance of his vassals. He was supreme law-maker and executor. To be sure, the feudal court and ecclesiastical court represented judicial power, and over ecclesiastical matters the ecclesiastical court was supreme. But each acted independently, and later there was the citizen class to be reckoned with. As early as the eleventh century, 1004 to be exact, according to one authority,[11] the different classes or "estates" were called together as a representative assembly in the provinces in France, Normandy, Artois, Vermandois, Burgundy, and others. In 1265 in England Earl Simon, because of financial necessity, issued a summons to burgesses and knights of the shire as well as to nobles and clergy. In 1295 Edward I was forced to repeat the summons, and so the Great Council of the Barons became a representative Parliament of the Realm. In 1302, in France, the first general representative assembly of the estates of the whole realm was called by Philip the Fair.[12] In the midst of his famous conflict with Boniface VIII over papal authority, the support of all the estates was imperative. In 1308, in Philip's war against the Knights Templars, and in 1314, to secure funds for war in Flanders, he summoned them again: chief lay vassals, chief clergy, representatives of cathedral chapters and monasteries, and representatives of the towns. The assembly divided into three estates: clergy, nobility, townsmen. They could submit grievances, but the session was short, lasting but a day, and there was no general debate. In no sense did the Estates General have the power of the English Parliament. They seldom agreed on a united program, and the king was not obliged to summon them. In the later reigns in the fourteenth century they showed some signs of independence of the Crown, but were never so effective as the English Lords and Commons. This early recognition of the necessity of representative government meant the crystallization of feudal classes into political machinery in most European countries for some time to come. The Estates General in France were summoned in cases of emergency until as late as 1789. The last began the revolution of that year. In the still

[11] Alphonse Callery, *Histoire de l'origine des pouvoirs et des attributions des États Généraux et Provinciaux depuis la féodalité jusqu'aux états de 1355,* Brussels, 1881.

[12] Georges Picot, *Histoire des États Généraux,* 2d ed., Paris, 1888, I, 20 ff.

existing Houses of Lords and Commons in England, feudal customs survive. With this crystallization into political machinery, the supremacy of the feudal myth was complete.

6. THE MEANING OF THE TERM "ESTATES OF THE WORLD"

The name *estates* for the feudal classes is also, of course, of medieval French origin. Coming down from the days when there were no France and no French language, it has all the flavor of the Latin still about it. With its prothetic *a* or *e* or *ae* prefixed to the Latin *status*, it is thinly disguised. The meaning of the Latin *status* and Old French *estat* or *astat* or *aestat* and Spanish *estado* and Italian *stato* and Middle English *estat* is at first identical, that of state or condition of being. But state or condition in medieval Europe must necessarily suggest feudal state of being. And so the term was applied to the classes of feudal society. Then it took on new significance, quite different from the simple meaning of its Latin original. It came to mean rank in society and all that went to make up that rank—one's property, style of living, form of land tenure. A person of high estate held his land as a lord or vassal of a lord, or, if of the clergy, he was canon, bishop, archbishop, cardinal, or pope. If of low estate, he was the lord's villein or serf, or, among the clergy, mendicant friar or poor parish priest. Later he might also be a townsman, a man of craft or trade or profession. In time the term *estate* came to be applied to the person of property, as well as to his rank before the law—in much the same way that *chivalry* meant either the system or the men in it, or as *clergy* meant learning and men of learning.[13] Lydgate, for example,

[13] *The New English Dictionary* does not include this meaning of *estate;* *The Century Dictionary and Cyclopedia* does. As Fr. Aurelius Pompen says in *The English Versions of the "Ship of Fools"* (London, 1925), p. 47 note, *"Estate* or *state* is used by Barclay time and again to denote a person of high rank, a noble. This seems a somewhat peculiar use of the word, for it has been overlooked by the *NED*. *The Century Dictionary and Cyclopedia* (*s.v.*, sub. 10) mentions it with an anonymous quotation from *Notes*

speaks of Holofernes and "al his host and al his chevalrie,"[14] of "Hanybal with al his chevalrie,"[15] and of the "carte & plowh, they ber up al the clergye & the chevalrye,"[16] in much the same way that any writer of the literature of estates would speak of men of rank as "estates." Similarly Caxton in his version of the *Mirrour of the World* praises the philosophers of olden times as unlike the people of his day, "ffor they were prudent alle and valyant, seen that they set to fore all other thynges clergye. . ." whereas "clergye goth now al to nought,"[17] and then shortly afterward he speaks of the necessary three estates of a commonwealth as "clergye, chevalrye and labourers."[18] "Herod on his birthday made a supper to his lords, high captains, and chief estates of Galilee," so read the early English version of Mark 6:21. Later, when people no longer thought in terms of estates, the word *estates* in that particular verse and others gave way to *men*. The same change in text occurred in the 1575 and 1578 editions of the *Mirrour for Magistrates*. A line reading "all states" in the four earlier editions was changed to read "all men" in the two later editions.[19] This derived meaning is common, however, in medieval and Renaissance literature, as will be seen in many of the works discussed in the following chapters. A typical medieval use of the word in this sense is Lydgate's "Lat estatis off ther berthe honurable, voide al raskail & wedde ther semblable"[20]; or Dunbar's "So many ane stait,

---

and Queries, one from Latimer, and one from the (unrevised) Authorized Version, Mark vi, 21." In *Modern Philology,* XXIII (Feb., 1926), 382, I have pointed out that this meaning was a common one in Barclay's day.

[14] *Fall of Princes,* ed. Dr. Henry Bergen, E.E.T.S., London, 1924, ext. ser., CXXII, Part II, 372.   [15] *Ibid.,* CXXII, Part II, 639.

[16] *The Pilgrimage of the Life of Man,* ed. F. J. Furnivall and Katharine Locock, E.E.T.S., London, 1905, LXXVII, 310.

[17] Ed. O. H. Prior, E.E.T.S., London, 1913, ext. ser., CX, 25-26.

[18] *Ibid.,* p. 30.   [19] Ed. Haslewood, London, 1815, II, 285, note 9.

[20] *Fall of Princes,* ed. Dr. Henry Bergen, E.E.T.S., London, 1924, ext. ser., CXXII, Part II, 372.

for the commoun weill sa quhein."[21] Typical sixteenth-century examples of this meaning are Alexander Barclay's praise of "pore man or estate" (a common phrase with Barclay) for keeping silence[22]; his condemnation of "any excellent or myghty man, outher lawyer or estate," who oppresses another[23]; his dislike for the life of a court poet, who, to earn a livelihood, must "make orisons before some great estate."[24] Similarly in the debate *Of Gentleness and Nobility,* now attributed to John Rastell,[25] the merchant uses the word *estates* to mean "men of rank" when he asks the knight the question:

> How can lords and estates have aught in store
> Except th' artificers do get it before?[26]

To Gascoigne and Dekker the word sometimes has the same meaning, as will be seen later. In the early seventeenth century the meaning still survives. It appears to be that of Shakespeare in Hamlet's remark to Horatio, as unknowing, they watched the funeral procession of Ophelia:

> This doth betoken
> The corse they follow did with desperate hand,
> Fordo its own life; 'twas of some estate.[27]

At any rate, Dr. Johnson, for his eighteenth-century readers, interpreted the word to mean "Some person of high rank,"[28] and not simply the rank itself. In the later seventeenth century the meaning survives in Milton's description of the fallen angels of *Paradise Lost* as "infernal States."[29] Feudal class conscious-

[21] *Poems,* ed. H. Bellyse Baildon, Cambridge, 1907, p. 280. See p. 139, note 78.

[22] *Ship of Fools,* ed. Jamieson, London, 1874, I, 110.

[23] *Ibid.,* I, 67.

[24] *Eclogues,* Spenser Society, Pubs., No. 39, p. 14.

[25] See A. W. Reed, *Early Tudor Drama,* London, 1926, pp. 106 f.

[26] Printed with *The Spider and the Fly,* ed. John S. Farmer, London, 1908, p. 435.

[27] *Hamlet,* Act V, Scene 1, l. 209.

[28] Furness ed., I, 399 note.

[29] *Poetical Works,* Oxford ed., London, 1925, p. 210, l. 387.

ness was still a constant force in the literature of the sixteenth and seventeenth centuries.

In medieval and Renaissance literature the word *estates* frequently has the meaning of political states, such as Troy, Rome, or Thebes.[30] Sometimes, too, it may signify eras in time, as in Geufroi de Paris' *Bible des sept états du monde*[31] of about 1243, where *états* refers to the eras of the Old Testament, the New Testament, Hell, Purgatory, Human Condition, Anti-Christ, and the End of the World. But these meanings have nothing to do with the literature of the feudal estates and so do not concern us here.

In modern times the old meaning of the word *status* survives in our word *state*, with its general meaning of condition and its political meaning of the commonwealth. Today the word *estate*, however, is rarely used except in a legal sense to mean property or in such reminiscent expressions as the Estates General or the Fourth Estate. Real property is still called *real estate*—recalling the land tenure of feudal days. "Land was once not regarded as property at all. People owned not the land, but an *estate* in the land; and these *estates* still continue to haunt, like ghosts, the language of real property law."[32]

Therefore, because the term *estates* is of medieval French origin, because the literature of estates mirrors a medieval feudal society, because it has well-marked literary traits, I have defined it as the literature of feudalism, a distinct and widely used literary form of the Middle Ages and Renaissance.

However, only by surveying its development from some of the earliest forms to its disappearance in other forms can one verify these conclusions and show the persistence and progress of the

[30] See p. 68 below.

[31] *Notices et extraits des manuscrits de la Bibliothèque Nationale et autres bibliothèques*, Paris, 1909, XXXIX, 255-322. Notice by Paul Meyer.

[32] Sir J. F. Stephen, *National Review*. Quoted in *Century Dictionary and Cyclopedia*.

form through the centuries. In the following chapters the Latin, French, German, and English specimens extant are compiled and summarized with some attention also to the author, when the author is known, to his estate, to the circumstances, political and otherwise, under which he wrote, and to some of the probable reasons why he wrote. The estate of the writer, of course, determines in large measure the nature of his arraignment of the classes, his philosophy, and his remedy. If he himself is of the nobility or the clergy or, as rarely happens in earlier literature of estates, of the commons, his own prejudices naturally color his views, political, social, economic, or religious. A member of the clergy is likely to treat the state and laity in general pretty harshly, until after the decline of papal power. After that, in the conciliar period, when talk of needed reform in the Church is in the air, he may be more critical of the Church than a member of the nobility or commons would be—and he may have first-hand knowledge, too, on which to base his criticism. Similarly a member of the nobility is likely, in early literature of estates, to treat clergy and commons with severity and to condone or gloss over the faults of his own class. Later, as we shall see, the writer of rank may be more severe with the faults of his own class than with those of any other. The lay writer of non-noble estate rails at both clergy and nobility, though, if a devout member of the Church, he may feel some scruples about attacking the representatives of God on earth. The "divinity" of the nobility seldom gets in his way. Sometimes the circumstances under which the writer decided to arraign his times and his reasons for writing can be only vaguely surmised, but often they are fairly obvious. After such a survey of the history of the *genre,* it will be possible, in the remaining chapters, to observe the development of its chief traits in individual works and finally to look briefly at its disappearance in other forms.

CHAPTER III

HISTORY OF THE FORM
CONTINENTAL VERSIONS

I F BY 1004 the estates of the world were so well defined as
to be called together as a representative assembly in several of the provinces of France, they were obviously distinct enough also for record in the catalogues of the literature
of estates. How soon after that date the first examples of the
genre were written and what they were like it is impossible to
say. Whether they grew out of general laments on the evils of
the time or out of laments on the defections of one estate, and
whether there were full-fledged laments on all three estates in
the eleventh century would be interesting to know. By 1170
both Latin and French laments on all three estates were being
written, and though they were not so numerous or so full in
their classifications as the later adaptations, they show that
by the late twelfth century the form was distinct and on its
way to a wider popularity. The Latin and French pieces soon
served as models for German adaptations and for other continental versions as well. By the latter half of the fourteenth
century, the fashion was at its height, in England as well as
on the continent, and its decline after that was as long and
gradual as the decline of feudalism itself.

The treatment of women in these catalogues of estates is significant for several reasons. A few writers include them in their
proper estates, with the men of those estates. That is, women of
the nobility are enumerated and berated along with the men
of that estate. Women who are "religious" are included in the
ranks of the clergy. The wives of physicians, lawyers, merchants,
and craftsmen are discussed with their husbands; and maid-
servants are ranked with the men-servants. The general practice, however, is to ignore the matter of estate so far as women

are concerned and to treat them all as women. Their estate seems not to matter so much as the fact that they are women, with duties and defections peculiar to themselves. They are included, by most writers, as the last group in the catalogue. The long diatribes concerning their pride, avarice, temper, or incontinence are very similar to those of medieval satire on women in general. Some writers say that they have no charges against women, but only praise. Some say that, though they berate bad women, they know some good women, whom they honor and esteem. The same apology is often made to good men, also. In one instance, as we shall see,[1] the faults of women form the major interest of the writer, and he expands the theme at such length that the rest of his catalogue of estates and their defections becomes an appendage to that of women's faults.

In the following summaries, for the sake of convenience and clearness, I have grouped the Latin, the French, the German, and the other continental specimens separately, though many of them run parallel in time. Since the earliest pieces were probably in Latin, we will look at them first.

1. LATIN ORIGINS

Among these earliest Latin pieces is the short poem called "De statibus mundi." Though its exact date and author are not certain, it has been attributed to both Gautier de Châtillon and Walter Mapes.[2] It enumerates the feudal classes and their vices, beginning with the clergy: "in illos quos operit pastoralis infula." Here the poet, whoever he was, has most to say about the vices of the clergy; it seems likely that he himself was of

[1] Pages 48-51.
[2] It is the first poem in W. Müldener's *Die Zehn Gedichte des Walther von Lille genannt von Châtillon*, Hanover, 1859. Müldener attributes it to Gautier. It had already appeared in Thomas Wright's *The Latin Poems Commonly Attributed to Walter Mapes*, Camden Society Collections, London, 1841, Volume XVI, and in E. du Méril's *Poésies populaires latines du moyen âge*, Paris, 1847.

that estate since he has first-hand knowledge of their defections. Of the sins of the other two estates he has less to say.
The charge that he makes against all three classes, however, is
one that persists throughout all the literature of estates: that
of avarice. In arraigning the clergy the poet seems to be con-
scious of the fact that he should name all the different ranks
within that estate, as if such enumeration were already an established form of procedure. Instead, however, he says that
there is really no use in going through all their separate orders,
since all of them are corrupt:

> Nam ab illis omnibus—quid irem per singula—
> defluxit in subditos vitiorum macula.

Moved by avarice, they buy and sell Christ nowadays, these
new Iscariots. They buy their benefices. Dean, bishop, archbishop, each desires promotion because of the greater revenues
in higher places. And where may an abbot or priest be found
who is worthy to serve Christ? He is a rare bird in the land.
Even the learned, the "artium doctores," now seek wealth, for
honor is in possessions. Many of the clergy delight also in lustful pleasures. They follow their desires under pretense of virtue. The other classes of society are corrupted by the clergy.
Old men, women, boys, and girls, all ages are full of avarice.
Even the poor love money and pleasure. So the world goes. The
priest is like the people: the blind lead the blind.

The classical inspiration of the author of this poem is not hard
to find. With several interspersed lines from Juvenal, three from
Ovid, and one each from Horace, Virgil, and Lucan, the poem
has a rather classical tone. For example, Juvenal's "Difficile est
saturam non scribere" forms a starting-point. In the course of
the lament Juvenal is also the authority of the poet in his assertion that the more the clergy have, the more they want: "Crescit
amor nummi quantum ipsa pecunia crescit." In another instance, when the poet wishes to name women as the most intolerable of all who have acquired wealth, he quotes Juvenal:

"Intolerabilius nihil est quam femina dives." In no instance, of course, does the poet name the source of his quotation. In spite of this classical coloring, however, the classes with whom the poet has to deal are distinctly medieval, and the poem serves as a good example of what the literature of estates was in its late twelfth-century form. Written at a time when the ranks of the clergy were becoming more and more powerful competitors of the temporal estates in wealth and influence, it lays down the lines which the *genre* was to follow.

In a thirteenth-century manuscript another Latin poem, of greater length, dating from about 1220, and its still longer German translation, dating from about 1276, were found. The *Sermones nulli parcentes*,[3] as the Latin form is called, apparently records the estates of the days of the newly crowned Hohenstaufen emperor Frederic II, when the conflict between empire and papacy was drawing to a head. The unknown author of the poem was perhaps a member of a newly organized preaching order which, feeling its independence of both pope and emperor, found much to criticize in both. The writer particularly warns the reader against pope and emperor, but, after a prologue of general lament on the evils of the times and the lack of correction by the clergy, and a recital of biblical examples of what men and women should be—Moses, Susanna, and so forth—he announces his intention of writing twenty-eight chapters on all the ranks of the three estates, "incipiens a papa usque ad ultimum clericum et ab imperatore usque ad ultimum rusticum, tam monialibus quam aliis mulieribus non oblitis." The women are not to be omitted. The rest of the poem fulfills the promise. The first chapter is addressed *Ad papam;* the next is *Ad cardinales;* the third, *Ad patriarchas* (the archbishops); and to each of the

[3] Ed. M. von Karajan, *Zeitschrift für deutsches Altherthum,* II (1842), 15-45. The Latin form has 1088 lines and the German has 1655. For discussion of authorship, see editor's comments, pp. 15 f. Du Méril, *op. cit.,* mentions the poem.

remaining ecclesiastical ranks a chapter is similarly devoted: *Ad episcopos, Ad praelatos generaliter, Ad monachos,* with additions reflecting the crusades, *Ad cruciferos, Ad conversos, Ad sarabyatas et girovagos, Ad sacerdotes saeculares.* The strict division of estates is broken here by a chapter of advice *Ad iurisperitos et phisicos,* one *Ad scolares,* one *Ad vagos,* and one *Ad moniales.* Then follows the advice to the military orders, beginning with emperor and kings and princes: *Ad imperatorem, Ad reges generaliter, Ad principes et comites, Ad milites, Ad nobiles, Ad scutiferos.* The last eight chapters are addressed to those of the third estate: *Ad cives, Ad mercatores, Item ad singulas res vendentes, Ad praecones et socios suos, Ad rusticos obedientes—* they must be patient and God-fearing and must pay their tenth —*Item ad rusticos qui sunt rebelles*—they are promised damnation and hell fire—*Item ad mulieres.* With a final pronouncement *De ipsis fratribus qui populo praedicant,* the poem closes. Each class is told its particular shortcomings, which will be discussed in a later chapter.[4]

Two other continental Latin poems of this type survive from the thirteenth century and are worthy of mention here as further evidence of its prevalence, even though they add little that is new about the defections of the classes. The one, for want of a title, is known simply as *Des diverses classes d'hommes.*[5] It is directed chiefly against churchmen, but finds all classes guilty of cupidity. Cupidity has ruled mankind ever since Adam fell. Even peasants, though of humble rank, are culpable because of their greed and arrogance:

> Quoniam inter se concupiscentiam
> et incredibilem habent jactantiam.

The soldiers are likewise arrogant. All the orders of the clergy are then enumerated and their cupidity described. The other

---

[4] See p. 347.
[5] Ed. Du Méril, *Poésies populaires latines du moyen âge,* p. 128. Republished by Du Méril in *Poésies inédites du moyen âge,* Paris, 1854, p. 313.

poem of estates also has no title but is usually known by its first line, *Viri fratres, servi Dei*.[6] Its tetrameter couplets swing along like Goliardic verse. The lament is that all classes have neglected the faith—all ranks of the clergy secular and monastic, all rulers, nobles, citizens, merchants, commons:

> Ubicunque fidem quaero,
> vel in plebe, vel in clero,
> vel in claustro, vel in foro;
> ubi fides sit ignoro;
> fides, nullibi apparet,
> totus mundus fide caret. . . .

The specific classes named are: "papa, cardinales, episcopi, praelati, canon regula, monachi et moniales, fratres mendicantes, Caesar, reges et marchio, dux, comes, miles, baro, cives, nobiles, communes, nautae, coloni, mercatores." The poem closes with an exhortation to all to return to Christ.

Meanwhile "the encroachments of ecclesiastical and civil tyranny" in England were also being set forth in the literature of estates. Several men, apparently university men, in the reigns of Henry II, Henry III, and Edward III protested in Latin verse against the abuses of the times. Such poems as "De diversis ordinibus hominum,"[7] "De nummo,"[8] *Contra avaros*[9] lament the abuses, enumerate the classes of society, and charge all classes with avarice. Of the three poems, the *Contra avaros* is the longest and gives the most information about the times. Rome, it in-

---

[6] *Ibid.*, pp. 136-44. It was printed in 1553 by Naogeorgus (Kirchmeyer) in *Sylva carminum in nostri temporis corruptelas* and also in part in Wolf's *Lectiones memorabiles* in 1600 and in 1671. Wolf dated this poem 1481 without giving any reason. See Du Méril, p. 136, note 3.

[7] Ed. Thos. Wright, *Latin Poems Commonly Attributed to Walter Mapes*, p. 229.

[8] *Ibid.*, p. 226. For other references to Sir Nummus see pp. 108, 145, 200, 201, 202, 257, 342-43.

[9] Ed. Thos. Wright, *Political Songs of England from the Reign of John to that of Edward II*, pp. 27-36. Footnotes contain an English prose translation by the editor. Revised edition by Edmund Goldsmid, Edinburgh, 1884.

forms us, is full of avarice and ambition. Cardinals, patriarchs, judges and notaries of the Curia are moved only by bribes:

> Coram cardinalibus, coram patriarcha,
> libra libros, reos res, Marcum vincit marca,
> tantumque dat gratiae lex non parco parca,
> quantum quisque sua nummorum servat in arca.
> Si stateram judicum quaeris, quaeras aere . . .
> commissus notario munera suffunde.[10]

The archbishops have their heels upon the prone necks of the clergy and force them to tears so that gifts will be tendered to dry them:

> Calcant archipraesules colla cleri prona,
> et extorquent lacrimas ut emungant dona.

The bishop loves a cheerful giver and dares right or wrong after the smell of a bribe:

> Diligit episcopus hilarem datorem,
> fas et nefas ausus post muneris odorem.

The archdean is no less base, for whomever he has once seized on, whether in earnest or jest, he holds, and he is merciful to neither needy nor naked:

> Nec archidiacono minor turpitudo,
> quem semel arripuit serio vel ludo
> tenet, nec misertus est inopi vel nudo.

The dean, born to eternal treacheries, putting on strange speech and garb, goes to the obscure taverns to spy:

> Decanus insidias natus ad aeternas,
> ut exploret symbolum et res subalternas,
> mutans linguae modulum et vestes hesternas,
> migrat in obscuras humili sermone tabernas.

The priest gives himself, and all that the dead or living give him, to his concubine:

> Presbiter quae mortui quae dant vivi, quaeque
> refert ad focariam, cui dat sua seque.

Lay folk follow the example of these corrupt clergy. Spendthrift

[10] Page 31.

princes stir up realms and states that they may lead armies.
They inflict the punishment of a tax on rustic and on wretched
citizen:

> Regna movent principes statusque lascivi,
> ut ducant exercitus, poenam donativi
> infligentes rustico miseroque civi.

Courtiers slander and smile at the same time; they flatter and
meanwhile they plot loss or dishonor:

> Qui regni vel curiae curis accinguntur,
> dum arrident detrahunt, et dum blandiuntur.
> Jacturam vel dedecus semper moliuntur.

A citizen appeases you that he may consume you: if you pay
your tenth, he puts off paying his to the future; he cheats you
of what is your own; look to it while it lasts:

> Si te civis percipit, demollit ut urat,
> si dena contuleris mutuum futurat,
> te de tuo submovet, percipe, dum durat.

So ambition and love of riches betray all men.

A classical tone, like that in the "De statibus mundi," creeps
into certain lines of this poem—epigrammatic sayings from
Horace and Juvenal: "Crescit amor nummi quantum ipsa pecunia crescit" and "Quicquid delirant reges plectuntur Achivi."
But the rest is distinctly medieval in its careful adherence to the
scheme of thought of the literature of estates.

With the *Vox clamantis*[11] of John Gower, in the latter fourteenth century, the identity of the author is at last certain. No
one, apparently, found this *genre* more to his liking than Gower,
for he used it in all of his major works and in some of his shorter
poems as well. Having already catalogued the estates and their
defections in French in the *Mirour de l'omme,* he repeated himself in Latin in the *Vox clamantis* and repeated himself again in
English in the Prologue of the *Confessio amantis.*

Of the estate of John Gower not much is known; he was cer-

[11] *The Complete Works of John Gower,* ed. G. C. Macaulay, Oxford,
1899, Vol. IV.

tainly not a member of the clergy or of the nobility. It has been said that he was a lawyer, but his harsh treatment of lawyers, apparently based on knowledge gained as a litigant, seems to bar him from that group. His treatment of physicians is similarly severe. He is most generous in his treatment of merchants,[12] and it has been assumed, from all his information about them and his kindly statements concerning their value to society, that he was a merchant. He was apparently a dealer in wool, which he regards as the most important of all products. He became a landed proprietor. Though a business man, and so a member of the group that was the chief force in breaking up the feudal caste system, his sympathies were with the landed nobility: he refers to the high cost of labor in his *Mirour* and to the unreasonable demands of the laborers. In the *Vox clamantis* he is appalled at the conduct of the peasants in their revolt of 1381, and his hatred and fear of the laborer estate appear more strongly than in the *Mirour*.

No more complete classification of feudal society, either continental or English, can be found than in the *Vox clamantis*. All the estates from pope and emperor to mendicant friar and day laborer are characterized fully as failing in their divinely ordained duties. They are not so exactly ordered here, however, as in some literature of estates; the estate of kings stands last, because Gower wished to close with an address to Richard II, and the merchants, craftsmen, and laborers come before the advocates, sheriffs, bailiffs, and jurymen at assizes, because he wished to discuss the latter in connection with the king. Otherwise there are few changes, and no estate is omitted. After the poet's famous description of his vision, in a June dawn, of the invasion of London, or New Troy, by peasants turned into beasts, fowls, and insects by the curse of God, and after his assertion that God's decrees, not Fate or Fortune as men say, govern all things earthly, the enumeration of estates begins:

[12] *Ibid.,* Intro., pp. lxi ff.

Hic tractat qualiter status et ordo mundi in tribus consistit gradibus, sunt enim, ut dicit, Clerus, Milicies, et Agricultores, de quorum errore mundi infortunia nobis contingunt. Unde primo videndum est de errore cleri precipue in ordine prelatorum, qui potenciores aliis existunt; et primo dicet de prelatis illis qui Cristi scolam dogmatizant et eius contrarium operantur.

The poet finds the world divided into three estates and proposes to examine the conditions of all of them, beginning with the clergy:

> Sunt Clerus, Miles, Cultor, tres trina gerentes,
> set de prelatis scribere tendo prius.[13]

The clergy are everything that Christ was not: they seek riches, earthly honors, and temporal possessions, and they lead gluttonous, lustful lives. These shortcomings are discussed in detail and will be further considered later.[14] Equally unchristian are the defections of the religious orders. Monks, friars, nuns, all break their vows. They live in luxury instead of poverty; lust, instead of chastity; pride, anger, envy, instead of brotherly love.

The laity—knights, plowmen, merchants, and craftsmen—receive similar treatment. The order of knights was founded for three things: to defend the Church, to protect the commonweal, and to support the cause of widow and orphan:

> Ecclesie prima debet defendere iura,
> et commune bonum causa secunda fovet;
> tercia pupilli ius supportabit egeni,
> et causam vidue consolidabit ope.[15]

Instead they follow the wars for gold or glory, and fall into the snares of deceitful women. The plowmen were ordained, by divine ordinance to Adam, to cultivate the soil. Instead they are lazy and avaricious:

> Sunt etenim tardi, sunt rari, sunt et avari,
> ex minimo quod agunt premia plura petunt.[16]

---

[13] Book III, chap. I, p. 105, 1-2.   [14] See p. 353.
[15] Book V, chap. I, p. 201, ll. 5-8.
[16] Book V, chap. IX, p. 217, ll. 577-78.

Moreover, there are few of them nowadays. A peasant now asks more pay than two received formerly, and one used to do as much as three do now. If the peasant won't work, he must be forced to. The day laborers are no better: they, too, must be punished if they fail in their duties. In the cities the two chief classes, the merchants and the craftsmen, pay honor to Usury and Fraud, daughters of Avarice. The merchants devote scarcely one day to God and his Sabbath. Those who sell food, such as meat, fish, bread, beer, and so forth, and those who work in gold and precious stones, or in cloth and fur, all practice various deceits. Fraud is everywhere.

With the defections of the legal profession, the advocates, sheriffs, bailiffs, and jurymen at assizes, and finally those of the king, Gower concludes his catalogue of estates. The advocate and his fellows falsely bear the name of men of law. They are concerned only with their profits:

> Hii sine lege dei sub lege viri quasi fictum
> usurpant nomen legis habere suum.[17]

Their subtle tricks are described in some detail and will be discussed later. As for the king, every subject must serve him; therefore he must rule justly, through love, not fear. Let him remember that death levels all. Alas, the poet laments in closing, the good old times are gone! Temperance and chastity are no more. The laws of marriage are broken, and women are now devoid of modesty, chastity, patience. A last warning, "Postquam de singulis gradibus, per quos tam in spiritualibus quam in temporalibus error ubique diffunditur," includes an account of Nebugodonosor's dream of the statue representing all mankind (already introduced in the *Mirour de l'omme*), a description of the conflict of the vices and virtues, a long account of the appearance of Death and his dealings, and a kind of summary of the defections of all estates.

A short Latin poem "On the Vices of the Different Orders of

[17] Book VI, chap. I, p. 230, ll. 3-4.

Society,"[18] also by Gower, indicates the defections in a much briefer and more general way. The theme is: Alas, all is darkness. There is no light to be found. Rome is in darkness. Among kings there is no light. Likewise, one cannot find the "lucem bellatorum" or that of the law: "Si lex scrutetur, ibi lux non invenietur." The "lumina mercatorum" are out, and the "via vulgaris tenebris vitiatur amaris." Every estate is corrupt:

Omnis in orbe status modo stat quasi praevaricatus.

Though the treatment of the theme is brief, the enumeration of classes is that of all the literature of estates.

Mention should be made here of the fourteenth and fifteenth-century Latin works which were translated into various other languages, even the Scandinavian, and which thereby introduced the literature of estates into almost every European country of the Middle Ages. Written in a time of schism in the Church and of social unrest and civil war, they can still make use of the scheme of thought of the literature of estates to preach the duties of each estate and to extol the resultant harmony if all do their duties. Most significant and most popular was the famous chess book of Jacobus de Cessolis of the early fourteenth century. Jacobus or Jacques was a Dominican, "Maitre en Théologie" of that order at Rheims. In the popularity of the game of chess, he saw an opportunity to drive home the lessons needed by the different classes composing the commonwealth. The chessmen represented these classes. Sermons were preached on them and were much enjoyed. So Jacobus de Cessolis wrote down his sermons in his *Liber de moribus hominum et officiis nobilium ac popularium super ludo scachorum*. It was widely read and translated. French versions were made by Ferron, a Jacobin friar, in 1347, and by Jehan de Vignay, also a Jacobin friar, in 1350, which were in turn translated by Caxton into

[18] Thomas Wright, *Political Poems and Songs Relating to English History Composed during the Period from the Accession of Edward III to that of Richard II,* London, 1859, I, 356 f.

English. The estates in the chess book will be discussed in detail as they appear in the English version of Caxton,[19] with his characteristic amplifications.

Similarly, Caxton translated his *Mirrour of the World*, in 1480, from a French manuscript written at Bruges in 1464; and the Bruges scribe says in his preface that his *Image du monde* was translated from Latin in 1245. The original Latin work was a poem of 6,594 lines. A second Latin version, with 4,000 lines added, was made in 1247. The work is a kind of encyclopedia of information, divided into three parts, of which the first part discusses the estates of the world in philosophic vein, explaining the origin and necessity and duties of estates, not their shortcomings. Like the other translated works, it will be discussed later in its final form, the English.[20]

Lydgate's *Fall of Princes* also has a Latin prose original, Boccaccio's *De casibus virorum illustrium*, written between 1355 and 1360. This appeared in French in the two prose versions of Laurence de Premierfait, *Des cas des nobles hommes et femmes.* Lydgate's versified form was begun in 1431. It has frequent enumeration of the estates and much philosophy concerning them.[21]

The French moralist Matheolus about 1290 saw fit to write his *Lamenta* in Latin, into which he introduced a long digression on the estates of the world. This whole work was found by the fourteenth-century cleric Jehan le Fèvre with much delight, and turned into French about 1370. It will be considered in its French form later;[22] the Latin text is corrupt and in places unintelligible.

Another Latin work, of which an abridged French version was made by the original writer, Jacobus Magni or Jacques le Grand,

[19] See p. 123.
[20] See p. 126.
[21] See p. 116.
[22] See p 48.

is the *Sophilogium,* called *Le Livre de bonnes meurs* in its French form. This long prose work, which appeared about 1468,[23] is divided into three books, each containing several tractates. The first two books have little to say about the estates of the world: they expand at great length on the love of wisdom among the ancients, on the value of various studies in the trivium and quadrivium, on the beauties of the virtues and the ugliness of the vices. In the third book, however, as the writer turns to a consideration of the brevity of life and the prevailing contempt for death, he is reminded of the necessity of telling each estate what its faults and duties are. First the duties of the clergy are enumerated: "Quomodo viri ecclesiastici debent habere curam subditorum in moribus & sciencia"; then those of nobles and princes: "De clemencia nobilium & principum. De bonis principibus"; and finally those of the third estate: "De divitibus & eorum statu. De pauperibus & eorum statu. De mercatura. De servis & laboratoribus." The usual duties are assigned: clemency, generosity, plain dress, defense of Church to the nobles; chastity, alms-giving, poverty to the clergy; patience and submission to the commons. The vices are the reverse of these virtues. The text is very generously sprinkled, in late medieval fashion, with references to authorities, both biblical and classical.

Such well-known works as the *De regimine principum* of Thomas Aquinas, completed by Guido de la Colonna, and the *Secreta secretorum,* regarded in the Middle Ages as Aristotle's advice to his pupil, Alexander, are addressed chiefly to one estate and so need scarcely be mentioned here as literature of the three estates, though they contain some of its philosophy, later reproduced in Hoccleve's *Regiment of Princes* and in Lydgate's and Burgh's *Secrees of Old Philisoffres.*

The Latin literature of estates appeared also in Spain and in

---

[23] I have used the copy of the *Sophilogium* in the New York Public Library, printed by the R printer in Strassburg about 1468.

Italy. The *Libro de Alexandre*,[24] written about the middle of the thirteenth century, and the *Speculum vitae humanae* of the Bishop of Zamora, Rodriguez Sanchez d'Arevallo, first published in Rome in 1468,[25] describe the different estates and conditions of men, lament their shortcomings, and warn them of the necessity of preparation for death. Peter Damiani, Italian moralist of the eleventh century, discusses, also in Latin, the choice of an anti-pope, the evils of the age, and the corruptions of the various classes of society.[26]

Such Latin laments were no doubt common in the earlier Middle Ages, particularly in France. That those named above are only a few of all that were written is quite probable. The few will perhaps serve to indicate the Latin orgins and development of the *genre*.

2. FRENCH ORIGINS

Of the vernacular treatments of the theme, the French are the earliest and the most numerous. Though *Les Vers de la mort*,[27] written about 1194 and ascribed to the Cistercian monk Hélinant, is too limited in its references to the classes of society to serve as an example of the literature of estates, it does touch upon the subject in a way to give an idea of how this *genre* probably began. Its theme, that of the power of death over all mankind, is a common one in later literature of estates. Here the theme simply suggests to the poet that he name the different classes. But his classification is very limited and is wholly incidental to the theme of death. Each stanza is addressed to Death: "Morz." The poet's remark that Death takes the highest leads him first to Rome, then to Rheims, then to Beauvais, where

[24] Ed. Alfred Morel-Fatio for the Gesellschaft für Romanische Literatur, Dresden, 1906, Vol. X. Described by A. Morel-Fatio in *Romania*, IV, (1875), 7-90.

[25] A. Claudin, *Histoire de l'imprimerie en France,* Paris, 1900, I, 45.

[26] Gröber's *Grundriss,* II, 359.

[27] Ed. Fr. Wulff and Em. Walberg, *Société des anciens textes français,* *Pubs.,* Paris, 1905, No. LIII.

lives the bishop "cui je aim tant." It next leads him "as contes et as rois," and he names some; also, to "toz noz prelaz communement" and finally "nos, povres chiens":

> Morz, tu abaz a un seul tor
> Aussi le roi dedenz sa tor
> Com le povre dedenz son toit.

A later writer of the literature of estates would not be content to dismiss each class so quickly. He would lament their defections in detail and then remind them that Death waits for them, not far ahead.

A full-fledged specimen of the literature of estates is *Le Livre des manières* of Étienne de Fougères,[28] one of the brilliant circle of lettered clerics in the French court of Henry II of England. First chaplain, later bishop of Rennes, he distinguished himself by various writings. His earliest works were "gay things" in verse and prose, all lost. Then, before his approaching death, came a marvelous vision, in which an apparition whispered, "Desine ludere." He turned in penitence from writing for the applause of men to that of saints' lives and moral doctrine. The saints' lives, in Latin, are of little importance. His literary reputation rests solely on the vernacular *Le Livre des manières*, of about 1174, or soon after. Étienne died in 1178. Various theories have been expressed about the sources of the work: it may have had a Latin original, or Étienne may have used earlier French poems and the *Polycraticus* of John of Salisbury, the twelfth-century political theorist, man of letters, and pupil of Abelard. Étienne's *Le Livre des manières* exists in a single manuscript, which is very corrupt. In forceful monorhymed tetrameter quat-

[28] I have used the Columbia University Library manuscript copy of MS 295 in the Library of Angers (France). No date. Most of the didactic pieces described by C. V. Langlois in his *La Vie en France au moyen âge*, Vol. II, *D'après des moralistes du temps*, revised edition, Paris, 1925, classify society and indicate the failings of the various estates. The dates and biographical material given here concerning those pieces are from Langlois.

rains, it furnishes much precise information about the conditions of the times in the various classes of society.

Étienne's theme is that of Solomon: "All is vanity." The theme at once suggests enumeration of classes, and the poet proceeds to name them. He divides his work into two parts, each one subdivided in turn. The first part is headed: "Première partie, contenant les devoirs des rois, des clercs, des évêques, des archevêques, des cardinaux, des chevaliers." Part two is headed: "Seconde partie, contenant les devoirs des vilains, des citoyens et des bourgeois, des dames et des demoiselles, et enfin l'enpression du repentir de l'auteur au souvenir de sa vie passée, et une «oraison final» pour implorer la miséricorda de Dieu, et l'intercession de la Vierge et des saints en sa faveur." The whole plan of the work is evident in these superscriptions. The duties of each class and their failures to do their duties are discussed in some detail, as will be pointed out in later chapters. It is to be noted that the author does not use the word *estat,* but names the classes only. It is also noteworthy that his ecclesiastical classification begins with the archbishop, not the pope. Of the pope he says that he is the head of all, fountain of doctrine, rod of discipline, wine and oil of medicine, milk of piety, our salvation. He has the sceptre and the purple. Let all the Church pray that God will keep him in the right path. The cardinals, too, are briefly treated: they are judges of last resort. As such they are constantly exposed to the evil of taking the law into their own hands and of not judging themselves guilty. God preserve them! All the other ranks are berated without restraint. The chief charge against clergy and laity alike is that of loose living. They would all rather eat and drink and dance than do their duties to society. Étienne's detailed advice to women of all ranks is also characteristic, as was noted above,[29] of the literature of estates.

The Norman cleric who, about 1200, wrote *Le Roman des*

[29] See p. 20-21.

romans also apparently intended to lament the defections of all the different classes of society.[30] But he stopped short after having satirized the clergy. In his opening stanzas he announces his all-inclusive plan; but he never completed it. His plan is as follows:[31]

> A cest romanz est li mundes matire,
> Cum il fu ja e cum il or s'enpire,
> Par quels manieres nus le veons defire
> Tant en nature tant en faire e en dire.
>
> Des granz miseires dirai premerement
> Que nus veons communals entre gent,
> Puis traiterai de l'establissement
> Ke sainte iglise reçut premerement.
>
> Oïr porrez ou il est bien tenuz
> E ou il est muëz e corrumpuz,
> Cume l'em change pur vices les vertuz
> E leist les biens pur les maus escreüz.
>
> Qui tel matire velt par reison traitier
> Par les treis ordres li estot repairier,
> Ke chascuns oie selonc le soen mestier
> Ke est a faire e que est a leissier.

In the early thirteenth century, probably before 1209, Guiot de Provins wrote *La Bible Guiot* in similar form, but somewhat different vein. For Guiot, an Epicurean monk, wrote to make his readers laugh, apparently, and not to reform them. Having tried several monasteries—among them the Cistercian abbey of Clair-vaux and the monastery at Cluny—he knows much about all the orders. Of those that live well, he approves; those that live austerely, like the black monks of which he is a member, repel him. The Carthusians and the lay-brothers and sisters of Saint-Antoine he scorns, the former because they live alone and do not tend their sick, and the latter because they are mere drudges out of avarice. Recluses are fools, and so are those who live without

---

[30] Ed. Irville C. Lecompte, Elliott Monographs, Princeton, 1923. See Intro., p. xxvi.   [31] *Ibid.*, p. 2, stanzas 5-8.

proper food and clothing. The Benedictines are full of envy and hypocrisy. Guiot also openly boasts of his cowardice and unwillingness to fight as the Templars do. In his later years, he lived much at the courts of princes. He recalls having been present at the magnificent court of Frederick Barbarossa at Mainz in 1184. He mentions almost a hundred great lords who gave him gifts as court jongleur. Apparently to amuse these old friends, says Langlois, Guiot wrote his *Bible*. The whole poem has a jesting, bantering tone that contrasts strangely with the moral earnestness of most literature of estates.

His purpose he announces at once:[32] to write a "bible" in which all people may see their faults mirrored. After lamenting the loss of the good old times when kings were kings, and lords were lords, he proceeds to tell the duties and failings of the three estates. Like Étienne de Fougères, Guiot does not use the word *estate*. First, the princes. They could not be worse. They are corrupt by birth and no longer keep the fine courts of the princes of the past. As a result, their vassals, too, are base-born villeins. One would wish to be dead when one recalls the nobility of former princes and lords. Then, the "Romans," the ecclesiastical hierarchy: pope, cardinals, archbishops, legates, bishops, canons, abbés, black monks, white monks, monks of Chartreuse and Grandmont, regular canons who dress in black, monks of Prémontré, monks of the Temple, monks of the Hospital, converts of Saint-Antoine, nuns and their converts. Guiot closes his catalogue with briefer attention to three of the professions: divines (theologians), men of law, and physicians. As a monk, who later lived at court, he knows most about the monastic orders and nobility, and of them he has much to say. Of the third estate he knows little, apparently, or is little concerned. Guiot is less wary of criticism of the pope than is Étienne. But even Guiot says little in comparison with the out-

[32] *Les Œuvres de Guiot de Provins*, ed. by John Orr, Manchester, 1915, p. 10.

bursts of later moralists in the time of the decline of papal hegemony. A probable reason for this early reticence was the fact that monastic orders were directly under the pope, and that most of the popes dealt generously with them as a check on the power of the secular clergy.

Probably in imitation of and in reply to Guiot's *Bible*, Hugues de Berzé wrote *La Bible au Seigneur de Berzé* sometime between September, 1220, and January, 1224. The two were confused until the eighteenth century, and only recently has the identity of Hugues as a young Burgundian knight of Berzé-le-Châtel, a crusader and man of the world, been fairly certainly determined.[33] Life to him has been pleasant, and his verse reflects his ease and grace of manner. Still, he has seen much that is evil in his eventful life, and so he proposes to preach a sermon on the evils of the time and to exhort men of all classes to seek the good. He boasts of his wide experience, in the Orient and elsewhere. He is neither cleric nor scholar; he has written this sermon because he knows the world thoroughly. He knows more than priests or hermits. He has learned that life is worth little. Like most of these moralists, Hugues begins with praise of the good old times,[34] when people were jolly and sang, smiled, and tourneyed. In those times, people sought pleasure. Now they think only of deceiving and cheating their neighbors. Man's troubles began with Adam and Eve. Christ atoned for their sin, and when God thus rescued us from hell, he ordained three orders:

> Quant Diex nous ot d'enfer rescous,
> S'ordena trois Ordres de nous.
> La premiere fu, sanz mentir,
> De Provoire por Diex servir
> Es Chapeles et es Moustiers:

[33] See C. V. Langlois, *La Vie en France au moyen âge*, Paris, 1925, II, 88-92.

[34] *Fabliaux et contes des poètes françois des XI, XII, XIII, XIV et XVe siècles*, pub. by Barbazan-Meon, Paris, 1808, Vol. II, ll. 79 ff.

Et l'autre fu des Chevaliers
Por justicier les robéors:
L'autre fu des laboréors.[35]

Here Hugues briefly lists the orders (he does not call them estates), and asserts their divine origin and their duties. God commanded them to observe chastity, charity, faith, penitence, and confession. They have failed in all. The clergy, the knightly order (of which Hugues knows most), and the peasants are all at fault. Hugues is not concerned with the hierarchies of each estate. He is more concerned with their shortcomings and, as a result, gives some very interesting information about the times.

Guillaume, another Norman cleric, calls his sermon on estates *Le Besant de Dieu*,[36] in reference to the parable of the talents. All are born with some gift from God. Guillaume's is that of eloquence in poetry. He proposes to use it: he will not cease to preach contempt of the world. But his title has little to do with the plan of the work itself. Guillaume has no sense of plan or order in writing. His theme turns out to be the conflict of vice and virtue in the world, more than any other one idea. In several places he says he is Norman, but apparently he spent a great part of his time in England. He was a cleric, with wife and children to provide for. He knew Latin, for his works contain many quotations or paraphrases. He mentions particularly, along with the Scriptures, the *De miseria humanae condicionis* of Pope Innocent III, from which he borrows several passages. Before 1226 or 1227, the date of *Le Besant de Dieu*, he wrote a romance, *contes*, and fables, so he tells us. He lived by his writings, as did many of his fellow clerks, composing the works for wealthier patrons. Then, one Saturday evening in bed, he began to think of the vanity of his time, of the uncertainty of life, and of the family he must support by his works. Life is short, and, strangely enough, man does not bother to ask whence he came and where he goes. He misuses the gifts of God. Then

[35] *Ibid.*, ll. 179 ff.　　　　　　　[36] Ed. Ernst Martin, Halle, 1869.

he dies, usually repentant. Life, for most men, is a yielding to vice, in the conflict between vice and virtue. With a good deal of independence, probably born of foreign residence, Guillaume first tells clerics, from bishops down, their faults: simony and all the other forms of avarice possible to the clergy. Then he turns to the rich laity. The following lines indicate how simply, how prosaically, he passes from one estate to the next:

> Si vus dirrai des plus puissanz,
> Des plus riches e des plus granz,
> Des reis, des contes, e des dus,
> Qui des regnes ont le desus.[37]

These over-lords are tyrants to the poor under them; they are merciless and covetous. Let them think of the brevity of life. Then the plowmen. They are no longer so patient as they were, but loaf on the job and consume their earnings in tavern and brothel. These faults will be fully treated in a later chapter.[38] Guillaume, in conclusion, moralizes at length on abstract sins in the world, with only occasional reference to classes. Incidentally he mentions the pope, whom he omitted before, and marvels that the head of the Church allows such evils in the ship of the world. Of the pope, however, one shouldn't speak ill, any more than of heaven. But those about him prove disloyal to God in every land:

> Cardenals, legaz e provoz,
> Qui por loier serront des noz
> Se nus avon cause a treiter
> Devreit l'en blasmer e tencier
> Quant l'apostoire les enveie
> En Engleterre ou en Gaweie
> Ou en France on en Alemaigne
> Ou en Galice ou en Espagne
> Ou en autres loingtaines terres
> Por apeiser les mortels guerres
> Il m'est avis qu'il ne font mie
> Tut solonc dieu lor legacie.[39]

---

[37] *Ibid.*, p. 22, ll. 765 ff.   [38] See pp. 350-51.   [39] *Ibid.*, p. 67, ll. 2349 ff.

So Guillaume's catalogue is completed, but in no such orderly fashion as characterizes most literature of estates.

Bishop, monk, knight, cleric—each we have seen concerned with the faults of the various classes of society. In the *Roman de carité*[40] and *Roman de miserere*[40] of the Recluse of Molliens, we have the version of the hermit—the life so despised by the amiable Guiot. Widely admired for their verse form and literary qualities, these works also reflect the life of the times in the early thirteenth century, about 1226. The Recluse was no longer young when he wrote, but he was well versed in fable, proverb, fabliau, and romance, and was not unaware of literary style and value. In spite of his love of retirement, he was a seasoned observer of the defections of all estates, and he, too, apparently, wanted to follow the fashion of enumerating them.

The Recluse begins with a lament for the good old times, when faith and charity abounded. He has sought everywhere for charity, among lay folk and lettered, and cannot find it. He went first to Rome, to see if the pope and his court had it. All there were covetous, not charitable. All Rome must be "greased" to function. He searched in Tuscany, Apulia, Hungary, Greece, Constantinople; he sought it among Germans, Saxons, Italians, and English. It is in none of them, nor in Ireland, Scotland, Denmark, Friesland, Holland, Flanders, the Holy Land, Burgundy, or Champagne. He thought that perhaps he would find it in France, since *French* means *free*. He begins with the king. The king is of first estate and should therefore be first in doing good:

> Rois, toi truis ou premier estal;
> Trover te doi en bien premier.[41]

This is the first use I have found of the word *estal* or *estat*. The Recluse uses the word *estal* frequently, also its plural *estaus*. It is from the Old High German *stal*, meaning "position," how-

---

[40] Ed. A.-G. van Hammel, *Bibliothèque de l'école des hautes études*, Vol. LXI (Paris, 1885).   [41] *Ibid.*, p. 17, stanza xviii, ll. 3, 4.

ever, and is not directly from the Latin *status*. In the *Roman de miserere, estal* and *estat* appear in successive lines. Having told the king his duties, the poet proceeds to the lords. Evidently the *genre* becomes burdensome, for he says he cannot name each class as he should, but will counsel all together:

> Je ne puis pas nomer cascun;
> Mais je doins mon conseil commun
> A vous, conte, duc et princhier.[42]

The knights are also addressed, and then the parish priests, and each class is told its duties. The abbé and the bishop follow. Charity is unknown to them. Perhaps it is to be found in the "little people" (petites gens). The Recluse soon discovers their faults, too, however, and so he ends his poem.

In the *Roman de miserere* the title has little to do with the content except in a general way. Miserere mei, Deus! God have mercy on all mankind for their wickedness. The Recluse first discusses the sins of Pride and Envy and their daughter, Evil-speaking, which prevail among all mankind. Then he proceeds to his main theme, that of enumerating the five senses and determining how they are used. Only in his discussion of taste does he introduce the classes of society. St. Paul is his authority for the doctrine that man, to eat, must work. He lists the duties of each class—each should serve the other:

> Labours de clerc est Dieu priier
> Et justiche de chevalier;
> Pain lor truevent li laborier.
> Chil paist, chil prie et chil deffent.
> Au camp, a le vile, au moustier
> S'entraident de lor mestier
> Chil troi par bel ordenement.[43]

Clerics and knights, if they do their duties, find plenty to do. The merchant works hard and therefore may eat. The jongleur

---

[42] *Ibid.*, p. 21, stanza xxxix, ll. 1-3.

[43] *Bibliothèque de l'école des hautes études*, LXII (Paris, 1885), 218, stanza clvi, ll. 6-12.

has no right to eat bread, though people gladly open their doors to him and turn away the poor. Let the jongleur eat nuts like the hog. Alas! those who do nothing in this world eat most, and those who work have a hard time getting their daily bread. The whole piece has a more democratic tone than *Carité*. At least the Recluse has much to say of the vices of the rich. But there is no attempt to enumerate all the classes as in most literature of estates. After the enumeration of these few classes, the poet proceeds to a new series of exhortations to old and young to remember death. He finally closes with the long prayer of a repentant sinner to the Virgin.

Robert de Blois, poet of courtesy, introduces into his advice about manners references to the estates of the world; but his *L'Enseignement des princes*,[44] of about 1260, like the numerous other medieval and early Renaissance books of conduct for rulers, is addressed to a single estate. It has no clear-cut enumeration of the classes of society; it merely reflects the writer's attitude toward all of them. As a member of the knightly order, Robert discusses the pride of lords, the avarice of the clergy, and the arrogance of the upstart serf who would rise out of his class. He is plainly interested in the classes of society and their duties, but his purpose, as his title indicates, is not to follow the fashion of the literature of estates, but to advise one estate only, that of rulers.

Though the characteristic form of the literature of estates is also incidental in the work of Philippe de Novare, skilled lawyer and man of the world, the member of a Lombard noble family, he is unwilling to conclude without cataloguing the classes as he sees them. With much *savoir-vivre* he tells in *Les Quatres ages de l'homme*,[45] a prose work of about 1273, how infancy, youth, middle age, and old age should be lived, and

[44] *Sämmtliche Werke*, ed. Dr. Jacob Ulrich, Berlin, 1889-95, Vol. III.
[45] Ed. Marcel de Fréville, *Société des anciens textes français, Pubs.*, Paris, 1888.

then in a postscript he enumerates the estates. Being a man of wide experience and observation, he is not bound strictly by the classification of most writers of the literature of estates. In view of the services they render each other, he says, there are three kinds of people in the world: "L'une des .III. menieres, si sont toutes les franches gens amiables et debonaires; l'autre toutes les gens de mestier; la tierce tuit li vilain."[46] When he explains his classification, it is easily seen to be a kind of cross-section of the feudal caste system, based not on actual practice but on ideals of service. Free people are all who have a free heart, who "debonairement et amiablement font servise a cels qui ammiablement les requierent; et cil qui a franc cuer, de quelque part il soit venuz, il doit estre apelez franz et gentis; car, se il est de bas leu et de mauveis et il est bons, de tant doit il estre plus honorez." Among the people of profession, he gives chief place to priests and clerks, who have care of souls, and second place to judges, advocates, and all others in professions. All are villeins who act basely and render service to no one except by force or through fear: "Et vilain sont cil qui vilainnement se contiennent, et en dit et en fet ne ne vuelent riens faire que a force et par paor; tuit cil qui ce font sont droit vilain, ausis bien comme s'il fussent serf ou gaeigneur as riches homes. . . ." A nice philosophy, but scarcely prevalent in practice in Philippe's day.

In the latter part of the thirteenth century the enumeration of estates was introduced into several other long works where one would scarcely expect to find it. Beginning with a theme that seems to be quite remote from that of the literature of estates, these writers, before they conclude, list the various classes of society apparently as a matter of course. Such a work is *Le Breviari d'amor* of Matfre Ermengaud,[47] written in Provençal about 1288. The estates of the world are there introduced into a symbolic Tree of Love. The connection between

---

[46] *Ibid.*, p. 112, ¶ 211.   [47] Ed. Gabriel Azaïs, Paris, 1862, 2 vols.

them and his allegory grows pretty vague before he is through
with his diatribe, but since the whole work is a kind of encyclopedia, a translation of parts of all preceding *Summae* and
Speculae and *Tresors* and *Images* and *Miroirs,* especially the
Speculum morale of Vincent of Beauvais (1256), an analysis
of the conditions of the classes of society could scarcely be
omitted. In the Tree of Love, says *Le Breviari d'amor,* there are
two planes or circles. In the first circle are God, the source of
all love, and three different hierarchies of angels. Contempla-
tion of this circle inspires a discussion of the contemporary
Catholic doctrine of demons, set forth by Vincent of Beauvais
and Thomas Aquinas, of the nature of Heaven and Earth, the
medieval sciences of zoology, botany, geography, and so forth.
The second circle is that of Nature and Natural Law. Con-
templation of this circle leads to an explanation of the nature
of the love of God; of the forbidden love of idols, stars, and
sun; of the Day of Judgment; and finally of the various classes
of society and their vices, omitting, however, all the clergy.
The writer begins with emperors and princes and other great
lords. They are accustomed to sell justice to their vassals. They
ruin them with expenses. They grant their favors to counsellors, seneschals, provosts who make exactions from which the
lords profit. They rejoice in murders on their domains in the
hope of securing the property of the guilty. The lesser nobility
follow the example of their over-lords. Then the writer proceeds
to the vices of the commons. Advocates, doctors, the bourgeoisie,
merchants, counsellors and administrators, journeymen, laborers, farmers, innkeepers, gamesters, jugglers, and women are
all guilty of defections peculiar to their degree. Ermengaud's
earnest desire, apparently, is to reform society. After this satiric digression, he returns to his tree allegory and discusses at
great length other kinds of love.

    Les Échecs amoureux,[48] a still unprinted early French love-

    [48] See E.E.T.S., London, 1901, ext. ser., No. LXXXIX, chap. VI, pp.

romance of more than thirty thousand lines, is a story of a game of chess played for love. Strangely enough, even into such a poem the estates of the world enter. The way the poet works around to them is interesting to see. He is lying in bed half-awake in lovely spring-time when a lady, Nature, appears. She bids him get up. There are two roads to choose between: eastward to heavenly things and reason; westward to sensuality. Take the east road, the lady advises. The poet strays far from his path, however, into a fair field where Minerva, Juno, and Venus are. Minerva asks him to go with her, but he prefers to go with Venus. She takes him to the beautiful Garden of Pleasure. Here the story of the *Romance of the Rose* is told, and here he plays a game of chess with a young lady who has also come for pleasure and love. At first, the lover loses. Then his whole concern is how to win. Encouraged and advised by Amor, he plays again. Minerva appears to tell him, in an extended sermon, that it is unworthy of a man to waste his time in the service of Venus. She gives him thirty-five rules, from Ovid's *Remedia amoris,* for overcoming passion. Two roads, she says, are open to him: the contemplative life and the active life. The best place for the first is the University of Paris. The second way is to be found in four stations of life: that of the king, that of his councillors, that of judges, and that of the people. This array of classes is not, of course, the three-fold classification. The fourth class, moreover, is made to include clergy, nobles, artisans, craftsmen, merchants, and peasants. Though the enumeration is not exactly that of other literature of estates, the philosophy of estates and their duties is as follows: the princes and lords must govern well; councillors must advise without flattery and deceit; judges must judge

---

59 f., has a discussion, by Ernst Sieper, of *Les Échecs amoureux* as the source of Lydgate's *Reson and Sensuallyte.* A fuller analysis of the poem, with quotations, may be found in *Litterarhistorische Forschungen,* IX (Weimar, 1898), 1 f.

according to the spirit of the law, not the letter; people must lead virtuous lives; knights must oppose the enemies of the realm and fight for right against wrong; and clerics must be high-minded and not of serf origin. The poet's theme is that the lover can be healed only by participation in the duties of life, and so he goes on to discuss the nobility of marriage, the duties of parents, and so forth. This poem was in part translated by Lydgate in the fifteenth century. Since his translation does not go beyond the beginning of the chess game, however, it does not contain reference to the classes of society.

Even in the anti-feminist tract *Les Lamentations de Matheolus*,[49] written about 1290 by the "bigamous" cleric and advocate of Boulogne-sur-Mer, Matheus or Matheolus, the estates of the world find a place. Having deliberately married, not a virgin as prescribed by the Church, but a widow, Matheolus was declared a bigamist and was deprived of all his rights as a cleric. At home, too, he had little comfort, for Perrette, with time, had become ugly and quarrelsome. To console himself, he wrote his *Lamentations* and sent them about to friends and to dignitaries of the Church. Let them take heed and avoid his fate. Matheolus probably based his work on such medieval classics as Theophrastus' *De nuptiis,* Alain de Lille's *De planctu naturae,* and Jehan de Meun's *Roman,* but most of his material is original. As was stated above, his work is in Latin and was not translated until about 1370, by Jehan le Fèvre, procurer of Parliament of Paris. Having had experience similar to that of Matheolus, Jehan le Fèvre was delighted to find the poem. His French version (it may be called a new version, for he makes a few wrong interpretations and some suppressions and amplifications) is much clearer than the Latin. After telling the thousand ways a woman has to torture her husband, after enumerating all the evil natural traits of women in general, and after

---

[49] Ed. A.-G. van Hamel, *Bibliothèque de l'école des hautes études,* Paris, 1892, Vol. I, facsimile 95.

advising his readers to choose a thousand lovers instead of marriage and one wife, he suddenly launches into a long enumeration of the estates of the world and their faults.[50]

The estates are discussed in regular order. In his enumeration of their faults, Matheolus has little to add that is new, except for judges and advocates and citizens. He has evidently tasted more of the greed of those classes than is to his liking. First, the faults of the clergy are described, from the court at Rome to parish priest. Then the knights' duty of defending the land is dwelt on at length, to show what they fail to do. Judges and advocates and physicians serve only for money. The "bourgois" are interested only in buying and selling. Lastly, the peasants live like beasts and are envious and niggardly. All estates are at fault, Matheolus concludes (he uses the word *estat* frequently):

> Le monde voy trop desguisé.
> Quant j'ay tous estas advisé,
> Et le bon et le mal eür,
> Je n'y sçay nul estat seür,
> Qui tous les pourroit experir.[51]

After his catalogue of classes, Matheolus proceeds to an "envoy" to one of his clerical friends, in the course of which he catches himself wishing for the extinction of the order of clergy, who oppress the laity. He stops short to remind himself that the order of clergy is one of the three of which God has formed society and that the world would be lost without them. This Matheolus expresses as follows, untranslated by Jehan:

> Praeterea tres janque status nostri statuerunt
> philosophi veteres; nam clerum preposuerunt,
> ut reliquos regeret, documentis. Inde locatur

[50] Book IV, p. 276, ll. 283 ff. C. V. Langlois comments on the singularity of the insertion of this "side-dish," and says that it is no doubt an adaptation of one of the numerous "états du monde" pieces which circulated then as independent poems.

[51] Book IV, p. 289, ll. 691 ff.

armatus miles et rem publicam tueatur;
istis agricole subsunt alii laicique,
quorum nanque labor victum largitur utrique.[52]

An interesting use by Matheolus of the familiar medieval tale of Satan's marrying off his daughters to the various classes of society occurs in Book II.[53] The Latin text says:

Ut quidam recitat sapiens, fastus dominabus
nubsit, et ypocrisis monachis necnon monacabus,
fraus mercaturis, clero symonia, lupina
nostris usura burgensibus, ipsa rapina
militibus, sacrilegium cupidisque jugatur
agricolis. Sathane sic filia queque locatur.
Ipsa sibi nullum sponsum Venus appropiavit,
immo venalis cum sit, se cuique jugavit.

This passage Jehan le Fèvre amplifies as follows:

Sathan ses filles maria,
Au siecle les apparia.
Orgueil fu marié aux femmes,
Dont orguelleuses sont les dames.
Clergié espousa Simonie,
Par qui loyaulté est honnie.
Ipocrisie, avec ses signes,
Est aux moines et aux beguines
Et aux autres religieus,
Qui se faignent les precieus.
Rapine, qui est pillerie,
Prist a mari Chevalrie.
Sacrelege est aux ahanniers
Et aux faulx laboureurs laniers.
Fraude, que l'on dit tricherie,
Se maria à Mercerie;
Les marcheans l'ont espousée
Et sont mouilles de sa rousée.
Aux bourgois se coupla Usure.
L'autre fille, qui est Luxure,
N'est encor a nulluy donnée,

[52] Book IV, ll. 5071-76.
[53] Pages 113-14, Latin ll. 1674-82, French ll. 2453-78.

Mais a tous est abandonnée,
Sans garder loy de mariage.
Luxure quiert son avantage
Et s'en va de sça et de la,
Car cil qui plus en donne l'a.

This device occurs in other literature of estates, as will be noted later.[54]

There are also fourteenth-century works in which references to the classes of society are numerous but incidental or unexpected, just as in these thirteenth-century pieces. It will be unnecessary here to describe them in detail, but they should be mentioned as showing the persistence of the theme. *Le Livre de bonne vie appellee Mandevie*[55] of Jean Dupin, published in 1485, but written about 1340, consists of eight parts—seven in prose and the eighth in verse giving a summary of all the classes of society, who pass in review before the poet in a dream, led by the knight Mandevie. The *Doctrinal le Sauvage*,[56] Friar Lorens' *Le Mireour du monde*,[57] and DeGuileville's *Le Pélerinage de la vie humaine*[58] also reflect the class distinctions of the time and eventually digress into discussions of the estates of the world. The last will be treated later[59] in connection with Lydgate's translation. *Le Mireour du monde* enumerates all the seven deadly sins and their numerous branches, and indicates the classes most guilty. The *Doctrinal le Sauvage* tells the various classes what their duties are, to society and to God.

In the fourteenth century, in France, the thought pattern of the literature of estates persists with a few changes. It reflects,

---

[54] See pp. 87 and 268.

[55] Described by Louis Karl, *Société d'émulation du bourbonnais lettres, sciences et arts, Bulletin*, XX, Moulins, 1912, 118-19, 184-94, 209-16.

[56] Ed. Achille Jubinal, *Nouveau recueil de contes, dits, fabliaux*, Paris, 1842, II, 150.

[57] Ed. Félix Chavannes, Lausanne, 1845.

[58] Ed. J. J. Stürzinger, London, 1893.

[59] See pp. 114-16.

on the whole, the decline of the Church and Empire. The long conflict between them for first place, the slowly growing strength of monarchy, the Great Schism, the Babylonian Captivity made them less and less formidable as French "estates of the world." Some writers of this period seem to be writing with the express purpose of stemming the tide of disregard or contempt for pope and emperor. Some, on the other hand, very plainly have no concern for any authority beyond that of king. The classification of each writer is usually significant of his attitude toward the new authority. In spite of changing politics, however, the form is still distinct. A few new literary devices appear, but through the new framework the deliberate conformity of the writer to the old scheme of thought is quite evident.

One of the most interesting specimens of the literature of estates of the fourteenth century is *Le Roman de Fauvel*[60] by Gervais du Bus. Not only is it one of the most interesting pieces; it is also one of the most complete in its enumeration of the estates. The purpose of the whole work is to list the classes and their faults by means of showing them currying Fauvel. The riding or the currying of the fallow horse, or mule, Fauvel, was a favorite way of denoting hypocrisy or deceit through flattery. Even walls of buildings were adorned with pictures of the different classes of society petting Fauvel, just as they were adorned with pictures of the Dance of Death. The English corruption, to "curry favor," is meaningless, but it persists in spite of the protests of the rhetorician.[61]

[60] Ed. Arthur Långfors, *Société des anciens textes français, Pubs.*, Paris, 1914-19, Vol. LXXII.
[61] The objection of George Campbell, *The Philosophy of Rhetoric*, London, 1776, I, 402, is interesting in this connection. In discussing his nine canons for good use in diction, he says: "Under the third sort, which can scarcely be considered as literally conveying any sense, may be ranked a number of vile, but common phrases, sometimes to be found in good authors, like *shooting at rovers, having a month's mind, currying favor, dancing attendance,* and many others."

Gervais was a Norman cleric, serving as a notary in the Chancellerie at the beginning of the fourteenth century. His *Roman de Fauvel* is clearly dated 1310. Though a member of the court of the king, he was strongly pro-papal. In the struggle between Philippe le Bel and Boniface his sympathies were all with Boniface, and he condemned the French bishops for their subservience to the king. By divine order, he says, there are two luminaries, the sun and the moon—spiritual and temporal power—of which the moon takes its light from the sun. Fauvel has made the moon pass over the sun. A sad eclipse. God gave no mastery to temporal sovereignty, and so it should be below the priesthood, an arm of the Holy Church. The arm should obey the head and put into execution what the head wants done. This is the political theory of the papal supporters of the thirteenth and fourteenth centuries: the comparison of the parts of the human body to parts of the body politic is a common one with political theorists and with writers of *belles lettres* as well, from John of Salisbury in the eleventh century to Nicholas of Cusa in the fifteenth century, and even later. The use of it in various pieces of the literature of estates will be noted later.

Evidently some of Gervais' contemporaries were no less puzzled by the pictures of Fauvel than is the modern reader, for he has composed his poem, he says, to explain them. In his introduction he finds that all estates of society curry Fauvel, and he enumerates them:

> Trop i a grant assemblement:
> Rois, dus et contes verrïés
> Pour torchier Fauvel alïés,
> Tous seignours temporels et princes
> I vienent de toutes provinces,
> Et chevaliers grans et petis,
> Qui a torchier sunt bien fetis.
> N'i a, sachiés, ne roy ne conte
> Qui de torchier Fauvel ait honte.

> Viscontes, prevos et baillis
> A bien torchier ne sont faillis;
> Bourjois de bours et de cités
> Torchent par grans subtilités,
> Et vilains de vile champestre
> Sont emprès Fauvel pour lui pestre.[62]

This list is complete except for the clergy, and Gervais has no intention of omitting them. A secular clerk himself, he particularly dislikes the monastic orders, especially the mendicant friars. So he lists the clerical curriers of Fauvel, all ranks of them, the pope first:

> Puis en consistore publique
> S'en va Fauvel, beste autentique,
> Et quant li pape voit teil beste,
> Sachiez qu'il li fet trop grant feste,
> Et les cardonneaux mout l'ennourent
> Et pour lui torchier tous aquourent.
> Li vischancelier, li notares,
> Audïenchiers, referendares
> Metent paine d'euls efforchier
> Pour Fauvel bien a point torchier.
> Prelas n'esparnent mont ne val
> Por torchier cel noble cheval.
> Abbeis, gens de religion
> I ont trop grant devocion.
> Jacobins, Cordelièrs, ou estes?
> A cest cop ne soiés pas bestes,
> Anciés penseis d'estudïer
> A Fauvel souef manïer,
> Si fetes vous, se Diex m'aït,
> Tant que cescun s'en esbahit.
> Augustins et nonnains et moines,
> Archediacres et chanoines
> Et clers d'iglise pourveiis
> Sont au torchier bien esmeiis,
> Et povres clers qui sont sans rente
> I metent trop bien lor entente,

---

[62] *Ibid.*, p. 5, ll. 34 ff.

Mès ne peuvent pas si près estre
Ne si avant com li grant mestre,
S'en sont courochiés et plain d'ire,
Si que souvent les ot l'en dire,
Que Fortune, qui n'est pas ferme
Et qui de torneir ne se terme,
Le plus avant retornera,
De haut bas, de loing près fera.
Ce que Fortune si tost torne
Et en son torner ne met borne
Fait les povres reconforter
Et de lour mals bien deporteir.
Et quant ne peuent avenir
A Fauvel torchier ne tenir,
Si dient il: «Dieu gart teil beste,
Mout a beau corps et bele teste».[63]

Gervais also describes the exact manner in which each estate strokes Fauvel: it is well for his readers, he says, to know the most effective ways. Again he commences with the pope:

Premier commencherei au pape;
Ce n'est pas drois que il m'eschape.[64]

The pope does reverence night and day. He takes Fauvel's bridle gently and strokes Fauvel's head and says, "He has a fine head." Cardinals follow his example. Kings, too, are not awkward at stroking Fauvel, one especially, probably Philippe le Bel. Counts, prelates and abbés, priors and deans and archdeacons, knights and squires, canons, chaplains, parsons, monks, nuns, are all adept at currying back, stomach, legs, and so forth. The poor, too, try to get close enough to caress Fauvel, but succeed only in holding his tail.

All of this, however, is purely figurative, and the poet has no intention of being obscure. The specific duties and defections of these different curriers must be pointed out. Fauvel has reversed everything in the world. Formerly things were different.

[63] *Ibid.*, p. 5, ll. 49 ff.　　　　[64] *Ibid.*, p. 7, ll. 97-98.

Now the moon outshines the sun. And with good reason: the pope is no longer holy like St. Peter, God's first vicar. Similarly, the cardinals are no longer like the first apostles. Prelates are busy counseling the king about temporal affairs and neglect their duties. In the other estates of the Church, Gervais likewise sees little good:

> Des autres estas de l'Yglise
> Poi en y voi de bonne guise:
> Tous sont mués de lour droit estre,
> Chanoine, moine, clerc et prestre.[65]

Fauvel has caused the deceit of the Templars, also, and Gervais laments their defections at length. Lords temporal don't give an onion that Fauvel is well curried. All are false. They have other faults, too, and all are named, as Gervais sees them. The third estate he mentions very briefly in a concluding summary. Evidently his sympathies are with the poor, for he has little to say of their forms of hypocrisy. He concludes:

> Puis que les rois sont menteours
> Et riches hommes flateours,
> Prelas plains de vainne cointise,
> Et chevaliers heent l'Yglise,
> Clergié est example de vices,
> Riches hommes sans charitei,
> Et marcheans sans veritei,
> Labourëurs sans lëautei,
> Hosteliers plains de cruauté,
> Baillis et juge sans pitei,
> Et parens sans vraie amistei,
> Voisins mesdisans, plains d'envie,
> Jennez enfans plains de boesdie,
> Desleal et fausse mesnie,
> Les seignours plains de tricherie,
> Trichirres en bonne fortune,
> Et ribaus governans commune,
> Les cors amés plus que les ames,
> Et fames de lor maris dames,

[65] *Ibid.*, p. 30, ll. 739 ff.

Sainte Yglise poi honouree,
France en servitute tournee,
Par Fauvel, cele male beste,
Par quoi nous vient toute tempeste.

Gervais includes women, parents, and children as well in his summary.

Shortly after Gervais du Bus had made his contribution to the literature of estates, the wise old "spicer" or pharmacist of Troyes in Champagne in 1319 sought to shun idleness by setting down his observations about the different classes of society in his *Renart le contrefait.*[66] Whether or not he tried to follow any definite form in his satire is uncertain. At any rate, his purpose was evidently not to enumerate all the orders of each estate, but to render an account of the life of the times as he saw it, in terms of the three estates. As a lover of old books, he knew well the stories of Reynard and also those of the fallow horse Fauvel; in his own satire he chose the guise of the sly fox who has smelled out the evils of the age. Though he found all classes corrupt, he berated the estates of clergy and nobility in a rather general fashion and then, in some detail, showed the commons how stupid they were to submit to the injustices put upon them by the other two estates. Perhaps, in the strictest sense, the voluminous, meandering, formless work should not be called a specimen of the *genre* that we have defined as the literature of estates. Nevertheless, the fact that the main interest of the writer is in the classes of society and their shortcomings makes his work significant here as a kind of corroboration of the charges of the writers of the literature of estates. Though he does not bother with the form of that literature, he has much of its subject matter.

Degraded from the clergy and socially ostracized for "bigamy," like Matheolus, the old pharmacist had had plenty of

[66] Ed. G. Raynaud and H. Lemaitre, *Le Roman de Renard le contrefait*, Paris, 1914, 2 vols.

time to look about him. His father had been a pharmacist before him; and except for his brief sojourn as a cleric, his contact had been chiefly with the bourgeoisie. His sympathies were plainly with the bourgeois and the villein.

Injustice is the chief fault of nobility and clergy. The poet has a great dislike for injustice. How did classes originate anyway? he asks. In the beginning all were equal. The first king was elected by an abused people who didn't know what they were doing. They had to choose a villein as king:

> Ung grant vilain entre eulx eslirent.

That was the end of equality. Since that time, the nobility have crushed the people. The nobility are always fighting, and their poor vassals must bear the burden. By taxation, feudal fees, laws of marriage and mortmain, the feudal lords grow rich and greedy. There is no gentility in them. The clergy, too, render poor justice. They arrest men, take away their possessions, and banish them through their provosts and mayors. Moreover, they exact the tenth greedily and excuse themselves by saying, "That's the custom." The high courts of law are a poor place to look for justice. Most of those who come there are looking for money or expect to "torchier Fauvel." The advocates are especially detestable. Here the poor pleader always loses, while the dignitaries of the Church and the nobility go scot-free. Why don't the cowardly villeins revolt?

The spicer's wrath at the base submission of the villeins leads him to turn his attention to their other faults. They have gross appetites, and they loiter at their work. They have numerous ways of loafing on the job when they work by the day; at piece work, however, they do in one day as much as they do in five days of the master's count. Day laborers, carpenters, vinegrowers, mowers, carters, herdsmen are all alike. After all, even the nobles have something to contend with.

The conditions of the bourgeois are the most enviable. He is most free and therefore really most noble. He lives and works in security. He may dress magnificently, sleep peacefully at home while the nobles go to war, and is protected by the law. To be sure, the bourgeoisie have their faults, too. Money-changers practice usury under cover, drapers sell goods in dark shops, goldsmiths sell alloy for solid metal, pharmacists adulterate their medicines, furriers misrepresent the quality of their furs, and so forth. As may be seen from the foregoing outline of *Renart le contrefait,* the spicer of Troyes makes no attempt to enumerate all the orders of clergy and nobility, but is fairly detailed concerning the estate he knows best, the commons.

Like medieval romance, the literature of estates grows longer and longer with increasing popularity. Gilles li Muisis, in the middle of the fourteenth century, wrote his interminable "register."[67] Voluminous to the point of exhaustion, it enumerates the estates of the world and reënumerates them. It is difficult to find any plan in the work; even the long table of contents is confusing. For, though the poet indicates that he intends to discuss the estates in order, he repeats himself and digresses until one loses one's way. Nor is his treatment of the estates as orderly as the table of contents seems to promise. In one place, Gilles apologizes for not following the enumeration of estates, and then complete disorder results. Finally he returns to the point where he left off. Nevertheless he furnishes much information about that troubled period of the Babylonian Captivity, and much that he says is most significant.

Gilles li Muisis was seventeenth abbé of the Benedictine monastery of Saint-Martin de Tournai, where he spent his whole life. When about twenty-four years old, he became blind, and he dictated his *Chronique, Annales,* and *Register* to occupy his leisure. He himself says that he began his "register" about Eastertime, 1350. So it is the work of a garrulous octogenarian, who hopes thereby to show what the present should be. He is cautious about offending by criticism of his contemporaries;

[67] *Poésies,* ed. M. le baron Kervyn de Lettenhove, Louvain, 1882, 2 vols.

he warns the would-be moralist of the futility of preaching, and of the danger it entails of loss of business. He expresses a resignation to human follies that has not appeared in the work of the other French moralists, a resignation probably due to his age.

It is impossible here to give anything like a complete idea of all that the abbé has to say about the estates of the world. After his lamentation and meditation on the virtues of the past, he turns to the estates of the world. He uses the word *estas* constantly. At times he uses it loosely. For example, he speaks of the three estates in Holy Church: "séculers rentés," "religieus rentés," and the mendicants. Later he speaks of two estates in the world: the clergy and the laity; and again of three estates: the rich, the middle class, the poor. After a long discussion of the condition of monks, nuns, and abbés, he announces his intention of showing the duties and faults of all estates, except the court of Rome:

De tous estas dou monde vollentiers parleroie,
De cescun un petit . . .
De princes, de prélats parlerai prumerains,
Excepté chiaus de Romme que je tieng souverains.[68]

Perhaps to the Abbé Gilles the close proximity of that court made prudence advisable. At any rate, he begins his category with king, princes, and nobles. Under the king, he says, are other orders:

Or sont, desous les roys, duc, prince, baron, conte
Et li chevalrie . . .[69]

All have duties to the other estates of society and all come far short. The pope follows, second in order—also significant of the state of affairs at the time. A prose prologue explains that the author will give a history of the popes of his time, beginning with Pope Célestin, "qui fu sainte personne." Of the popes before him, he will say nothing: he was a little boy then and

[68] *Ibid.*, I, 288, stanzas 1, 2.
[69] *Ibid.*, I, 295, stanza 3.

so doesn't know anything about them. His historical account of seven popes, their election, life, and death, is very thin because, as he says, he is usually writing from hearsay. The prelates of all ranks follow the pope: cardinals, deans, and canons of cathedral and collegiate churches, curés, and chaplains. In a digression the abbé admires a book of the Recluse of Molliens and the *Romance of the Rose* because:

> Il parollent de tout et de tous et de toutes.

The medieval desire to be exhaustive applies to humanity as well as to science: all mankind must be properly catalogued. After his thorough treatment of the prelates, the abbé characteristically adds another chapter: "Ch'est encoires des prélas." Then another: "Ch'est encoires des cannones." Then another: "Ch'est encoires des curés et des capelains."

The second volume of the "register" takes the poet back to his table of contents: "Des estas de tous gens seculers." He has already spoken of some lay folk, he says, but no matter. He will put in a little prologue to make a comparison of the present age with other times. If he were to discuss the estates of today fully, he could make a book as large as the Bible. All the faults of the laity are now given in detail. The poor get the worst of it in this world: they work out of fear and are often beaten. The middle class is best. Women receive their usual condemnation in this list of secular estates. Merchants (for the most part praised, not condemned), farmers, and servants conclude the review. But, not satisfied with this exhaustive treatment, the abbé adds three more short chapters on kings, princes, knights, and squires, repeating what he said before.

About the same time that Gilles li Muisis was writing this voluminous register, across the channel, in England, John Gower was very deliberately following the fashion in the *Mirour de l'omme*,[70] the first of his three works enumerating the estates

[70] Ed. G. C. Macaulay, *The Complete Works of John Gower*, Oxford, 1899, Vol. I.

of the world. To be quite uniform with his French models, he even wrote in French. Though less exhaustive than the abbé's register, the *Mirour de l'omme* is a complete catalogue of feudal society, the same catalogue, as has been pointed out,[71] as reappears in his later *Vox clamantis* and *Confessio amantis*. "Gower, in fact, was a man of stereotyped convictions, whose thoughts on human society and on the divine government of the world tended constantly to repeat themselves in but slightly varying forms. What he had said in one language he was apt to repeat in another."[72]

The device for introducing the estates in the *Mirour* is also identical with that in the *Confessio amantis,* namely, the origin of the seven deadly sins and their offspring. Wedded to the World, they each produce five daughters, and Man succumbs to all of them. To contend with the Vices, God gives seven Virtues in marriage to Reason, and each of them, likewise, has five daughters. The Vices and Virtues battle for Man; Flesh yields to the Vices and Soul to the Virtues. To determine the result of the conflict, one must pass all human society in review. With the Vices and Virtues thus arrayed, the setting is complete for the introduction of the estates of the world: "Puisq'il ad dit les propretés des vices et des vertus, sicome vous avetz oï, ore dirra en partie l'estat de ceux q'ont nostre siecle en governance; et commencera primerement a la Court de Rome."[73] No rank of the clergy is omitted: pope, cardinals, bishops, archdeacons, officers, deans, curates, parish priests, chantry priests, students, members of religious orders, and mendicant friars. The ranks of clergy are immediately followed by the ranks of the laity, noble and non-noble: "Ore q'il ad dit l'estat de ceux qui se nomont gens du sainte eglise, il dirra en part

[71] See p. 27.
[72] G. C. Macaulay, *The Complete Works of John Gower,* Oxford, 1899, Vol. I, Intro., p. xxxvi.
[73] *Ibid.,* p. 214.

l'estat de ceux qui ont le siecle en governance, et commencera primerement a parler de l'estat des Emperours au temps q'ore est."[74] Alas, Rome is no longer the head of the world: now, with two heads, she has no head. Alas, when those who ought to be for all the world, each in his own place, let nobility decline. After the emperor, the kings. They were divinely ordained for certain duties, and they have failed in all of them:

> Apres l'Empire le seconde
> Pour governer les gentz du monde
> L'estat du Roy fuist ordiné:
> Ly Rois, sicome le livre exponde,
> S'il a sa Roialté responde,
> Doit guarder toute honesteté:
> De sa primere dueté,
> Doit sainte eglise en son degré
> Defendre, que nuls la confonde,
> Et puis doit de sa Roialté
> Selonc justice et equité
> Guarder la loy dedeinz sa bonde.[75]

The king does none of these things. He fights the Church, he promotes ignorant clerics, he covets and takes Church property, he lives wantonly. But Death regards no class:

> Ne truist le Roy plus defensable
> Q'un povre vilein labourer.[76]

After the kings, the lords, who in various cities and countries are "comme Roy regent":

> Et si ne portont nequedent
> Le noun du Roy, ainçois sont ditz
> Ducs, Princes, Contes et Marchis.[77]

Let them beware of tyranny, avarice, pride. All are sons of Adam. Gower, the self-made man, naturally does not fail to remind the nobility of their lowly origin, as French moralists did before him:

[74] *Ibid.*, p. 246.
[76] *Ibid.*, ll. 23105-6.
[75] *Ibid.*, ll. 22225 ff.
[77] *Ibid.*, ll. 23212 ff.

> Tous suismes d'un Adam issuz,
> Combien que l'un soit au dessus
> En halt estat, et l'autre en bass; . . .
> Tous suismes fils de dame Evain.
> Seigneur, tu qui me dis vilain,
> Comment voes dire q'es gentil?
> Si tu le dis, je dy nenil:
> Car certes tout le flom de Nil
> Ne puet hoster le sanc prochain
> De toy, qui te fais tant nobil,
> Et du vilein q'en son cortil
> Labourt pour sa vesture et pain.[78]

Gervais du Bus wrote similarly:

> Tous summes neiz d'une semence,
> Si q'il n'a point de difference
> Entre vilain et gentil homme:
> Tous summes d'Eve et d'Adan neis,
> Et tous fusmes a mort dampneis
> Pour ce qu'il mordrent de la pomme.[79]

And so did the pharmacist of Troyes, speaking of the over-lord:

> N'est il aussi homs com vous estes? . . .
> Comme vous est il d'Adam nez?[80]

Having continued for some time in this vein, Gower proceeds to knights and men of arms. They, too, are an important estate if they only do their duty. But they don't. Instead they oppress the poor through avarice and never go to war. They fight only with their tongues. The third estate is represented by men of law, judges, sheriffs, bailiffs, jurors, merchants, artificers such as goldsmiths, apothecaries, furriers, drapers, saddlers, victualers such as taverners, bakers, and butchers, and farmers. Fraud has corrupted "l'onour des tous estatz." All estates blame, not themselves, but the times: "Le siecle est mal, le siecle est mal!" Man alone is the source of all evil. The concluding two sections are devoted to Gower's remedy, salvation through return to

[78] *Ibid.*, ll. 23389-91, 23404-12.   [79] *Roman de Fauvel*, ll. 1107 ff.
[80] *Renart le contrefait*, ll. 37614 f.

Christ, and to a long account of the life and death of Christ.

The great similarity between the *Mirour de l'omme* and the *Vox clamantis* is quite evident throughout. In the *Vox clamantis*, as was noted above, the estate of kings appears last, because Gower wished to address King Richard II in his conclusion, and the merchants, artificers, and farmers come before the judges, lawyers, and sheriffs, because these were to be treated in connection with the king. Otherwise the two works offer almost identical classifications, even to divisions of city population into merchants, artificers, and victualers, and of the ministers of the law into judges, sheriffs, bailiffs, and jurors. The charges made against the estates are also very similar.

All of these more or less voluminous twelfth, thirteenth, and fourteenth-century moralists saw fit to preach in terms of classes of society. Most of them classify humanity into the three feudal groups, and agree that these three estates, necessary to the world, were ordained by God to serve him and each other. Their method is sufficiently consistent, one with another, to indicate that they are consciously working in a tradition. Sometimes their classification constitutes the basis of the whole work, as in *La Bible Guiot;* sometimes it is only tacked on at the end or lugged in unexpectedly in the midst of other material, as in the *Lamenta* of Matheolus. In addition to these long works arraigning the classes of society, there were also many shorter poems in which the formula is no less distinct, though less expanded.

An Anglo-Norman manuscript, probably written in the first half of the thirteenth century and surviving in fragmentary form, contains a poem[81] of twenty-five stanzas which is quite typical of these shorter pieces of the literature of estates. Three estates were ordained by God, says the poet, each with their separate duties. The devil is very courteous; like him, in olden

[81] G. Paris and P. Meyer have printed the best possible text of it in *Romania,* IV (1875), 388-91.

times, the richest undertook to maintain the land and laity in loyalty and to support holy Christendom everywhere. The clergy were ordained to teach the world what is good and to pray for them; the knights were ordained to defend the land from the Saracens and other heathen adversaries; the villeins were ordained to provide food for the others. The duties of the estates are set forth in the following stanzas:

Mult est [li] diables curteis:
Les plus riches suprent ançois
De ces que Deus parti en trois
Pur tenir la tere et les lais
En leauté,
Pur alever partut sainte Cristienté.

Ben vus sai dire queus ce sunt
Qui deivent guverner le mond:
Li clers qui les corunes unt.
Quant le bien sevent e nel funt
Mar furent né.
Que que seit des lais li clerc sunt perdut.

Car il devoient preier pur les lais
Pur la terre et pur le pais
Et enprendre e charges e fès
Pur çous qui sunt verai confès.
Li ordené
Deivent doner al pople esample de bonté.

Après [les] clers sunt chevalers
Pur [garder] terres et musters
De Sarazins et d'aversers,
Qui Deu ne ses sainz n[en] unt chers,
Que poesté
N'aient sur li mescreant ne li malfé.

Puis establi le vilain
Pur gaanier as altres pain:
Cum plus labure de sa main
Tant est plus halegre [s] et sain;
Ja n'ert lassé.
En un jur pert quanque ad aüné.

But all these estates "love the devil." Look at Rome and the archbishops and bishops and archdeans and deans and canons secular and the Templars and Hospitalers. They are full of avarice and lust. The cross and mitered crown are sold dearly nowadays. The bishop distributes his favors to his sons and daughters and parents, knowing full well that they are damned thereby. Meanwhile they give mantles and cloaks to their lady-loves. These are they who preach to us and pardon our sins. With the line:

Jo nel di mie pur nul mal

the poem closes. So the defections of the remaining estates are not described. The poem was apparently copied in England from a French original.

Raimon del Cornet in his *Gesta*[82] similarly lists "Totas las gens del mon," and says that all go the way of mammon. He mentions pope, cardinals, archbishops, bishops, clergy, priests, doctors, advocates, notaries, student clerics, treasurers, bailiffs, judges, merchants, ribald minstrels, poor mendicants, jugglers, and hostlers. His purpose is to show all of them the way to the tree of life.

Some of the laments of Rutebeuf in the thirteenth century and of Deschamps in the fourteenth century likewise lament the shortcomings of all the classes. Rutebeuf's "De l'estat du monde"[83] mourns the loss of the good old times and the vices of the "religieus premierement" and then those of the "genz laies." Deschamps' "Le Lay des douze estas du monde"[84] shows, with many others in similar vein, his complete adoption of the philosophy of the feudal classes of society. Instead of naming

[82] "Pièces diverses," *Lexique roman*, ed. F. J. M. Raynouard, Paris, 1838, I, 464-73. Raynouard labels the poem "Aissi comensa la gesta de Fra Peyre Cardinal." Authorship corrected by Paul Meyer, *Romania*, IV: 386.

[83] *Œuvres complètes*, ed. Achille Jubinal, Paris, 1874, II, 15-23.

[84] *Œuvres complètes*, Société des anciens textes français, Paris, 1880, II, 226.

only the three estates, however, he names all the degrees in each estate and arrives at a total of twelve. Each degree has duties to others, and in times past these duties were performed. Not so now. Now all estates fail, and there are "paine et labour en tous les cas de ces .XII. mondains estas." In the ballade "De l'exces des convoitises"[85] he admonishes:

> Princes, foulz est qui fait tele entreprinse;
> Face chascuns l'estat ou il est mis.

In another ballade,[86] advising all of whatever estate, each stanza closes with the refrain:

> Fay ce que doiz, et aviengne que puet.

In two ballades, "Néant des conditions humaines"[87] and "Les Pauvres gens voient mourir quatre rois,"[88] he specifically names "prince," "roy," "chevalier," "prelat," "bourgeois," "marchant," "laboureur," "advocat," and says they are all in disorder through war and avarice. Another ballad is called "Tous les états périssent sans la crainte de Dieu," but here he refers, not to the classes of society, but to states, Troy, Rome, Thebes, and others.

Further evidence of the use of the form in shorter poems is found in "Ch'est li dis des estas dou monde,[89] by Jean Condé. He enumerates the following classes and their duties: clergy, princes, knights, citizens, farmers, women, and girls.

In another didactic poem of the fourteenth century, about 1352, called *L'Exemple du riche homme et du ladre*,[90] the canon of Fére-sur-Oise used the device of the parable of the rich man and Lazarus (Luke 16) as a pretext for exhortations to avoid the seven deadly sins. Just after his discussion of the evils of

---

[85] *Ibid.*, I, 136.   [86] *Ibid.*, I, 152.   [87] *Ibid.*, I, 154.   [88] *Ibid.*, I, 320.

[89] *Bibliothek des litterarischen Vereins in Stuttgart*, ed. A. Tobler, LIV-LVI, 177-85.

[90] Found by Paul Meyer in the Phillips Library in Cheltenham in 1886. See article by Paul Meyer, *Notices et extraits*, XXXIV, 176 f. Prologue, parts "Des grommes" and "Des campions," and "L'escusance de l'acteur" are quoted.

avarice, he saw fit to pass in review "les divers états du monde" in this order:[91] "du pape, des cardinals, des prelas, des religieus, des curés, des canonnes seculers, des dames de religion, des prestres petitement rentés; des rois, princes, justices, juges, advocas, executeurs, usuriers, hoirs des useriers, notaires et tabellions, fauls tesmoins, murdreurs, faus dimeurs, taverniers, devins, guerrieurs, grommes, flateurs as signeurs, esracheurs des bonnes (bornes), religieus proprietaires, faus monoyers, faus courretiers, campions, jueurs as dés." After this review of estates, the author treats a number of unrelated subjects: disobedience, the Sabbath, feast-days, prayer, and so forth. Some of the fifteen thousand verses are original ("faits"); some are borrowed ("compilés"). The author borrows most, apparently, from the Recluse of Molliens' *Carité* and *Miserere*.

A far more entertaining treatment of the *états du monde* material, however, is that of a narrative like *Des estats du siecle*,[92] by an unknown poet. It is the story of the attempts of a rather unstable youth to find his place in the world. First he decided to try "l'estat de Clergie." The clergy, he had observed, lived a life of ease and various delights. They had preference of various kinds, rents, holdings, fine horses, old and new wines; and above all they held places of authority over the rest of the people. So he went to school to become a cleric, but his disillusionment was complete: he saw all that one must do to become a cleric—get up early in the morning and go to bed late at night, think by day and sing by night—and he decided, after four or five years of such a life, that merchandise was a much better profession. Merchants grew rich, lived at ease, acquired profit on land and sea. Having put on sailor's togs and gone to sea, he became frightened at the dangers of sailing and returned

[91] *Ibid.*, p. 180.
[92] *Recueil général et complet des fabliaux des XIIIe et XIVe siècles imprimés ou inédits*, ed. A. Montaiglon and G. Raynaud, Paris, 1872-90, II, 264-68.

home, to become a farmer. For a time he of the fickle mind
derived profits from his venture without great labor and peril
and without going away from home. Then, one season, his seed
perished in the earth and he got no grain. So he thought the
villein a fool and decided to be a "chevalier": chevaliers have
honors and the "estas de grans seigneurs." As a knight, he
could have everything without turning his hand over. Everyone
would respect him. Whoever harmed him would be in danger
of his life. But, having become a knight, he had to go to war
for his country. He had no plumes, there were no sports or
feasts, and when he saw the enemy approaching, he wished he
were elsewhere and thought that if anyone would save him he
would give him ten livres. Then he saw that, "entre tous les
estas," the profession of the advocate was the most profitable.
Advocates made money without labor. When a man brought
his case to an advocate, the advocate couldn't help smiling, because, if the man had money in his pocket, he was sure to lose
it in fees. When the fickle youth came to plead a case, however,
he was completely routed by his adversaries, who were well
versed in the customs and canons of the day. The "estas" of
marriage remained to him. When a man has a wife, wise and of
good fame, she governs the house and all its interests with
reason. She gives her husband much ease; if she sees that his
heart is sad, she comforts him sweetly. Once married, however,
he realized that his "estate" was not what he had expected. So
he despised marriage, became a recluse, and proposed all the
rest of his life to study astronomy. Henceforth he would know
the nature of the heavens, and of the earth have no more care.
This delightful bit of satire is not, like most of the *états du
monde* material, an array of the faults of the classes, but rather
that of the folly of the individual who neglects the duties of his
own estate to try those of various others. In other words, he
is guilty of "injustice," in the Platonic sense of the word—
minding other people's business, not his own.

The short Anglo-Norman poem "Sir Pride the Emperor"[93] also secures added interest by an unusual device. It is the story of the crowning of the emperor of all countries and classes. The court of Rome demands to know who he is. He replies that he is Emperor Pride, and cites ancient and modern instances of his power. Rome is still not satisfied. So he sends letters to all his lieges, demanding service. The letters go to the court of Rome itself and to the court of the king, commanding them to show no pity. Other letters go "à prelaz," "à les bachilers," "à vavasours," "as esquiers," "a genti femmes," "a les chapeleyns seculers," "a religiouns," and finally "a veisins du payes," and "à matrones." The interest of this inverted form of the lament becomes especially lively in the letter to the chaplains secular, to put on the dress and manners of squires:

> "Gardez," fet-il, "la chevelure,
> E mettez la coyf pardesure;
> Fetez tayller la vesture
> A fur de esquiers à mesure.
> Vos matins dites roundement,
> La messe chauntez brevement.
> A diner venez prestement;
> A tables juhez jolivement.
> Ne esparnez nul serement,
> Ne jà ne chargez dit le gent.
> A boys alez à la chace;
> Si vous avez de chanter grace,
> Ne lessez pas de karoler
> En coumpanye de esquier.
> Si jelouz fusez de vostre estat,
> Vos serrez tenu un papelard . . ."

Now the poem concludes: Pride has assembled his host and goes over land and sea to show his trade.

In the fifteenth century in France, the specimens of the literature of estates are by no means so numerous as in the thirteenth

[93] In *Reliquiae antiquae,* ed. Thos. Wright and J. O. Halliwell. London. 1845, II, 248.

and fourteenth centuries. Civil war and foreign invasion gave less opportunity for writing. Even though the theme of the literature of estates was more suited to the almost hopeless state of affairs in the first half of the century than were those of many other medieval literary forms, there was probably little time or incentive to versify lengthy laments like those of the preceding century. The *genre* continued, however, in verse, prose, and combinations of verse and prose. The works, in almost every case, reflect the changes that have come over France and so, like their predecessors, are valuable for the light they shed on the times.

Early fifteenth-century evidence of the relative importance of the three estates may perhaps be found in the political treatise of Christine de Pisan, *Le Corps de policie*.[94] Always a loyal adherent of the king's cause, she wrote with strong faith in his final victory. Hence his estate is highest and noblest in her classification of society: "premièrement le chief de tous c'est le Roy de France." Pope and emperor have no place here. Knights and nobles she addresses next, as the king's necessary source of strength and support. The position of the clergy in her scheme of classes is significant of her sense of their importance. They become a part of the third estate, that of "all people," along with merchants, craftsmen, and day laborers. "En la communité du peuple," she says, "sont compris trois estas, c'est assavoir: par especial en la cité de Paris et aussi en autres cités, 1° le clergié, 2° les bourgeois et les marchans, 3° et puis le commun, si comme gens de mestiers et laboureurs." If by "le clergié" Christine means, as she seems to imply later, all those who are educated, such as writers like herself and people of profession, then the representatives o.' the Church are of still less importance to her, for they are not even a third part of the third estate.

[94] It is still in manuscript, but is described by Raimond Thomassy, *Essai sur les écrits politiques de Christine de Pisan,* Paris, 1838, pp. 127 f.

No piece of literature of estates shows to better advantage the possibilities of adaptation of this *genre* to changing social and political conditions, however, than does Alain Chartier's eloquent *Quadrilogue invectif*,[95] written about 1422. This is no mere enumeration of classes, but a vehement and stirring piece of prose propaganda. All the sad plight of early fifteenth-century France, harassed by barons' wars and English invasion, is reflected in this four-fold debate, in which France addresses her three sons, nobility, clergy, and people. As secretary to the dauphin in 1422, Alain Chartier exerted all his powers as a writer to urge the cause of France against Henry V and the English. In 1420, by the treaty of Troyes, all of France had been forfeited to the English king. By 1422 the discouraged dauphin had withdrawn to his holdings south of the Loire. In this apparently hopeless situation, the *Quadrilogue* was written. A few months later, however, the tide turned with the death of Henry V.

The cause of France's condition, says the *Quadrilogue,* is the defections of the three estates: the sloth and cowardice of the nobles, the weakness of the clergy, and the discontent and fickleness of the people. In his opening address to his readers, the author pledges his devotion "a la treshaulte et excellente majesté des princes, a la treshonnouree magnificence des nobles, circonspection des clers et bonne industrie du peuple françois." God ordained the estate of nobles. He raised them aloft, but he also lowers them again if they fail in their duties. Even so whole realms and principalities suffer mutations. We impute to Fortune what is the just vengeance of God on our faults. Now the hand of God is on France. Alain has been reading the Holy Scriptures, among them Isaiah 3, and has been much moved.

---

[95] Ed. E. Droz, Paris, 1923. This work is the original of a large part of the anonymous *Complaynt of Scotlande* of 1549 (see p. 167), as was pointed out by W. A. Neilson, *Journal of English and Germanic Philology,* I (1897), 411.

So he writes his *Quadrilogue invectif*. Let the reader read all, lest he believe that "tout le blasme soit mis sur ung estat."

The device used is the familiar one of the dream-vision. About break of day, the writer suddenly woke, to see in his imagination the sad plight of France. He thought of her still glorious realm, and realized that lack of order and discipline was the cause of her persecution. As he wavered between hope and despair, a light sleep came over him, and he seemed to see in a green field a lady of very noble bearing. She was sad, however, and had plainly fallen from higher honor. She was also fearful of greater grief to come. Her golden hair lay in disorder on her shoulders, and her crown was much awry. She wore a marvelous mantle, adorned with three kinds of designs: first, at the top, were embroidered, with precious stones, the noble fleur de lis and the ensigns of old French kings and princes; in the middle, were cut the letters and figures of diverse sciences; below, reaching to the ground, were drawn pictures of animals, plants, fruits, and seeds. Though the estates are not named here, the designs clearly represent them. This beautiful mantle was so torn, however, that the three parts could hardly be seen. After the long labor of destruction of a tottering palace nearby, symbol of past glory, the lady suddenly saw three of her children: the one standing upright in arms, thoughtful and troubled; the second in long vestments, sitting in silence on a seat beside the first; the third in mean habit, fallen on the ground, plaintive and languorous.

The four-part debate which follows begins with France's reproach of the three estates for their sloth. They think only of themselves, she says, and show only ingratitude to her. They are unnatural sons, since they care not "au commun besoing." Even animals do better. What illustrious service the subjects of ancient realms rendered! But the French estates are worse than their enemies. The enemies of France fight as enemies; her own sons fight her under the name of friends and defenders.

Where are the knights who want to seek glory "en ces condi-
cions chevalereuses"? Where is the prudence "des clers et conseilliers"? What has become of the constancy and loyalty "du
peuple françois"?

Je me doubte que tous trois soient rabaissez et avillez de la dignité
et devoir de leurs estaz. Pluseurs de la chevalrie et des nobles crient
aux armes, mais ilz courent a l'argent; le clergé et les conseilliers par-
lent a deux visaiges et vivent avecques les vivans; le peuple veult
estre en sceurté gardé et tenu franc, et si est impacient de souffrir
subgection de seigneurie.[96]

All they think of is getting and spending. Night and day, they
hunt and shoot in the woods and fields or buy offices, estates,
honors; they sleep and eat like swine, and dress extravagantly,
"sans garder difference des estaz." Let them remember the ice
of winter, the contagious diseases, the good fortune of their
enemies, and not the labor of carrying arms.

After a long silence, the third estate, "Le Peuple," who lay
on the ground, defended himself. He has lost all hope, he says,
since he is like an ass who sustains an insupportable burden
and is only beaten in return. The rest live off him, and he dies
for them: "Ilz vivent de moy et je meur pour eulx." They ought
to protect him from the enemy, but all they care about is eating his bread in safety. He sees no way out, "sinon par desespoir
laissier mon estat pour faire comme ceulx qui ma despoille en-
richit, qui mieulx ayment la proye que l'onneur de la guerre."[97]
Nevertheless the people are a necessary and honorable estate,
"sans lequel les nobles ne le clergé ne pevent suffire a faire corps
de police ne a soustenir leurs estas ne leur vie."

To this lament, "Le Chevalier" replied. No matter what happens, he said, the people are always grumbling. They can't
endure the ease of peace or the hardships of war. They are
always complaining about the noblity and crying to God for
vengeance for the evils they have caused themselves. By their

[96] *Ibid.*, p. 12.   [97] *Ibid.*, p. 18.

impatient murmuring and desire for mutations of government they have brought the war on themselves. Don't they know that the "nobles hommes en leur estat aient a souffrir autant que tu as"? They and their ladies, exiled from their homes, suffer many discomforts. They are often without cover over their heads, lose horses and goods, and are ever in danger of death. Many have sold their lands to serve their country and are now living in poverty. Meanwhile, "ung grant bourgois, qui compte ses deniers par default d'autre besoigne, ou ung riche chanoyne, qui exploicte le plus du temps a menger et a dormir,"[98] calls them to protect him and his goods. The nobles can't live and fight on air. While the purses of the people are being filled, those of the nobles in war are empty of the fees and rents owed them.

People and nobility each replied again—the former to say that, not they, but the disorder and extravagance of the nobility have brought on the war, and the latter to say that it is the people who have been extravagant in their imitation of the nobility, especially those in the city who have swallowed all the money of the realm—before "Le Clergie" broke his silence. Instead of replying to charges of clerical defection, hinted at in preceding complaints, he set forth a three-fold remedy. It is useless, to argue, he says. Three things are necessary: skill, revenue, and obedience. The prince needs faithful subjects. He has been moving about constantly for four years. All must discipline themselves to support the prince in every way.

To this need of discipline, the nobility added that of "clemence et debonnaireté" on the part of the prince, to inspire confidence. With that France closed the debate. Let each estate apply himself to his own chastisement rather than to vituperation of his neighbor. Let all join in one desire, that of the common welfare. Let all their words be written down. So she called Alain, since he had heard all, and since he was unable to fight,

[98] *Ibid.*, p. 26.

to write down the disputation, "faicte par maniere de quadrilogue invectif." All the sorrows and sufferings of waning French feudalism are reflected in this piece of literature of estates.

The unknown author of *L'Instruction de la vie mortelle,*[99] a poem of some forty-seven thousand verses, like the Recluse of Molliens, sets out to treat the five senses, but he wanders from his plan. After a long, dry, unoriginal discussion of history and philosophy before his time, he turns his attention to instruction for living a Christian life and to the historical development of the estates that compose Holy Church. The following lines indicate his concern with those estates:

> Apres l'estat des papes et emperours
> Et maintes choses qu'avindent en leurs jours,
> Bien appartient, pour mieulx l'œuvre parfaire,
> Des cardinalz et autres estas retraire,
> A celle fin que l'en sache comment
> En sainte Eglise sont ordonnéement
> Tous les estas par ycelle estaublis,
> Et qu'il y a, des grans jusques aux petis . . .

In *Le Doctrinal rural du temps présent*[100] the comparison of the present with the past gives the writer cause to treat the "divers états." A prince is said to be lacking in valor if he isn't proud, and is called "chevallereux" if he is proud; men of war pillage; monastics spend their time outside the cloister; merchants deceive their customers; women are perverse and coquettish; and so forth. Most of the charges are not very new or different from those of former times.

Robert Gaguin's *Le Débat du laboureur, du prestre et du gendarme*[101] reflects the conditions and relations of the three estates in the fifteenth century in verse form that is briefer than

---

[99] The poem is still in manuscript in St. John's College, Cambridge, but is described by Paul Meyer, *Romania,* XXXV (1906), 531-54. Long quotations are included from the prologues to its five parts.

[100] *Notices et extraits,* V, 533 ff.

[101] *Roberti Gaguini epistole et orationes,* ed. Louis Thuasne, Paris, 1904, II, second supplement, 350-65.

the *Quadrilogue invectif*, but it is similar to that prose lament in content. It records a conversation of the three estates, concerning their hardships, the results of the Hundred Years' War. The plowman complains of the evil treatment that the men of war make him submit to:

> Fier, inhumain et trop cruel gendarme,
> C'est or en droit qu'à toy je hue et crie . . .

The priest adds his complaint to that of the plowman. The gendarme replies that he is the most unfortunate of all, since he has to endure privations and the severity of his commander, and is always in danger of death. He adds that, if he sometimes oppresses the priests and peasants, they have merited such treatment by their sins. They have nothing to complain of; they will know utter oppression if they have recourse to the English, their enemies.

Le Débat de félicité[102] of Charles Soillot, secretary of Charles, Count of Charolais, son of Philip the Good, and Duke of Burgundy after the death of his father, also avoids a mere enumeration of the estates by having them appear in person and make philosophic prose and verse speeches on happiness. However, there is nothing definitely characteristic of the fifteenth century in the speeches. The conclusion of the dispute is that happiness is not found on earth, but dwells in heaven. The possessions of this world are only means of losing it. The three orders constituting the nation are represented by three women: Dame Église, Dame Noblesse, Dame Labeur, each of whom thinks that she alone possesses happiness. Unable to agree, they decide to plead their cases before the Sciences, assembled in court of judgment. Dame Église speaks first and boasts of her power and riches. Though kings command the body, she has power over both body and soul. One word from her is more powerful than the arms of Noblesse, her rival. With due effort, she knows how to secure all the advantages of life and is sur-

---

[102] *Notices et extraits*, V, 542 f. Notice by C. Legrand d'Aussy.

prised that Noblesse pretends to be as happy as she. Dame Noblesse finds these pretentions of Dame Église wholly false. Dame Église is powerful only because sustained by Dame Noblesse. If certain bishops and archbishops have become powerful, it is because they have taken domains belonging to Dame Noblesse, and they hold them to her detriment. Arms give Dame Noblesse riches, preëminence, authority. She commands all: all render her honor and tremble in her presence. Chivalry surrounds her with glory; and without glory one is not happy. Dame Labeur, without daring to compare herself with the two superior orders, declares humbly that, if they are happy, it is through her labors; and that, after all, a good workman, like them, can be happy, too. The court of Sciences decides against all three. It declares that no one has happiness.

But the debaters are not satisfied. They demand reasons for the judgment. The court replies that it considers happy only him who in his estate has the necessities of life and who is free from care, desire, and fear. The Church, though it thinks itself more fortunate than the other two, is really much more miserable. Though it enjoys great power, what remorse it should feel for having used it so badly! What torments it goes through to increase its dignities and revenues! What distress its members evidence because they cannot marry and leave a heritage to their children! As for Dame Noblesse, she is besieged by flatterers and financiers who propose taxes and new laws with which the people are oppressed. She is guilty of pride, sloth, prodigality, cowardice, and debauchery. If Noblesse were what she should be, she would have only eulogies. As for Labeur, she is quarrelsome and jealous; she is always complaining. If she were upright, just, and industrious, the court would call her happy. The three then ask, What is happiness? and the rest of the work is a dissertation, with much display of learning, on ancient and modern opinions.

Fifteenth-century conflict no doubt suggested Honoré Bonet's

L'Arbre des batailles, published by Antoine Vérard in Paris in 1493.[103] The device used is that of a tree, but it is not the tree of love or the tree of life noted in the works of Ermengaud and Raimon del Cornet.[104] The whole treatise is an elaborate account of the requisites of war, but incidentally the author arranges all society: cardinals and bishops are the topmost branches, the rulers just below them, then knights and plowmen. All the branches are necessary to the life of the tree.

That French interest in the literature of estates did not end with the close of the Middle Ages is evident from the continued representation of classes in the *sottie.* The close connection between the *sottie* and the didactic literature of the Middle Ages and early Renaissance is quite apparent. Many of the French *sotties,* as well as the German *Fastnachtspiele,* consist of nothing more than the appearance, in order, of the members of the various classes, to state their grievances. The number of estates is usually four: Clergié, Noblesse, Marchandise, and Labour. The necessity of separating citizen and plowman became more urgent as time went on. These four figures appear again and again.[105] A *sottie* played in Paris in 1514, called *Sotise a huict personnaiges,*[106] included Le Monde, Abuz, Sot dissolu, Sot glorieux, Sot corrompu, Sot trompeur, Sot ignorant, Sotte folle. The Sot dissolu was dressed to represent a gendarme, the Sot corrompu to represent magistrates, the Sot trompeur to represent merchants, the Sot ignorant and the Sotte folle to represent the people, men and women. In 1535 at Rouen was presented a *Sottie moral de tout le monde,* in which Le Monde, a fool, was dressed in a costume that represented three

[103] Claudin, *op. cit.,* II, 460. I have used the original text in the John Pierpont Morgan Library.

[104] See pp. 45 and 67.

[105] See Petit de Julleville's *Répertoire du théâtre comique en France au moyen âge,* Paris, 1886, p. 344.

[106] *Romania,* VII: 270 and *Société des anciens textes français, Pubs.,* III, 34.

estates: Noblesse, Église, Labeur. In 1541 another morality was played at Rouen in which Église and Noblesse forced Pauvreté to wash their dirty clothes and carry them on his back. But these are only a few examples of the very popular representation of estates for the auditor rather than the reader.

Even into the late sixteenth century the literature of estates goes in France. There, too, as will be seen in the literature of estates in England, it took on new significance with new political and social conditions and is no longer the enumeration of the duties and faults of the classes. The very popular *Satyre menippée de la vertu du catholicon d'Espagne et de la tenue des estats de Paris*,[107] a burlesque account of the meeting of the Estates, was published in 1594. The Estates-General met in 1593 in the interests of the Spanish party. The satire, in witty political verse, attacked that assembly. The procession of elaborately garbed estates, the order of seating in the tapestried assembly hall (even the tapestries are given significance relative to the occasion), the harangues of the representatives of the three estates are all described with delicate irony. The first two estates favor the Catholic Party and Spanish interference. The last harangue, that of Monsieur d'Aubray "pour le tiers estat," comes like a thunderbolt.[108] After a vivid description of the miseries of the people, he argues against foreign domination in France and against Catholicism. The assembly sits in silence at his conclusion. The work was translated and published in England[109] in 1595, where the literature of estates was still familiar.

[107] Ed. C. E. Nodier, Paris, 1824, 2 vols. Also ed. C. Labitte, Paris, 1841, and C. Read, Paris, 1876.

[108] Ed. Nodier, II, 1 f.

[109] By P. Le Roy and others, under the title *A Pleasant Satyre or Poesie: wherein is discovered the Catholicon of Spayne, and the Chiefe Leaders of the League.* See R. M. Alden, *The Rise of Formal Satire in England*, p. 43, note 2.

3. GERMAN ADAPTATIONS

The estates of the world also found their way into German literature, but with some few differences. In the first place, the German literature of estates is not nearly so voluminous as the French. Moreover, the catalogues of German society are usually not so distinct or precise. The word *estat* does not appear in the German, of course, as it does in the English adaptations. The chief reason for these differences no doubt lies in the fact that class distinctions were never so clear-cut in feudal Germany as in France. The line between the lord and his men was never so nicely drawn. Until the end of the thirteenth century, for example, serfs in attendance on rich lords as *ministeriales* or *Dienstmannen* were sometimes made knights and given fiefs, though they still remained serfs, subject to the restraints of serfs.[110] Such a confusion of ranks would have been inconceivable in France. The form of the literature of estates was, therefore, less applicable in Germany than in France.

Nevertheless, there are German adaptations of the form, beginning, as in the French literature of estates, with more or less general laments on the sins of the various orders of society, pride, avarice, envy, and so forth, and becoming more detailed in the later pieces. Earlier, the characterization of classes is likely to be only an incidental part of a hodge podge of other material; whereas later, as in *Des Teufels Netz*, it becomes the chief concern of the whole work. A good many of the stock medieval devices for introducing the discussion of classes are used. As in France, the literature of estates in Germany furnishes a very good idea of the manners and customs of the time.

German literature of estates seems to begin in the latter part of the thirteenth century. Before that time, such extended

[110] Charles Seignobos, *The Feudal Régime*, pp. 48-49.

moral treatises as *Der wälsche Gast* of Thomasin von Zirclaera and Freidank's *Bescheidenheit* refer constantly to the evils of various classes but do not enumerate them. As early as 1160, the *Memento mori* of Heinrich of the cloister Melk in Austria, like *Les Vers de la mort* ascribed to Hélinant,[111] bewailed the weaknesses of all classes except women and reminded them that death takes all. Here, too, however, there is no enumeration or characterization of each class. About 1275 the Latin poem *Sermones nulli parcentes,* discussed above,[112] was translated into German and contains exact enumeration of the three estates and of the various ranks within the estates. By that time, then, the scheme of thought was known in Germany in the vernacular as well as in the Latin.

The *Renner* of Hugo von Trimberg,[113] begun in 1296 and completed about 1313, is full of class consciousness. However, the work is a truly medieval mixture of abstract moralizing, allegory, lament for the good old times, praise of poets, beast fable, and pseudo-science, and the rather brief enumeration of classes and reflections on the follies of the classes of society are incidental in the poet's comments on what he has seen of life in general. The scribe of the manuscript of 1350 explains the title as follows:

> Renner ist ditz buch genant,
> wanne ez sol renne durch di lant.[114]

[111] See p. 34.   [112] See pp. 23-24.

[113] Ed. Gustav Ehrismann, *Bibliothek des litterarischen Vereins in Stuttgart,* Vols. CCXLVII-XLVIII (1908-09) and CCLII (1909). Also, Bamberg historischer Verein, 1833.

[114] Cf. B.L.V.S. ed., pp. 4, 46. Also, B.H.V. ed., p. 8. Quotation is from the latter. A similar explanation of the title of the *Cursor mundi* occurs in the Fairfax manuscript of that poem:

> Cursur o werld man aght it call,
> For almast it overrennes all.

There seems to be no relation between the poems, however, for the *Cursor mundi* is what the *Renner* deliberately avoids: a paraphrase of the Scriptures.

The poet is now fifty years old and regrets his evil youth. He realizes that death takes all and so will write a book on God's goodness. His allegory is that of a meadow hemmed in by mountains, in which grows a tree bearing fruit. The meadow is the Earth, where God put Adam and Eve. They sinned. Abel and Cain were their children. Cain killed Abel. All this you can read in Genesis. The writer says that he might go on with the story, but that, after all, God ordained priests to tell those stories, out of Latin into German, and to give the laity a good example:

> Diu rede wêr mir ze lenge
> Und ouch diu wort ze strenge,
> Daz ich si sölte brenge
> Von latîn ze diute:
> Der suln klôsterliute
> Pflegen und ander pfaffen,
> Die got dar zuo geschaffen
> Hât, daz si guot bilde geben
> Uns leien an lêre und ouch an leben.[115]

So, instead of paraphrasing the Bible, he goes on to moralize on the vices and virtues of the various classes of society. The fruit on the tree in this beautiful meadow represents mankind, shaken off by the wind, curiosity, into thorns, springs, and a lake below, representing arrogance, avarice, and sloth. These three are the chief sins. The other four are also discussed later. But, once started, the poet soon forgets his allegory and simply moralizes about the faults of the various classes, as well as those of women, of whom he has much to say. The treatment of the sin of arrogance is typical of that of the other deadly sins. The very thought of it suggests the enumeration of all classes, for all classes are guilty of it:

> Hôchfart lît an ritterschaft,
> Hôchfart lît an meisterschaft ...
> Hôchfart kan arme liute erstecken ...
> Hôchfart wont bî küenen recken,

[115] B.L.V.S. ed., CCXLVII, 7-8, ll. 176 ff.

> Hôchfart wont bî betel secken . . .
> Hôchfart füert an irem reien
> Müniche, pfaffen unde leien . . .[116]

This arrogance, the author declares, is all wrong, for all mankind are of one stock—the theme also, as we have seen, of Gervais du Bus, Gower, and the pharmacist of Troyes:

> Pfaffen, ritter und gebûre
> Sint alle gesippe von natûre
> Und süln gar brüederlîchen leben.[117]

The French moralists, however, usually drove home the distinctions ordained by God between the classes and their duties to each other and the state. Here, in the *Renner,* there is much questioning of class distinctions—a characteristic of German feudalism. At one point in the *Renner,* for a group of villagers who throng about him as he rides into their town, asking him why there are such class distinctions, the poet gives the somewhat common medieval explanation that Noah, uncovered while asleep and drunk by his son Ham, cursed Ham and said that all his descendants should be servants. But, the writer continues, virtue makes nobility, not birth or possessions—a favorite theme—and, after all, the good go to heaven, noble or non-noble, all alike.

Arrogance is especially common among court people and office holders, Hugo continues:

> Hôchfart vil manigen hât betrogen.
> Keiser, künige und herzogen,
> Grâfen, fürsten unde frîen . . .[118]

The good old times are gone: nobles are no longer modest and generous. Formerly nobles' sons were sent away to learn manners. Now they go to the taverns, where they soon lead common folk astray. The author is careful to add, however:

[116] *Ibid.,* pp. 19-20, ll. 475 ff.
[117] *Ibid.,* p. 21, ll. 505 ff.
[118] B.L.V.S., CCXLVII, 21, ll. 523 ff.

Pfaffenfürsten meine ich niht,
Bî den nieman kein unzuht siht . . .
Swelhe stete stênt ûf hôhen bergen . . .[119]

Arrogance is also found among the common people. The strong sympathies of the author for the poor are very evident in several places, and he promises "hellische feur" to those nobles and clergy who oppress them. At the same time, he complains of the arrogance of those who rise from low estate:

Wir sehen die trahten nâch grôzen êren,
Die nie wurden herren kint
Und weder gebûre noch ritter sint.
Gewaltiger ûf hôhen pferden . . .
Diz ist grôz übermuot, dâ von
Sprach hie vor künic Salomôn.[120]

Much further on in his poem, he lists those of the commons whom arrogance affects as burgers, villagers, citizens, storekeepers, smiths, millers, brewers, tailors, painters, even murderers and thieves.

Another chief sin, that of avarice, is also found among all the classes. Like other writers of the literature of estates, Hugo von Trimberg seems to feel obliged to enumerate the different degrees of society; but the cataloguing has apparently become burdensome, for here he asks, Why name them all again?

War zuo sölte ich si alle nennen?
Ir müget daz selber wol bekennen,
Daz geistliche liute und werltlîche
Alle würden gerne rîche.[121]

Further evidence of the interest in estates in German literature is found in the popularity of the Latin chess book of Jacobus de Cessolis. Besides the Latin text, there were four independent German translations, all in verse.[122] The work will be considered later in the discussion of Caxton's English trans-

---

[119] *Ibid.*, p. 23, ll. 555 ff.   [120] *Ibid.*, pp. 44-45, ll. 1064-67 and 1083-85.
[121] *Ibid.*, p. 182, ll. 4403 ff.   [122] Paul's *Grundriss*, 2d ed., II, 324.

lation of it.[123] It was well known in almost all European countries in the fourteenth century.

In the fifteenth century, the *genre* was well established in Germany, as is evident in Hans Vintler's *Die Pluemen der Tugent* and especially in *Des Teufels Netz*. *Die Pluemen der Tugent*[124] is, however, a German adaptation of an Italian piece of literature of estates, the *Fiori di virtú* of Tomaso Leoni. Leoni's poem was written about 1320 and was often republished in the fifteenth century, after the introduction of printing. Vintler made a rhymed translation of it in German, adding whatever he saw fit.[125] The translation was finished by 1411[126] and was published in 1486. Vintler's sermons, like those of his original, are built up on the popular allegory of the Devil and his seven daughters, already noted in Matheolus' *Lamenta*.[127] The daughters are paired off somewhat differently here. For example, arrogance, married by Matheolus to women, is now espoused to the lords. The second daughter, greed, is married to the citizens; falsehood, to the peasants; envy and hate, to craftsmen; hypocrisy, to priests and spiritual folk in general; the sixth, whom he couldn't marry off, he sent among women; the seventh, whom he made a prostitute, went all over the world to get money for him. Vintler, though a member of one of the most prominent and wealthiest Tyrolean noble families of the time, especially attacks the faults of the nobility and the arrogance of women, and, in the democratic vein of the *Renner*, he spares the "bauer" as few French moralists do. Goaded by the evils of the times, he often throws off his tone of mild censure, to burst forth into the fiery speech of violent condemnation. Only the clergy he treats somewhat reservedly; when he talks of their hypocrisy he is translating,[128] but later

---

[123] See p. 123.   [124] Ed. I. V. Zingerle, Innsbruck, 1874.
[125] *Ibid.*, Einleitung, pp. xv-xvi.   [126] Paul's *Grundriss*, II, 325.
[127] See *Modern Philology*, IX:440 and *Romania*, XXIX: 54 f.
[128] Line 3494.

he charges them, also, with ambition and avarice, and with teaching magic and heresy. Twice he talks of the falsity of the "bauers." The first accusation,[129] however, is from Leoni: "la terza fu Falsità, e quelle diede a'villani." One "bauer" is worth three degenerate nobles, he says later,[130] the medieval commonplace noted above. The nobility are accused of the usual faults. They fail utterly in the duties of their rank and might better become serfs. Like Hugo von Trimberg and most medieval moralists, Vintler asserts that moral uprightness, not blood, makes nobility, for between the blood of a lord and that of another man there is no difference. The long ten-thousand-line poem also has a passage on the power of Herr Pfennig everywhere, a chapter on the different kinds of fools and folly, the usual compilation of biblical and classical references, and the listing of vices and virtues with stories to illustrate them.

The most complete piece of literature of estates in fifteenth-century Germany is, however, *Des Teufels Netz*.[131] A long satiric-didactic poem, apparently written between 1415 and 1418, at least before 1441,[132] it catalogues all society from pope to innkeepers and dyers—no rank is omitted. The device is at once apparent. The prologue calls all, men, women, rich, poor, to listen to this story of one who, like the Recluse of Molliens, describes himself as a hermit. The Devil seeks to get all into his net, by means of seven servitors, the seven deadly sins. May God preserve me from the Devil, says the poet, for giving this warning. Once, before Christmas, he sat thinking and writing of all that God has done for mankind. To him came the Devil to boast of his power on earth. The ensuing dialogue composes the rest of the poem. The Devil discloses the secrets and preaches in a strange way for the Devil: if only such a one were not avaricious or proud or otherwise sinful, he would be spared hell fire. The hermit commands him

---

[129] Lines 3465 f.   [130] Line 6707.
[131] Ed. Dr. K. A. Barack, *Bibliothek des litterarischen Vereins in Stuttgart*, Stuttgart, 1863, Vol. LXX.   [132] Paul's *Grundriss*, II, 325.

to tell of the sins of all from the highest down. The Devil complies, beginning with the Church Council, which has failed to achieve needed reform in the Church. This is the Conciliar Period, and the poem reflects the evils peculiar to the time.[133] The Devil first caused a schism and then lied to the heads of the Council until they were befuddled and did nothing, the Council weakened, and no reformation followed. Arrogance, avarice, envy, hate entered, and the Devil got them all in his net. Then he ensnared pope, cardinals, bishops, prelates, and all other religious orders. All are guilty of some one or more of the seven sins. The sins of women and children follow, before the laity are classified. As usual, the latter list begins with emperor and kings. The defections: "Von den Kurfürsten," "Von den Hertzogen," "Von den Grafen," "Von den Freyen," "Von Rittern und Knechten" complete those of the estate of the nobility. Various feudal officers and servants are also included: "Von den Schützen und Schintfesseln," "Von dem Keller und dem Koch," "Von dem Amman (Amtmann) und dem Schreiber," "Von den Jegern (Jägern)," "Von den Torwarten," "Von den Kuchin Knabcn (Kücheknaben)," "Von den Aufftragern," "Von den Stubenhaizern (Steubenheizern)," "Von den Wachtern (Wächtern)." The third estate is minutely subdivided as to its different trades and professions: the burgomasters, merchants, tailors, bakers, millers, butchers, fishermen, shopkeepers, apothecaries, physicians, weavers, leather-workers, shoe-makers, masons, smiths, waggoners, saddlers, armorers, manure-carriers, shipmen, fools, schoolmasters, minstrels, gentlewomen, maids, midwives, peasants, herdsmen, ruffians, harlots, robbers, murderers, innkeepers, dyers, and others too numerous to mention. In conclusion the Devil asks Christ to divide good and evil. Christ does so, and the Devil drives the evil off to his domains.

Medieval interest in the literature of fools and folly found

[133] Line 2919. The editor thinks that the poet was probably a Hussite, because of his interest in reformation.

its most popular and most influential expression in the German *Narrenschiff* of Sebastian Brant, of 1494. Into that literature, too, the enumeration of the classes of society went. Catalogues of fools and lists of political orders were easily correlated. The whole matter of estates in the *Ship of Fools* will be treated in some detail in the discussion of the last important version, that in English by Alexander Barclay.[134] Suffice it here to say that the original version reflects the literature of estates, and that each succeeding version becomes more and more concerned with estates. The chapter in the *Narrenschiff* on fools who "curry Fauvel" was long unintelligible to commentators and to German lexicographers, who dated the expression from manuscripts of the fifteenth and sixteenth centuries.[135] Other chapters as well show Brant's knowledge of and interest in the literature of estates. Locher, Riviere, and Barclay amplified and elaborated Brant's references, until the English version properly has a place in the literature of estates in England as well as in the literature of folly. The numerous successors of the *Ship*, both in England and on the continent, frequently mention classes of society, though usually not clearly divided into three estates.

The German *Fastnachtspiel*, like the French *sottie*, shows a concern with the faults of the classes of society similar to that of the didactic poetry. Even a cursory examination of several of them reveals this concern. Kings, princes, lords, the professions, tradespeople, peasants, clergy of all ranks, and women appear in very undramatic sequence to complain of their troubles or to be complained about.[136] This medieval interest in estates in the *Fastnachtspiel* persisted into the sixteenth cen-

[134] See p. 143.

[135] See comments of Gaston Paris, *Histoire littéraire*, XXXII, 115.

[136] See *Bibliothek des litterarischen Vereins in Stuttgart*, "Fastnachtspiele aus dem fünfzehnten Jahrhundert," Vols. XXVIII-XXX, XLVI, ed. A. von Keller, 1853. See XXVIII-XXIX, 378 ff. for an example of more or less complete classification.

tury, just as in the *sottie* in France. For example, Mistress Truth can find shelter with no estate in one of Hans Sach's plays. She meets a peasant and his wife and begs for lodging. She has been stoned and beaten and thrust out by townsmen, farmers, merchants, tradespeople, the courts of justice, the courts of the nobility, even from God's temple. Finally the peasant and his wife also refuse her lodging.[137]

The theme of the origins of the classes of society also found repeated treatment in sixteenth-century German literature in the form of the interesting fable of the unlike children of Eve. According to this fable—this "lovely fable," as Hans Sachs called it—Adam and Eve, after the loss of Paradise, labored hard for a living for themselves and their children. Some of their sons (they seem to have had no daughters) were handsome, and some were ugly and deformed. One day God decided that it was only right that he should visit them. He sent an angel to announce his coming. Eve was delighted. She swept the house and adorned all the rooms with grasses and flowers and green boughs. Then she washed and dressed her beautiful children and taught them how to bow and shake hands with the Lord when he should come. The ugly, deformed ones, however, she hid in the hay and in the stove. When the Lord came, the beautiful children received him politely, as their mother had taught them. God laid his hands on them and blessed them and, best of all, he instituted for them estates of high degree. When they grew up, he said, they should be kings, princes, counts, knights, wealthy citizens, merchants, and learned doctors. When Eve saw the Lord's kindness, thinking that he might be generous with her other children, she brought them in from the hay and out of the stove. Dirty, ragged, awkward, they stood before him. The Lord had to laugh to see them; but he

[137] *Neudrucke der Litteratur der XVI und XVII Jahrhunderte*, "Dreizehn Fastnachtspiele aus den Jahren 1539-1550 von Hans Sachs," XXXI-XXXV, 130-140.

pitied them, too, and blessed them and instituted for them also certain estates to provide them with a livelihood. Since they were unfit for high estate, he ordained them to hard work as farmers, craftsmen, fishermen, shipmen, messengers, and servants. Such a blessing made Eve sad. God showed her, however, that the world could not endure without the different classes, and she was satisfied.

It is in this simple form, free from all moral or religious implications as to the origin of estates, that the story appears in the sixth eclogue of Mantuan, first printed, along with the other nine, in 1498. The eclogues were immediately popular and were widely read in France, Germany, and England, as well as Italy. In Germany they were printed at least three times before 1512.[138] The sixth eclogue may have served to revive interest in the old story of Eve's children in the sixteenth century. In Germany, it was retold at least thirteen times, and in England, as we shall see later,[139] Alexander Barclay reproduced it in his paraphrase of Mantuan's sixth eclogue.

In some of the numerous retellings of this story in Germany in the sixteenth century the simple version is kept. Hans Sachs, who versified it in four different forms (once in every form he tried his hand at), in 1546 wrote a *Meisterlied, Die ungleichen Kinder Eve*, in which there is no suggestion that God dealt out the estates according to goodness or badness, but only according to external fitness for the rank assigned. When God arrived, he was so pleased with the beautiful children that he rewarded them with high estate:

> Sprach zu eim: "du ein künig sei!"
> zu dem darbei:
> "sei ein fürst!" und zum dritten: "du ein grafe frei!"
> zum vierten: "sei ein ritter schon!"
> zum fünften sprach er: "und du sei ein edelmon!"

[138] See *Eclogues of Baptista Mantuanus,* ed. W. P. Mustard, Baltimore, 1911, p. 35, footnote.
[139] Page 149.

zum sechsten: "ei,
du sei ein burger reich!"[140]

When Eve produced the ragged, dirty children, he laughed and
gave them low degrees:

Der her tet des rostigen haufen lachen,
tet bauren und hantwerker aus in machen,
zum malen und zum bachen,
schuster, weber und lederer
schmit und hafner, waidleut, fischer
furleut und der geleich.[141]

To Eve's query as to why children of the same parents should
be so differently rewarded, he replied with the simple philosophy of the necessity of all classes:

Got sprach: "es stet in meiner hant,
das ich im lant
mit leuten muß besetzen ein ieglichen stant,
darzu ich dan leut auserwel
und iedem stant seines geleichen leut zu stel,
auf das niemant
gebrech, was man sol han."
Also durch dise fabel wirt bedeute,
das man zu iedem stant noch findet leute;
darbei man spüret heute,
wie got so wunderbar regiert,
mit weisheit ziert, er ordiniert
zu iedem werk sein man.[142]

Twelve years later, in 1558, Hans Sachs in a *Spruchgedicht*
told the fable again in its simplest form.

A somewhat more elaborate version, however, appeared in
Germany in the sixteenth century in the works of several writers. As early as 1516, at Easter time, a five act play was presented at Freiberg, Saxony, before the duke and his court, concerning "den ungleichen Kindern Adam's und Eve, wie sie
Gott der Herr angeredet und examiniert," in which the distri-

[140] *Deutsche Dichtungen des sechzehnten Jahrhunderts,* IV, 213.
[141] *Ibid.*
[142] *Ibid.,* p. 214.

bution of estates is no longer a matter of ugliness and beauty, but of goodness and badness.[143] The text of this play is not extant, but another one, a *Tragedia von Adam und Eva*, of 1553, is extant and gives the content of the Freiberg play, the number of persons in it and their names, as well as its addition of angels, devils, and snakes. Just after the *Tragedia* had been published, Hans Sachs' *Spiel, wie Gott der Herr Adam und Eva ihre Kinder segnet* and also his five act comedy, *Die ungleichen Kinder Eve. Comedie, wie sie Got der Herr anret,* a working over of the *Spiel*, appeared. They, too, closely follow the version of the Freiberg play. Evidently all three plays were based on the Freiberg version. In the prologue of this comedy, however, Hans Sachs merely says that he has derived his theme from Philipp Melancthon. Melancthon did tell the story in a Latin letter to one Graf Johann von Wied, March 23, 1539. He says that he, in turn, has found it in a Latin poem. If it was Mantuan's poem that Melancthon used he changed it considerably in the telling: for in his version, as in all these expanded forms of the tale, he has God catechize the *good* and *bad* children of Adam and Eve, of whom Abel and Cain are the best and the worst respectively. There are five other good children and five other bad children, making six of each. Abel and his kind prove model boys, well versed in the Lord's Prayer, the Creed, and the Ten Commandments. Cain and his kind defy God and show their scorn by misstating all that they should have learned. The good sons God ordains to high estate, and the bad ones he promises hard labor and low estate forever. Cain, inspired by Satan to seek revenge, then kills Abel and is condemned to exile, a fugitive from all mankind. This is the story that Hans Sachs presents in his comedy. To the good children God gives the following estates:

> Wil auch in diser zeit euch geben
> glück unde heil auf diser erden,

---

[143] See *Deutsche Dichtungen*, VI, Einleitung, xxxvi-xl.

das groß leut aus euch sollen werden,
als köng, fürsten und potentaten.
gelert, prediger und prelaten.[144]

The bad children God condemns to hard labor:

derhalben so müßt ir auf erden
hart und armutselig leut werden,
als baurn, köbler, schefer und schinder,
badknecht, holzhackr und besenbinder,
taglöner, hirten, büttel und schergen,
kerner, wagenleut unde fergen,
jacobsbrüder, schustr und lantsknecht.[145]

The persistence of the story in Germany in the sixteenth century is further shown by its reappearance in several other works. Erasmus Alberus made a Latin dialogue of it, which Leonhart Jacobi turned into German in 1541. It also found a place in collections of stories: in Schumann's *Nachtbüchlein*, in Chyträus' *Fabeln*, published in 1571, and in Widmann's *Faust*, published in 1599.[146] As an explanation of the origin of feudal classes, the fable could scarcely be taken seriously in the sixteenth century. As a pleasant sermon on the practical advantages of being good, it must have made its appeal; for most of the works prefer the expanded version, in which the moral and religious implications predominate. But it is interesting to note that the non-moral form survives, too, no doubt because of its simplicity and naturalness and humanity.

4. OTHER CONTINENTAL VERSIONS

Other continental adaptations of the literature of estates should be noted. A Dutch version is that of Jacob van Oestvoren's *Die blauwe Schute*, 1413, a probable source of Brant's *Narrenschiff*.[147] The poem has two parts. In the first part is the list of classes of people belonging on the ship. One group, that of the men, is divided into the three estates: nobles, clergy,

[144] *Ibid.*, VI, 196.   [145] *Ibid.*, VI, 201.   [146] *Ibid.*, IV, 212, note.
[147] Friedrich Zarncke ed., *Das Narren Schyff*, Leipzig, 1854, p. lxiii.

citizens. Another group is that of the women: young maidens, unmarried women, married women. In the fourteenth century, about 1331, Boendale's *Jans Teesteye* was written, a *débat*, in which the poet complains of the times and expects improvement, especially from the merchants and peasants. The nobility and clergy are despaired of. Women's conduct, too, is scorned by the writer. There were other didactic pieces in similar vein. The *Miserere* of the Recluse of Molliens was partly translated into Dutch, as was also the shorter *Doctrinal le Sauvage*. That the literature of estates appears in Italian is evidenced by the *Fiori di virtú* discussed above. In Spanish, as has been noted,[148] the fashion of estates appeared in the *Libro de Alexandre*. Gower's *Confessio amantis*, the earliest English work to be translated, appeared in translation in both Spain and Portugal.[149]

[148] See p. 34.
[149] Macaulay ed., Intro., p. vii.

CHAPTER IV

HISTORY OF THE FORM: EARLY ENGLISH DEVELOPMENT

1. THE PROCESS OF ADOPTION

LIKE most forms of medieval French literature, the literature of the estates of the world found ready adoption in England. The literature of feudalism followed the institution, and though at first it found expression in French and Latin, English versions appeared in the early fourteenth century. In the latter half of the fourteenth century Gower, after putting his criticism of estates into French and Latin, finally catalogued them again in English. In the fifteenth century the literature grew in volume and reached its culmination with Lydgate and Caxton. But interest in it continued into the sixteenth and seventeenth centuries, in various guises, as will be indicated in the following chapters.

Conditions in fourteenth-century England lent interest to a form that could set forth the conflict of classes. By that time the three estates had become more or less crystallized into the political organization of the English government. The gradual development in the thirteenth century of a "parliament," or meeting to talk things over, meant representation in government of all three estates, even the commons. The commons, however, in this case, consisted of representatives of land-owning knights, two from each shire, and of prosperous burgesses, two from each of twenty-one towns. These representatives had little interest in the lower classes of working-men, gradually rising from the rank of villein or serf, and so there followed the social upheavals of the fourteenth century. The population was still mainly rural, and their occupation agriculture; but the process of substituting money rents for labor service, which had begun as early as the twelfth century, became general in the fourteenth. This new freedom from the soil, the growth of the towns, the development of new crafts and professions, and the loss of laborers through the Black Death, all tended to upset the old system of the three estates. With a tyrannous nobility, a luxury-loving clergy, and an arrogant, self-asserting commons, the writer of the literature of estates had plenty to say. What he says is often, though not always, indicative of his estate. Some writers have sympathy for the over-lords and despise the commons. Some, on the other hand, are champions of the commons and denounce the nobility. Almost all of them, lay and clerical writers alike, find fault with the clergy. The earliest works, however, like those on the continent, usually denounce all three estates and make general rather than specific charges.

2. Fourteenth-Century Adaptations

The Simonie,[1] "a poem on the evil times of Edward II" (1307-27), is probably one of the earliest Middle English pieces of the literature of estates. Though it breaks off abruptly and is evidently incomplete, it lists all the estates and charges them with avarice. The specific forms of avarice named are the familiar ones of French literature of estates; and this poem may quite probably have had a French original. It is distinguished, however, by a peculiar stanza form.

If you wish to know why the times are so bad, the poet will tell you the truth:

Whii werre and wrake in londe and manslauht is i-come,
Whii hungger and derthe on eorthe the pore hath undernome,
Whii bestes ben thus storve, whii corn hath ben so dere,
ȝe that wolen abide, listneth and ȝe muwen here
                                        the skile.
Inelle liȝen for no man, herkne who so wile.

The cause is simony, he says, and it begins "at the court of Rome":

[1] Thomas Wright's *The Political Songs of England from the Reign of John to that of Edward II*, Appendix, pp. 323-45.

Alle the popes clerkes han taken hem to red,
If treuthe come amonges hem, that he shal be ded.
There dar he noht shewen him for doute to be slain,
Among none of the cardinaus dar he noht be sein,
                                        for feerd,
If Symonie may mete wid him he wole shaken his berd.

If a wise man comes to Rome without silver, he will get nought. If a base wretch comes with money, he will gain his quest. The other ranks of clergy are no better than the court of Rome. Archbishops and bishops ought to inquire as to the lives of all churchmen under them; but some of them are fools themselves and lead such sorry lives that they dare not speak for fear of raising counter-accusations among the lower ranks of the clergy. Archdeacons, sent to visit different churches, all learn how to work most shrewdly: they will take bribes from this one and that and let the parson and priest have wives at will. Anything at all may go on in their parishes if money is there to pay for it. Meanwhile the archdeacons themselves lead a gay life with their "i-gadered markes and poundes." Abbots and priors ride with hawk and hound, and act like knights. They should leave off such pride and be religious. Pride, as well as simony, is master in the house of every religious order. If a poor man comes to the abbey for help, he gets none. If a man comes with "a litel lettre, in a box upon his hepe," he speeds the better, even if he is with someone who will harm the abbot. The Minorites, Jacobins, Carmelites, and Augustines would preach more for a bushel of wheat than for the salvation of a soul. They take into their orders men with money and turn out those without it. To an evil rich man who is sick they pay many visits: to a poor man they do not go. Officials and deans of cathedral chapters will give leave to sin if they receive a present. False physicians, an estate akin to the clergy, help a man to die. They swear that he is sicker than he is. They frighten the wife, get her money, spend it on wine and ale, and bring the sick man roots and rinds that make him worse. The rest of the laity are also avaricious. Earls, barons, knights, all ordained to uphold Holy Church and to fight for it, are the first to assail it. Thus is the whole "ordre of kniht turned up-so-doun." Justices, sheriffs, mayors, bailiffs are full of deceit and slander when it pays. By them "the pore is thus i-piled, and the riche forborn." Merchants used to buy and sell honestly, but no more. Now business is all treachery, and all merchants are false cheaters. So closes the list of estates. The rest of the poem is a much more general lament on the prevalence of simony and pride.

The prose tracts of Wycliff are full of references to the classes of society and of criticism of the defections of the three estates, with chief attention, of course, to those of the clergy. Fighting for reform in the Church in the days of papal captivity and schism, he has much to say about the shortcomings of all classes. In his "Schort Reule of Lif,"[2] for example, he names the "þre statis: prestis, lordis, laboreris," and discusses the duties of each. Similarly, in his tract "On Seven Deadly Sins,"[3] he divides the Church "in þese þre partis;—in prechoures, and deffendoures, and þo þridde part ben laboreres." Envy, pride, sloth are rife among them all. In "Of the Leaven of the Pharisees"[4] he analyzes the faults of lords and concludes that "Generaly ypocrisie regneþ among alle statis of cristen men," but that the faults of the "religious" are much the worst: "Clerkis possessioneris fordon presthod, knyȝthod & comineris."[5] Curates "maken lordis & comunes bi blynd devocion & ypocrisie to mayntenen worldly clerkis in pride, coveitise & ydelnesse & false techynge of anticristis errours undir colour of fredom & worschipynge of holy chirche & goddis lawe."[6] To put an end to the activities of make-believe friars, "lordis,

[2] *Select English Works,* ed. Thomas Arnold, Oxford, 1871, III, 204 ff.
[3] *Ibid.,* III, 130.
[4] *English Tracts,* ed. F. D. Matthew, London, 1880.
[5] *Ibid.,* "Of Clerks Possessioners," chap. I, pp. 116-18.
[6] *Ibid.,* "The Office of Curates," chap. XXXII, p. 162.

clerkis & comunes shulden helpe."⁷ Wycliff's firm belief in the
necessity of the three classes and in their divine origin is em-
phasized by his discovery of an analogy between them and the
three persons of the Trinity: "Almyȝty god þe trinyte, fadir,
sonne and holy gooste, boþe in þe olde lawe and þe newe haþ
fowndid his chirche up-on þre statis, awnswerynge or acordynge
to þes þre persones and her propirtes. . . ."⁸ Secular lords
are the Father, the clergy are the Son, and the commons are
the Holy Ghost. "And so þes þre statis ben, or schulde be, sufficient in goddis chirche." The clergy say that they have no
private property but hold all in common. They say, too, that
they do not occupy it as lords, but by perpetual alms. This
is untrue. They hold property just as the knight or baron does,
and execute lay justice. Instead of living like lords, they should
preach. God ordained knights and lords to defend the Church
and priests to preach.⁹ Other classes of society as well as the
clergy, however, need reform. Although "false confessouris ben
cause of alle þe synne þat regneþ among clerkis, among lordis,
among comunes, . . . also false men of lawe disceyven moche
þis world . . . & wynnen hem a litil worldly stynkynge muk
wiþ goddis curs. . . . Also false marchauntis bryngen up &
susteynen moche synne to distroie þe world."¹⁰ Lawyers and
merchants are guilty of "diverse gilis or disceitis & falsnesses."
From "lordis courtis to þe comyns," pride, gluttony, and lechery
are everywhere. The necessity of performing the duties of one's
estate Wycliff emphasizes in the tract "Of Servants and
Lords."¹¹ "First, servauntis schullen trewely & gladly serve to
here lordis or maistris & . . . holde hem paied of þe staat of
servauntis, in whiche god ordeyned hem for here beste." Later
he discusses also "hou lordis schulden lyve in here astaat."

⁷ Ibid., "Tractatus de Pseudo-Freris," p. 323.
⁸ Ibid., "The Clergy May Not Hold Property," pp. 362, 384.
⁹ Ibid., "De Officio Pastorali," pp. 408 ff.
¹⁰ Ibid., "Three Things Destroy His World," pp. 181 ff.
¹¹ Ibid., pp. 227, 230.

Wycliff's tracts are scarcely literature of estates in the strict sense in which the term is used to describe the French fashion of exact and orderly enumeration of classes in all their ranks. But they reflect distinctly the estates philosophy of the time and therefore may properly be included here.

Chaucer's relation to the literature of estates has been the subject of some discussion.[12] The knight of Chaucer's Prologue has been compared to "des chivalers et des gens d'armes" of the *Mirour de l'omme* of Gower; his monk, to the characterization "de monachis" in the *Vox clamantis* and "des Religious . . . possessioners" in the *Mirour;* his friar, to the long treatment of mendicant friars in both the *Mirour* and the *Vox clamantis;* and similarly his merchant, clerk, man of law, apothecary, and poor parson, to related treatment in Gower's works. Only Chaucer's plowman is different from Gower's. Chaucer's plowman is like Langland's, loyal to truth and duty, whereas Gower, having acquired the landowner's dislike of the laborer's demands for twice as much pay while doing only a third as much work as formerly and wanting to live as his master did, belabored the rude "servant of the plow," with none of Chaucer's tolerance or sympathy. Chaucer's Prologue has been said to have been influenced by the literature of the threefold estates of the world: nobility, clergy, and commons, with women as a necessary adjunct.[13] Certainly it does portray some of the most interesting types of people in those three classes, but Chaucer's superior artistry did not permit him to be satisfied with the customary exhaustive classification of estates and their defections. He was more interested in character than in denunciation, and for Gower's more or less morbid preachment Chaucer gives us a company of living personalities.

[12] See Ewald Flügel's "Gower's *Mirour de l'omme* und Chaucer's Prolog," *Anglia,* XXIV (1901), 437 f. and H. S. V. Jones' "The Plan of the Canterbury Tales," *Modern Philology,* XIII (May, 1915), 45.

[13] H. S. V. Jones, *Modern Philology,* XIII: 45.

Where Gower attempted an exhaustive catalogue, Chaucer, the artist, is brief. In the strict sense of the term, Chaucer's Prologue, like Wycliff's tracts, is not a piece of literature of estates. As a portrayal of fourteenth-century classes of society, it must, however, be considered. No doubt Chaucer was thoroughly familiar with the earlier literature of estates. His possible knowledge of the *Roman de carité* has been pointed out.[14] No doubt he was also thoroughly familiar with the literature of estates of his own time.

Neither is *The Vision of William Concerning Piers the Plowman* literature of estates in the strict sense of the term. For Langland, too, is not content with mere enumeration of all classes but introduces them wherever they serve his allegory in any order he sees fit to use. The term *estates* does not appear. Nevertheless, in the course of the long vision-allegory all classes are introduced and their duties and defections described. The nearest the poet comes to enumeration of estates is the following passage, descriptive of the gathering for Meed's marriage:

> And al þe riche retynaunce · þat roteþ hem on fals lyvynge
> Were bede to þat brudale · on boþe half þe contreie,
> Of many maner men · þat were of medes kunne;
> Of knyȝtes, of clerkes · of oþer commune puple,
> As sysours and somners · shereyves and here clerkes,
> Budels and bailifs · and brokours of chaffare,
> [Forgoers] and vytailers · and vokettus of [þe] Arches,
> Ich kan noȝt rekenye þe route · þat ran a-boute mede.[15]

The duties of each class of society are also described, in the following paraphrase of Isaiah 2: 4:

> Ech man to pleye with a plouh · a pycoyse oþer a spade,
> Spynnen, and spek of god · and spille no tyme:

[14] *Ibid.*, p. 46 and G. L. Kittredge, "Chaucer and the Roman de Carité," *Modern Language Notes*, XII (Feb., 1897), 113-15.

[15] Ed. W. W. Skeat, E.E.T.S., London, 1873, orig. ser., LIV, C-Text, Passus III, 30 ff.

> Prestes and persons · *placebo* and *dirige,*
> Here sauter and here sevene psalmis · for alle synful preyen.
> Haukyng oþer hontyng · yf eny of hem hit usie,
> Shal lese þer-fore hus lyve-lode · and hus lif paraventure.
> Shal noþer kyng ne kny3t · constable ne mey:e
> Over-cark þe comune · ne to þe court sompne,
> Ne putte men in panell · ne do men plighte here treuthe;
> Bote after þe dede þat ys ydo · the dome shal recorde,
> Mercy oþer no mercy · as most trewe a-corden.
> Kynges court and comune court · constorie and chapitre,
> Al shal be bote on court · and on berne be Iustice;
> That worth trewe-tunge a [tydy] man · þat tenede me nevere.
> Batailles shulle nevere eft be · ne man bere eg-tool,
> And yf eny man [smyþie] hit · smyte þer-with to deþe.[16]

Conscience is here comparing the corruptions of Meed with the peace and order that prevail when "kynde love" comes to take her place. In the literature of estates, common love or love of one class for another is often cited as the only remedy for the corruption of the times.[17] The sermon of Reason also discusses the duties of the humbler classes, the pomp and arrogance of the prelates and priests and monks, and the duties of kings and popes:

> He bad wastours go worche · and wynne here sustinaunces
> Þorw som trewe travail · and no tyme spille . . .
> And sitthe he preide prelates · and prestes to-geders,
> That hij precheþ to þe puple · proven hit hem-selve . . .
> And amende 3ow monkes · moniales, and chanons,
> And putte 3ow to 3oure penaunce · *ad pristinum statum ire* . . .
> And sitthe he consailed þe kyng · hus comune to lovye;
> For þe comune ys þe kynges tresour . . .
> And sitthen he preide þe pope · have pyte of holy-churche . . .[18]

Women, meanwhile, may spin wool and flax for the poor and sew chasubles for chaplains. There are other passages in the same vein, interspersed with, and incidental to, the allegory of Piers Plowman's search for Truth.

[16] *Ibid.,* Passus IV, p. 67.   [17] See below, pp. 369-76.
[18] *Ibid.,* Passus VI, pp. 89, 92.

The shorter poem *Richard the Redeles,*[19] ascribed also to Langland, names three "degrees" as necessary to a realm. Sympathizing with Richard II in his conflict with Bolingbroke, the poet warns that Richard's courtiers have plucked away his power while he, in turn, has despoiled the people. Allegiance is secured only by law and love. All three degrees have rights and duties:

> ffor tristith, als trewly · as tyllinge us helpeth,
> þat iche rewmw undir roff · of þe reyne-bowe
> Sholde stable and stonde · be þese þre degres:
> By governaunce of grete · and of good age;
> By styffnesse and strengthe · of steeris well y-yokyd,
> Þat beth myȝthfull men · of þe mydill age;
> And be laboreris of lond · þat lyfflode ne ffayle.[20]

Of this enumeration the editor says that the numbers 1, 2, 3 are prefixed in the manuscript to the lines beginning "By governaunce," "By styffnesse," and "And be laboreris." "These refer," he says, "to the 'thre degres,' viz. 1. *Oratores* (here Counsellors); 2. *Bellatores* (Warriors); and 3. *Laboratores* (Labourers); according to the old three-fold division." Without aid it would be exceedingly difficult to recognize the three estates in this Middle English poem. Perhaps the poet, whoever he was, was referring to the three feudal classes, and perhaps he was not. The rest of the poem is devoted to discussion of a ruler's duties and does not concern us here.

John Gower's great concern with the estates of the realm has already been indicated in consideration of his *Vox clamantis* and *Mirour de l'omme.*[21] His third long work, the English *Confessio amantis,* also has, in its thousand-line Prologue, an enumeration of the estates of the world and their faults in ex-

---

[19] Ed. W. W. Skeat, bound with *Piers Plowman,* E.E.T.S., London, 1873, orig. ser., No. LIV. The editor says that it is unquestionably by Langland. Thomas Wright, who published it twice before this printing, said it is not by Langland.

[20] *Ibid.,* p. 495.

[21] Pages 28 and 61-65.

actly the same fashion as that of his French and Latin poems. The description of the corruptions of the classes in the *Confessio amantis* is more general, but the form and content are almost identical. The rest of the poem is, as everyone knows, a series of love stories, and at first thought, one wonders how Gower can possibly prefix a prologue on estates to such a book. The explanation is simple, to a medievalist. The cause of discord and corruption among the classes is lack of love. The poet has found that, with all his previous sermons to the universe, he has been unable to change it. He has found it a hopeless task. So he proposes to discuss that which the world lacks, namely, love, as a more hopeful subject, because it does wonders in the world.

> I may noght strecche up to the hevene
> Min hand, ne setten al in evene
> This world, which evere is in balance:
> It stant noght in my sufficance
> So grete thinges to compasse,
> Bot I mot lete it overpasse
> And treten upon othre thinges.[22]

Perhaps the fact that Gower had no other language at his command into which to put his philosophy of estates also made some considerable difference in his decision to turn to a new theme. Nevertheless, the old theme proved irresistible for the third time; and so he put it into English as well as Latin and French.

After a few lines of introduction, announcing that the Prologue is to consider the present evil times, as compared with the good old times, the three estates, Temporal Rulers, the Church, the Commons, are described as the causes of the evil in the world. Formerly temporal lords kept peace and administered justice; the clergy lived exemplary lives and cared for their flocks; the commons kept their place. Now, in the six-

[22] *The Complete Works of John Gower,* ed. G. C. Macaulay, I, 35, Liber I, ll. 1 ff.

teenth year of the reign of King Richard II, there are only war
and plunder on the part of the rulers, simony and high living
among the clergy, arrogance and sloth among the commons.

> The world stant evere upon debat,
> So may be seker non astat . . .

Man alone is cause of all this discord, and love is the only
remedy.[23] In conclusion, the theme of the destruction of the
four monarchies is introduced to prove the evil effects of division.

Brief references to the estates occur in various long works
in the fourteenth century. Those in the *Pricke of Conscience*
are typical. It is the familiar theme that death comes to all
that causes the poet to dwell on the classes subject to it:

> Emperour, kyng, duke, ne caysere,
> Ne other þat bers grete state here,
> Ne riche, ne pure, bond ne fre,
> Lered or lawed, what-swa he be.[24]

And again:

> Ded wil na frendshcpc do ne favour,
> Ne reverence til kyng ne til emperour,
> Ne til pape, ne til bisshope, ne na prelate,
> Ne til nan other man of heghe estate,
> Ne til na religiouse, ne til na seculere,
> For dede over al men has powere.[25]

These brief references, though entirely incidental to the subject matter and purpose of the whole work, are interesting as
further evidence of the wide occurrence of the theme.

In addition to the longer treatments of the fourteenth-century English estates there are many short poems in manuscripts
of the fourteenth and fifteenth centuries lamenting the corruptions of the times and referring to the classes giving evidence

---

[23] *Ibid.*, Prologue, ll. 8-16, 115-21, 148-50, 183-87, 1048-50, etc. See
below pp. 369-76.

[24] Ed. Richard Morris, Berlin, 1863, Book I, p. 25, ll. 882 ff.

[25] *Ibid.*, Book III, p. 52, ll. 1884 ff.

of those corruptions.[26] Sometimes only one class is named, sometimes all three. It was out of such brief laments, perhaps, that the longer literature of estates grew. The one called "Syr Peny" is typical. Like the Latin poem "De Nummo,"[27] it enumerates all that bow to him:

> Pope, kyng, and emperoure,
> Byschope, abbot, and prioure,
> Parson, preste, and kny3t,
> Duke, erle, and baron,
> To serve sur Peny are they boen,
> Both be day and ny3th.[28]

The similar Anglo-Norman poem in the same volume called "Sir Pride the Emperor" has been described above.[29]

About half of the poems in a certain fifteenth-century manuscript[30] tell the three estates of the realm their faults in no gentle terms. The poems reflect the corruptions of the reigns of Henry IV and Henry V. The poet, probably an abbot or prior of the south-midland part of England, has strong democratic sympathies.[31] He probably occupied a seat in Parliament and voted with the commons. He repeatedly asserts that the commons make a kingdom, that it is they who uphold the honor of lords and Church and are the jewels of the king's crown. The commons, however, have been oppressed by nobility and clergy; and so most of the advice is addressed to the latter in favor of the commons. He who robs the poor will not prosper. Law must rule; justice, truth, and peace must prevail. Prosperity means a

---

[26] See *Political Poems and Songs on English History 1327-1483,* ed. Thos. Wright, London, 1861, 2 vols. Also *Reliquiae antiquae,* ed. Thos. Wright and J. O. Halliwell, London, 1845, 2 vols.

[27] See p. 25. For other references to Sir Nummus, see pp. 145, 200, 201, 202, 257, 342-43.

[28] *Reliquiae antiquae,* II, 108. Poem also printed in appendix to *Latin Poems Commonly Attributed to Walter Mapes,* ed. Thos. Wright.

[29] See p. 71.

[30] *Political and Other Poems,* ed. Dr. J. Kail, E.E.T.S., London, 1904, orig. ser., No. CXXIV.   [31] See Intro., p. ix.

full treasury. But what is a kingdom's treasury? Cattle and grain are important, but so are loyal estates of the realm:

> Bestayle, corn stuffed in store,
> Riche comouns, and wyse clergy;
> Marchaundes, squyers, chivalry
>   That wol be redy at a res
> And chevalrous kyng in wittes hyȝe,
>   To lede in were, and governe in pes.[32]

The sworn duty of king and knight is to maintain right:

> Eche kyng is sworn to governaunce
> To governe goddis puple in riȝt.
> Eche kyng bereþ swerd of goddis vengeaunce
> To felle goddis foon in fiȝt.
> And so doþ everons honest knyȝt
>   That bereþ þe ordre as it wes;
> The plough, þe chirche, to mayntene ryȝt,
>   Are goddis champyons, to kepe þe pes.[33]

God made one law "for eche astate": do no wrong; and "eche astate" deserves according as he obeys it. All the world is like a cherry fair, often changing, for death takes "popes, prelates and lordynges"; all are mortal, even kings. Let the kings, therefore, protect their subjects, let the clergy preach as they are charged to do, let judges administer justice, and commons support all. All estates must support the Crown. The estates of the realm are the stones and flowers in the king's crown:

> What doþ a kynges crowne signyfye,
> Whan stones and floures on sercle is bent?
> Lordis, comouns, and clergye
>   To ben all at on assent . . .
> Þe leste lyge-man, wiþ body and rent,
>   He is a parcel of þe crowne.[34]

But the short poem of most interest so far as the literature of estates is concerned is "The Descryvyng of Mannes Membres,"[35] apparently written about 1418. These anatomical verses

---

[32] *Ibid.*, p. 11, stanza 9.

[33] *Ibid.*, p. 13, stanza 18.

[34] *Ibid.*, p. 51, stanza 2.

[35] *Ibid.*, pp. 64 f.

are an English version of the medieval theory that represented the commonwealth as a body of articulate members, working together, much as the members of the human body work together. It has already been noted in the French in the *Roman de Fauvel* of Gervais du Bus.[36] "The heved, y likne to a kyng," and mouth, nose, eyes, and ears are his chief of counsel. The neck is a justice, judging rightly. Man's breast is "presthod in good degre." The shoulders and backbone are the lords of the land; the arms, the knights; the hands, the squires; the fingers, yeomen. Man's ribs are men of law. The legs are "all craftes þat worche wiþ handes." The feet are "alle trewe tylyers of landes." Even the toes have their representatives in true servants, who serve in all kinds of weather and under any circumstances. "He may not stonde, þat haþ no toon," nor do any thing else. Servants need not feel insulted, therefore, by their lowly position.

Fifteenth-century literature of estates in England is somewhat more extensive than that of the fourteenth century, chiefly in the work of Lydgate and Caxton. With the gradual decline of feudalism and the growing tendency toward monarchy, old social classes gave way to new. Those of high estate more often fell to low, and those of low estate found it much easier to rise aloft. The consequent unrest made class consciousness keener than it had ever been before. Moralists felt the necessity of telling people to stay in the class to which they belonged, for the welfare of the realm. Moreover, the industry and skill of Caxton made possible the translation and publication in England of French fashions as yet not widely known.

3. Lydgate's Use of the Form

"Lamenting Lidgate," a sixteenth-century writer[37] said of him, "lurking emong the Lilies with a balde skons, with a gar-

---

[36] See p. 53; also pp. 119-20, 165, 261-62, 263-64, 315, 369-70.

[37] Wm. Bullein in his *Dialogue Against the Fever Pestilence*, E.E.T.S., London, 1888, ext. ser., LII, 17.

land of Willowes about his pate: booted he was after Sainct
Benets guise, and a black stamell robe with a lothly monsterous
hoode, hanging backwarde; his stoopyng forward *bewayling
every estate,*[38] with the spirite of providence forseyng the falles
of wicked men, and the slipprie seates of princes, the ebbyng
and flowyng, the risyng and falling of men in auctoritie, and
how vertue doth aduaunce the simple, and vice ouerthrowe the
most noble of the worlde." No doubt Bullein was referring particularly to the *Fall of Princes,* but Lydgate sees fit to "bewail
every estate" in some way or other in several of his most important works. Even in such pieces as his *Troy Book,*[39] where
he must turn his attention to non-feudal society and tell the
story of the destruction of Troy as he found it already written
in the version of Guido de la Colonna, he talks of King Peleus'
assembling his "estates of degre," and of the Greeks' finding
Colchos a place where "all estatis, bothe hie and lowe, hadden
her lyf in sovereyn suffisaunce." In Priam's new palace, Ilion,
in rebuilt Troy, Lydgate tells us, he had seats arranged for
nobles according to rank: "Only þe statis by ordre to devyde."
In Priam's "parlement" only his lords sat, but Priam thought
that the decision of the lords to make war, "of all þe comoun"
should be confirmed. The two Egyptian merchants in Lydgate's
translation of the *Fabula duorum mercatorum*[40] also become
estates: "In Egipt whilom, as I reede and fynde, Ther dwellyd
a marchaunt of high and gret estat," who later "gan to pleyne
his sodeyn poore estaat." In his translation of the *Secreta secretorum* he also frequently uses the term *estat.*

Some of Lydgate's works, like the *Temple of Glas* and the
Siege of Thebes, contain no references to estates; nor is the
route of folk described in the *Assembly of the Gods,* sometimes

[38] Italics mine.
[39] Ed. Henry Bergen, E.E.T.S., London, 1906, 1908, 1910, ext. ser., Nos.
XCVII, CIII, CVI. Quotations from XCVII, 23, 50, 173, 234.
[40] Ed. Dr. Gustav Schleich, *Quellen und Forschungen zur Sprachgeschichte,* Vol. LXXXI-LXXXIII, Strassburg, 1897, stanzas 1 and 79.

ascribed to Lydgate, but certainly not his,[41] that of the literature of estates found elsewhere. There, on the battlefield of Microcosm, Vice contends with Virtue. Vice is followed by the seven deadly sins as well as other sins. In the train of Idleness is a host of commons: boasters, braggers, bribers, liars, heretics, backbiters, glosers, renegade knights, double-tolling millers, jolly tapsters, keepers of stews. Virtue's helpers are the cardinal virtues, likewise followed by a great company of commons, but not one tenth of Vice's army: famous doctors, conscientious priests, discreet confessors, fowlers, despisers of vain riches, peacable prelates, just governors, founders of churches, well-meaning merchants, true artificers, virgins pure, holy matrons, pilgrims and palmers, true laborers, holy hermits, monasterial monks, well-disposed friars, canons, and nuns. These are rather haphazard armies, and they bear no evident relation to the literature of estates.

Lydgate's *Horse, Sheep, and Goose*[42] is somewhat more typical of the *genre*. Here the poet describes a dispute or trial that he saw painted on a wall. The horse, sheep, and goose dispute as to which is more valuable to the *re publica*. The Lion and the Eagle, of "estat roiall," act as judges. Each disputant cites famous animals of each kind in history and shows the practical uses of each. The sheep, too shy to speak for himself, is extolled by the ram. The decision of the judges is that all three are necessary to the commonwealth:

> Thus all vertues / allone hath nat oo man:
> That oon lakkith / god hath yove a-nothir:
> That thou canst nat / parcas a-nothir can:
> So entircomon / as brothir doth with brothir;
> And, if charite / governe weele the tothir,

[41] Ed. O. L. Triggs, E.E.T.S., London, 1896, ext. ser., No. LXIX. See also MacCracken's "The Lydgate Canon," *The Minor Poems of John Lydgate*, E.E.T.S., ext. ser., CVII, xxxv f.

[42] Ed. F. J. Furnivall, E.E.T.S., London, 1866, ext. ser., No. XV, re-edited 1903.

> And in oo clausë / speke in wordis pleyn,
> That no man shold / of othir ha disdeyn.

The philosophy is that of the literature of estates, but the poem nowhere identifies the animals with any particular estates. The reader, apparently, was to make the identification for himself.

A complete classification of feudal society is found in Lydgate's *Daunce of Machabree,* "wherein is lively expressed and shewed the state of manne and howe he is called at uncertaine tymes by death, and when he thinketh least thereon: made by thaforesayde Dan John Lydgate Monke of Burye."[43] It was translated from a French poem on the same theme. Lydgate's version begins with a prologue, in which he states his theme, that death spares no one, "Popes, kynges, ne worthye Emperours," and then tells how he came to write:

> Considereth this, ye folkes that been wyse,
> And it emprinteth in your memoriall,
> Like thensample which that at Parise
> I fonde depict ones uppon a wal
> Full notably, as I rehearse shall,
> Of a Frenche Machabrees daunce.

The warning in this poem is to serve as a "mirrour" for all estates in the pilgrimage of life. The poem proper is in dialogue form: "Death fyrst speaketh unto the Pope, and after to every degree as foloweth." Each degree replies, after being spoken to. To the Pope Death says:

> Ye that been set most high in dignitie
> Of al estates in earth spirituall,
> And like to Peter hath the soveraintee
> Over the church and states temporall,
> Upon this daunce ye first begin[ne] shall,
> As most worthy lord and governour;
> For al the worship of your estate papall,
> And of [al] lordship to God is the honour.

---

[43] Appendix to Lydgate's *Fall of Princes,* ed. Dr. Henry Bergen, E.E.T.S., London, 1924, ext. ser., CXXIII, Part III, 1025-44.

The Pope replies:

> Fyrst me behoveth this daunce for to lede,
> Which sat in earth [e] highest in my see,
> The state ful perilous, whoso taketh hede,
> To occupie Seynt Petris Dignitee;
> But for al that [fro] Death I may not flee,
> Upon this daunce with other for to trace;
> For which al honor, who prudently can see,
> Is litle worth that doth so some passe.

Death speaks similarly in turn to the Emperour, the Cardinal, the Kyng, the Patriarche, the Cunstable, the Archebishop, the Barone, the Princesse, the Bishop, the Squyer, the Abbot, the Abbesse, the Bayly, the Astronomer, the Burgis, the Chanon Seculer, the Marchaunte, the Chartreux, the Sargeaunte, the Monke, the Usurer, the Phisicien, the Amerous Squyre, the Gentlewoman, the Man of Law, Master John Rikil Tregetour (juggler of Henry, King of England and conqueror of France), the Person, the Iurrour, the Minstral, the Labourer, the Frere Menour, the Chylde, the Yong Clerke, and the Hermite. Each time Death reminds the one addressed that the "Daunce" is inevitable and that much must be left behind. The reply admits folly, usually, and says, Yes, death is inevitable. It is interesting to note that to the Labourer Death is kindly:

> And cause why that I thee assoyle
> Is onely this: from thee to discever
> The false world that can so folkes fayle.

The poem concludes with the usual references to the work of the worms. A "King ligging eaten by Wormes" speaks:

> Howe I lye here whylom crouned kyng,
> To al estates a true resemblaunce,
> That wormes foode is fine of our livyng.

Machabree, the Doctor, advises all to live well and be ready when Death comes.

In his translation of DeGuileville's *Pélerinage de la vie hu-*

maine[44] Lydgate sets forth the whole philosophy of the literature of estates. It has no detailed enumeration of all ranks as in
the *Daunce of Machabree,* but it has the philosophy of estates
that the *Daunce of Machabree* lacks. Lydgate was translating
for Lord Salisbury, who had fought in France, and the doctrine
of the *Pilgrimage* no doubt was his own politics as well. In the
allegory, the philosophy is put into the mouth of Labor, a
humble net-maker. The pilgrim, on his way to Jerusalem, comes
to a forked road: on the left sits Miss Idleness; on the right,
Labour, the Net-maker. When pilgrim is advised to take the
right road, he asks the Net-maker why he follows so simple a
craft. Net-maker replies that each one must work according
to his powers. And in the world there must be diversity of ranks
and crafts:

> Lerne ek off me, thys sentence,
> Ther muste be a dyfference
> (Pleynly yiff thow lyst to knowe,)
> Off Estatys hih & lowe,
> And off crafftys ek also.
> And tak also good heed herto,
> Yiff all ffolk in a Regioun
> Hadden On occupacioun
> In the Rychest crafft of alle,
> Demë thanne what sholdë falle.[45]

If all were in one craft, all would be alike—"the ffoot as good
as ys the hed." Then a knave, by his working, would be equal to
a king, and that would be "no maner polycye, But rather a
confusïon In every maner Regïoun." Every degree has a duty
to perform for the good of the realm:

> Wherfor, in Townys & cytes,
> Lat men lyven lyk her degres:
> Wysë ffolk that kan dyscerne,
> Lat hem by wysdam so governe

[44] E.E.T.S., Nos. LXXVII, LXXXIII, XCII (1899, 1901, 1904). Also *Rox-burghe Club Pubs.,* ed. F. J. Furnivall and Katherine Locock, London, 1905.
[45] *Roxburghe Club Pubs.,* CXLV, **310-11**, ll. **11363** ff.

That no man ne have no wrong;
And swych as myghty ben, & strong,
Wyth myghte lat hem the lond dyffende;
And clerkys to ther studye entende;
And labourerys, lat hem werche;
And spyrytual ffolk off the cherche,
Lat ther occupacïoun
Ben in contemplacïoun,
In devocioun & prayere;
Voyde hem ffrom offyce seculer;
Lat hem go lyve lyk ther bond;
And swyche ffolk as tyle the lond,
Lat hem do trewly ther labour,
Bothe in drouht & ek in shour;
ffor trewly (yiff I rekne shal)
Carte & plowh, they ber up al
The clergye & the chevalrye.[46]

Every craft, no matter how lowly, is necessary. Therefore, says the Net-maker, do not scorn even mine. Though poorly clad, I am not to be despised. Nowadays he who is richly clad is thought wisest in the world, and, though a man had studied at Paris every science and were poorly clad, men would think his wisdom folly and him a fool. No wonder men think Labour a fool since his clothes are all torn. And yet, he concludes,

<blockquote>I sustene & ber up al.</blockquote>

Nowhere in Lydgate's work, however, is the philosophy of estates set forth at such length as in his *Fall of Princes*. He is "translating" from the French prose paraphrase of Boccaccio's *De casibus virorum,* and reflects the French point of view, even though he constantly has his eye on "Bochas," his authority. The differences in the three versions have been clearly indicated.[47] To Boccaccio, princes, spiritual or temporal, were fit only for his scorn. In his dedicatory epistle he said that no

[46] *Ibid.,* ll. 11378 ff.
[47] By the editor, Dr. Henry Bergen, E.E.T.S., London, 1924, ext. ser., CXXI, Intro., ix-xxvii.

pope, emperor, or king was worthy of his dedication—they all
"made him sick."[48] The corruptions of the world were due to
its rulers. The people were contaminated by their example. To
be sure, this epistle made a fitting introduction to a work on the
stories of the sad ends of the illustrious personages of mythol-
ogy and history. Strangely enough, Boccaccio's fate was to be
translated by two men in the service of such "great ones" as
Boccaccio despised—both known for their unquestioned loyalty
to their ruler and for their reverence for the political systems of
the time. Laurence de Premierfait's *Des cas des nobles hommes
et femmes* was translated for and dedicated to an unscrupulous
tyrant, the Duke of Berry, and Lydgate's version was made at
the request of and dedicated to Humphrey, Duke of Gloucester,
no less unscrupulous. Nevertheless, into the French version crept
a plea for agricultural laborers that is reflected in Lydgate's
version, though his attitude is always that of the aristocrat with
a good deal of contempt for the political abilities of the people.
So the work changes from a treatise written in scorn of rulers
to one equally disdainful of the people they rule; it begins with
the belief that no ruler is fit to rule and therefore falls, and
ends with the belief that subjects of rulers exist to be ruled and
for their benefit. Boccaccio was not steeped in the philosophy
of the estates of the world whereas Laurence and Lydgate were
and wrote accordingly. Because that philosophy included analysis of the faults of the nobility, even the French and English
versions lament in general terms the tyranny and avarice of the
feudal lords, but the tone is always friendly and supplicating,
not scornful like Boccaccio's. Lydgate's work was immensely
popular in England for at least a hundred and fifty years.

The dedication of Laurence introduces the philosophy of
estates. His purpose is to explain why men are subject to Fortune. The explanation consists of an analysis of the faults of

[48] "Quadpropter nausea quadam vexatus . . . ab indagine destiti."
Ibid., p. 1.

the three estates: "Comment lacteur parle du cas de leglise presente et des prestres," "Laucteur parle du cas de noblesse mondaine," and "Ci parle lacteur du cas des laboureux champestres."[49] It begins with a lament: "Helas, las, et troys foys las, par faulte de ceste sapience." What hearts or eyes but must be saddened by the sight and must weep "quant les hommes voient clerement et cognoissent les cas ia aduenus des troys estatz du monde? Cest assauoir, des prestres, des nobles hommes, aussi des laboureurs de cestui temps." The priests are berated for their ignorance and avarice, the nobles for their lack of noblesse, and the laborers are not berated but commiserated for their unhappy lot. Laurence takes Virgil for his authority that the life of a laborer is a happy one: "Il nest aulcun aultre estat qui ait en soy teles excellances en profis en delitz et en honnestetes publiques et priues comme la vie et estat des laboureurs, par qui les hommes sont sousten et nouris en necessite de corps et les sacrifices diuins sont admenistres selon la religion publique." They cannot be abased by Fortune's wheel. But now, alas, they suffer hardships. They no longer are sure of a living. After paying their tithes and rents, they are not even sure of what is left. Surely God intended a man to have a home and the necessities of life. Laurence exhorts the Duke of Berry to help them. Laws should be passed to improve their condition. They suffer through the avarice of the other estates.

Lydgate's version reflects this same concern with estates. He says that Laurence was required "Off estatis" to write and also that "Bochas" wrote of "Grete emperours, estatis and degrées." These who have fallen have supposed "Ther estatis sholde be durable," only to find that Fortune's wheel sent them downward. Lydgate's stories begin with Adam and Eve and end with King John, taken prisoner in France by Prince Edward. The incongruity of the fall of Adam and Eve "from ther estat roiall" is

[49] *Ibid.*, p. liv.

THE WHEEL OF FORTUNE
From Lydgate's *Fall of Princes*

amusing, to say the least. Similarly Nimrod, Cadmus, Gideon, Œdipus fell:

> Who clymbeth hiest, his fal is lowest doun;
> A mene estat is best, who koude it knowe,—
> Tween hih presumyng & bowyng down to lowe.

The story of Saul is used to show the fate of one who became king, though of low estate. As long as he ruled with wisdom, God aided him. When he became willful and proud and no longer obeyed God, God withdrew his grace. Saul fell. The poet asks:

> What thyng in herte mor froward mai be thouht
> Than is the sodeyn fals presumpcioun
> Off a wrechche that cam up off nouht,
> To yeve hym lordshepe and dominacioun?
> And for to make a pleyn comparisoun,
> Men sholde resoun dreede a leoun lasse
> Than the reudnesse off a crownyd asse.

All this is no rebuke of poverty, however, the poet says very generously, for a poor man may have true nobility, and God may raise him up "Onto thestat off vertuous noblesse." Any poor man who is wholly virtuous may be called "gentil veraili in deede," no matter what his "kynreede." This same idea is expressed again several times. Some of low estate have arisen and been powerful, as, for example, Socrates, Euripides, and Demosthenes.

The story of Rehoboam in the *Fall of Princes* is a sermon to princes who disdain their subjects. The poet's chief argument is the familiar analogy between the estates of the commonwealth and the members of the human body.[50] Let princes remember that all lordship first rose out of labor. The fame of emperors, princes, even the Nine Worthies rested on the labor of the people. The prince is the head, but there must also be warriors to defend the body politic:

> Ther mut been handis & armys off diffence,
> Which shal this ymage manli keepe and guie

[50] E.E.T.S., ext. ser., CXXI, Part I, 223-24. For other uses of the analogy see pp. 53, 165, 261-62, 263-64, 315, 369-70.

From all assautis off foreyn violence,
Which shal be named noblesse off chevalrie—
Ther trewe office iustli to magnefie,
Sustene the chirch & make hemsilven strong
To see that widwes nor maidnes ha[ve] no wrong.

There must also be judges:

Prudent iuges, as it is skele and riht,
To punshe wrong and surfetis to redresse.

The body of the figure represents the people of various degrees:

Mid this ymage there is a bodi set,
An agregat off peeplis and degrees,
Be parfit pes and unyte I-knet
Bi thestatis that governe comountees,—
As meires, provostes & burgeis in citees,
Marchauntis also, which seeke sundri londis,
With othir crafftis which lyven bi ther hondis.

To the second estate, the clergy, is ascribed the part of the soul,
a common ascription in medieval political theory. The Church
was the soul of government; the temporal authority, the body.

This bodi must have a soule off liff
To quyke the membris with gostli mociouns,
Which shal be maad off folk contemplatiff,
The cherche committed to their pocessiouns,
Which bi ther hooli conversaciouns
And good exaumple[s] sholde as sterris shyne,
Be grace and vertu the peeple [t] enlumyne.

Lastly, the part of the laborers is described in the usual fashion:

Folwyng upon, off entent ful cleene,
Laboreris, as ye han herd devised,
Shal this bodi bern up and susteene
As feet and leggis, which may nat be despised;
For trewe labour is iustli auctorised,
And ner the plouh upholden be travaile,
Of kynges, pryncis farweel al governaile.

If all parts of this body do their duty, then the image is well
wrought:

Thus first yiff pryncis governed been be riht,
And knyghthood suffre the peeple to ha[ve] no wrong,

And trouthe in iuges shewe out his cleer liht,
And feith in cites with love be drawe a-long,
And hooli cherche in vertu be maad strong,
And in his labour the plouh ne feyne nouht,—
Thanne be proporcioun this ymage is weel wrouht.

Other stories in the *Fall of Princes* illustrate the various faults of the estates. Such faults did not exist in the good old times, according to "Bochas." In olden times, each estate did its ordained duty:

Lordshipe that tyme avoided meyntenaunce,
Hoolichurch lyved in parfitnesse;
Knyhthod tho daies for trouthe whet his launce,
And fals extorsioun hadde non interesse;
Marchantis wynnyng cam al off rihtwisnesse,
Artificers the werkdai wer nat idill,
And bisynesse off labour heeld the bridill.

In a digression later on, this former "golden worlde" is again described, and, incongruously enough, it is assigned to the time of Noah and Abraham. In Noah's day, says the poet, the estates of knighthood, clergy, merchant, and labor were upright and dutiful:

Knyhthod in prowesse gaff out so cleer a liht,
Girt with his suerd of trouthe & equyte,
Heeld up the cherch in spiritual dignite,
Punshed hertikes, because attemperaunce
Had in that world hooli the governaunce . . .
The trewe marchaunt be mesour bouht & solde,
Deceit was non in the artificeer,
Makyng no balkis, the plouh was treuli holde,
Abak stood idilnesse ferr from laborer.

In another digression the writer laments that all estates, lords, men of church, knights, and merchants, have enough and to spare, but that poor poets must go a-begging. In still another, also according to Bochas, the proper apparel of all estates is described, since nowadays all estates dress beyond their ranks. Thus, in story and occasional digression, the estates are told their defections.

Many of Lydgate's minor poems also revolve about the theme of the existence or the conditions of the estates of the world. "A Prayer to St. Thomas of Canterbury,"[51] for example, closes with specific enumeration of those to be prayed for:

> Sith Crist ech day doth miracles for the werche,
> Of grace and mercie have first in Remembraunce,
> Pray for the states of all hooly Cherche,
> For the kynges vertuous governaunce,
> For hys Prynces Marcial Puissaunce,
> That high discrecioun may ther Brydel leede,
> Lyke ther degrees lyve to thy pleasaunce,
> And pray for alle that calle the in ther neede.

> Pray for thy Capeleyns, be to hem gracious,
> Which ever in oon abide in thy servise,
> Monckes professed, Preestes religious,
> To pleese Ihesu at mydnyght thay arise,
> Thou as ther Patroun, defende hem in sich wise,
> Thy Cherch, thy Toun, that noman hem mysbede,
> For thy Monasterie soo graciously devyse
> To be ther support and cheef help at ther neede.

> For Knyghtes, Squyeres, and yomen for the werre,
> In al juste Title make hem to prevaile,
> Pray for marchauntes that saile fro soo ferre,
> For Artificeres that lyve by ther travaile,
> For trew ti[t]he[r]es, and pray for the poraile,
> Lat thy blessynge on all these ffolkes sprede,
> Pray Iesu stynt blood-shedynge and Bataile,
> And pray for alle that calle the in ther neede.

The estates of the world fashion must have been very convenient for prayer, for having gone through the whole hierarchy, the priest could be sure that he had omitted no one—just as today a prayer for world, nation, state, city, and congregation is common, probably for the assurance of order and completeness that it gives.

The admonitions to the estates in the English version of the

[51] *The Minor Poems of John Lydgate,* ed. Henry Noble MacCracken, E.E.T.S., London, 1911, ext. ser., CVII, 140.

"Duodecim abusiones," ascribed to Lydgate, also include the whole hierarchy. The twelve Latin phrases, which were apparently familiar also in Anglo-Saxon and Middle English,[52] list the classes as follows:

Rex sine sapiencia.	Episcopus sine doctrina.
Dominus sine consilio.	Mulier sine castitate.
Miles sine probitate.	Iudex sine Iusticia.
Dives sine elemosina.	Populus sine lege.
Senex sine religione.	Servus sine timore.
Pauper superbus.	Adolescens sine obediencia.

Lydgate's admonitions follow:

Goo forth, kyng, reule the by sapyence;
Bysshop, be able to mynystre doctryne;
Lord, to treu counceyle yeve audyence,
Womanhed, to chastyte ever enclyne;
Knyght, lete thy dedes worshyp determyne,
Be rightuous, Iuge, in savying thy name;
Ryche, doo almes, lest thou lese blys with shame.

People, obeye your kyng and the lawe;
Age, be thou ruled by good religyon;
True servaunt, be dredfull & kepe the under awe,
And thou, poure, fye on presumpcyon.
Inobedyence to yougth is utter destruccyon.
Remembre you how god hath sette you, lo!
And doo your parte, as ye ar ordeyned to.

4. Caxton and the Estates of the World

Caxton's contribution to the literature of estates was no less important than Lydgate's. The most conspicuous example of it is his version of the famous chess book of Jacobus de Cessolis, *Game and Playe of the Chesse.*[53] Translated from the French, in 1474, the book was printed in England about 1480, shortly after the press of Caxton was set up. The English text follows the French pretty closely, but at times Caxton expands the theme in

[52] Ed. J. Schick, E.E.T.S., London, 1891, ext. ser., LX, clx. The text quoted concludes the volume.

[53] Reprint of 1st ed. by Wm. E. A. Axon, London, 1883.

the usual medieval fashion. Though his title suggests a book of
instructions on how to play chess and the work is usually found
in libraries with just such books of instruction, *The Game and
Playe of the Chesse* is an elaborate allegory of the estates of the
world.

The ideal of the commonwealth of the middle ages finds an interesting expression. The sharp lines of demarcation between class and
class are stated with the frankness that comes of a belief that the
then existing social fabric was the only one possible in the best of
worlds. There is no doubt in the author's mind as to the rightful
position of king and baron, of bishop and merchant. The "rights
of man" had not been invented, apparently, and the maxim that the
king reigns but does not govern, would have perplexed the souls of
Cessoles and his translators. They had no more doubt as to the
divine right of the monarch, than the Thibetan has of the divine
right of the grand lama. The Buddhist thinks he has secured the
continuous re-appearance of supernatural wisdom in human form, and
the regular transmission of political ability in the same family was
the ideal for which the devotees of medieval despotism had to hope.
Nothing could be further from the aspirations of our author than a
race of mere palace kings seeking enjoyment in self-indulgence. The
king was to be the ruler and leader of his people. The relation and
interdependence of the several classes is emphatically proclaimed,
and the claims of duty are urged upon each.[54]

As a result, the book is of little use to one who is learning to
play chess, but is "ful of holsom wysedom and requysyte unto
every astate and degree." It aims to teach all classes their duties
by means of biblical, classical, and contemporary lore of all
kinds.

The chessmen represent the classes of society, the board represents the commonwealth in which they move, the position of
the chessmen on the board is significant of the relation of class
to class, and the moves of the chessmen represent the duties of
the classes. In discussing the position of each man on the board,
Caxton invariably says: "And hit is reson that he shold be so."
This is a *reasonable* array of estates—the only right ordering of

[54] *Ibid.*, Intro. by editor, p. liii.

them. The tone of the whole treatise is that of the common sense political philosopher. The writer's democratic sympathies are evident: he frequently lauds the third estate. In fact, his political theory is that of communism. He takes the word *commonwealth* literally to mean the profit of all in common. "And also hit is to be supposyd that suche as have theyr goodes comune & not propre is most acceptable to god."[55] The Trojans are cited as an example of a people of "one herte and one sowle." Plato, too, is an authority:

And acordynge thereto we rede in plato which sayth y^t the cyte is well and Iustely governid and ordeyned in the whiche no man may saye by right · by custome · ne by ordenance / this is myn / but I say to the certaynly that syn this custome cam forth to say this is myn / And this is thyn / no man thought to preferre the comyn prouffit so moche as his owen.[56]

Interest in the "comyn prouffit" is the standard by which all the classes are judged in the *Game and Playe of the Chesse*.

The table of contents indicates the subject matter of the four "traytees" or tractates of the book as follows: the first on the origin of chess; the second on the king, queen, alphins, knights, and rooks; the third on the pawns; and the fourth on the chess board and the moves the men may make. The alphins or elephants (the modern bishops) represent the judges. The rooks represent the vicars or legates of the king. The pawns represent the common people—laborers or tillers of the soil, smiths, drapers, notaries, merchants, money-changers, physicians, surgeons, apothecaries, taverners, guards of the city, toll-takers, customs officers, dice players, and messengers. As may be seen from this classification of society, the estate of the clergy is not included. The usual characteristics and duties assigned to each chessman will be discussed later. The interesting traits of the political philosophy of the work are its expansion of the theme of common profit and its emphasis on the importance of the commons.

[55] *Ibid.*, p. 88. [56] *Ibid.*, p. 88.

Like most literature of estates, it laments conditions nowadays as compared with those of former times:

But now a dayes ther is nothynge ellys in the world but barate Treson deceyte falsenes and trecherye Men kepe not theyr covenantes promyses · othes · writynges · ne trouthe / The subgettis rebelle agayn theyr lorde / ther is now no law kepte · nor fidelite / ne oth holden / the peple murmure and ryse agayn theyr lord and wole not be subget / they ought to be pietous in herte / whiche is availlable to all thinge. . . . For pite is nothynge ellis but a right grete will of a debonaire herte for to helpe alle men.[57]

This is the theme of sedition so often met with in sixteenth-century versions of the literature of estates.[58]

Caxton's prose *Mirrour of the World*,[59] translated from a fifteenth-century manuscript of the *Image du monde*, translated in turn from a thirteenth-century Latin verse original, is likewise interesting here for the philosophy of estates that it contains in the first of its three parts. The whole was a popular medieval encyclopedia, shorter than most others, and was Caxton's first work published in England. Part I treats of God's creation of the world and man. Part II discusses other inhabitants of the earth—beast, bird, fish. Part III discusses the stars, eclipses of sun and moon, Virgil's miracles, the making of money, and the structure of the universe. Part I only is of importance here. Again it is interesting to see by what a devious route the encyclopedist finally gets round to a discussion of the estates of the world. He begins with a eulogy of science or philosophy or "clergy." In ancient times, he says, philosophers or clergy nobly gave themselves up to the study of the universe. They even suffered persecution for their devotion. By means of their science, certain philosophers—among them Virgil—were able to foretell the coming of Christ. The seven liberal arts resulted. Nowadays, however, "clergye goth . . . al to nought, that almost it is perisshid." Nowadays knowledge is not held a virtue. Nowa-

---

[57] *Ibid.*, p. 61.   [58] See pp. 161-63, 180, 192, 246, 321-23.
[59] Ed. Oliver H. Prior, E.E.T.S., London, 1913, ext. ser., No. CX.

days men are interested only in getting money. Even the clergy
turn away from their estate and "take them to the wynnyng,
lyke as marchants doo and brokers." All good things, however,
come from the "seven sciences," that the philosophers founded,
"ffor therby had they understondyng to love God and his ver-
tues, and that God is alway and shal be withouten ende." It is
to emphasize the need of clergy still further that the writer next
launches into a discussion of the three estates and the necessity
of all three to society. His explanation is most illuminating of
medieval adaptation of classical philosophy. The discussion is
headed: "Of thre maner of peple and how clergye cam first in to
the Royamme of Fraunce." It came westward from Athens, to
Rome, then to Paris, and now is most flourishing in Paris. In
old Athens the philosophers named three kinds of people and
the duties of each. This, of course, is a reference to the political
theory of Plato and Aristotle, but the language of medieval
adaptation is incongruous, to say the least:

> The philosophres that thenne were, and whiche that oughte to teche
> and lerne other, accompted but thre maner of peple in the world after
> their understandyng: and that were clerkes, knyghtes, and labourers.
> The labourers ought to pourveye for the clerkes and knyghtes suche
> thinges as were nedeful for them to lyve by in the world honestly;
> and the knyghtes ought to defende the clerkis and the labourers,
> that ther were no wronge don to them; and the clerkis ought to en-
> seigne and teche these ii maner of peple, and to adresse them in
> their werkis in suche wise that none doo thinge by whiche he sholde
> displese God ne lese his grace.[60]

Nor should any of the three classes take upon itself the duties
of another, for the duties of one class are enough for each man,
according to the philosophers.

> Thus setted somtyme the wise philosophres thre maner of peple in
> the world, as they that knew that no man myght sette his corage in
> that he myght be wise a right in ii maners or thre; ffor it happed never
> day of the world that clergye, chevalrye and labourers of therthe
> myght be well knowen by one only man in alle his lyf, ne lerned, ne

[60] *Ibid.,* p. 29.

reteyned. Therfore he that wold lerne byhoveth hym only to lerne one of the thre; and therfore the philosophres sette thre maner of peple without moo in the erthe, ffor they wold seche the very trouthe.

This medieval adaptation of the philosophy of classes of the ancients apparently comes, in the Latin original, from the time of Albertus Magnus and Thomas Aquinas and their correlation of Christian and classical doctrine. The simplicity of these statements of the *Mirrour of the World* contrasts with the more involved philosophy of the sixteenth-century literature of estates, which reflects all the complexities of medieval changes of polity and political theory.

In addition to these works concerning the philosophy of estates, Caxton produced a book of *Dialogues in French and English*,[61] adapted from a fourteenth-century book of dialogues in French and Flemish, the purpose of which was to "fynde all be ordre," or, in other words, to classify some sixty-two kinds of phenomena, including humankind. A "book for travelers" it has been called and also "a vocabulary." It probably served both those purposes, with its French catalogue on one side of the page and the English on the other. Beasts, birds, fish, trees, drinks, towns, metals, and so forth are all classified, and then the estates of the world are indicated as follows:

Des prelats de saincte eglyse,	Of the prelates of holy chirche,
Du pape, cardinaulz, evesques,	Of the pope, cardinals, bisshops,
Archevesques, abbes, et officiaulx,	Archebisshops, abbotes, and officials,
Des moynes et gens de lordene;	Of monkes and folke of ordre;
De lempereur, roys, et roynes,	Of themperour, kynges, and quenes,
Des ducs, countes, et princes,	Of dukes, erles, and princes,
Barons, chevaliers, escuyers;	Barons, knyghtes, and squyers;
Les noms dhommes et des femmes,	The names of men and of wymmen,
Et des mestiers, selon lordre de a b c.	And of crafts, after thordre of a b c.

[61] Ed. Henry Bradley, E.E.T.S., London, 1900, ext. ser., No. LXXIX.

But this list suffices only for the table of contents. All the ranks in these estates are given in great detail in the text proper. The finest shades of precedence are noted. It is not sufficient to show the superiority of one estate over another; the precedence of one king, or one archbishop, or one bishop, or one duke, or one earl, over another of the same title, is indicated. It must have taken nice judgment to produce such a list. Its authority, moreover, could scarcely hold for long, since Fortune's wheel was ever turning.

Caxton's *Dialogues* have a definitely utilitarian purpose that the literature of estates that we have so far examined has not. Most of the literature of estates apparently aimed to please the reader, as well as to improve him, and to bring literary fame to the writer. If in the case of the *Dialogues* the desire to instruct obscures the literary aims of the writer, the reader must not too quickly conclude that he has none. The very nature of the subject matter, that of learning a new language, has, in a certain sense, a literary value, and its form, that of dialogues, is a common literary device. It is interesting to examine the work here, in connection with other fifteenth-century literature of estates, for the light shed on the important part the estates played in the life of the times.

5. UTILITARIAN PIECES

Other utilitarian pieces dealing with the estates of the world survive from the fifteenth century. Most of them, like the *Dialogues*, have to do with the all-important matter of precedence. If it was important for a traveler to know who was who, how much more necessary it was for a butler, an usher in chamber, a marshall in the hall, or a director of a funeral to know exactly how to usher guests into the hall, seat them at table, or garb them for a funeral procession. The purpose of these pieces is distinctly that of instruction, but that is no reason for assuming that they were without literary pretensions. One of them is in monorime quatrains, considered very effective in their day. An-

other, printed in 1557, is also in verse. Their lists of estates, like
that of the *Dialogues,* show in a practical way the same caste
system as that about which the rest of the literature of estates
grew up.

A Book of Precedence,[62] or "The Copie of a Booke of Precedence of all estates and playcinge to ther degrees," as its full
title reads, is interesting for the detailed description that it gives
of both order of precedence and dress for each estate. The
"Cloth of Estate," "Mantell or Robe of Estate," "Capp of
Estate," of a duke, a marquis, an earl, a viscount, a baron, and
of the wives and children of each, are described. The duke, for
example,

must goe after his creation, and not after his Dukedome; the Dutchesse his wife to goe according to the same; he to have in his howse a
Cloth of Estate, and in evry place Els out of the princes presence,
so that the same Com not to the ground by halfe a yarde; likewyse a
dutchesse may have her Cloth of Estate, and a barones to beare up
hir trayne in her owne howse.[63]

And no "Earle of Duty ought to washe with a Duke, but at
the duke's pleasure." The term *estate* in this book is obviously
restricted to members of the nobility. The term was coming
to mean, more and more, "people of rank and property," and to
have slight connection with those classes who had no "estate" to
boast of.

The curious *Ordering of a Funerall for a Noble Person in
Hen. 7. Time*[64] and the account of *A Funeral in Popish Times*[64]
both tell the proper trappings for the funeral of a member of
the nobility. The number of mourners allotted to different degrees is given as follows: "a King, 15; a Duke, 13; a Marcus,
11; an Earle, 9; a Baron, 7; a Knight, 5." Liveries for noblemen
at interments are described, "every man acordyng to his eastat."
A duke might have sixteen yards at ten shillings per yard for his

[62] Ed. F. J. Furnivall, E.E.T.S., London, 1869, ext. ser., VIII, 13-28.
[63] *Ibid.,* p. 13.
[64] *Ibid.,* pp. 29-33.

cassock and mantle; an earl, sixteen yards at eight shillings per yard; a baron or banneret, who is a Knight of the Garter, six yards for gown and hood; a knight, five yards at six shillings eight pence per yard; a squire, like a knight; all other gentlemen, five shillings per yard.

John Russell's *The Boke of Nurture,*[65] another of these utilitarian pieces, is typical of the books giving instruction for serving in a gentleman's house. It is written in verse, however, not prose. An added descriptive title identifies the author: "Folowyng Englondis gise, by me John Russell, Sum Tyme Servande with Duke Umfrey of Glowcetur, a Prynce Fulle Royalle, with whom Uschere in Chamber was Y, and Mershalle also in Halle." A young man, in this instance, wishes to be a butler, and so is taught all that pertains to serving at table. In addition, however, he must be able to perform the "office of ussher and marshalle," in order to seat the different degrees of guests at dinner. The list of estates extends to the degrees of clergy and commonalty as well as to the nobility, down to parish priests and "worshipfulle merchaundes and riche artyficeris." It begins: "The pope hath no pere." The other estates are then given their proper order:

> Emperowre is nex hym every where;
> Kynge corespondent; þus nature shalle you lere.
> high Cardynelle, þe dignyte dothe requere.
> Kyngis sone, prynce ye hym Calle;
> Archebischoppe is to hym peregalle.
> Duke of þe blode royalle,
> bishoppe / Marques / & erle coequalle.

In similar monorime quatrains, all other orders of nobility, clergy, and commons are listed. The instructions as to the seating of these estates are quite complicated. Certain estates, for example, are so "worthy" that they may not sit together or be seen eating:

[65] Ed. F. J. Furnivall, E.E.T.S., London, 1868, XXXII, 115-99.

Pope, Emperowre / kynge or cardynalle,
Prince with goldyn rodde Royalle,
Archebischoppe / usyng to were þe palle,
Duke / alle þese of dygnyte owȝt not kepe þe halle.

Other great and honorable estates may be seated in chamber or
hall, two or three at a table, if they are congenial:

Bisshopes, Merques, viscount, Erle goodly,
May sytte at .ij. messeȝ yf þey be lovyngely.
þe meyre of london, & a baron, an abbot myterly,
the iij chef Iusticeȝ, þe spekere of þe parlement, propurly.

The other estates may be placed by fours, those of the knight's
rank being seated together, and those of squire's rank. The most
interesting part of the instructions concerns the puzzles in rank,
blood, and wealth, that reflect the social changes incident to
declining feudalism. For example, what should the poor usher
do about seating a poor noble and a wealthy commoner? The
answer is definite: "The substaunce of lyvelode is not so digne
as is blode royalle." If a lady of blood royal is married to a man
of lower rank, or if a "poore lady" is married to a man of blood
royal, the lady of blood royal must keep her original place, but
the "lady of low blode" takes the rank of her husband. The
father and mother of the pope or cardinal must not expect to
sit with their son, but are assigned a chamber by themselves.
The real test of a marshall, however, is that of his ability to
seat strangers from other countries. The problems of seating
the commonalty conclude this book of "Curtesie of court."

The *Boke of Kervynge*,[66] a briefer prose work on carving, also
gives the duties of the marshall or usher in seating the different
estates at the table. The list and instructions are so similar to
those of John Russell as to be very probably an abstract or outline of his work.

The list in *The Ordre of Goyng or Sittyng*[67] is still briefer.
The order of estates is given, without instructions, from pope

[66] *Ibid.*, pp. 261-86.   [67] *Ibid.*, p. 381.

and emperor to artificer and yeoman. An interesting emendation occurs in the fifteenth-century manuscript: "A pope hath no pere" is struck through with a heavy black line, and "the popes colectour" with several thin lines. A sixteenth-century marshall probably no longer had any concern as to how the pope or the pope's collector ranked. He no doubt eliminated them with pleasure.

The Schoole of Vertue[68] was printed in 1557 with the subtitle: "and booke of good Nourture for chyldren, and youth to learne theyr dutie by. Newely perused, corrected, and augmented by the fyrst Auctour F. S[eager]. With a brief declaracion of the dutie of eche degree." It is a kind of hornbook, concluding with versified instructions as to the "dutie of eche degres. (so) brefely declared." Princes, judges, prelates, parsons, vicars, men of law, craftsmen, merchants, and magistrates are advised in the usual fashion, but the term *degree* here is loosely used, and there are also stanzas addressed to fathers, mothers, children, masters, servants, husbands, wives, landlords, rich and poor.

Another kind of book of instruction that has a philosophy of estates as well as a catalogue of them is the treatise on coat armor in the *Boke of St. Albans*.[69] Its philosophy makes some rather astounding original contributions but parallels that of other literature of estates in some instances. It is, apparently, "the first English treatise on heraldry . . . derived chiefly from Nicholas Upton's *De officio militari*."[70] Some of the extremes to which theory about nobility and commonalty went in the Middle Ages are found in it. Before the equally elaborate myths regarding the coat armor of the various estates can be explained, the question of the origin of nobility and commons must first be

---

[68] *Ibid.*, pp. 333-55.

[69] Facsimile reprint, introduction by Wm. Blades, London, 1899. I am indebted to Alice B. Campbell, a former student of mine, for this reference and for the use of the reprint.

[70] *Cambridge History of English Literature,* IV, 429.

settled: "How Gentilmen shall be knawy^en from churlis & how they^e first began." In the sons of Adam and Eve, the difference began. Cain, by killing Abel, became "a chorle and all his ofspryng after hym by the cursyng of god and his owne fadre adam." Seth was made a "gentilman thorow his fadres and moderis blissyng." Noah, a descendant of Seth, was a "gentilman by kynde." The rest of the world, the "ungentle," were destroyed by the flood. But of Noah's three sons ungentleness was reborn in "Cham," who, while his father slept, treated him with indignity. To him Noah gave the north part of the world to dwell in, "where sorow and care colde and myschef as a churle thow shalt have · in the thirde parte of the worlde wich shal be calde Europe that is to say the contre of churlys." Jafeth and Sem continued the gentility of their father. Jafeth was given the west part of the world, "which shall be calde asia that is to say the contre of gentilmen." Sem was given the east part of the world, "which shall be calde affrica · that is to say the contre of tempurnes." The directions of the writer seem strangely confused, and his terminology exceedingly individual. Jafeth had a famous line: "Habraham," "Moyses," "Aron," the "profettys," and also "that gentilman Jhesus." Jesus was by "his modre mary prynce of Cote armure."

The question of the origin of coat armor is settled with equal ingenuity. Jafeth first made a shield, and in it he put a ball to represent the world. Then, some two thousand years before Christ, coat armor was designed and used at the siege of Troy, as one can read in the "gestys troianorum." This was the beginning of the law of arms—before any law in the world except natural law—even before the ten commandments. The law of arms was based on the nine orders of angels, crowned with nine diverse precious stones of nine different colors and having nine different virtues. These stones were preserved in coat armor, and so now whoever wears one of these stones represents that particular virtue.

Just as there are nine orders of angels, so there are nine dignities of royalty: five noble—gentleman, squire, knight, baron, lord—and four excellent—earl, marquis, duke, prince. There are also nine kinds of gentlemen, as well as many other things in nines. The four evangelists were gentlemen, of the right line of that worthy conqueror Judas Machabeus, whose kindred later fell into poverty and had to labor and were then no longer gentlemen. Likewise, "the .iiii. doctoris of holi chirch Seynt Jerom Ambrose Augustyn and Gregori war gentilmen of blode and of cotarmures." The nine orders of gentlemen are: gentlemen of ancestry and blood; gentlemen of blood; gentlemen of coat armor, secured by king's gift or by holding of a lordship or by killing a Saracen; gentlemen "untriall that is to say made up emong relygyous men as priorys Abbottis or Bysshoppis"; gentlemen "appocrifate that is to say made upp and gouyn to him the name and the lyveray of a gentylman"; gentlemen spiritual; and gentlemen both spiritual and temporal. The estates of this treatise are all "gentlemen." There is no attempt to catalogue all society.

One would scarcely look in a treatise on hawking[71] for a catalogue of estates, but even there they may be found, listed for a definite purpose, that of telling the reader which hawks are suitable for the various classes of society. The eagle, "bawtere," and "melowne," by their powerful nature, belong to an emperor. A "gerfawken" and a "tercell gentill" are for a prince. A duke should have a "fawken of the rock"; an earl, a "fawken peregryne"; a baron, a "bastarde"; a knight, a "sacre" and a "sacret"; a squire, a "lanare" and a "lanrett." A lady should have a "merlyon." A young man's hawk is the "hoby." "And yit ther be moo kyndis of hawkes" to be distributed. So the yeoman is allotted the "goshawke"; the poor man, the "tercell"; the priest, a "spare hawke"; and "an holiwater clerke" may have a "muskyte."

[71] In the *Boke of St. Albans*.

6. Minor Adaptations in the Fifteenth Century

In addition to the prose and verse works of Lydgate and Caxton and these handbooks of instruction, the verses of some of the poets of the late fifteenth century also found the theme of estates an important one. The poems of George Ashby,[72] Clerk of the Signet to Queen Margaret of Anjou, are full of references to the estates of the realm. Addressing Edward, Prince of Wales, he hints at the "great changes of high estates." He advises the Prince in all the virtues of nobility and reflects the conditions of the times as well. His sympathies are not with the people, and he bids Edward beware of the commonalty. In "A Prisoner's Reflections," for example, he has occasion to mention the uncertainty of Fortune. Christ, the Virgin, St. John the Evangelist, St. John the Baptist, and numberless other saints have suffered. So must all classes of society:

> Right so kyng, Quene, Duke, Prynce and Emperoures,
> Erle, Baron, lord, knyght, and many squyers,
> Bysshop, Abbot, Pryour and conquerours,
> And many gret estates and Rewlours,
> Clerkes, marchauntes and eke counseylours
> Have be put in trouble and gret grevaunce
> For theyr soules helth by humble sufferaunce.[73]

The poems of Henryson and Dunbar likewise revolve frequently about the theme of estates. In his *Moral Fables*[74] Henryson says he writes for all classes in the vein of Æsop, who had no scruples about incurring the disdain of high or low estate. In the Moralitas appended to the fable of "The Twa Myss," he makes the usual point that the highest are most likely to fall and that the mean estate is sure. In "The Fable of the Fox and the Wolf," the Fox is a climber, who pretends to "gen-

---

[72] Ed. Mary Bateson, E.E.T.S., London, 1899, ext. ser., No. LXXVI.

[73] *Ibid.*, p. 9, stanza 38.

[74] *Poems*, ed. G. Gregory Smith, Scottish Text Society, Edinburgh, 1906, Vols. LV, LVIII, LXIV.

till stait." In "The Trial of the Fox," the animals come "in ordour sett as to thair stait efferit." The mouse in "The Lion and the Mouse" pleads guilty to offense to the estate of the lion and wins mercy. Later he saves the lion. The lion represents a prince or emperor, or a king with crown. The mouse represents the commonalty. Let the king have mercy. The fable of "The Wolf and the Wether" is another sermon to social climbers:

> Thairfoir I counsell men of everilk stait
> To know thame self, and quhome thay suld forbeir,
> And fall not with their better in debait;
> Suppois thay be als galland in thair geir,
> It settis na servand for to uphald weir,
> Nor clym so hie, quhill he fall of the ledder.

In "The Wolf and the Lamb," the lamb signifies the poor people: "As male men, merchandis, and pure lauboreris." The wolf is one of three kinds: "pervertairs of the lawis," "mychty men, haifand ennuch plente" but wanting more, and "men of heretage." To these three the poet says: be honest. Even the *Testament of Cresseid* becomes, with Henryson, the story of one who fell from high estate.

Dunbar, the sometime Franciscan friar and ambassador of the King, in the troublous times of James II, James III, and James IV, also found much to criticize in the estates of the Scottish realm. To preach a half-jesting sermon "Of Discretion in Taking,"[75] he describes the avarice of the three classes:

> The clerkis takis beneficis with brawlis,
> Sum of Sanct Petir, and sum of Sanct Pawlis;
>   Tak he the rentis, no cair hes he,
> Suppois the divill tak all thair sawlis:
>   In taking sowld discretioun be.
>
> Barronis takis fra the tennentis peure
> All fruct that growis on the feure,
>   In mailis and gersomes rasit ouir hie,

---

[75] *Poems*, ed. H. Bellyse Baildon, Cambridge, 1907, p. 125, stanzas 2, 3, 4.

And garris thame beg fra dur to dure:
In taking sowld discretioun be.

The merchantis takis unleisum win,
Quhilk makis thair pakkis oftymes full thin,
  Be thair successioun ȝe may see
That ill-won geir riches nocht the kin:
  In taking suld discretioun be.

Dunbar is particularly critical of the clergy, whose profits he apparently did not share in as did many of his fellow friars. "Of the Warldis Instabilitie," addressed to the King,[76] belabors first the people, then the nobility, and then the clergy at some length:

The pepill so wickit ar of feiris
The frutless erde all witness beiris,
The ayr infectit and prophane;
  Quhilk to considder is ane pane.

The temporale stait to gryp and gather,
The sone disheris wald the father,
And as ane dyvour wald him demane;
  Quhilk to considder is ane pane.

Kirkmen so halie ar and gude,
That on thair conscience, rowme and rude,
May turne aucht oxin and ane wane;
  Quhilk to considder is ane pane.

I knaw nocht how the kirk is gydit,
Bot beneficis ar nocht leill devydit;
Sum men hes sewin, and I nocht ane;
  Quhilk to considder is ane pane.

And sum, unworthy to browk ane stall,
Wald clym to be ane cardinall,
Ane bischoprik may nocht him gane;
  Quhilk to considder is ane pane.

In "Dunbar's Remonstrance. To the King" he lists the King's "kirkmen, courtmen, and craftismen" as worthy of the King's consideration. He, too, in his "Lament for the Makaris," treats the theme of death and laments that:

[76] *Ibid.*, pp. 131 ff., stanzas 9, 10, 11, 12, 13.

Unto the deth gois all estaitis,
Princis, prelattis, and Potestaitis,
Bayth riche and pure of all degre;
Timor Mortis conturbat me.[77]

"A General Satyre"[78] again belabors all estates: prelates, priests, clerks, lords, judges, merchants, and women, for their failure to do their duty. Sometimes, however, Dunbar lists the estates to praise them, as in "A Treatise of London," probably recited at a banquet given by the Lord Mayor of London to the Scotch Embassy who were in London to arrange a marriage between James IV and Henry VII's daughter Margaret. Dunbar's English sympathies are evident:

London, thow art of townes a per se,
Soverayn of cyties, semlyest by sight,
Of high renown, riches & royalte,
Of lordis, barones, & many goodly knyght,
Of famowse prelates in habytis clerycall,
Of merchantis full of substance & myght:
London, thow art þe flour of cytes all.[79]

Such was the course of this French fashion in England in the fourteenth and fifteenth centuries. In both verse and prose, writers consciously sought to reproduce in English the laments and warnings to all the feudal classes with which the continent was already familiar. It remains to see how the *genre* fared in the following centuries.

[77] *Ibid.*, p. 146, stanza 5.

[78] *Ibid.*, pp. 162 f., stanzas 2-7, 13. The editor suggests difficulty, footnote p. 280, in understanding the line: "So mony ane stait, for the commoun weill sa quhein" (careless). He says, *"So mony ane stait* is not very clear. *Stait* to make sense with the context must mean 'estate'—'so many an estate given to individuals and so little for the common good all over the country.' Ed." *Stait* undoubtedly means here what it meant so often in the Middle Ages and later, a *person* of estate. The phrase means simply: so many men of estate, so careless of the commonweal.

[79] *Songs, Carols, and Other Miscellaneous Pieces,* ed. Roman Dyboski, E.E.T.S., London, 1907, ext. ser., No. CI, stanza 1.

CHAPTER V

HISTORY OF THE FORM: LATER ENGLISH DEVELOPMENT

THE literature of the estates of the world continued in the sixteenth century in England as it did on the continent, but usually with a different emphasis. Feudalism had given way to monarchy, and though the feudal classes of society still existed—as they continue to exist in present-day England—the relations between those classes were much altered. Consequently the old political philosophy would no longer fit. The feudal theory of government no longer needed propagation. Many new conditions affecting the old feudal classes did need airing, and so the fashion survived.

1. CHANGING CONDITIONS: THE DECLINE OF FEUDALISM

It was a time of great changes in the social and economic order as well as in government. The practice of enclosures was, of course, only one evidence of these changes. The villein and serf had for some time been free from the dictates of an overlord. They had become more or less independent farmers, deriving their whole subsistence from the produce of the land they leased from wealthy landowners. As the raising of wool for foreign manufacture proved a more and more profitable source of income, leases were canceled, and the cultivated land was turned into pastures for sheep. With no other source of livelihood these ejected farmers and their families often drifted about until the only professions open to them were those of vagabond and harlot. Legislation helped little. It could not stem the tide of a new industrial era, of which the practice of enclosures was a far-reaching, but by no means exclusive, feature. The nobility and clergy, no longer bound by feudal ties to the commons of the realm, felt no obligations to protect or provide for them in need. They themselves were subject to the king as they had never been before. The Reformation brought such a change in the estate of the clergy that they were finally unable to do for the poor what they had once done, even if they had wanted to. Deprived of their benefices, abbeys, and monasteries, many of the lower ranks of clergy also became vagabonds or, perforce, doffed robe and cowl to enter the ranks of the Anglicans. Meanwhile, however, the wheel of Fortune swung upward as well as down. New opportunities opened to townsmen: crafts, trades, business of various kinds. Never before was there such possibility of becoming wealthy and of rising thereby to social prominence. Changing one's estate now became fairly common practice. Cardinal Wolsey was never permitted, in all his glory, to forget his origin as a butcher's son. The Tudors themselves took their rise from a middle-class Welsh family. The ranks of the nobility, depleted by the Wars of the Roses, were filled up by the early Tudors with middle-class men like themselves. The servant consequently looked forward to occupying his master's seat, the merchant aspired to knighthood or nobility, and the humble cleric hoped some day to achieve political influence as bishop or even chancellor.

Thus, though feudalism had declined, class consciousness was never more acute, and it found its way into the literature of the period just as it had in earlier days. To be sure, the strict censorship of the Tudors meant suppression of much that might otherwise have been written. The literature of estates might have flourished more widely than it did had it not been for that censorship. To enumerate the faults of king or queen in sixteenth-century England required courage that medieval critics did not need or know. To lament the faults of the nobility and clergy was rather dangerous business, also, since all such criticism might spell sedition to an ever-watchful sovereign. To belabor the commons, particularly the agricultural classes, was rather futile, since they were the chief sufferers of the distress incident to the rapidly changing order. Nevertheless, those who could not be silenced did challenge the sovereign and nobility at times and set forth the hardships of the commons. Such critics represent the ever-growing spirit of democracy, which, though it did not deny that the classes of society were a divine institution, nevertheless fiercely denounced the oppression of the lower classes by the higher. These new democrats were opposed by the conservatives, who, in rather indifferent imitation of a past fashion, enumerated the estates of the realm, or who philosophized abstractly about government, and who usually found opportunity to extol the reigning monarch as a ruler "a per se." These conservative writers carefully avoided any grappling with immediate problems. The democrats, on the other hand, filled their diatribes with as much information as to the conditions of the times as they dared. The estates of the different authors of these sixteenth-century pieces explain their views in almost every case. Nobility and Anglican clergy cry down sedition and cry up the old philosophy of estates. Those who happen to belong to the ranks of the commons or dissenting clergy protest against the social and political evils of the day and usually find king, nobility, and high clergy to blame. As in most periods of history, those who were on the lower spokes of Fortune's wheel found fault with the existing order of things, and those who rode aloft were quite content with things as they were. Occasionally, as with Dekker, the writer felt the necessity of clinging to both parts of the wheel. He must conciliate both royalty and his own class, the commons. Such utterances must be read with an eye on the author's circumstances and on his probable immediate reasons for writing. In the late sixteenth century and first half of the seventeenth century, when the estates of both bishops and nobility were in danger of extinction in the rising tide of democracy, the tone of their opposition became fainter and fainter, but in the first half of the sixteenth century their staunch adherence to the philosophy of estates was sounded full and clear.

2. THE ESTATES IN THE FIRST HALF OF THE SIXTEENTH CENTURY

Sixteenth-century literature of estates appeared in various guises. In didactic verse like the *Shyp of Folys*, the *Mirrour for Magistrates*, and Gascoigne's *Steele Glas;* in Reformation poems and sermons; in the political philosophy of Dudley, Cheke, Elyot, Starkey, and the *Complaynt of Scotlande* in the first half of the century and in that of Hales, Stubbs, Hooker, and Smith in the latter half; in the political drama of Lyndsay; in morality and interlude; in political ballads; in political poems of Greville and Breton; in some of Dekker's non-dramatic pieces; in books of husbandry and travel; in English imitations of classical satire and eclogue; in early seventeenth-century essays; in all these forms the analysis and criticism of the three estates went on. The pieces are in both verse and prose. Whereas in earlier times the verse forms far outnumbered those in prose, the sixteenth-century prose works just about equal those in verse. The total number of pieces dealing with estates in this century is large, much larger than that of the fourteenth and fifteenth centuries together.

Among the earliest sixteenth-century users of this fashion of decrying the abuses of the estates of the world is Alexander Barclay in his *Shyp of Folys*.[1] A Franciscan friar and a loyal supporter of Roman Church and Tudor rule, in 1509, the very year of Henry VIII's accession, he published his lament on the increasing evidences of change of estate all about him. To be sure, he was supposed to be translating a late fifteenth-century arraignment of folly. Careful comparison of his text with his original, however, convinces one of Barclay's having interpreted and added as he saw fit. His version grows in the process of

---

[1] Discussion based on a facsimile of Brant's first (1494) edition, a copy of the March, 1497, edition of Locher's version, a copy of the first (1509) edition of Barclay's *Shyp*, all in the New York Public Library, and a photostatic reproduction of the Grenville copy of Riviere's version in the British Museum.

translation. At the beginning of this study I made a line by line comparison of Brant's German version, which Barclay did not use, the Latin text, which was his original, and the French text of Riviere, at which he perhaps glanced occasionally, with Barclay's own 1509 edition;[2] and I was impressed by Barclay's great concern with this theme of the estates of the world. Whereas the German and Latin and French versions have only occasional references to the estates of the realm, Barclay's has many. The general, moralizing tone of the German version frequently is lost in the political and social references of Barclay's pointed satire. Sometimes, to be sure, Barclay follows Locher pretty closely. Frequently, however, on the slightest provocation—such as the word *populus* or *res publica* or *senatus* or *gradus* or *status* —he launches forth on an original discussion of the particular class or classes guilty of the folly under consideration. Moreover, he has many original additions in the form of envoys appealing to various estates to mend their ways, and in the form of stanzas labeled "Addition of Alexander Barclay."

Barclay has much to say about the faults of all estates, but his chief concern seems to be with that of change of estate or the desire to rise above one's class. Later, in Reformation times, he himself was to have a change of estate thrust upon him. Later he saw the dissolution of religious orders and became a vicar in the new Anglican Church. He attacked Wolsey as a tyrant and was denounced and chastized as a heretic rebel against the new order. He resisted the change boldly until threatened with death. "Will not that cowl of yours be left off yet?" he was challenged by Cromwell, who found him in a shop near St. Paul's churchyard. "And if I hear by one o'clock that this apparel be not changed, thou shalt be hanged immediately for example of all others." So he put his cowl away and "durst never wear it after."[3]

[2] See conclusions of Fr. Aurelius Pompen, *The English Versions of the Ship of Fools,* London, 1925, p. 309.

[3] See "The Life of Alexander Barclay" by John Richie Schultz, *Journal of English and Germanic Philology,* XVIII (1919), 360-68.

Barclay's frequent introduction of the theme of estates would seem to indicate his thorough familiarity with preceding literature of estates. The themes of Fortune's wheel, the dance of death, the fallow horse, the love of Sir Nummus, and many others furnished him ample opportunity to use his knowledge of estates and the literature of estates. In his prologue he assures the reader that in his book are to be found "The fautes . . . of all estatis as degrees temporall." His text forced him into listing fools instead of estates, but he nevertheless treats of estates whenever possible. His Argument calls his work a satire, which may serve all men as "a bright Myrrour." Excusing the rudeness of his translation, he says his terms are more suitable to "rude people" than to "estates"—meaning there, of course, persons of high rank. It is impossible here to indicate many of Barclay's references to estates. A few will perhaps suffice.

In his chapter "Of Newe Fassions and Disgised Garmentes" he declares that

> Mannys fourme is disfigured with every degre
> As Knyght Squyer yeman Jentilman and knave . . .[4]

> For both States / comons / man / woman / and chylde
> Are utterly inclyned to this inconvenyence . . .[5]

> Alas thus al states of Chrysten men declynes.
> And of wymen also disfourmynge theyr fygure.[6]

Here the word *states* means persons of high rank in one place and merely ranks in the other.

In his chapter "Of the Mutabylyte of Fortune," Barclay introduces references to estates where his original has none:

> That man whiche hopyth hye up to ascende
> On fortunes whele / and come to state royall

---

[4] For the sake of convenience in reference, the following footnotes indicate places in the Jamieson edition of the *Ship of Fools*, London, 1874, as well as in the first edition of 1509. The quotations are from the text of 1509. This one is found on Folium XIX of the 1509 edition and in I, 35, of the Jamieson edition.

[5] Ed. of 1509, Folium XXI; Jamieson ed., I, 37.

[6] Ed. of 1509, Folium XXI; Jamieson ed., I, 39.

> If the whele turne / may doute sore to descende
> If he be hye the sorer is his fall . . .

> Promote a yeman / make hym a gentyl man
> And make a Baylyf of a Butchers son
> Make of a Squyer knyght / yet wyll they if they can
> Coveyt in theyr myndes hyer promosyon.[7]

All this is folly, for death comes to all:

> There is no lorde Duke kynge nor other estate
> But dye they must / and from this worlde go . . .

> Therfore me thynke of all thynge it is best
> Man to be pleased and content with his degree.[8]

"Of the Abusion of the Spiritualte" is devoted to the folly of those who enter the ranks of the clergy. Men enter the Church to avoid labor. Following Locher, Barclay says:

> Every man laboures nowe with all theyr myght,
> Unto the order of presthode to promote
> His soñe: howe beit he be a very sote . . .

Then he adds himself:

> From the kechyn to the quere and so to a state
> One yester day a courter is nowe a prest become
> And than have these folys theyr myndes so elevate
> That they disdayne men of vertue and wysdome . . .

> O cursyd hunger of sylver and of golde
> For your love and desyre iṁoderate
> To folys and boyes presthode is nowe solde
> And to men myschevous fyllyd with debate
> The godly honour longynge to a state . . .[9]

and more in like vein. Similarly other estates fail in their duties.

"Of the Extorcion of Knyghtis Great / Offycers / Men of War / Scribes and Practysers of the Lawe" expands the theme of the oppression of the poor by these dignitaries, all because of the "cursyd hunger of sylver and of golde."

[7] Ed. of 1509, Folium LXXVII; Jamieson ed., I, 186.
[8] Ed. of 1509, Folia LXXVIII, LXXIX; Jamieson ed., I, 188, 190.
[9] Ed. of 1509, Folium CLIIII; Jamieson ed., II, 59-60.

> The knyght is ordeyned by manhode to defende
> Wydowhode and age from wronge and iniury
> With fatherles children / and suche as lyve in penury
> And with dynt of swerde to defende the comon welth
> Expellynge thevys / savynge true mannys helth

> The scribe is ordeyned hym self to exercyse
> To wryte with his pen iust lawes and verytable
> And shewe by his craft the rule of right iustyce.[10]

Instead, by oppression they increase their estate.

One of the most interesting chapters for its evidence of sixteenth-century change of estate is that "Of the Arrogance & Pryde of Rude Men of the Coutrey," in which all versions more or less agree. Formerly in the good old times, rustics were so given to "symplenes" and other virtues

> That the godly trone of fayth and righwysnes
> Had left great townes lordes and men royall
> And taken place amonge these men rurall.[11]

But now their manners are quite changed:

> Theyr clothes stately after the courters gyse
> Theyr here out busshynge as a foxis tayle
> And all the fassions whiche they can devyse
> In counterfaytynge they use in aparayll. . . .

> Nowe Carles ar nat content with one grange
> Nore one ferme place / suche is theyr insolence
> They must have many / to support theyr expence
> And so a riche / vyllayne proude and arrogant
> Anone becometh a covetous marchant.
> Than labours he for to be made a state
> And to have the pryvelege of hye nobles
> Thus churlys becomyth statis nowe of late
> Hye of renowne without all sympylnes
> But it is great foly and also shame doutles
> For Carles to coveyt this wyse to clym so hye
> And nat be pleasyd with theyr state and degre.[12]

[10] Ed. of 1509, Folium CLXIII; Jamieson ed., II, 84.
[11] Ed. of 1509, Folium CLXVIII; Jamieson ed., II, 96.
[12] Ed. of 1509, Folia CLXVIII, CLXIX; Jamieson ed., II, 97, 98.

In the chapter "Of Folys that Despyse Deth Makynge No Provysion Therefore," Barclay again follows his original, for the theme in the Middle Ages immediately suggested the introduction of the various classes of society. Pope, emperor, king, prince, lord, bishop, workmen, and beggars—Death leads all by the sleeve in his "cruel daunce."

Other chapters are devoted to judges, lawyers, physicians, craftsmen, laborers of all kinds, so that no estate is overlooked. The philosophy of estates, which is so frequently evident, will be indicated later.[13]

Barclay's later works—those extant and certainly by him— also show keen interest in the estates of society and in their duties to the commonwealth. Though feudal restrictions no longer bind them, they are still bound by social necessity, so Barclay seems to say. These later works are also translations or adaptations; but in them, as in the *Shyp of Folys*, Barclay expands the theme whenever he sees fit. It is interesting to observe that many of his expansions occur when opportunity has arisen for discussion of the estates of the world. In the *Mirrour of Good Maners*, some dozen times he tucks in his references to a man's estate when the Latin text says nothing of rank or class. In his *Certayne Egloges*, some twenty times he speaks of a man's estate. "Gathered out of a Booke named in Latin, Miseriae Curialium, Compiled by Eneas Silvius, Poet and Oratour," and also from two of Mantuan's, the eclogues record the usual dialogues of shepherds on life in town and country. All the undesirable features of a courtier's life are described, and the conclusion is that of Wyatt's shorter poem of the town and country mice: the mean and sure estate is best. Coridon replies to Cornix's defense of country life that

> Such feare and daunger doth happen commonly
> On all degrees with sodeyn ieopardy,
> For plowmen, shepheardes and citizens also
> By warre endureth great dammage, losse and wo.[14]

[13] Pp. 280, 295, 302, 314, 333-34.   [14] *Spenser Society Pubs.*, No. 39, p. 28.

Cunctis mortalibus mors debetur

THE DANCE OF DEATH

From Lydgate's *Fall of Princes*

The last of the five eclogues, paraphrased from Mantuan's sixth, contains the explanation of Amintas of the origin of estates in God's distribution of degrees to the unlike children of Eve.[15] It begins with Adam and Eve:

> First when the worlde was founded and create,
> And Adam and Eve were set in their estate,
> Our Lorde conioyned them both as man and wife.

One day when God came, Eve hid some of her numerous children, lest he think her lustful. God said:

> O woman let me thy children see,
> I come to promote eche after his degree.

To the eldest:

> He saide: have thou sceptar of rowme imperiall,
> Thou art the eldest thou shalt have most honour,
> Justice requireth that thou be Emperour.

To the seconde He gave the honor of a king; to the third, that of duke; others He made earls, lords, barons, squires, knights, and so forth. He also made some judges, mayors, governors, merchants, sheriffs, aldermen, and burgesses. Eve regretted then that she had hidden some of her children, and so she brought them out, all black with dirt. God said:

> No more will I make, howbeit that I can,
> Of a vile villayne a noble gentleman,
> Ye shall be plowmen and tillers of the grounde,
> To payne and labour shall ye alway be bounde.

Faustus, to whom this story is told, scorns it as an empty fable. He tells the true story. Shepherds and plowmen were first— Cain and Abel. The first to see Christ were shepherds. Their descendants were promoted to high estate. A similar theory is expressed in the *Shyp of Folys:* the world began in poverty. Then as it grew more prosperous, kings and other estates were established.

[15] *Ibid.,* p. 41. For German versions of the story, see above, pp. 91-95. Barclay's version is retold by Anne Kimball Tuell in the New York *Nation,* "How Digging Began" (March 26, 1930), p. 361.

In the same year that the friar Barclay was preaching the necessity of being content with one's estate, the same lesson was taught by another conservative, but one of different estate and with very different motives. The writer was no other than Edmund Dudley, or Edmonde Dudlay, as the title page has it, "Barrister-at-law, Sometime Speaker of the House of Commons; President of the Privy Council of Henry VII; and one of that King's Commissioners for receiving the Forfeitures of Penal Statutes." In the reign of Henry VIII, however, he and his associate Empson were recognized for the notorious extortioners they were and were put into the Tower. There, under sentence of death for high treason and in the hope of being spared, Dudley wrote his *Tree of Common Wealth*.[16] In spite of his efforts he was beheaded on Tower Hill on August 17, 1510.

The work is an elaborate allegory, in which the commonwealth of England—that is, the common or public weal, good, or happiness—is represented as a great and mighty tree, with five various roots and fruits. The roots are five abstract virtues: Love of God, Justice, Truth or Fidelity, Concord or Unity, and Peace. From each root springs a certain fruit, destined for some one estate of the realm: from the first root, Love of God, comes Honour of God, to be eaten by all estates; from the second root, Justice, comes Honorable Dignity, the fruit for the king and those to whom he gives it; the third root, Truth or Fidelity, comes Worldly Prosperity, the fruit for the nobility; from the fourth root, Concord or Unity, comes Profitable Tranquillity, the fruit for the commonalty; and from the fifth root, Peace, comes Good Example, the fruit for the clergy. All the fruits, except the first, have a poisonous core, which must be destroyed if the fruit is to remain sound. The parings are what we have seen listed elsewhere as the duties of the various estates, and the cores are their defections. Only by doing its duty and

[16] Printed for the first time in Manchester, in 1859, for the Brotherhood of the Rosy Cross.

ridding itself of its faults may each estate enjoy the fruit destined for it: Dignity for the king, Prosperity for the nobles, Tranquillity for the commons, and Good Example for the clergy. The parings—or duties—of the several estates are: Compassion for the king; True Defence for the nobility; Timely Exercise for the commonalty; and Increase of Virtue and Knowledge for the clergy. Their poisonous cores are: Unreasonable Elation or Pride for the king; Vain Delectation for the nobility; Lewd Enterprise for the commons; and Subtle Glory or Glorification for the clergy. Even with paring and coring, the fruits are dangerous to eat unless served with the "payned sauce" of the Dread of God, coming from the tap root, Love of God. The first fruit, Honour of God, is so good in and of itself that it needs no paring or coring, may be eaten by all in as large amount as can be digested, and, served with the other fruits, will turn the evil cores into good. The Unreasonable Elation of the king will become True Elation; the Vain Delectation of the nobility will become True Exaltation; the Lewd Enterprise of the commons will become Noble Enterprise; and the Vain Glory of the clergy will become Perfect Glory. Commons, nobility, clergy, and king, if they use their proper fruits in due manner, will prove the beauty and value of the Commonwealth.

Though the allegory seems vague and far removed from actual life, the author, from his intimate knowledge of the evils of his time, gives much detailed information about the vices and virtues of all the estates of the realm. The king is divinely ordained, we are told, and his duties are to maintain the commonwealth, to support his magistrates, to protect his poor subjects that they be not oppressed by their superiors, and to maintain peace. In return for all this, his subjects must, "from the highest degree to the loweste," be faithful to him, honor and revere him, be obedient to all his lawful commandments, fight for him, and render him all just revenues without fraud. Thus concord and harmony will prevail.

The estate of the clergy, "in the wch are contayned Archbisshops, Bisshops, Abbotρ, Priors, Archdeacons, and Deanes, and all priestρ, religious and seclars,"[17] must devoutly pray for the prosperity of all the subjects of the realm, "aswell nobles as other, ev^er'y man well to prosper and speede in his lawfull busynes." Besides they must give godly example: distribute alms, dress soberly, and repair their churches and mansions. The property of the Church is not theirs to give to their kinsfolk when they marry.

The estate of chivalry, or nobility, must also work for unity and harmony:

And as to the sure fasteninge thereof in all the Chevalrie of this realme, wherein be intended all Dukes, Erles, Barons, Knightρ, Esquires, and other gentlemen by office or aucthoritie, that is to saie, ev^er'y man after the hon^r and degree that god and his prince hath called him to, and after that parte or porcon to leade his lief, and not to maligne or envy his superio^rs, nor disdaine or set at nought his inferio^rs, But ev^er'y man to knowe other wth his dutie, and to help and guide them as his powre maie extende.[18]

Nobles should scorn supporters of false quarrels and perjurers; they must not retain bullies or rascals, must be gentle and courteous in words and deeds, must keep their word to rich and poor, arrange "lovdaies," relieve the poor, punish murderers, robbers and thieves, serve their prince, and "defende the church ρ the Comynaltie."[19]

The estate of the commons, too, must add to the concord of the realm by performing certain duties:

Yet it is requisite that this roote be well rooted in the Comynaltie of this realm, for there resteth the greate nomber; therein be all ye merchantρ, Craftes men and artificers, laborers, franklins [freeholders] grasiers, farmers, tyllers, and other generallie the people of this realme. Theise folkes maie not murmur nor grudge to live in labo^r and paine, and the most parte of their tyme wth the sweat of theire face, nor let anie of them presume or counterfet the state of his better, nor let them in anie wise exceede in theire apparell or

---

[17] *Ibid.*, p. 17.   [18] *Ibid.*, p. 18.   [19] *Ibid.*, p. 19.

dyet, But to use them as theire expence will surelie serve them. Let theise folkes remember theire rente and paymᵗˢ that they muste make, and rather pinch theire Bellie then to sell theire necessarie, and *let them beware of pollers, pillars* [cheaters, extortioners] *and of Westminster hall,* or else theire purse wilbe thynne. To Sessions and assizes make they not haste, except that neede enforce them. Let them *sequester themselves from costlie Courts, leaste care be their carroll when theire silver is spente;* cloath not themselves in lyverie of Lorde, yet bettʳ weare the lyverie of their wyves. And good it were not to use any unlawfull game, The tavᵉʳnes and alehouses are not to theise folkes much agreable. If theie use hawking and hunting, at length they will saie fye on their wynninge: And the chief of theis folkes, as the substanciall merchante, the welthie grasiers and farmʳˢ, let them not use nor covet over great lucoʳ [lucre] and be to yoᵘ unkinde that are lesser then they, but be they unto their under-linges loving and charitable, and destroy them not wᵗʰ yoʳ accompt wares and prises excessive, from daie to daie given, and not ovᵉʳ hastelie caste them in prison for breaking of a daie or twoe: or take a greate gaine for a long daie to be given, or to delivᵉʳ them yoʳ mony to be the losse, and you to have the profit and yoʳ mony also: and beware of usurie both plaine and colored, for to god both be indif-ferentlie knowne. Beware of deceipte of buyinge and selling, and amende not yoʳ wares wᵗʰ subtiltie and crafte, wᵗʰ oathes and lies sweetlie forged, for *if yoʳ gaines be reasonable, the better it will abide.* Make not yoʳ ware to rise or to fall by yoʳ assemblie shortlie at a pointe, for that is but a Crafte the poore people to polle; and consider howe yoʳ thrifte generallie encreaseth by lending of wares to great men for daies, though yoʳ prices you knowe best yoʳ selves, but secretlie to yoʳ conscience, as a scraping it is: And though you lefte the purchasing of lande, and sometimes buildinge and feast-ing, till yoʳ riches were greatlie grounded, it forced not much. Yee meane occupiers and begynners, make not yoʳ bargaines, but soe as ye be able to paie, leaste Westminster, St. Katherines [probably some court for recovery of debts] or yoʳ boulted dores, be your reckoning place, and then yoʳ credence [credit] for evᵉʳ is gone. And mynish not yoʳ stockes for yoʳ wives pleasure, though shee behigh [promise, pro-fess to] yoʷ to love yoᵘ. All the [? ye] craftesmen and artificers, work dilligentlie and trulie: let not slouth guide yoᵘ, neither earlie nor late. Disdaine not to learne of men that have coninge [knowl-edge], Straungers though they be. If yoʳ worke and yoʳ stuffe be substanciall and true, yoʳ customers will not faile yoᵘ. *Yoʳ bellies and yor back℘ are enemyes to yor thrifte:* but temperaunce will helpe all. Ye s^rving men and s^rvaunt℘, be true and dilligent to yor masters, exceede not yor wages in gamyng and expences. Be not loath to lerne, least ye be longe lewde [ignorant]. Thinke yor master not to bad, leaste yo" chaunge for the worse. All ye laborers, be not wearie of yor sweate; it beseemeth yo" best. Let not Idlenes lead yo" into the daung^r of Indigence; And thus the roote of concorde shalbe surelie rooted in the Com̃ynaltie of this realme,[20]

as well as in the clergy and nobility, to the glory of the commonwealth. Thus did the notorious agent of Henry VII, famed for his oppressive exactions, preach to all estates.

Nor does this conclude his sermon. He expands the theme at greater length when discussing the parings and cores of each fruit.[21] The folly of changing one's estate is enforced on the commons repeatedly. The spirit of discontent may make them murmur at payment of taxes or "fyfteenes," and at subservience to their betters. The spirit of arrogance may persuade them that they are of the same "moulde and mettall" as their betters. Why, they may ask, should their betters sport and play and enjoy the wealth of the world while they themselves labor and till and have little? All are born of Adam. Yet some live in royal castles and manors, while others have but poor tenements and cottages. Let the commonalty beware of such temptations. God, in his divine wisdom, ordained degrees in society just as in all the rest of the universe, and God desires that we keep our due degree.

With the satire of Barclay and the political allegory of Dudley, sixteenth-century literature of estates, in both verse and prose was begun. Other verse and prose pieces soon followed. By the time of Elizabeth, Barclay's appeal to the estates of the realm was duplicated several times, and Dudley's treatise was one of a considerable line of political and economic prose treatises which sought to analyze, if not always to reform, the evils of the time.

[20] *Ibid.,* pp. 19-21.   [21] *Ibid.,* pp. 25-51.

A work that followed shortly after the *Tree of Common Weal* and that inspired much comment on estates in later treatises, though it cannot be included in the literature of estates itself, was Sir Thomas More's *Utopia,* of 1516. To Dudley's conservative approval of the *status quo,* More opposed the doctrine of communism in an ideal realm, which was to be truly a "common wealth" because in it all was to be owned in common. The plan was only a jest, but a jest with profound meaning. Many of More's successors took him seriously enough and replied adversely or favorably. Whereas other realms only talk much of the common wealth, says More, here "nothing is private," and the "commen affaires bee earnestlye loked upon."[22] Justice prevails, as a result.

For what justice is this, that a ryche goldesmythe [banker], or a usurer, or to bee shorte anye of them, which either doo nothing at all, or els that whyche they doo is such, that it is not very necessary to the common wealth, should have a pleasaunte and a welthie lyvinge, either by Idlenes, or by unnecessarye busines: when in the meane tyme poore labourers, carters, yron-smythes, carpenters, and plowmen, by so great and continual toyle, as drawing and bearinge beastes be skant hable to susteine, and againe so necessary toyle, that without it no common wealth were hable to continewe and endure one yere, should yet get so harde and poore a lyving, and lyve so wretched and miserable a lyfe, that the state and condition of the labouringe beastes maye seme muche better and welthier?[23]

In the so-called commonwealths of the time, "which now a dayes any where do florish, so God helpe me, I can perceave nothing but a certein conspiracy of riche men procuringe theire owne commodities under the name and title of the commen wealth."[24] In Utopia husbandry is a science common to all, both men and women, and is practiced of "all estates."[25] In such a society all pride and covetousness, the chief failings of the medieval estates of the world, are utterly unknown. With the desire of

[22] Trans. by Ralph Robynson. Ed. George Sampson, Bohn Library, London, 1914, p. 184.   [23] *Ibid.,* p. 185.   [24] *Ibid.,* p. 186.
[25] *Ibid.,* p. 93.

money utterly banished, "howe greate a heape of cares is cut away!" With such a doctrine, Sir Thomas More substitutes an extreme popular sovereignty, unheard of before or since, for the feudal régime with its classes of society, which in many countries are as familiar today as they were in the Middle Ages. The *Utopia* is, consequently, not a treatise in which to look for the estates of the world and the propagation of the feudal philosophy of estates. It is, in fact, the literature of estates turned inside out. The old system is what should not be; the communism of Utopia, devoid of differences of estate, is what should be.

Sir Thomas Elyot was one of those who had small faith in the doctrine of communism. To him, those who talked of having all things in common were "fantasticall foles."[26] His *Boke Named the Governour* is, of course, a treatise of advice for one estate only, that of rulers or magistrates. However, Elyot also, at considerable length, refutes the arguments of communists like More and preaches the old doctrine of the estates of the world—the necessity of estates and their duties. The first part of the *Boke Named the Governour* reads like a reply to the *Utopia*. Elyot is neither the political idealist that More is, nor simply a religious dogmatist, though he is finally satisfied with the explanation of divine origin of government and of classes of society. He says that he bases his arguments on "reason and commune experience" and on the authority of Plato and Aristotle,[27] but his chief argument is that of divine order, and thereby he reaches the position of conservative adherence to the old doctrines of the necessity of monarchy and of gradations of society.

First, he has much to say, in the tone of the knightly school-

[26] *The Boke Named the Governour,* ed. Henry Herbert Stephen Croft, 2 vols., London, 1883, I, 5.

[27] *Ibid.,* editor's footnote, p. 11, says that Elyot shows bias, for the sentiments he expresses could scarcely have been inspired by a perusal of classical writers.

master that he was, of the meaning of the terms *res publica* and "publik weale." They are usually misunderstood, he says. His explanation of their real meaning is most interesting in the light of all that philosophies of estates have said before him. He defines a "publik weale" as "a body lyvyng, compacte or made of sondry astates and degrees of men, whiche is disposed by the ordre of equite and governed by the rule and moderation of reason."[28] Thus he commits himself at once to differences in degree. The term *res publica* is nothing but the Latin word for "public weal." *Res* means more than "a thing"; it may mean also "estate, condition, substance, or profit." Now *profit* is only another word for "weal." And the word *publica* is derived from the word for "people," *populus*. "Wherfore hit semeth that men have ben longe abused in calling *Rempublicam* a commun weale," if by commonwealth they mean "that every thinge shulde be to all men in commune, without discrepance of any astate or condition." Those that give it such a meaning "be thereto moved more by sensualite than by any good reason or inclination to humanite. And that shall sone appere unto them that wyll be satisfied either with autorite or with naturall ordre and example." A very simple explanation solves the apparent contradiction: the word *populus* includes "all the inhabitantes of a realme or citie, of what astate or condition so ever they be." If one wishes to speak of the commonalty only, one must use the word *plebs,*

wherein be contayned the base and vulgare inhabitantes not avanced to any honour or dignite, whiche is also used in our dayly communication; for in the citie of London and other cities they that be none aldermen or sheriffes be called communers. And in the countrey, at a cessions or other assembly, if no gentyl men be there at, the sayenge is that there was none but the communalte, whiche proveth in myn oppinion that *Plebs* in latine is in englisshe communaltie and *Plebeii* be communers.[29]

[28] *Ibid.*, I, 1.
[29] *Ibid.*, I, 3.

Thus, he proceeds, there is as much difference between "public weal" and "common weal" as between *res publica* and *res plebeia*. If the public weal is to be a *res plebeia*, then in it the commoners only must be wealthy and the nobility needy and miserable, or all must be of one degree and sort.

In such a communism, Elyot has no interest. For it would destroy the "discrepance of degres, whereof procedeth ordre." This order runs through the whole universe, natural and supernatural. By it the incomprehensible majesty of God, as by a bright light of torch or candle, is declared to the blind inhabitants of this world. Moreover, without such order, only chaos would result and perpetual conflict. Nor can anything or anyone exist of himself; for if he destroys others on whom he depends, then he too of necessity must perish. The result is universal dissolution. All this is true of the realm supernatural, but those things within the compass of man's knowledge are similarly ordered, by "degrees and astates." The elements of the body, herbs, animals, trees, birds, fishes, all show order. Similarly order exists in the realm of humankind, "so that in every thyng is ordre, and without ordre may be nothing stable or permanent; and it may nat be called ordre, excepte it do contayne in it degrees, high and base, accordynge to the merite or estimation of the thyng that is ordred."[30] In the "astate" of mankind, one would naturally expect more perfect order than among the inferior creatures who have not man's knowledge and wisdom and who were ordained by God for the use of man. God does not give to every man the same gifts, but some have more, some less, as pleases God's divine majesty. Therefore they cannot be all of one estate. Such as think they can have all things in common, therefore, are "fantasticall foles."

One man excels another in understanding, and so shulde the astate of his persone be avanced in degree or place where understandynge

[30] *Ibid.*, I, 5.

may profite. . . . And unto men of suche vertue by very equitie appertaineth honour, as theyr iuste rewarde and duetie, whiche by other mennes labours must also be mainteined according to their merites. For as moche as the saide persones, excelling in knowlege wherby other be governed, be ministers for the only profite and commoditie of them whiche have nat equall understandyng: where they whiche do exercise artificiall science or corporall labour, do not travayle for theyr superiours onely but also for theyr oune necessitie. So the husbande man fedethe hym selfe and the clothe maker: the clothe maker apparayleth hym selfe and the husbande: they both socour other artificers: other artificers them: they and other artificers them that be governours. But they that be governours . . . nothinge do acquire by the sayde influence of knowlege for theyr owne necessities, but do imploye all the powers of theyr wittes, and theyr diligence, the only preservation of other theyr inferiours." Moreover the slothful person should not share equally with the industrious; for, if he did, the industrious workman would become discouraged and idle. "Wherfore it can none other wyse stande with reason, but that the astate of the persone in preeminence of lyvynge shulde be estemed with his understandyng, labour, and policie.[31]

He should have honor and substance, as a reward for himself and also as an incentive to those below him. Where all things are common, there is no order, he repeats, and he enforces the repetition by an original analogy: that of household furniture. Pots and pans adorn the kitchen well enough, but they would scarcely be ornaments in the bedchamber; neither would the beds and pillows be fitting in the hall, or carpets and cushions become the stable.

Semblably the potter and tynker, only perfecte in theyr crafte, shall littell do in the ministration of iustice. A ploughman or carter shall make but a feble answere to an ambassadour. Also a wayver (weaver) or fuller shulde be an unmete capitaine of an armie, or in any other office of a governour.[32]

Without these different estates there is no public weal, any more than a house is sufficiently furnished without its necessary ornaments.

[31] *Ibid.*, I, 7.   [32] *Ibid.*, I, 7.

Elyot similarly demonstrates the necessity of monarchy by the argument of order. A tyrant is not desirable, of course, but neither is a "communaltie." The latter "of all rules is moste to be feared." For the commons, without bridle, order everything without justice, and with vengeance and cruelty. A king or prince, on the other hand, provides the most sure governance, for he rules only for the welfare of his people, and that kind of government is best approved and has longest continued and is most ancient. With such assurance does Elyot juggle facts to further his argument. In addition to the king there should be inferior magistrates, chosen by the king and compared by Aristotle to the king's eyes, ears, hands, and legs. Such magistrates should be chosen from "that astate of men whiche be called worshipfull, if amonge them may be founden a sufficient nombre, ornate with vertue and wisedome, mete for suche purpose, and that for sondry causes." However, if such virtue and learning "do inhabite a man of the base astate of the communaltie," then he too is worthy to be so advanced.

The rest of the work is devoted chiefly to the proper training for a member of the nobility. All the finest human qualities are those of gentility. By his majesty such a one "may be espied for a governour." Even his apparel is important. God has ordained certain apparel for certain ranks of society.

And what enormitie shulde it nowe be thought, and a thinge to laughe at, to se a iuge or sergeant at the lawe in a short cote, garded and pounced after the galyarde facion, or an apprentise of the lawe or pleder come to the barre with a millaine bonet or frenche hatte on his heed, sette full of plumes, poudred with spangles. So is there apparaille comely to every astate and degree, and that whiche exceedeth or lackethe, procureth reproche, in a noble man especially.[33]

[33] *Ibid.*, II, 17. A footnote, p. 17, refers to a very similar passage in Puttenham's *Arte of English Poesie*, ed. 1811, Liber III, p. 237, where the author says that "every estate and vocation should be knowen by the differences of their habit: a clark from a lay man: a gentleman from a yeoman: a souldier from a citizen, and the chiefe of every degree from their inferiours, because in confusion and disorder. there is no manner

Strangely enough, Elyot later[34] asserts that in the beginning people had all things in common and that private possessions and dignities were bestowed by the consent of the people on those at whose virtue they marveled and by whose industry they received a common benefit. This readiness to labor for the common benefit was called "gentilnesse" in English, "And the persones were called gentilmen, more for the remembraunce of their vertue and benefite, than for discrepance of astates." Apparently Elyot has forgotten his earlier argument. This is another instance of how in the philosophy of estates one argument may be made to work both ways, according as the author is addressing one estate or another. On the nobility, the acquisition of estate from the commons puts a great responsibility. To the commons, nobility is said to be ordained of God, for the sake of their submission. Here Elyot proceeds to say that God is responsible for the good children of these "gentilmen," who, in turn, strove to retain the gentility of their fathers. Thus the estates of the nobility originated. Let no man think that lineage and riches make him noble: only true nobility of character can do that. The idea of divine origin of estates is asserted again toward the close of the work, however, with the same examples from nature.[35] With equality of degree, we should, like savage beasts, desire to slay one another.

To Sir John Cheke, tutor of Edward VI, secretary of state, and one of the principal restorers of Greek learning in England, the doctrine of communism was no more agreeable than it was to Sir Thomas Elyot. His *True Subiect to the Rebell* or the *Hurt of Sedition, How Greivous It Is to a Common-wealth*,[36] written in the summer of 1549 at the time of the insurrection in Devon and Cornwall to demand their old form of religion,

---

of decencie." He must have had Elyot's passage in mind, says the editor. Other references to the necessity of suitable apparel are also cited.

[34] *Ibid.*, II, 26 f.   [35] *Ibid.*, II, 210-11.
[36] First ed. 1549. Reprinted by G. Langbaine, Oxford, 1641.

and of Ket's rebellion in Norfolk against enclosures, is an expostulation, at first quietly reasonable and then denunciatory, against the "great misorder of sedition" and the cry of "equality in the commonwealth." The king or magistrate is the "ordinance of God," and therefore what is done by him is done "by the ordinance of God." The rebels are bound by God's word to obey their king just as the members of the natural body obey the head.[37] They rise in the name of religion and "pretend a commonwealth." "How amend yee it," he asks, "by killing of Gentlemen, by spoiling of Gentlemen, by imprisoning of Gentlemen? A marveilous tanned commonwealth." In all countries some must rule and some obey: "Every man may not beare like stroke, for every man is not like wise." If it is the riches of the gentlemen that the rebels envy, they seek only to impair another man's estate without amending their own.

And to have no Gentlemen, because yee be none your selves, is to bring down an estate, and to mend none. Would yee have all alike rich? That is the overthrowe of labour, and utter decay of work in this Realme. For who wil labour more, if when he hath gotten more, the idle shall by lust without right, take what him lust from him, under pretence of equalitie with him. This is the bringing in of idlenesse, which destroyeth the commonwealth, & not the amendment of labour, that maintaineth the commonwealth. If there should be such equalitie, then yee take all hope away from yours, to come to any better estate than you now leave them. . . . And think beside that riches and inheritance be Gods providence, and given to whom of his wisedome he thinketh good. . . . God hath made the poore, & hath made them to be poore, that he might show his might, and set them aloft when he listeth, for such cause as to him seemeth; and pluck downe the rich to this state of povertie, to shew his power, as he disposeth to order them. . . . But what meane yee by this equality in the commonwealth? If one be wiser than another, will yee banish him because yee intend an equalitie of all things? If one be stronger then another, will yee slay him because yee seek an equalitie of all things? . . . Why would yee have an equalitie in riches, & in other gifts of God there is not meane sought? . . . Yee should submit you

[37] Oxford ed., p. 13.

by humilitie one to another, and yee set up your selves by arrogancy above the Magistrates.[38]

The king had expected to right the evils quietly and in due order, considering "all states that none should have just cause to grudge against the other." Instead sedition has arisen and martial law must prevail. Now what the rebels refused to do of themselves they must be compelled to do. The only remedy is love among all classes: "For love is not the knot onely of the Commonwealth, whereby divers parts be perfectly joyned together in one politique bodie, but also the strength and might of the same, gathering together into a small room with order, which scattered would else breed confusion and debate."[39] Thus Sir John Cheke also preaches the old doctrine of the estates of the world, changing it only in so far as necessary to fit a specific case.

No less certain, though less harsh, are the assertions of Thomas Starkey concerning the necessity of estates and of their just performance of their duties to one another. In his *England in the Reign of King Henry the Eighth*,[40] a dialogue between Cardinal Pole and Thomas Lupset, lecturer in rhetoric at Oxford, of 1536, Pole is usually the liberal thinker and Lupset, the conservative. In a tone of calm reasoning, they discuss theories of government, the classes of society, the faults of those classes, and the possible remedies. The whole is a sixteenth-century adaptation of the familiar theme. The abuses named and the remedies suggested are those of England of that particular time; but the theories of estates are those of the preceding centuries. In fact, like others before him, Starkey has Cardinal Pole cite Plato's *Republica* as a source of his doctrine. As chaplain of Henry VIII, at the time of the negotiations between Henry and Cardinal Pole about the legality of Henry's

---

[38] *Ibid.*, pp. 8-11.   [39] *Ibid.*, pp. 52-53.
[40] Ed. J. M. Cowper, E.E.T.S., London, 1878, ext. ser., Nos. XII, XXXII.

marriage with Katharine, his brother's widow, and about the supremacy of the pope in England, Starkey was in the midst of Reformation activities. Though earnest and sincere in his approval of all of Henry's Reformation acts, he was easily persuaded and was regarded as a tool by his party.[41] Before his dedication of the *Dialogue* to Henry VIII he inserted a letter, in which he explained his desire to have Lupset (now dead) and Pole (now cardinal) discuss three things: first, "what thing hit ys that men so much speke of and call a commynwele"; secondly, "the most commyn and notabull abusis"; and thirdly, "how thes abusys both in custum and law may be reformyd and the treu commyn wele a-mong us restoryd." The plan is that of most literature of estates.

Though the treatise expresses the theories of estates of its predecessors, it is full of statements that to Elyot and Cheke would seem heretical. In the assertions of Cardinal Pole there is none of the blind adherence to monarchy that Elyot and Cheke showed. Pole does not hesitate in the least to point out the abuses of all classes, high as well as low, and his whole discourse has the tone of scientific analysis. No longer are abuses and remedies vaguely enumerated, but there is evident an honest attempt to get at real causes and cures. And the cures suggested have a satisfying quality that the impractical or supernatural medieval remedies never had.

The first part of the *Dialogue*, that on theories of government, has been called a "dry discussion."[42] To the student of the literature of estates it is not dry, but most illuminating. Pole disagrees with Lupset's belief that man is born to civil or political life. Man lived many years without prince or council or cities or towns, and during that time he lived more virtuously than now. Even now, in the country where there are

---

[41] *Ibid.,* pp. x ff., in *Starkey's Life and Letters,* ed. Sidney J. Herrtage, prefixed to the *Dialogue* as Part I of *England in the Reign of King Henry the Eighth.*   [42] Preface, p. cxxv.

fewest laws, men are most virtuous. In cities, vices flourish. Lupset complains that Pole misunderstood him: by "civil life" he meant living together in good order, one ever ready to do good to another. Such a life is most advantageous to man. Pole agrees, and as his contribution to the rule of their most wise prince, he proposes to discuss the three topics named above. The discussion of the nature of the commonwealth revolves about the familiar analogy of human body and body politic. Just as man is composed of body and soul, so the commonwealth has body and soul: "Thys body ys no thyng els but the multytude of pepul, nombur of cytyzns, in every commynalty, cyty, or cuntrey."[43] Just as man's body is strong "when every parte can execute quyckly and wel hys offyce determyd by the ordur of nature," so "the strength of thys polytyke body stondyth in every parte beyng abul to dow hys offyce and duty." The heart is the king, or the rulers of the commonwealth, if there be more than one, "accordyng to the governance of the commynalty and polytyke state; for some be governyd by a prynce alone, some by a conseyl of certayn wyse men, and some by the hole pepul togyddur." Pole has plainly been reading Plato and Aristotle. The head, with its eyes, ears, and other senses, is the king's officers. The hands are the craftsmen or warriors, "wych defend the rest of the body from iniury of ennymys utward, and worke and make thyngys necessary to the same." The feet are the plowmen and tillers of the ground, "because they, by theyr labur, susteyne and support the rest of the body." All parts must be strong and healthy or the whole body suffers. To be healthy, it must have a due proportion of parts: there must be craftsmen, plowmen, and other classes in sufficient number. Without this due proportion, the body politic is deformed. There must also be abundance of all things necessary, and good order. That end is achieved by every one's doing "hys duty to other wyth brotherly love, one

[43] *Ibid.*, pp. 45 f.

lovyng a nother as membrys and partys of one body." No civil order, whether monarchy or oligarchy or democracy, can prosper unless its members think more of public than of private good. This idea, of working together "in perfayt love and unyte; every one dowyng hys offyce and duty," is stressed at length. The duty of the ruler is "to se the admynystratyon of justyce to the hole commynalty," for which purpose he is maintained in pomp and pleasure and in quiet life, without bodily labor. The duty of his subjects is, "with common quietness, to apply themselfys to theyr laburys and paynys for the susteynyng of the hole body . . . gyvyng also reverently to theyr pryncys and lordys al humbul servyce and meke obedyence requyryd to theyr state and degre." Lupset objects that all this is Utopian. Pole agrees that the present state is imperfect, but the best so far evolved. He proposes, at their next meeting, to "spye out the commyn fautys and mysordurys."

Their two succeeding meetings are devoted to the detailed discussion of abuses and remedies. Some of them have been hinted at in previous pages. They are too numerous for treatment here, but will be considered in later chapters.[44] All three estates are denounced, in all their different ranks. Specific remedies are suggested for the various abuses. The analogy of the body is carried on through the discussion. The body politic is sick, and the different members have diseases peculiar to them. The idleness of feet and hands, for example, is gout; the disagreement of parts is a deformity; the idleness of the body proper is palsy, and so forth.

The Complaynt of Roderyck Mors of Henry Brinkelow corroborates that of Starkey, but without the philosophy of estates that the latter introduces. The outspoken, heterodox yeoman-friar, Brinkelow, had little time for philosophizing about estates in the manner of the mild-tempered, aristocratic, orthodox Cardinal Pole. He finds in the "lawe of love" the remedy for

44 See pp. 361-65, 375-79.

the ills of the time, and cites those ills, but without the inclusion of the estates of the world in the manner of other sixteenth-century pieces.

The Complaynt of Scotlande vyth Ane Exortatione to the Thre Estaits to be Vigilante in the Deffens of Their Public Veil,[45] of 1549, by an unknown author, is an analysis of the abuses of the Scottish estates and the possible remedies similar to that of Starkey concerning the English estates. The device is different, however, since it is lifted bodily out of Alain Chartier's Quadrilogue invectif. Like the Quadrilogue, it uses the old form of complaint or lament, made by Dame Scotia to her three sons, "callit the thre estatis of Scotland": nobility, clergy, and commons. Out of her three centuries of independence, often under the rule of infant kings, Scotland emerged with greater abuses than those of English laments. Chronic anarchy and confusion prevailed. During the infancy of James V, after the disaster of Flodden Field, "the barons, unawed by any superior, assumed prerogatives of more than sovereign power, the ecclesiastical dignitaries stretched their pretentions to unparalleled limits, while the body of the clergy revelled in the grossest depravity, only equalled by the rapacity with which they plundered the miserable commons."[46] In addition to such abuses, Scotland suffered from English sympathisers among the Scottish nobility and from English invasions. Tracts appeared defending English claims and urging the union of England and Scotland. Partly to answer such tracts and chiefly to call all estates to the performance of their duties in this crisis, the Complaynt was written.

The author, like some of his medieval predecessors, reaches his discussion of estates by a devious route. The work is divided

---

[45] Ed. James A. H. Murray, E.E.T.S., London, 1872, ext. ser., No. XVII. The relation of the Complaynt of Scotlande to Alain Chartier's Quadrilogue invectif has been mentioned, p. 73 note.

[46] Ibid., Intro. by editor, p. ix.

into two chief parts: the author's discourse on the misery of
Scotland and his dream of Dame Scotia. Between them he introduces, by way of transition, a "Monologue Recreative," in
which he tells how he came to end his discourse and to have
the vision of Dame Scotia and her sons. Preceding the whole
work is a "Prolog to the Redar," in which the writer defends
his craft. Every craft, he says, is necessary "for the public
veil." Aristotle is his authority

that nature hes nocht maid ane man abil for everye craft or office,
bot nature hes maid ane man abil to be ane prince, ane abil to be
ane servand, ane abil to be ane clerk, ane abil to be ane craftis man,
be rason that oure hurt nature hes dividit oure complexions to be of
diverse qualiteis . . . for that cause aristotil hes said in his politiques,
that in ilk communite ther is ane multitude, ande ilk ane of thir degreis ar ordand til help uthirs in necessite.

The discourse continues, at some length, on mutations of monarchies, with many examples. This first part of the work has
nothing to do with the estates of the world. It assails as pagan
the theory that Dame Fortune and her wheel caused mutations,
and reasons out that of the six thousand years that the world is
to endure only four hundred and fifty-two remain. The "Monologue Recreative" now abruptly represents the writer as men-
tally and physically worn out by writing. To prevent himself
from falling asleep right away, he goes for a walk through the
beauty of the short midsummer night. The morning brings
laborers going to work. He lies down on the cold ground, with
a gray stone for a pillow, and goes to sleep. He dreams of
Scotia and her three sons. In a subsequent revision, as the editor points out, the writer interpolated here his praise of the
pastoral life—its freedom from the vices of the city and its
glory as the source of all science: astronomy, cosmography,
botany—and all that he himself knew about those sciences.
From that eloquent digression he turned to the Vision of Dame
Scotia, which fills the rest of the work.

Translating the words of Alain Chartier, the author of the

Complaynt introduces "Ane lady of excellent extractione ande of anciant genolygie, makkand ane melancolius cheir for the grite violens that sche hed sustenit and indurit." Her hair is in disorder, her crown is tottering on her head, and she is carrying a shield in her hand, bearing a red rampant lion hurt in many places. Her whole appearance, in fact, is identical with that of France in the *Quadrilogue*. Her torn mantle represents the three estates, as does that of France. The lady weeps as she sees her three sons coming toward her.

The eldest of them vas in harnes, traland ane halbert behynd hym, beand al affrayit and fleyit for dreddour of his lyve. The sycond of hyr sonnis vas sittand in ane chair, beand clethed in ane sydegoune, kepand grite gravite, heffand ane beuk in his hand, the glaspis var fast lokkyt vitht rouste · hyr ȝongest sone vas lyand plat on his syde on the cald eird, ande al his clathis var revyn ande raggit, makkand ane dolorus lamentatione, ande ane piteouse complaynt · he tuke grite pane to ryise up on his feit, bot he vas sa grevouslye over set be violens, that it vas nocht possible til hym to stand rycht up.[47]

The author of the *Complaynt* adds his own touches here. The lady begins to reproach them, first all together and then individually, and here the *Complaynt* is all Scotch. Again, as in Starkey's *Dialogue*, the charges are those peculiar to that time and to the country in which the work was written. The sons are all guilty of degeneracy, of selfishness, of lack of patriotism, of sacrificing their country to selfish ends, and especially of taking "assurance of England." More than three thousand "renegat Scottis" with their families have gone to live in England during the last fifty years. They will learn the fate of traitors in the end. English and Scottish history is here reviewed to show that the English king does not legally represent Trojan Brutus, but is of the blood of Sergest and Hengest and so is a usurper. Moreover, there have been many other breaks in the legal succession.

To the charge of treason, Dame Scotia's third son, "callit

[47] *Ibid.*, p. 70.

laubir," answers with a lamentable complaint. Though the nobles are traitorous, the poor are not. They can't be, because
they are crushed. The laborer has both the damage and the
reproach. He is kicked and prodded like a dull ass (Alain
Chartier's words) to do what is beyond his power. Though he
works night and day to sustain the other two estates, they are
more cruel to him than are his old enemies of England. His
land and cattle are taken from him, or his rents are raised until
he has nothing left. Or, if he is a merchant or craftsman, he
must loan to his two cruel brothers, and if he asks for the
return of his money, he is bullied and often slain. Such are the
daily abuses of "my tua brethir nobilis and clergie quhilk suld
defend me." This last statement leads to further original philosophy of estates: "the lauberaris ar ane notabil membyr of
ane realme, vitht out the quhilk the nobilis & clergie can nocht
sustene ther stait nor ther luif." The laborer is, in fact, not the
youngest brother, but the oldest. He created the estate of the
other two:

for i vas gottyn and borne lang befor them and it vas i that first
instituit there faculteis · for the pollice that vas inventit be me & my
predecessouris eftir the creatione of the varld, hes procreat the stait
of my brethir · the faculteis and the begynnyng of nobillis and spirit-
ualtie, hed bot pure lauboraris to there predecesouris, bot nou sen
thai ar cum to stait and digniteis t[h]rocht me, thai ar be cum in-
grat, and lychtleis (slight) me.

When nobility and clergy make up their genealogical tables,
they should begin at Adam and his successors, "quhilkis var
lauberaris of the grond, and be there prudent invention and
pollice, hes procreat the stait that thai posses." Instead they
imagine themselves descended from angels and archangels. If
the blood of noble and laborer were let in one basin by a surgeon, it would be all of one color. Let the nobles and clergy
do their duty in defence of Scotland, and the commons will
prove as good Scotchmen as the rest.

Dame Scotia reproves her youngest son by enumerating all

his faults. He is as guilty as the rest. If he were in the seat of nobility or clergy he would be more cruel than the wild beasts of Arabia. It has always been true of the commons that, unbridled, they perpetrate intolerable exactions. All the insurrections in any realm have proceeded from the ignorance and obstinacy of the common people. They must be daily subdued and held in subjection. They are so ignorant and inconstant that their meetings are all disorder, and they follow the loudest shouter. Therefore the civil law forbids assemblies of the commons. They are also intemperate and lustful. If one of them does rise aloft, he is more arrogant than any noble or member of the clergy.

The next accusation is of the eldest son, the nobility: "ther is nocht ane sperk of nobilnes nor gentrice amang the maist part of ʒou."[48] To let them know how far short they come of nobility and gentleness, Dame Scotia proceeds to give a long dissertation on the nature of true nobility, in the manner of Elyot's *Governour*. In the "gude ancient dais," the golden world as some call it, there was no difference of estates, "for at that tyme al men var egal, & nocht partial nor devidit, for the pepil lyvit al to gydthir in ane tranquil & lovabil communite, ande thai left no thing to there posterite bot regrettis for the alteratione of that gude varld." Now the iron age has superseded that golden world, and all is changed. The cause of this alteration was the oppression by some men of their neighbors. To escape such oppression, the people chose certain men, the most robust and prudent, to be their defenders. These defenders were so noble that they distributed most of the spoils among the people who had supported them and gave nothing to those that were cowards. "Of this sort began the fyrst nobilnes ande gentreis in the varld, for thai that var vailʒeant, thai var reput for nobilis ande gentil men, ande thai that var vicius & couuardis, var reput for vilainis and carlis." A nobleman's coat

[48] *Ibid.*, p. 144.

of arms is a sign of his obligation to follow in the steps of his predecessors. No Scotch nobles deserve honors, because of their imbecility and avarice. They forget their predecessors and the fact that gentility proceeds from virtue. Those who are unworthy should be compelled to do "vile mecanyk laubir," to keep the ranks of nobility free from pretended gentlemen. And, on the other hand, "ane sone of ane mechanyc plebien, beand verteous, he is ane gentil man." Death levels all, anyway. The sermon closes with some local color: Scottish gentry are inordinately fond of costly clothing beyond their estate, and they are not reputed gentlemen unless they spend more on horses and dogs than on their wives and children.

The exhortation to the clergy, the second son, which is lacking in the *Quadrilogue,* charges him with worse faults than those of his two brothers. For they are ignorant, but he is learned. God has set the clergy "abufe the stait of thy tua brethir," to teach them and to dispense his gifts among them. The clergy should promote unity and concord among all estates. Instead, the clergy and temporal rulers fight like cats and dogs. Without doubt the abuses of the clergy are the cause of schism and diverse sects that trouble all Christianity. The schism can be healed only by reform of the clergy. If England annexes Scotland, Henry VIII will no doubt take their goods and heritage, just as the English clergy lost theirs. These he will distribute among "ane certan of grit personagis of his realme, quhilkis adherit till his tirran opinion." The highest prelates he had his butcher behead, and he hung their quarters in certain byways for all to see. The lower orders, both "regular and religiouse preistis, monkis, and freris," he required to learn trades, some shoemakers, some tailors, some mariners, and so forth. Let the Scotch clergy change their clerical habits for coats of mail and help to defend their land. They should not be scrupulous about the matter, for all estates must help defend the common weal. The lament of Dame Scotia closes with another exhortation to all three sons to reform.

All of these earlier sixteenth-century prose discussions of the estates of the realm show conservative acceptance of the organization of society as it was when they were written. No one questioned the necessity or desirability of all three estates. Though all the writers disapproved of the defections of the estates, they had no quarrel with the form of government itself. Moreover, with the exception of the *Complaynt of Scotlande,* they analyze their theories of government and reprove the faults of the estates in rather mild and traditional tone, to which no censor could take offense. The Scotch author of the *Complaynt,* though he too uses a traditional device for his charges, is much more outspoken. He seems to feel that he has a desperate cause to fight, and he fights it as best he can, under cover of a familiar literary device.

The poems of Sir David Lyndsay, written about the same time as these prose pieces, are, like the *Complaynt of Scotlande,* full of Scotch frankness. Though an "estate" himself, the author belabors high estate as well as low in no uncertain terms. *The Dreme,*[49] of 1528, using the same dream-vision device as the *Complaynt,* takes the dreamer into "the lawest hell," where he sees all the classes of society. Prelates and rulers are first enumerated, as they should be:

> Thare sawe we divers Papis, and Empriouris,
>   Without recover, mony cairfull Kyngis;
> Thare sawe we mony wrangous Conquerouris,
>   Withouttin rycht, reiffaris of utheris ryngis;
>   The men of Kirk, lay bounden in to byngis:
> Thare saw we mony cairfull Cardinall,
> And Archebischopis, in thair pontificall;
>
> Proude and perverst Prelatis, out of nummer,
>   Priouris, Abbottis, and fals flatterand Freris;
> To specifye thame all, it wer ane cummer.[50]

The poet goes on, however, to specify the remaining orders of Holy Church:

[49] *The Poetical Works of Sir David Lyndsay,* ed. David Laing, Edinburgh, 1879, 3 vols.   [50] *Ibid.,* I, 8, ll. 169 ff.

> Regular Channonis, churle Monkis and Chartereris,
> Curious Clerkis, and Preistis Seculeris:
> Thare was sum parte of ilk Religioun,
> In Haly Kirk quhilk did abusioun.[51]

The causes of their punishment are those of most literature of estates, namely, covetousness, lust, and ambition. They have failed in the duty of their estate:

> Als thay did nocht instruct the ignorent
> Provocand thame to penitence, be preicheing . . .
> Be symonie, was thair promotioun,
> More for deneiris, nor for devotioun.[52]

They have not properly dispensed their money: one third for the Church, the "secund part, to sustene thair estaitis," and one third for the poor. They have spent all on themselves. With medieval disregard for anachronisms, the dreamer sees, among these sinful prelates, some famous biblical sinners: "Symon Magus, bischop Caiphas, bischop Annas, and the tratour Judas." Then he turns and sees the temporal sinners:

> Than we beheld ane den full dolorous,
> Quhare that Prencis, and Lordis temporall,
> War cruciate with painis rigorous: . . .
> Sum catyve Kingis, for creuell oppressioun,
> And uther sum, for thair wrangous conquest, . . .
> Dukis, Merquessis, Erlis, Barronis, Knychtis,
> With thai Prencis, wer punyst panefullie.[53]

Ladies were being punished, too, in their different ranks:

> Emprices, Quenis, and ladyis of honouris,
> Mony Duches, and comptes, full of cair.[54]

Next the commons:

> Than we beheld, quhare mony ane thousand
> Commoun pepill lay, flichterand in the fyre:
> Of everilk stait, thare was ane bailfull band;

[51] *Ibid.*, I, 8, ll. 179 ff.   [52] *Ibid.*, I, 8, ll. 190-91, 195-96.
[53] *Ibid.*, I, 10, ll. 239-41, 246-67; 11, ll. 260-61.
[54] *Ibid.*, I, 11, ll. 267-68.

Thare mycht be sene mony sorrowfull syre;
Sum for invy sufferit, and sum for yre,
And sum for laik of restitioun
Of wrangous geir, without remissioun.

Mansworne merchandis, for thair wrangous winning,
Hurdaris of gold, and commoun occararis,
Fals men of law in cautelis rycht cunning,
Theiffis, revaris, and publict oppressaris:
Sum part thare was of unleill lauboraris;
Craftismen, thare saw we, out of nummer;
Of ilke stait to declare, it war ane cummer.[55]

After a roundabout journey through purgatory, limbo, earth, the surrounding elements of water, air and fire, the heavens where the dreamer sees God, Christ, Mary, and the angels "in Ordouris nyne," in turn divided into "Hierarcheis three, And three Ordouris in everilk Hierarchie," the dreamer returns to earth, and a geography lesson follows. He finally reaches Scotland, and describes Scotland's resources with great fervor. All is not well with her, however. The rulers are negligent. Just listen to the complaynt of ragged John the Commonweill, who now comes over the heath on foot. The poet asks him why he is so miserable. Policy and justice are gone, he says; wrong rules. Why is this? The estates are to blame: spiritualty, lords, commons. As a final exhortation to the king, the poet reminds him that none may flee death:

Kyng, Quene, nor Knycht, of lawe estait, nor hie,
Bot, all mon thole of Deith the bitter schouris.[56]

Ane Pleasant Satyre of the Thrie Estaitis of about 1540 recites the shortcomings of the estates of the realm in the form of dramatic allegory. In the manner of the old morality, the Vices and Virtues contend for sovereignty in the realm of Rex Humanitas. Diligence, the king's messenger, appears first to ask for silence. The nation has been corrupt, but reformation is at hand:

---

[55] *Ibid.*, I, 12, ll. 302-15.   [56] *Ibid.*, I, 43, ll. 1122-23.

> I wairne, in name of his magnificence,
> The THRIE ESTAITIS of this Natioun . . .
> And first, I wairne the Spiritualtie . . .[57]

When Rex Humanitas appears, he says he is "Tanquam tabula rasa"—"Redie for gude, and ill." So he tries both good and ill. Placebo, Wantonnes, Solace—three rascals—offer to show him some sport. Wantonnes, to prove that lechery is no sin, says, Look at the Church. Rex Humanitas decides to enjoy Sensuality. She boasts of her prowess with every estate:

> Till everilk stait I am so greabill,
>   That few or nane refuses me at all;
> Paipis, patriarks, or prelats venerabill,
>   Common pepill, and princes temporall,
>   Ar subject all to me Dame Sensuall.[58]

Gude-Counsall, who has been driven from Scotland to England, Italy, and France, arrives to oppose Sensuality, and she, too, makes her boast:

> Princes, or potestatis, ar nocht worth ane leik,
>   Be thay not gydit, be my gude governing;
> Thair was never Empriour, Conquerour, nor King,
>   Without my wisdome, that might thair wil avance . . .[59]

Flattrie, Falset, Dissait also seek Rex Humanitas, each showing his true nature in a lively speech. Disguised, they are received by the king as his secretary, treasurer, counsellor, and confessor. Veritie, opposing them, advises rulers and clergy to walk uprightly for the sake of the easily led commons. Instead, the "Spritual Stait" threatens her and finally imprisons her. Chastitie and Diligence lament that they, too, are banished from all estates. Chastitie makes an appeal to Temporalitie and is told that they would keep her if their wives would allow it, but they won't. So she turns to the "men of craft." A shoemaker and a tailor welcome her "till it be June." But their wives won't have her, and she is driven out of the

[57] *Ibid.*, II, 12-13, ll. 47-48, 51.   [58] *Ibid.*, II, 32, ll. 507-11.
[59] *Ibid.*, II, 34, ll. 565-68.

country on the advice of Sensualitie. She blames Emperor Constantine for her fate:

> For, sen he maid the Paip ane King.
> In Rome I could get na ludging . . .[60]

The turning-point comes with the arrival of Divyne Correctioun, who has newly landed to reform the realm—"Evin all the Thrie Estaits." The three vices, Flattrie, Falset, and Dissait, are frightened, but Flattrie says he'll preach or keep quiet in some cloister; Dissait says he'll dwell with the merchant men, his masters; and Falset says he'll live merrily among "the men of craft." Divyne Correctioun announces his plan. He will do nought without the convening of "ane Parliament of the Estaits all":

> To rich and puir, I beir ane equall band,
>   That thay may live into thair awin degrie . . .
> Quhat is ane King? nocht bot ane officiar,
> To caus his leiges live in equitie.[61]

Veritie and Chastitie are first freed, at Gude-Counsall's advice. Then all go to find Rex Humanitas. They free him from Sensualitie, who finds easy refuge among the Spiritualitie. Rex Humanitas assembles a Parliament of all three estates. Gude-Counsall states the duties of king and other estates. A king's office is to do every man justice, tempered with mercy. All other estates, "Baith Sprituall Stait, and Temporalitie," must be obedient to their king.

The second half of the play shows the three estates coming to Parliament and the reformation of the evils of the realm. All three classes are led across the stage backward, to represent their complete subjection to their vices. They are here called Spiritualitie, Temporalitie, and Merchand. Each announces his desire to do his duty. They sit down to take counsel. Spiritualitie advises against correction: the people can't stand it. Correctioun reproves Spiritualitie. Into the midst of their

---

[60] *Ibid.*, II, 78, ll. 1461-62.   [61] *Ibid.*, II, 85, ll. 1606-7, 1612-13.

debate, Johne the Commonweill enters rather unceremoniously. The trouble with Scotland, he says, is that the three estates all go backward. Rex Humanitas asks who leads them so, and Johne replies that Spiritualitie is led by "Covetice, and cairles Sensualitie," Temporalitie is led by Publick Oppressioun, and the merchants and the craftsmen are led by Falset and Dissait. Two sergeants put the evil leaders in stocks, though Spiritualitie protests at being separated from Covetice and Sensualitie. They assure him that they will soon be back with him. Temporalitie agrees to the changes advised by Gude-Counsall, and the stage direction follows: "Heir sall the Temporall Staitis, to wit, the Lords and Merchands, imbrasse Johne the Commonweill." Other evils of the realm are recited by Johne: the clergy take the property of the people; they take the wives of other men and maidens, any number; they hold pluralities; the consistory, or ecclesiastical court, decides temporal matters; the clergy do not preach; money and priests go to Rome that should no longer go there; the clergy hold land that should be given to laborers to till, so that when war is declared, they will be ready to fight. Correctioun says that all these evils shall be remedied. Johne's simple creed is that of true Christianity. The tailor and the shoemaker show their trades and are commended for doing better work than the clergy. Correctioun seeks those who can teach the truth, and who cares not "quhat estait sa ever he be." A doctor of divinity and two licentiates are asked to purge Spiritualitie. The only remedy is love—love, the ladder of two rungs: love God and love your neighbor as yourself. Friar, Prioress, Abbot, Parson, all the Spiritualitie are disrobed as unnecessary to the Church. Johne the Common-weill is given a fine garment and a seat in Parliament. Diligence and her Scribe proclaim fifteen acts of Parliament, the first of which is that Holy Church shall be protected "With the avyce of the Estatis Thrie." The other evils are also remedied, and the Vices are hanged, after each tells how he has corrupted the three estates.

The play closes with the appearance of Folly and his sermon on "Stultorum numerus infinitus." He has a fool's cap for every estate.

Some of Lyndsay's other poems are more briefly or only incidentally concerned with the theme of estates. *The Deploratioun of the Deith of Quene Magdalene* describes the display of the three estates of Scotland at a royal funeral, and *The Tragedie of the Cardinall,* lamenting the murder of the ambitious prelate, David Beaton, is a tale of a fall from high estate in the manner of those in the *Mirrour for Magistrates. Ane Dialog Betuix Experience and Ane Courteour* lists all the ranks of the estate of the clergy but not those of nobility and commons.

In this first half of the sixteenth century, like the *Fastnachtspiel* and the *sottie,* the morality and interlude also found the theme of the corruptions of the estates a profitable one. Lyndsay's *Pleasant Satyre of the Thrie Estaitis,* as we have seen, used it with a good deal of force and interest to show the abuses of the Scottish estates. John Bale's *Kynge Johan* introduced it into that famous English morality. The sedition of the realm of King John is due to the defections of Nobylyte, Clargy, and Cyvyle Order. He charges all three with their duties to the state:

> For the love of God, loke to the state of Englond!
> Leate non enemy holde her in myserable bond;
> Se yow defend her as yt becummyth Nobilite;
> Se yow instructe her acordyng to yowr degre;
> Fournysh her yow with a cyvyle honeste:
> Thus shall she florysh in honor and grett plente.[62]

They themselves declare their duties to the Church, when King John demands an explanation of their adherence to the pope:

K. JOHAN. One questyon more yet ere ye departe from me
　　　　　I will fyrst demaund of yow, Nobelyte:

[62] *Specimens of the Pre-Shaksperean Drama,* ed. J. M. Manly, Boston, 1897, I, 543.

	Why leve ye yowr prince and cleave to the Pope so sore?
Nob.	For I toke an othe to defend the Chyrche evermore.
K. Johan.	Clergy, I am sure than yowr quarell ys not small.
Clargy.	I am professyd to the ryghtes ecclesyastycall.
K. Johan.	And yow, Cyvyle Order, oweth her sum offyce of dewtye.
S. Order.	I am hyr feed man; who shuld defend her but I?[63]

And Imperyall Majestye, after they have been freed from Sedycyon, again proclaims their future duties to their state:

The adminystracyon of a princes governaunce
Is the gifte of God and hys hygh ordynaunce,
Whome with all your power yow thre ought to support
In the lawes of God to all hys peoples confort:
First yow, the Clergye, in preachynge of Gods worde,
Than yow, Nobilyte, defendynge with the sworde,
Yow, Cyvyle Order, in executynge justyce.[64]

The divine origin of kingship, "how he was of God a magistrate appoynted," is frequently stressed, and the defections of the three estates are described at length. With Sedycyon banished, they are dutiful again. In the morality *Respublica,* written on the accession of Queen Mary, avarice is the chief affliction of Respublica, the "ladie of Estate."[65] Her realm is purged only when she has been able to "punishe in all eastates."[66]

The interlude, too, provided opportunity for enumeration of estates and for discussion of the philosophy of estates. *Of Gentleness and Nobility,*[67] "a Dialogue between the Merchant, the Knight, and the Ploughman, disputing who is a very Gentleman, and who is a Nobleman, and how men should come to authority," now attributed to John Rastell,[68] is an example of fairly thorough adaptation of the philosophy of estates to that early dramatic form. In rough heroic couplets the three estates

[63] *Ibid.,* I, 576.   [64] *Ibid.,* I, 616.
[65] Ed. L. A. Magnus, E.E.T.S., London, 1905, ext. ser., XCIV, 8.
[66] *Ibid.,* p. 58, l. 1791.
[67] Printed with *The Spider and the Fly,* ed. John S. Farmer, London, 1908, pp. 431-72.
[68] See A. W. Reed, *Early Tudor Drama,* London, 1926, pp. 106 f.

debate their claims to gentility and authority. Each maintains that he is the true gentleman: the knight by virtue of his ancestors and their possessions, the merchant by virtue of services rendered to the commonweal, and the ploughman by virtue of his independence of all the rest. The origins of nobility and authority form the subject of a second debate. The knight maintains that he, and he only, is a gentleman because he is "born to great lands by inheritance" and bears the name and arms of ancestors who have borne them for the last five hundred years. The merchant, born of artificers, "as smiths, masons, carpenters, or weavers," is a churl to consider himself a gentleman. Not so, says the merchant. His definition of a gentleman is one who renders services to others:

> For I call him a gentleman that gently
> Doth give unto other men lovingly
> Such thing as he hath of his own proper.[69]

The ancestors of the merchant have always given their labors to help the ancestors of the knight, building their houses, making their clothes, and so forth. The merchant's progenitors, therefore, were gentlemen. Well, says the knight, they never gave anything unless they were paid for it. Yes, but how did the lords get their money? asks the merchant. Only by the labor of the artificers. The knight's retort is that of relative competence: artificers do the work they do because they have little wit, whereas gentlemen have more wit and therefore serve as justices at sessions and leaders in the army. Into this contest of wits the ploughman enters, to present his claims to gentility by force. When the knight bids him "Avaunt," he hits both knight and merchant with his whip. Neither wants to fight; and the ploughman scorns them for doing nothing. The ploughman, after all, is noblest, he says, since of all estates he is most independent of others. God is "the noblest thing that is" because he needs the help of no one. The ploughman is therefore

[69] Ed. Farmer, p. 435.

most like God. The disputants meet a second time to reopen the question. It's foolish, says the ploughman, for the knight to say he is a gentleman because of his ancestor's possessions:

> For when Adam delved and Eve span,
> Who was then a gentleman?
> But then came the churl and gatherèd good,
> And there began first the gentle blood;
> And I think verily ye do believe
> That we came all of Adam and Eve.
> Then to speak by reason; great possessions
> Make no gentleman, but gentle conditions.[70]

Well, says the knight, if "gentle conditions" be the cause of nobility, he can well compare with the other two, for he and his ancestors have "ever used gentle manner." As for the origin of nobility, it began with no churlish desire of acquiring possessions, but as a reward for service and virtue. The ploughman objects. Possessions began by extortion. There is apparently no solution to the question. Merchant and knight agree that it is useless to try to convince the ploughman: they are sure that gentle conditions are most commonly found in the noble born. The ploughman also decides that words are useless, and he goes back to work. The conclusion of the "Philosopher" is that of most literature of estates: virtue makes the gentleman.

English balladry and Reformation verse and prose of the first half of the century also concern themselves with the theme of estates. Like Lyndsay's *Satyre*, they have moɪe vehemence of expression than have the conservative prose philosophers, and it is the estate of the clergy that is belabored with most energy. Those that give attention to all three estates may properly be noted here.

The ballad *Now a Dayes*[71] enumerates the abuses of all three

---

[70] *Ibid.*, p. 449.

[71] Ed. F. J. Furnivall, *Ballads from Manuscripts*, I, 93-100. Printed for the Ballad Society, London, 1868-72. The editor says, Intro., p. 3, that the MS belongs to the middle of Henry VIII's reign.

estates, apparently without fear of censor. It presents a nice picture of conditions in England in the days of enclosures. It begins with a typical medieval lament that the good old times are past:

> We Englisshemen beholde
> Our auncient customs bolde,
> more preciouser then golde,
>   be clene cast away,
> And other new be fownd,
> the which (ye may understand)
> that causethe all your land
>   So gretly to decay.

In former days, noble men thought only of the good of the realm. They built churches where men's lives might be amended. Many a knight was sworn to defend Holy Church with all his might. All men pledged themselves to obey their prince. The king, in turn, gladly took their counsel and made no statute save for the commonweal. He was loved in those days, even by his commons. Few of them were poor or lacked necessities. Then one could ride with merry heart through prosperous towns and cities. The lament ends here, and the charges of defections begin. Now, says the poet, all is changed:

> The townes go down, the land decayes;
> Off cornefeyldes, playne layes;
> Gret men makithe now a dayes
> A shepecott in the churche.

Now all the people live at variance, and each estate blames the others for their troubles. Each class is trying to outdo the others: the spiritualty, the commonalty, and the nobility. Priors and abbots are now "grete grosyers." They openly buy and sell, always grasping for greater possessions and for promotion. Similarly the commonalty apply themselves right marvelously to learn subtle crafts with which to beguile their neighbors. Temporal lords are almost gone. They no longer maintain households and great retinues; and so many a good man must beg his bread. If he steals, he is shortly hanged. The result is great disorder. Great men are wise in gathering goods unto themselves, but they can devise nothing for the commonweal. They will not "break their wits" on that problem. And if a man speak against them, he is carried straight to jail. May all the persons of the Trinity help us!

The verse and prose of the Reformation naturally give most attention to the clergy. The song of Watkyn in *Rede Me and Be Nott Wrothe*[72] by Roy and Barlowe begins in genuine medieval fashion with the theme: "The worlde is worsse then evyr it was." Then, when the second stanza promises "Fyrst to begynne at the spretualte," the reader expects to hear of the other estates as well. But the whole song never gets beyond the spiritualty. Some of the Reformation verse in the second half of the century, however, is addressed to all estates and will be examined later.[73]

The sermons of Latimer, also, are chiefly concerned with the faults of the clergy. They do not enumerate all the estates, but they have recourse to the old philosophy of estates in order to prove one point or another. In his famous *Sermon on the Ploughers*,[74] with characteristic vehemence, Latimer enumerates the duties of all estates to emphasize that of the clergy:

But they that wil be true ploughmen muste worke faythfullye for Goddes sake, for the edifiynge of theyr bretherne. And as diligentelye as the husband man plougheth for the sustentacion of the bodye: so diligently muste the prelates and ministers labour for the fedinge of the soule: boeth the ploughes muste styll be doynge, as mooste necessarye for man. And wherefore are magistrates ordayned, but that the tranquillitie of the commune weale maye be confirmed limiting both ploughes.

Instead, prelates are "lording it." They live in elegant palaces, gather in their rents, pamper their paunches, and perform temporal duties unmeet for the clergy. Let every man, for the sake

[72] Arber's *English Reprints*, No. 28, London, 1871, pp. 66 ff.

[73] See p. 209.

[74] Arber's *English Reprints*, No. 2, London, 1869.

of the commonwealth, do his own business and follow his own
calling: "Let the priest preache, and the noble men handle
the temporal matters . . . Well, I woulde al men woulde loke
to their dutie, as God hath called them, and then we shoulde
have a florishyng christian commune weale." If the plowers of
the soil were made lords, they would stop plowing too. Then,
with both plows idle, there would be nothing but hunger in
the commonweal. In the series of seven Friday sermons preached
before Edward VI,[75] Latimer treats of the duties of a king and
the divine origin of kingship. His authority is the Scriptures,
which are good for all, "Kynges, Prynces, Byshops, and for
all states." The king, God's high vicar, must labor like all the
other estates:

Every man must labour, yea though he be a Kynge yet he muste
labour, for I knowe no man hath a greater laboure then a Kynge.
What is his labour? To studye goddes boke, to see yat there be no
unpreachynge prelates in his realme, nor bribing Iudges, to se to all
estates, to provyde for the poore, to see vittailes good chepe. Is not
this a labour trowe ye?

About the middle of the sixteenth century, the criticism of
the three estates is embodied in the work of two writers who
are as different in attitude as conservative and democrat could
well be. In these turbulent years, when the religious fate of
England wavered uncertainly between Protestantism and Catholicism, class unrest was increasingly evident. The need of
warnings about the dangers of falling from high to low estate
or of rising from low to higher estate was felt more keenly
than ever. Neither of these two mid-century writers questions
the old philosophy of estates, the divine ordination of estates,
the need of all three, and the duty of each to the other; but
one in very restrained and traditional fashion warns of the
dangers of change of fortune of those in high place, and the
other, with great sympathy for the hardships of the commons
and little complaint of their faults, nevertheless warns them

[75] Arber's *English Reprints*, No. 13, pp. 25, 39, 169, 181.

of the necessity of their remaining content in their own estate.

No more emphatic statement of the philosophy of the estates of the world is to be found in the literature of the sixteenth century than is that of the poems of Robert Crowley. Printer, preacher, Archdeacon of Hereford, and finally Vicar of St. Giles, Cripplegate, he was a Protestant of the most ardent sort. His long and stormy career was full of controversy on religious matters. Anything that savored of popery was anathema to him. At the same time, he was the champion of the poor, and his works show keen observation of the social evils and injustices of the time. His adaptation to those evils of the philosophy of the literature of estates is complete, but he uses the term *estate* loosely, and his enumeration of estates is not the rigid catalogue of the medieval moralists. His estates and abuses are those of 1550 in Tudor England.

One and Thyrtye Epigrammes, "wherein are bryefly touched so many Abuses, that maye and ought to be put away,"[76] lists those abuses in alphabetical order. In "Of Allayes" he laments the avarice of all:

> For the charitie of rich men
>   is nowe thorowe colde.
> And this is a Citye
>   in name, but, in dede,
> It is a packe of people
>   that seke after meede;
> For Officers and al
>   do seke their owne gaine,
> But for the wealth of the commons
>   not one taketh paine.
> An hell with out order,
>   I maye it well call,
> Where everye man is for him selfe,
>   And no manne for all.[77]

In "Of Almes Houses" he tells of how "men of greate riches"

---

[76] Ed. J. M. Cowper, *Select Works,* E.E.T.S., London, 1872, ext. ser., No. XV.　　　　　[77] *Ibid.,* p. 11, ll. 191 ff.

have bought even the alms-house site and turned the poor out. In "Of Baylife Arrantes" he characterizes the bribed bailiff and closes: "Thus pore men are pold." Class unrest is plainly evident in "Of the Colier of Croydon," in which he describes the wealth of the collier and of the coal barons among the knighthood:

> For his riches thys Colier
> myght have bene a knight;
> But in the order of knighthode
> he hadde no delyght.
> Woulde God all our knightes
> dyd minde colinge no more,
> Than this Colier dyd knyghtyng,
> as is sayde before!
> For when none but pore Colyars
> dyd wyth coles mell,
> At a reasonable price,
> they dyd theyr coles sell;
> But sence oure Knyght Colyars
> have had the fyrste sale,
> We have payed much money
> and had fewe sackes to tale.[78]

"Of Marchauntes" similarly bids merchants keep to their merchandise and thus serve the commonwealth. Instead they buy farms, rent them at high rents, loan money at usury, and so forth. Women are scrmonized in "Of Nice Wyves" in the usual fashion. "Of Obstinate Papistes" shows Crowley's prejudices against popery.

The Voyce of the Laste Trumpet, "blowen by the seventh Angel (as is mentioned in the eleventh of the Apocalips) callyng al estats of men to the ryght path of theyr vocation, wherin are conteyned .xii. Lessons to twelve several estats of men, which if thei learne and folow, al shall be wel, and nothing amis," lists twelve estates as follows: beggars, servants, yeomen, lewd priests, scholars, learned men, physicians, lawyers, merchants, gentlemen, magistrates, and women. Each is taught a

[78] *Ibid.,* p. 20, ll. 488 ff.

lesson. The series of lessons is ordered by rank, beginning with beggars and rising to magistrates or rulers. The tenth lesson is for gentlemen, those of noble birth, the eleventh is for magistrates, the twelfth for women (last, as usual), and the other lessons are all for members of the third estate, though Crowley does not group them. Preceding the first lesson, that to the beggars, is a statement of the philosophy of the estates of the world:

> Whoso woulde that all thynges were well,
> And woulde hymselfe be wyth out blame,
> Let hym geve eare, for I wyll tell
> The waye how to performe the same.
> Fyrste walke in thy vocation,
> And do not seke thy lotte to chaunge;
> For through wycked ambition,
> Many mens fortune hath ben straynge.[79]

Crowley's lesson to the beggar, on this text, is humorous, to the modern reader at least:

> If God have layede hys hande on the,
> And made the lowe in al mens syght,
> Content thiselfe with that degre,
> And se thou walke therin upryght.[80]

Even beggardom is of divine origin! If ill or hungry, trust God, the beggar is told. God fed Daniel in the lion's den and Elias.

> Yea though thou shouldest perishe for fode,
> Yet beare thou thy crosse patientlie;
> For the ende shal turne the to good,
> Though thou lye in the stretes & die.[81]

"The Servauntes Lesson" similarly preaches content with one's estate. The poet proposes, he says, to turn them from "stout & stubborne mynd" to their duty:

> Fyrst, consider that thy callyng
> Is to do service, and obey
> All thy maisters lawful biddynge;
> Bearyng that he shal on the laye.[82]

[79] *Ibid.*, p. 57, ll. 1 ff.

[81] *Ibid.*, p. 58, ll. 61 ff.

[80] *Ibid.*, p. 57, ll. 9 ff.

[82] *Ibid.*, p. 60, ll. 101 ff.

Not doing one's duty brings a worse fate. Even if the servant prosper for a time and rise from his estate, misery will be his end. God will plague such a one and in eternity will put him in eternal pain, where he will wish to be a slave again. Repent, he advises, and serve willingly. In other words, remember your estate. "The Yeomans Lesson" is a long sermon to the tiller of the soil to be content with his lot. There is much repetition of the need of his being content and of his due obedience to the God-appointed king:

> Thou that arte borne the ground to tyll,
> Or for to laboure wyth thyne hande,
> If thou wilt do nought that is yil,
> Desyre not idle for to stande.
> But se thou do plowe, plant, and sow,
> And do thy nedeful busines,
> As one that doth his duty knowe,
> And wyll not the Lords wyll transgresse.
> For what doste thou, if thou desyr
> To be a lord or gentleman,
> Other then heape on the Gods ire
> And shewe thy selfe no Christian?[83]

Whether he prosper or be poor, let the yeoman pay his rents to his landlord and tribute to the king without fail. On the greedy landlords' head he will heap coals of fire, and to his prince he must always be obedient:

> See thou paye it him for Goddes sake,
> Whose officers al princes are.
> For in his need both thou and thine
> Are his to maintaine his estate . . .
> For it is God that appointeth
> Kinges and rulers over the route:
> And with his power he anointeth
> Them for to be obeyede, no doubte.[84]

If wrong is done, God will avenge. Only let the yeoman keep his own estate. A final threat is added to enforce the lesson:

[83] *Ibid.*, p. 63, ll. 225 ff.   [84] *Ibid.*, p. 67, ll. 347 ff.; p. 68, ll. 401 ff.

> Thus leave I the, wyth threatenyng
> To the thy soulles damnation,
> If thou, mislykynge thy callynge,
> Wylt nedes change thy vocation.[85]

No medieval moralist ever preached the doctrine of estates more forcefully than does Crowley, particularly to those of low estate. "The Lewde or Unlerned Priestes Lesson" and "The Scholars Lesson" are short but pointed: let them teach the people. For that they were ordained. If they rise aloft, let them not leave the people desolate. "The Phisicians Lesson" tells them that they were ordained of God to heal the sick, but everyone knows that they have slain many thousands. Moreover, they cater to the rich. Let them aid the poor who cannot pay. God will reward them. "The Lawiars Lesson" is less severe than most diatribes against the legal profession. It is a good calling, the poet says, if only those who follow it walk in it justly. But they, too, are greedy and ambitious to rise. Let them assist poor as well as rich, and serve no wrong cause. Let them fear no man's power, "be he king, a duke, an earle, a lord, or knight," in their just service. "The Marchauntes Lesson" begins with the usual adjuration:

> The ende why all men be create,
> As men of wisdome do agre,
> Is to maintaine the publike state
> In the contrei where thei shal be.[86]

Merchants who get goods from abroad at a good price should sell reasonably to the poor. They should not buy up land to rent out and make more money. They even make prices of wood and coal go up. They even buy benefices and lend for interest. Why should they thus strive to rise aloft? Sixteenth-century lack of realization of the existence of a new economic order is everywhere evident in Crowley's poems. Only the old motive—that of changing one's estate—is ascribed to the different estates as their reason for misusing their class. Why should

---

[85] *Ibid.,* p. 70, ll. 453 ff.   [86] *Ibid.,* p. 86, ll. 1025 ff.

merchants' daughters be made ladies and their sons gentlemen? asks the poet. There are already enough who bear the name of gentle blood, and everyone should keep to his estate:

> For in the worlde ther can not be
> More greate abhomination,
> To thy Lorde God, then is in the,
> Forsakeyng thy vocation.[87]

"The Gentlemans Lesson" preaches the duty of wise rule and the necessity of knowledge for that purpose:

> Thou arte a man that God hath set
> To rule the route in thy countrey;
> Wherfore thou hadste nede forto get
> Good knowledge rather then money.[88]

They are as much bound in their duty as is any other estate and must answer for failure much more strictly than must the poor man who tills the ground. They may not raise rents or levy fines more than is customary, for just as they hold of the king, so their tenants hold of them and are as much entitled to a living in their estate as is the gentleman. "The Maiestrates Lesson" addresses rulers as those "that God doeth call, To beare the swerd of punishment." Let them ever bear in mind their duty: to rule all justly. They must not sell offices. Nor must they covet greater empire:

> Thou must not covet imperye,
> Nor seke to rule straunge nacions;
> For it is charge inough, perdie,
> To aunswere for thyne owne commons.[89]

"The Womans Lesson" is the usual sermon on dress and conduct.

Crowley's *Pleasure and Payne, Heaven and Hell:* "Remembre these foure, and all shall be well," describes the last judgment. Though the several estates are not named, they are implied throughout, and the philosophy of estates is there. God

[87] *Ibid.*, p. 90, ll. 1173 ff. [88] *Ibid.*, p. 91, ll. 1181 ff.
[89] *Ibid.*, p. 99, ll. 1473 ff.

made the different estates, and at the last judgment he will reward them according as they have performed their separate duties. Judgment is based on Matthew 25 where Christ says his friends clothed, fed, took him in when he had nothing. Them he receives into heaven. Others he casts into hell. Here Crowley is explicit about the origin of estates. Those who served God say:

> "We know that thou gaveste all thynge
> To all estates, boeth hygh and lowe.
> There is no myghty lorde nor kynge,
> But he is in thyne hande, we knowe."[90]

The rich are first belabored because they did not aid the poor. As usual, Crowley's sympathy for the poor is evident. Instead, the rich have raised rents and then wasted their money in pleasures. False prelates are next addressed. They, too, have neglected their poor, wasted tithes, and practiced simony. They are guilty even of the princes' faults because they have not shown them their duty. They feared that their own livings would decay if kings and rulers of the land understood their duties. Fathers and mothers, too, have been negligent through the fault of the prelates. The faults of the commons are here omitted. The poem concludes with a plea for corrections of evils: let the poor enjoy his copyhold, open up the enclosures for tillage, restore undue fines and rents, do away with leasing out lands, restore unjust tithes, give up pluralities, rob the people no more. Let all pray to God for mercy.

When Crowley turns from verse to prose to arraign the estates of the world, he becomes even more vehement. In *The Way to Wealth*, "wherein is plainly taught a most present Remedy for Sedicion,"[91] he denounces the faults of all the three estates and makes a stirring exhortation to them to mend their ways. His theme, as the descriptive title indicates, is the familiar one of sedition. If higher rank means greater guilt, then the

---

[90] *Ibid.*, p. 110, ll. 50 ff.

[91] Ed. J. M. Cowper, E.E.T.S., London, 1872, ext. ser., No. XV.

nobles are most guilty, the commons least guilty, and the clergy half way between. Each estate, if asked the cause of sedition in the land, would point out the faults of the other estates. So Crowley proposes to point out the faults of each estate in turn. He condoles with the poor man first: "Alasse, poore man, it pitieth me to se the myserable estate that thou arte in! Both for that thou arte so oppressed of them by whom thou shouldest be defended from oppression," (the nobles' fault), "and also for that thou knowest not thy dutye in thys great misery," (the prelates' fault). But, he goes on, are you sure that you haven't been at fault in any way?

Consider, firste, if thou have loved thy neighboure as thy self; consider if thou have done nothing unto him that thou wouldeste not that he shoulde do unto the. Loke if thou have not gone about to prevent him in any bargen that thou hast sene him about; loke if thou have not craftely undermined him to get some thing out of his hand, or to deceive him in som bargein.

At any rate, they must not rebel, for God appointed rulers, and he will put down rebels. Next, the prelates: "Ye Byshoppes, ye Deanes, Archdiacons and Canons; ye Persons and ye Vicares, what soever ye be, that receyve any parte of the tenth of mens yerelye encrease, or any other patrimony of preachers, geve eare to the prophet Ezechiel!" Woe to the shepherds of England that have fed themselves. Let the clergy of the realm give up their pluralities. Let them marry, if they wish, but let their wives not deck themselves in fine frocks and French hoods. Lastly, Crowley attacks the rich gentry. He begins craftily, with the stock arguments of the rich against the poor. Apparently he is sympathetic toward the rich. The "paisant knaves" who want to be wealthy, who regard no laws, who would have no gentlemen,

thei wold have al men like themselves, they would have al thinges commune! Thei would not have us maisters of that which is our owne! They wil appoint us what rent we shal take for our groundes! We must not make the beste of oure owne! These are ioly felowes!

Thei wil caste doune our parckes, & laie our pastures open! Thei wil have the law in their own handes! They wil play the kinges!

They must be taught their place: "And because they wold have al comone, we wil leave them nothing." If they stir again, "we wil hang them at their own dores!" Then Crowley turns on these wealthy accusers of the poor. To be sure, he says, the commons have their faults, "yet if their offence wer laied in an equall balaunce with yours (as no doubt thei are in the sight [of] God) doubt not but you should sone be ashamed of youre parte." Whatever the commons have done or been, they have had an example in the nobility:

For without a law to beare you, yea contrarie to the law which forbiddeth al maner of oppression & extortion, & that more is contrarie to conscience, the ground of al good lawes, ye enclosed frome the pore theire due commones, leavied greater fines than heretofore have bene leavied, put them from the liberties (and in a maner enheritaunce) that they held by costume, & reised theire rentes.

Willingly, then, they have disobeyed God and King. Let them, too, reform. Crowley's prose work *An Informacion and Peticion agaynst the Oppressours of the Pore Commons of This Realme* also shows his strong sympathies for the poor, but without analysis of the faults of the three estates.

Robert Crowley's works are the utterances of one who earnestly desires reform of the manifest abuses of the time, but who does not see that the old philosophy of estates will no longer correct those abuses and restore order. It is well enough to tell a member of feudal ranks to remain in his estate and thus help maintain order. He will probably do so perforce if not by desire. To tell a member of a modern industrial society not to seek greater gains and thereby acquire greater social prestige is futile. There is no law to hinder such a one, and he will change his estate as rapidly as he can.

The other mid-sixteenth-century criticism of estates contrasts strongly with Crowley's denunciation. It is almost entirely tra-

ditional. It has nothing particularly characteristic of the sixteenth century in it except its added evidence of more and
more frequent change of estate. The *Mirrour for Magistrates*,[92]
of 1559, and some six succeeding issues, is another of the numerous "mirrors" that discuss the origin, duties, and fates of
various classes of society. In its purpose and in its constant references to the estates, it is much like its model, Lydgate's *Fall
of Princes*. In its five extensive parts, it shows particularly
the attitude of thirteenth to sixteenth-century writers to the
theme of the fall from high estate, by means of its stories of
the fates of legendary and historical notables, men and women.
Sackville's complaint of Henry Duke of Buckingham, Drayton's tragedy of Cromwell, Skelton's tragedy of Edward IV, and
the others by less familiar poets are all full of consciousness
of estates, and the term is used frequently. Also, authors' prefaces to each part, envoys, dialogues, and so forth frequently
refer to the estates. Though the stories are of "those exalted
hye," they are for the instruction of all, rich and poor, "Which
way to love, and live in due degree." They constitute "a worke
by all men wonderfully commended, and full of fitte instructions for preservation of eche estate."

Since the theme of the whole work is that of estates, it is
difficult to give any particularly significant and quotable references to them. A few passages, however, chosen more or less
at random, will show how the theme is stressed and restressed.
The first Induction, by John Higgins, explains the appropriate-
ness of the theme to the season of the inception of the work.
As winter drew on, he went to a printer's shop to buy a book
to read. He found there, so he pretends, the *Mirrour for Magistrates*, and he decided that its mournful theme was suited to
the sad time of year:

> For some, perdy, were Kinges of highe estate,
> And som were Dukes, and came of regall race.

[92] Ed. Joseph Haslewood, London, 1815, 3 vols.

Som Princes, Lords, and Judges greate that sate
In councell still, decreeing every case.
Som other Knightes, that vices did imbrace,
Som Gentlemen, som poore exalted hye:
Yet every one, had playde his tragedye.[93]

The general conclusion of most of the stories is that the "meane contented state of all is best." Therefore let him who is of mean estate be content. For even if, with all his newly acquired wealth, he manages to achieve a stately appearance, he will still be only a "countrey clowne":

Then is the meane estate commended well for meaner sorte
And golden meane is best in every trade of life:
For though a countrey clowne doe keepe a stately porte,
[And in expenses great, and idle charge is rife;
Although he bravely builde his house and proudly paint his wife,
Yet is he but a clowne, and makes (in deede) himself a scorne:
Full hard it is to make such one a gentill borne,
Except some noble gifts of grace his gentill minde adorne].[94]

And again:

The [setled] man [reposde,] content, is bleste and best at ease,
Which [hath decreede] in meane [e] state both God and man to
please.

Sometimes the introduction of "estates" produces an anachronism, as in the complaint of the British Guidericus, who refused to pay tribute to Caesar and who lost his life in a tempest. As ruler of Britain, he says, he sought to restore order after the invasions of the Romans. To do so he called a parliament of the three estates:

The three estates in court to *parle*, I
In hast did call, amongst which royal route,
As one who ment for welthe of commonty,
Howe to restore their ancient libertie,
Pronounst the speache which here I shal recite.[95]

The soldier-poet, Blenerhasset, was over in the Isle of Guernsey with no books, he explains, and was relying on memory.

[93] Ed. Haslewood, I, 16.   [94] *Ibid.*, p. 311.   [95] *Ibid.*, p. 356.

The explanation, however, would probably not cover his intro-duction of a "parle" of estates into legendary Britain.

Another narrative of a British king, that of Cadwallader, finds the best estate to be that of the clergy. It tells "How Cadwallader the last king of Brittaynes, after he had behaved him*selfe very valiantly against the Saxons, resigned his crowne, and* went to Rome, where he lived in a religious house. This *storye contayneth in it the estate of al estates.*" While king, he lived in fear. As churchman, he lived at ease. The comparison of estates reminds one of the disillusionment of the unstable youth in *Des estats du siecle:*

The king must wage his warres, he hath no quiet day,
The noble man must rule with care the common-weale,
The countreyman must toyle to tyll the barren soyle,
With care the marchant man the surging seas must sayle,
With trickling droppes of sweat the handcraftes man doth thrive:
With hand as hard as bourde the woorkeman eates his bread,
The souldiour in the fielde with paine doth get his pay,
The serving man must serve and crouch with cap and knee,
The lawier he must pleade and trudge from bentch to barre,
Who phisicke doth professe, he is not voyde of care:
But churchmen they be blest, they turne a leafe or two,
They sometime sing a psalme, and for the people pray,
For which they honour have, and sit in highest place:
What can they wishe or seeke, that is not hard at hande?
They labour not at al, they knowe no kinde of payne.[96]

Were they not in this serious moral tale, the lines would sound most satiric; but no such thought is in the mind of the harassed king, who found a real retreat in the estate of the clergy.

3. THE ESTATES IN ELIZABETHAN VERSE AND PROSE

Throughout the reign of Elizabeth, there is still plenty of evidence of the survival of the literature of estates in both verse and prose. With Tudor monarchy becoming more and more secure and with a censorship that proved more and more effec-

[96] *Ibid.,* pp. 423-24.

tive, it is not strange that the conservative attitude still prevails, except in an occasional piece of political prose and in the more outspoken verses of the Reformation. The political prose begins to question the age-old charges against the estates, in the light of new conditions; and the Reformation verse and prose still reflect the struggle between Catholicism and Protestantism and between Anglicanism and Puritanism with a frankness that tells much about social and religious conditions of the time. Elizabethan verse of estates, as might be expected, falls more easily into the old mould and so maintains the form most distinctly. In the prose that deals with the estates the predominant traits of the *genre* are less evident, and seldom do all appear. The writers of both prose and verse, however, are content to follow the old mode, in order to arraign the abuses of their time. Even Elizabethan drama, in one way or another, finds need of reference to the estates of the realm, but there is no enumeration of classes and abuses and no philosophy of estates such as we have seen in the morality and interlude.[97] Shakespeare's lines in *Troilus and Cressida,* Act I, Scene 3, reiterate the old belief in the necessity of classes in a stable society and in the importance of the monarch:

> Degrees in schools and brotherhoods in cities,
> Peaceful commerce from dividable shores,
> The primogeniture and due of birth,
> Prerogative of age, crowns, scepters, laurels,
> But by degree, stand in authentic place?
> Take but degree away, untune that string,
> And, hark, what discord follows!

But Shakespeare's concern, like Chaucer's, was with character and the resultant drama, and not primarily with political formulas. None of his drama analyzes in detail the organization of society or the philosophy on which such organization was based. The traditional structure of the literature of estates was naturally not suited to drama. We will examine some of the earlier

[97] See pp. 179 f.

Elizabethan verse of estates and then proceed to the prose.

The eclogues of Barnabe Googe, of 1563, should be mentioned for their brief treatment of the theme of estates, even though, as in Barclay's eclogues, it is incidental and the term *estate* is used loosely. The questions of which is the best estate and where it is found, in city or in country, receive the answer, in the third eclogue, that the town's "estate" is void of virtue and nobility. Then follow the familiar assertions of change of class and of the inability of the lowly to assume high estate and of the desirability of the mean and sure estate. The old-time lords and ancient gentlemen are gone, Googe laments, and upstart courtiers take their place. "But Fisshe bred up, in durtye Pooles, wyll ever stynke of mudde," or, in other words, "An Ape, wyll ever be an Ape, thoughe purple garments hyde." It is folly, he adds, for the laborer to become a knight, for the duties of one estate can never be done by another:

> Unfitte are dunghill knights to serve
> the towne, with Speare in fielde:
> Nor strange it semes, (a sudain Chop)
> to leape from whip, to shielde.[98]

However, the eight "satyrs" of Edward Hake in his *Newes Out of Powles Churchyarde*,[99] of 1567, show more definite adaptation of the old pattern of the literature of estates to English classes of the second half of the sixteenth century. They give evidence of the poet's concern about the new abuses of his own time and his ardent desire of reform of those abuses. As a lawyer and resident in Gray's and Barnard's Inns, he has most to say of the abuses of the law, but as protégé of the Earl of Leicester, head and defense of the Puritan party, Hake also shows his strong hatred of the papists. His courage in so openly attacking the abuses of his time is considerable, though he says

[98] Barnabe Googe's *Eglogs, Epytaphes, & Sonettes,* Arber Reprint, London, 1871, pp. 40-41.

[99] Ed. Charles Edmonds, London, 1872. A reprint of the amplified 1579 ed.

nothing of those in authority, and Tudor censorship no doubt found little to cavil at in his satires. However, as some of the orders of commons became more and more wealthy and influential, Hake must have felt the burden of their dislike. When, in 1588, he was elected to Parliament for Windsor, he sat for only a few months and was not reëlected. What prestige he won was due to his services to the Earl of Leicester, a member of the estate with which he found no fault.

In several ways Hake's satires show their kinship with earlier literature of estates. In the first place, his form, that of dialogue, is found in many medieval specimens of the *genre*. In the second place, he enumerates the estates and their abuses, one estate in each satire. The first satire is devoted to the clergy; the second, to the men of law; the third, to physicians; the fourth, to the merchants; the fifth, to a new Elizabethan class, the "banckrowtes" or money-lenders; the sixth, to the papists; and the seventh to another new class, the brothel bawds and brokers. The eighth satire considers no estate, but is addressed to the reader. A third way in which the *Newes Out of Powles Church-yarde* is traditional is in its general theme or charge: that of avarice, or "excessive and unlawfull seeking after riches, and the evill spending of the same."

A brief summary of Hake's charges will show how these traditional traits are worked out in Elizabethan satire. All estates are lying in wait for "Syr Nummus," so Paul tells Bertulph as they are overheard by the author in the aisles of St. Paul's:

> This Nummus nowe (quoth he)
> Is straightly watchte, and hardly kept
> with men of each degree.[100]

The clergy first. To be sure, most of them don't have much chance to hoard Nummus:

> Their lyvinges are so lopt,
> That from th' inferiour Clergie men,

[100] *Ibid.*, p. 4 of the first satire. For other references to Sir Nummus see pp. 25, 108, 145, 257, 342-43.

long since syr Nummus hopt.
I meane not pompous Prelates here,
　　nor Chaplens of degrée,
These flaunting fellowes by your leave,
　　will haat ift had maye bée
I meane, I meane poore Ministers,
　　some plaste and some disperst;
Whome powling Patrons and such lyke,
　　have greevously amerst.
And yet forsoothe our Baldockes bleate,
　　and say they kéepe no chéere.
They catche syr Nummus from them still,
　　and yet would have him héere.[101]

Perhaps it would be well, however, not to talk of the clergy,
lest it breed rancor. Everyone else is seeking money, too, in
country and city. Since the time is short, Paul proposes to leave
out those in the country and consider "the most estates" in the
city. The second satire is devoted to men of law: "judges,"
"practisers at the law," "petypractisers," "petyfogging mates,"
"clarks," "attorneys," and so forth. Judges take bribes and decide for him who gives them most. They delay justice and twist
the law to make wrong right and right wrong. Lawyers fleece
their clients, and finally, when they have nothing left, turn
them out of house and lands. Because they dislike poor people
in their neighborhood, lawyers acquire large estates and build
princely houses. To tell all that the "crewes of greedy griping
crowes" among the clerks and attorneys do would take the pens
of twenty skillful men. In brief, they enlarge their private gains
by foul deceits and spend them "in pompe and prowde arraye."
The third satire makes similar charges against physicians. They
put on stately airs: "Wee must beseche his Maistership our
Patient to see." Even so his lordship won't come unless Nummus
is plainly visible. Then he comes in haste and assumes the bed-
side manner, "with solempne face and grave devised porte."
With all their money, physicians do no good. They spend it on

---

[101] *Ibid.*, p. 5 of first satire.

gay apparel; they buy a pretty nag to ride on; they have a
footcloth, a gown with a great cape, and a swinging velvet cap;
then they assume "mighty lookes." In doctoring, they care little
whether they kill or cure, if only they get money. In the fourth
satire, the poet passes over the apothecary with his "filthy
stincking drugges" and the surgeon with his "fowle deceyte"—
both are moved only by love of Nummus, and, if hell were
searched for them, they'd be found in Pluto's own house. He
turns instead to the merchants. They run all over the seas, "to
the Indes, to Gynnie, Spaine, Calecut," to bring back such
dainties as peacocks' plumes, silks, velvets, spices and hops.
They sell so dear that they become rich and live like peers. They
loan money and make bankrupts of their neighbors. Their wives
and daughters are dressed in the best. The daughters must marry
wealthy men. These merchants can't endure beggars. They never
think of Charon's boat, or, if they do, they evidently expect the
pope to save them "all for chinke." The theme of death is continued in the fifth satire and so is that of bankruptcy. This new
class of commons appears frequently in other Elizabethan lists
of estates: the "banckrowtes." By their hellish business of
money-lending and borrowing and then shutting up shop when
they are rich in the name of bankruptcy, they are able to live
like epicures. Other fools and roysterers dissipate the wealth of
their dead fathers and end at Tyborn on the gallows. The sixth
satire gives a fairly detailed account of the abuses of St. Paul's,
particularly the secret work there of the papists. "Great Sacks of
newes," of the pope's power abroad, of the landing of his champions in Ireland and of Irish rebellion, are poured forth in the
papists' aisle. Brothel bawds and brokers, who practice their
own peculiar kinds of trickery, are considered in the seventh
satire. In the eighth and last one the author addresses the reader
again, on the sin of avarice. Though Hake's list of estates is incomplete, his satires are interesting for the information they give
of most of the Elizabethan classes of society.

The Elizabethan poem that most thoroughly adapts the old pattern of the literature of estates, in enumeration of classes, their duties, and their defections, is Gascoigne's *The Steele Glas*, of 1576.[102] Unlike Hake, Gascoigne belabors all estates. Moreover, he does so in mildly conventional manner that also makes his "mirror" seem more traditional than Hake's satires. There are some sixteenth-century additions and changes, but they give no such definite information about the times as do Hake's charges. Dedicated to Lord Gray of Wilton and lamenting a misspent youth at court, *The Steele Glas* presents the point of view of the conservative reformer, who finds much fault with the third estate, but who also chides king and nobility with the understanding of a former courtier.

The traditional elements are at once evident. The poet's device is an old one, that of a "mirror." He looks into his steel glass to see the abuses of the world, and he muses on "this weak and wretched world." In olden days a steel glass was used because it "both trusty was and true." Nowadays people use "christal glas, which glimseth brave and bright, And shewes the thing much better than it is." The poet's charges are also the long familiar ones. In his steel glass he sees that pride and avarice "doth al the world possesse." Everyone wants to seem to be what he is not. The array of classes that he observes is also that of the three estates, with a few sixteenth-century English additions. It is interesting to compare Gascoigne's classes with those of his medieval pattern. He has no pope or emperor, of course, and he has none of Hake's concern about the papists. His first estate is now composed of kings, lords, knights, and gentlemen. His second estate, the "clergie," is tucked in obscurely after the plowmen and craftsmen. The third estate is conspicuous for its added sixteenth-century ranks. It has the long-familiar officers, lawyers, merchants, craftsmen, and plowmen, but new names are those of soldiers, roysterers, and syco-

[102] *Complete Works*, ed. John W. Cunliffe, Cambridge, 1910, II, 133 f.

phants. The roysterers we have already found in the ranks of
Hake. In strictly medieval fashion Gascoigne's list closes with
the ladies. Gascoigne himself seems to feel the need of defining
his classes. Apparently he recognized that they were not so distinct as in the days of his medieval predecessors in the fashion.
When discussing the rank of knight, for example, he defines it as
follows:

> Yes out of doubt, this noble name of Knight,
> May cŏprehend, both Duke, Erle, lorde, Knight, Squire,
> Yea gentlemen, and every gentle borne.[103]

When defining the rank of peasant, however, he becomes face-
tious and deliberately includes in low estate all money-grabbers
or those who "get goods greedily," no matter what their rank:

> And here to write, the summe of my conceit,
> I do not meane, alonely husbandmen,
> Which till the ground, which dig, delve, mow, and sowe,
> Which swinke and sweate, whiles we do sleepe and snort
> And serch the guts of earth, for greedy gain,
> But he that labors any kind of way,
> To gather gaines, and to enrich himselfe,
> By King, by Knight, by holy helping Priests,
> And al the rest, that live in common welth,
> (So that his gaines, by greedy guyles be got)
> Him can I compt, a Peasant in his place.
> Al officers, all advocates at lawe,
> Al men of arte, which get goodes greedily,
> Must be content, to take a Peasants rome.[104]

He realizes the unusualness of his classification and so adds:

> A strange device, and sure my Lord wil laugh,
> To see it so, desgested in degrees.

The duties and defections of all the classes are, as has been
said, those of some of the earliest medieval literature of estates.
In the list of duties, the king has a place of importance never ac-
corded him in medieval enumeration. Gascoigne gives him an
estate by himself and makes a total of four estates:

[103] *Ibid.*, p. 155.   [104] *Ibid.*, p. 160.

> Againe I see, within my glasse of Steele,
> But foure estates, to serve eche country Soyle,
> The King, the Knight, the Pesant, & the Priest.
> The King should care for al the subjectes still,
> The Knight should fight, for to defende the same,
> The Peasant he, should labor for their ease,
> And Priests shuld pray, for thē & for thēselves.[105]

The duties, however, are unchanged. Like his medieval predecessors, Gascoigne also finds that none of these estates do their duty. They are all guilty of avarice and pride, in a manner peculiar to their individual ranks:

> This is the cause (beleve me now my Lorde)
> That Realmes do rew, from high prosperity,
> That kings decline, from princely government,
> That Lords do lacke, their auncestors good wil,
> That knights consume, their patrimonie still,
> That gentlemen, do make the merchant rise,
> That plowmen begge, and craftesmen cānot thrive,
> That clergie quayles, and hath smal reverence,
> That laymen live, by moving mischiefe stil,
> That courtiers thrive, at latter Lammas day,
> That officers, can scarce enrich their heyres,
> That Souldiours sterve, or prech at Tiborne crosse,
> That lawyers buye, and purchase deadly hate,
> That merchants clyme, and fal againe as fast,
> That roysters brag, above their betters rome,
> That sicophants, are counted jolly guests,
> That Lais leades a Ladies life alofte,
> And Lucrece lurkes, with sobre bashful grace.[106]

The poet, again like his precedessors, exhorts the different estates to mend their ways and do their duties. Of all of them Piers Plowman is worthiest, he adds:

> Stād forth good Peerce, thou plowmā by thy name, . . .
> Thou winst the roome, by verie worthinesse.

As if to be traditional to the last, Gascoigne closes with an epilogue containing a satiric description of women's clothes.

[105] *Ibid.*, p. 150.
[106] *Ibid.*, p. 148.

Some of Gascoigne's *Posies*,[107] also, show his interest in the theme of the faults of the estates. Particularly his *Dulce bellum inexpertis*, with its theme that "war is pleasant to those who know it not," finds ample opportunity to belabor all estates. The theme of the poem, that war is the scourge of God, is treated at some length, and then the poet abruptly turns aside to address "Prince, Nobilitie, Prelacie, Lawyers, Merchants, Husbandmen, Comunaltie." Let them all desist from their greedy grasping: the prince, of more land; dukes, earls, barons, knights, and squires, of more possessions; bishops, deacons, prelates, priests, of more tithes, glebe-land, fees, pluralities, and new degrees; lawyers, of wealth; merchants, of coin; husbandmen, of more gain; let common people of all ranks "clayme nothing but right." All this address, Gascoigne admits, is straying from his subject, but when he returns to his main theme, he again finds need of belaboring the estates, who follow wars only for glory or for gain. Each estate in war hopes for some profit from it:

> Th'ambitious Prince doth hope to conquer all,
> The Dukes, Earles, Lords, & Knights hope to be kings,
> The Prelates hope to pushe for Popish pall,
> The Lawyers hope to purchase wonderous things,
> And Merchaunts hope for no lesse reckenings,
> The peasant hopes to get a Ferme at least,
> All men are guestes where *Hope* doth holde the feast.[108]

In the *Peroratio* of the same poem Gascoigne begs pardon of all estates for his satiric remarks, and he names members of each class whom he reveres, to show that some are good. He concludes:

> But to conclude, I meane no more but thus,
> In all estates some one may treade awrye,
> And he that list my verses to discusse,
> Shall see I ment no more, but modestly
> To warne the wise, that they such faults do flie
> As put downe peace by covine or debate,
> Since *warre* and *strife* bryng wo to every state.[109]

---

[107] *Complete Works*, Cunliffe ed., Vol. I.
[108] *Ibid.*, p. 158, stanza 88.   [109] *Ibid.*, p. 182, stanza 207.

Even in his apology Gascoigne is traditional, for many a medieval cleric thought best to remind his readers that not all were included in his jeremiad.

Though the *Poems of Monarchy*[110] of Fulke Greville do not list estates or types, as do those cited by Gascoigne, they show in verse as many others tried to show in prose the efforts of the conservative political theorist to oppose the force of changing estates and their influence toward democracy. As a member of the nobility, who held many offices under Elizabeth and James I, he was naturally in favor of monarchy, and the old philosophy of estates, with its more or less static doctrine, is manifest in these poems. Monarchy, he says, was established for the sake of order. People came to expect too much of kings: a protecting popularity

> As gives, forgives, intends no other things
> But in a crown a common slave to be.[111]

Such over-valuing of an estate makes for treason. In fact, monarchy declined through tyranny. Order may be maintained by a strong tyrant, but if he be evil, let him beware. People, then, must wait for divine intervention, living in "their duties shrin'd,"[112] as their only safety, until God pluck off the monarch's crown. In the poem "Of Laws" the poet asserts the importance of assemblies of estates even in a monarchy:

> Yet above all these, tyrants must have care,
> To cherrish those Assemblies of Estate
> Which in great Monarchies true glasses are,
> To shew men's griefs; excesses to abate;
> > Brave moulds for Laws; a medium that in one
> > Joyns with content a people to the throne.[113]

Such assemblies of "all States" show who are nursing peace, who are multiplying contentions, what the people want, what the nobility want, and whereby sovereignty remains firm. Such a par-

---

[110] *Works,* ed. A. B. Grosart, St. George's, Blackburn, Lancashire, 1870, 4 vols., Vol. I.   [111] *Ibid.,* p. 15, stanza 30.

[112] *Ibid.,* p. 74, stanza 191.

[113] *Ibid.,* p. 107, stanza 288.

liament is not "for the end of one State but of all," and each
estate must consider the needs of the other. The poem "Of Nobility" explains the origin of estates and the necessity of all of
them working together. With a Renaissance flourish he ascribes
to Prometheus the rôle of Creator:

> When wise Prometheus had his fine clay drest
> To fashion MAN, he nothing more did shun
> Then Nature's uniformity in beasts,
> Of which by Art there can be nothing won;
>   Whence in these creature's frame He did comprize
>   Many both strong and strange varieties.

> That as there divers kinds be of complexions,
> So in them there might be preheminence,
> Divers of spirit, vigor, and affections;
> To keep up which degrees of difference,
>   Reason, of life the guardian, was ordain'd,
>   As conscience to Religion was chain'd.

> And to confirm this inequality
> Have not the feignèd gods in orbs above
> Gloriously plac'd that specious hierarchy
> Whose influence doth inferior spirits move;
>   And in slack or swift courses, high or low,
>   The divers honours of each being show?[114]

Differences of estate, then, are justified by like inequalities
throughout the universe. In the midst of this "differing nobleness," however, there must be unity:

> By which consent of disagreeing movers,
> There will spring up aspects of reverence,
> Equals and betters quarrelling like lovers,
> Yet all confessing one omnipotence,
>   And therein each estate to be no more,
>   Then instruments out of their Maker's store.[115]

No monarch should create too many nobles, lest the rank be
cheapened. He should create some, however, to show esteem of

[114] *Ibid.*, p. 119, stanzas 322, 323, 324.
[115] *Ibid.*, p. 122, stanza 331.

worth. In "Excellency of Monarchy," Greville shows little liking for the names *republic* or *commonwealth:*

> Besides, where this name 'Publick shall have pow'r
> To bind reward with wreath'd frugality;
> Where sad stil'd Justice shall mankind devour,
> Thorough a bloody stern severity;
>   Must not these glorious stiles of Common-weal,
>   Wound even that worth wherewith it should deal?[116]

Similarly Democracy levels achievement or rather kills it. No great state ever grew out of a system that cannot create estates:

> Whence I conclude, that since DEMOCRACY
> In her craz'd moulds great empires cannot cast,
> Of force, these frail confusèd policies,
> Which cannot breed States, can make no State last;
>   But as the viper doth, must tear the womb
>   Of monarchy, whence her foundations come.[117]

Meanwhile the estates of the realm were also receiving some attention in the later sixteenth-century verse of the Scottish Reformation. The *Satirical Poems of the Time of the Reformation*[118] in Scotland are also usually concerned with a single estate, but occasionally one of them is addressed to all estates. They cover a period of nearly twenty years, from 1565 to 1584, and treat of the "fierce struggle between Catholicism and Protestantism, the avarice and tyranny of the nobles, the unsettled and lawless condition of the commons."[119] They take the form of complaints, lamentations, exhortations, proclamations, admonitions, and premonitions. There are several exhortations to the lords to rid the land of the papists and to relieve the poverty of the laborers. "The Lamentatiõ of the Cõmounis of Scotland"[120] is a nice presentation of their ills, naming the different kinds of craftsmen. And there are other similar lamentations. "The Lamentation of Lady Scotland, compylit be hir self speik-

---

[116] *Ibid.*, p. 214, stanza 604.   [117] *Ibid.*, pp. 226-27, stanza 640.
[118] Ed. James Cranstoun, Scottish Text Society, Edinburgh and London, 1891, Vol. I.   [119] *Ibid.*, Intro., p. ix.   [120] *Ibid.*, pp. 221 f.

ing in manner of ane Epistle, in the Moneth of Marche, the ȝeir of God 1572,"[121] however, contains an address by Lady Scotland to all three estates, asking them to aid her. In her charges Lady Scotland reminds one of Dame Scotia in the *Complaynt of Scotlande*. The poem is a kind of versified summary of that prose work. The charges enumerated here, as in the *Complaynt*, are full of specific evidence of the conditions of the times. Once, she says, she and her husband, "Johne, the Cõmoun-weill," were prosperous, but no more. Civil wars now distress her and have robbed her of husband and children. Her hope now is in the young Prince, son of her daughter, who was Queen Mary. Let church, nobility, commons (the commons comprising burgesses, craftsmen, merchants, commons) assist, the church first:

> And ȝe, my Kirk, my Faithful Mother deir,
> That purgit art of Channoun, Monk, and Freir,
> Of Papist Priest, Papist, and Papistrie,
> Bot not, allace, clene of Hypocrasie,
> Of avarice, pryde and ambitioun,
> Thocht ȝe have left all Superstitioun:
> I grant the word of God is trewlie Preichit,
> And in the schullis Exercise trewlie teichit;
> Ȝit, sayis the Commounis, ȝe do not ȝour office,
> For upaland thay have not dew service:
> The rowmis appointit pepill to confidder,
> To heir Gods word, quhair they suld pray togidder,
> Ar now convertit in scheip Coits and Fauldis,
> Or els ar fallin, becaus nane thame uphauldis.[122]

The parish churches cannot be used because of wind and rain. It is no pleasure, either, to come where there is nothing to contemplate but crows and doves, crying and making their uproar, so that no one can hear the minister. Moreover, feathers and filth lie where folk should sit. As a result, people make fun of the church. They go anywhere but to church. The church, after all, is not to blame for all this, but the lords and commons of the parish, who do not pay enough to support the church. Let the

---

[121] *Ibid.*, pp. 226 f.   [122] *Ibid.*, p. 231, ll. 149 ff.

church exhort them to aid it, as well as to support the poor. This introduction of contemporary local abuses into the old *genre* of the literature of estates gives it a strange new significance that contrasts rather oddly with the old. Here the colleges and university are also exhorted to amend, to settle this "Civile difference," and to show forth charity and brotherly love. The nobility are next addressed:

> And 3e, my Barrouns and Nobilitie,
> That dois oppres my pure Communitie,
> Quhair is 3our wit, 3our ressoun, sence, and feill,
> To fle away my husband Commoun-weill?
> Quhat have 3e wyn sensyne? lat se 3our ganis:
> Gar pryse 3our proffeit, & esteme 3our panis.[123]

They have set France and England against them. They have failed to be true to the king, as they promised to be. Ambition, vainglory, greediness rule them. Their tenants complain that they are oppressed. Their rents are raised. They can scarcely pay them. Whereas they used to eat goose and hen, and have plenty of bread, drink, and bedding for hospitality, now they drink milk and new ale and are glad to get "Peis breid and watter Caill." Whereas they used to ride to town with their landlord, where they played games to exercise their bodies, now they must labor, puff, and pant, to pay their master's exorbitant rents. They are so weak that they can't carry a coat of mail. They beget weak children, ill-nourished. Thus the commons decrease in numbers. Finally Lady Scotland addresses burgesses, craftsmen, merchants, commons:

> Now 3e, my Burges, Craftis, & Merchand men,
> And 3e, my Commounis, with my hynd 3emen,
> To 3ow I have sum purpois for to say,
> How, quhen, and quhy, my husband fled away.
> First, thair come in, lurkand upon 3our gait,
> Pryde and Invy; with Falset and Dissait.
> Thir four socht ludgeing all the towne about.[124]

[123] *Ibid.*, p. 233, ll. 215 ff.   [124] *Ibid.*, p. 236, ll. 293 ff.

Lady Scotland charges the women of the commons with having taken in Pride and Envy as their guests, and the men with having harbored Falsity and Deceit. Moreover, she finds them guilty of prodigality in their efforts to dress like their betters:

> To ʒow, my Commouns, quahat mair can I say?
> I pietie ʒow as far furth as I may;
> Now pure ʒe ar, ʒit purer wald ʒe be
> For using proud pure Prodigalitie.
> Thair is na Lord nor Laird in all this land,
> Bot ʒe man counterfait in claiths fra hand,
> Fra top to ta, thocht ʒe suld beg and borrow.
> Johne, ga ʒour way, for it will not be for ʒow:
> ʒe suld ʒour ground grub with Simplicitie,
> And mak ʒour claiths conforme to ʒour degre;
> Bot ʒe, ʒour wyfe, and bairns, can tak na rest,
> Without ʒe counterfait the worthyest;
> Buft brawlit hois, Coit, Dowblet, sark, and scho:
> ʒour wyfe and bairns conforme mon be thairto.
> Leif of, and leirne ʒour bairns to saw and teill:
> Sic doings chaist away the Commoun-weill.[125]

The two pictures of the commons, that of their extreme poverty and that of their prodigality, seem quite contradictory. Sometimes, as we have seen, the writer of the literature of estates finds it necessary to contradict himself in order to preach on the same text to two different classes. The result is an interesting study in emphasis, showing how humankind suits its evidence to the point it wishes to prove.

The prose treatment of the estates in these earlier years of the reign of Elizabeth, like that of the first half of the sixteenth century, is mainly a conservative restatement of the philosophy of estates that survived from the days of medieval feudalism. To be sure, there is usually the different emphasis of the writer who lives in new surroundings and under a new form of government. The enumeration of estates has some sixteenth-century changes; the duties and defections ascribed to each estate have

[125] *Ibid.*, p. 236, ll. 293 ff.

the variations of a new social and political order; the remedies, when any are suggested, are adapted to new conditions. But on the whole, the old doctrine is revived with amazing persistence. In only one work are the changes in the philosophy of estates so out-standing as somewhat to startle the reader with their modern tone, and to remind him of the calmly rational method of Cardinal Pole in Starkey's *Dialogue*. The rest apparently have no desire to upset long established beliefs about the necessity and duties of the three feudal estates. They are quite content to let their minds run along the old grooves of medieval political theory.

The work that gets farthest out of those grooves is the so-called William Stafford's *Compendious or Briefe Examination of Certayne Ordinary Complaints of Divers of Our Countreymen in These Our Dayes*.[126] As the probable author of the work, which he called a *Discourse of the Commonweal of This Realm of England,* John Hales analyzed England's ills without bias and with some of the acuteness of a scientific economist. Though written in 1549, the work was far in advance of its time and was not published until 1581. Realizing that the enclosures, though they caused immediate suffering, meant ultimate prosperity, that the debasement of the coinage, not the enclosing and raising of prices of lands, increased costs, and that England's future welfare lay in the development of home manufactures, he had a very different attitude toward the shortcomings of the various estates of the realm from that of most of his contemporaries. To him, the true cause of the "dearth," or high prices, was "the great store and plenty of treasure, which is walking in these parts of the world far more in these our dayes then ever our forefathers have sene in times past." What were formerly regarded as luxuries, "such as glass, china, and earth-

---

[126] Published for the New Shakespeare Society, ed. F. J. Furnivall, London, 1876. For evidence of John Hales' authorship see Miss Elizabeth Lamond's Introduction to her edition of the work, Cambridge, 1893.

enware, watches, and ornaments of all sorts, were in the hands of people whose fathers would not have dreamed of indulging in such extravagance."[127]

In an examination of the literature of estates, Hales' plan, as well as his subject matter, is significant. In his device he is traditional. He puts his work into the form of three colloquies among a knight, a merchant, a doctor, a husbandman, and a craftsman, in order to get all points of view. It is a maxim, he says, that every man is to be credited in the art in which he is most experienced. "Then, I perceave every man findeth himself greeved at this time, & no man goeth cleare, as farre as I can perceave. The Gentleman, that hee cannot lyve on his Landes onely, as his father did before; the Artifficers cannot set so many a worke, by reason all manner of victayle is so deere; the Husbandman, by reason his Lande is deerer rented then before; then we that bee Merchaunts pay much deerer for everything that commeth over sea." The ills discussed have already been briefly indicated. In addition to those named, religious difficulties, such as non-residence, pluralities, lack of care in ordaining men and in holding Visitations, are also considered. The remedies are, on the whole, practical, pointed suggestions for improvement. They will be discussed more fully later.[128]

In 1583, about the same time as that of the publication of Hales' *Discourse,* the Puritan Bishop Stubbs in his *Anatomie of Abuses,*[129] Part II, set forth the defections of the estates of the realm, "such imperfections, blemishes, and abuses, as now reigning in everie degree, require reformation." The estates and their faults are enumerated in traditional fashion, with little doctrine that is new. The form, like Hales', is that of dialogue, between Theodorus and Amphilogus. First the abuses of the

---

[127] *Ibid.,* Intro. by Frederic D. Matthew, p. xvi.   [128] See p. 379.
[129] Ed. F. J. Furnivall, *New Shakespeare Society, Pubs.,* Series VI, No. 12, London, 1879.

Temporalitie are cited: the Country, the Queen, Her Council, Shires, Judges, Prisoners, Landlords, Tailors, Starchers, Tanners, Shoemakers, Brokers, Laws, Universities, Schoolmasters, Merchants, Drapers, Clothiers, Goldsmiths, Vintners, Butchers, Grasiers, the Poor, Beggars, Husbandmen, Ingraters or Forestallers, Chandlers, Barbers, Surgeons, Physicians, Astronomers, Astrologers, Prognosticators, Almanac-Makers, Sheepmasters. This list of nobility and commons and their abuses is very evidently altered by the times in which Stubbs wrote. Contemporary references are, of course, frequent. There is little philosophy of estates, but the usual abuses of each class are described. Having heard of the defections of the first and third estates, Theodorus requests a similar treatment of the abuses of the Spiritualitie:

Having now spoken sufficiently of the corruptions and abuses of the temporalitie, if I might be so bold, I would request you somewhat to say concerning the corruptions and abuses of the spiritualitie, or (as some call it) of the ecclesiastical hierarchie. For I am fully persuaded, that the one being so corrupt, the other can hardly be without blemish.

The Amphilogus of the Puritan Stubbs replies: "I am verie loth to enter into that fielde, the view whereof offereth such store of matter to intreat of, as if I shoulde enter the same, I shoulde rather not knowe where to end, then where to begin." Consequently the faults of the clergy are omitted. Part I of the *Anatomie of Abuses*, which is concerned chiefly with abuses, not with classes, also now and then applies an abuse to a certain class, as, for example, in the discussion of extravagant clothing:[130]

I doubt not but it is lawfull for the potestates, the nobilitie, the gentrie, yeomanrie, and for everye private subiecte els to weare attyre every one in his degree, accordinge as his calling and condition of life requireth; yet a meane is to be keept, . . . every extreme is turned into vice.

[130] *Ibid.,* pp. 33-34.

The nobility and magistrates may properly "set forthe their byrthes, dignities, functions, and callings" by means of rich apparel. The private citizenry should under no circumstances wear silks, velvets, satins, damasks, gold, and silver. At present there is such confusion of dress that

it is verie hard to knowe who is noble, who is worshipfull, who is a gentleman, who is not: for you shall have those which are neither of the nobylitie, gentilitie, nor yeomanry; no, nor yet anie Magistrat, or Officer in the common welth, go daylie in silkes, velvets, satens, damasks, taffeties, and such like, notwithstanding that they be both base by byrthe, meane by estate, & servyle by calling. This is a great confusion, & a general disorder: God be mercyfull unto us!

This complaint is one of long standing and can scarcely be regarded as typically Elizabethan. On the whole, Stubbs' treatment of estates is quite conventional.

Shortly before Hales' and Stubbs' very different statements of the faults of the estates of the realm appeared, another analysis was published which, for all its sixteenth-century changes, is also quite conventional in its philosophy of estates, defections, and remedies. Sir Geoffrey Fenton, translator and statesman, in 1574 contributed *A Forme of Christian Pollicie*[131] to the prose literature of estates. As his own description of the work indicates, "gathered out of French," he did not pretend to be original,[132] and the tone of the whole work is continental rather than English. No doubt, however, he makes some additions of his own, suitable to English readers.

[131] I have used the copy of the original edition, London, 1574, in the Columbia University Library.

[132] Fenton's sources for this work have apparently not been determined. In several ways, his work reminds one of Jean Bodin's *Six livres de la république*. That work, however, did not appear until 1577, three years after Fenton's was published. Bodin published his first work, *Oratio de instituenda in republica juventate*, in 1559, and Fenton's fifth book is *Of the Institution of Youth, Which is a Thing Profitable and Necessarie in a Common Weale*. Both are treatises on the education of youth. It would seem as if Fenton may have done some of his gathering from that source.

Fenton's use of the word *estate* is varied. He first calls religion and justice or Church and Government the "two estates" which form the true foundations of the commonweal. Here *estates* means institutions rather than classes of society. Without these two estates, he says, countries "slyde into vices and imperfections, which breede the revolucions and ruines of all estates." Here he obviously refers to states or governments. In still another instance, he announces his intention of treating the "office of every estate," and his estates, in the following discussion, prove to be those of man and woman in marriage, fathers and mothers and their children, masters and servants, mistresses and their handmaids, and so forth. Finally, however, he uses the term in its strictly feudal sense, to mean classes of society, and he enumerates the classes, their duties, their faults, and the remedies in the traditional fashion.

The work is full of medieval political theory. Though it is planned particularly "for all Magistrates and governours of common weales, for their more happy Regiment according to God," and though it is addressed to "Sir William Cecill Knight, Baron of Burghley," its purpose is to set forth the proper conduct of "al sorts of people generally." The familiar medieval analogy is frequently made, in the course of the discussion, between the human body and the body politic. Just as in the human body there are two parts, the corporal and the spiritual, so there are *two* estates in the commonweal, that of the magistrate or ruler and that of the clergy. The two must work together as harmoniously in the realm as they do in the action of man. They were conceived in the very beginning, in the law of nature or reason and in written law. Since then they have existed, each content with his own duty and work. But these two estates, after all, are not the total number necessary to the commonweal, for Fenton finds that

It falles nowe to convenient purpose, that wee adde to these two estates, two others. . . . I meane the Maistres of Schooles with their

Ushers, and Phisitions with their Surgeons and Pothicaries, even as under the Title of Pastours, wee comprehende also Priestes, and other orders, and with the name of gouvernours, wee signifye Judges and all such as are incident to them in the action of Justice.

Fenton is always careful to justify his inclusion of new estates and the order of precedence that he gives them in his discussion. It is unfortunate, he remarks, that physicians, out of their one estate, have "made three, yea, a fourth." The four are now: physicians, surgeons, apothecaries, and "arborists" or herbists. To these estates, Fenton adds those of gentlemen, advocates, merchants, tradesmen, and husbandmen. The old array of estates is finally complete. Women receive their due attention in the discussion of the authority of husbands over wives. If all three estates perform "the care and dutie of their office," the "body politike . . . can not erre nor much faile to live togither in happie conversation."

The estates, however, do not perform their divinely appointed duties. The magistrate fails to rule according to law; the clergy do not preach and teach; physicians are justly called abusers, robbers, poisoners of men; apothecaries sell old drugs at high prices; teachers are ignorant; gentlemen set a bad example; advocates serve the rich but not the poor; merchants buy at wholesale and sell at retail; tradesmen use various deceits. In husbandry, the writer concludes, "is least guile, for he tilles his ground, and laboreth his viniard with simple industrie." Even he, however, has been found guilty of subtle tricks to evade payment of tithes and rents.

The author also suggests definite remedies for these abuses, some of which are wholly traditional and some of which are characteristic of the time. Magistrates must show true nobility; the clergy must preach; physicians must study philosophy diligently, have "resolute practice in physic" for three years, in "medicine Theorical" for ten years, in anatomy, herbs, and "pharmacopole" for two more years, besides a number of years of apprenticeship in cities, not in uplandish towns, where there are only "fat monkes which beare no importaunce in the worlde" to practice on; apothecaries must not be allowed to practice without swearing to be honest; teachers must instruct thoroughly, concerning the body as diligently as the mind; advocates must serve rich and poor alike; merchants must abide by the golden rule; tradesmen must remember that there are plenty of chances to make money without deceit; husbandmen must be taught by their pastors to deal justly.

In addition to Fenton's traditional array of classes, defections, and remedies, he has much discussion of the origin of nobility in true nobleness, the dignity and power of the magistrate, the need of friendship and love in the relations of the estates one with another. There is scarcely a topic characteristic of the literature of estates that he does not introduce, though the reader must hunt to find it. The effect of the whole discussion, as I have said, is that of a rather haphazard importation that has no very close connection with conditions in Elizabethan England.

Such sixteenth-century utilitarian pieces as Fitzherbert's *Boke of Husbandry*[133] and Harrison's *Description of England* also do not fail to introduce some discussion of the three estates of the realm and are much more English in tone than is Fenton's *Forme of Christian Pollicie*. The way in which they get round to the theme is interesting. Fitzherbert's prologue propounds the question: "whereunto is every manne ordeyned?" Job says that man is ordained to labor, as a bird is ordained to fly, and Paul says that he who does not labor should not eat. These texts the author finds hard to apply literally. For king, queen, lords spiritual and temporal should not eat, "without they shuld labour, the whiche were uncomely, and not convenyente for suche estates to labour." The solution of the problem

[133] Ed. W. W. Skeat, *English Dialect Society, Pubs.*, London, 1882. Series D.

Fitzherbert finds in "the boke of the moralytes of the chesse," wherein one may read that every man, from the highest degree to the lowest, is placed in his estate to do some kind of labor. He proceeds to describe the contents of Caxton's *Game and Playe of the Chesse:*

and that boke is devyded in vi. degrees, that is to saye, the kynge, the quene, the byshops, the knightes, the iudges, and the yomenne. In the which boke is shewed theyr degrees, theyr auctorytyes, theyr warkes, and theyr occupations, and what they ought to do. And they so doynge, and executynge theyr auctorytyes, warkes, and occupatyons, have a wonders great study and labour, of the whiche auctorytyes, occupations, and warkes, were at this tyme to longe to wryte. Wherfore I remytte that boke as myn auctour therof: The whiche boke were necessary to be knowen of every degree, that they myght doo and ordre them selfe accordynge to the same.[134]

Since to the yeomen is ascribed the duty of laboring for, defending, and maintaining "all the other hyer estates," and since "the whiche yomen[135] represent the common people, as husbandes and labourers," Fitzherbert proposes to speak first of husbandry, and so he never reaches the other estates.

Harrison's *A Description of England*[136] includes an enumeration of the three estates of the realm that rule and a fourth estate of "daie labourers, poore husbandmen, and some retailers (which have no free land), copie holders, and all artificers, as tailers, shomakers, carpenters, brickmakers, masons, &c," who, though free men, have no voice in the government. His four

[134] *Ibid.,* pp. 1-2.

[135] The editor here notes that Caxton has eight pawns on each side, a number which suggests to him "the well-known formula which divides men into the eight classes of 'soldier, sailor, tinker, tailor, gentleman, apothecary, ploughboy, thief'; which is sometimes otherwise varied." The modern "rich man, poor man, beggar man, thief, doctor, lawyer, merchant, chief" maintains the same eight-fold division. They are "estates of the world," though not the three-fold division of the medieval and early Renaissance moralists.

[136] Ed. F. J. Furnivall, *New Shakespeare Society, Pubs.,* London, 1877, Book II, chap. 5, pp. 105-41.

divisions he indicates in his opening sentence: "We in England divide our people commonlie into foure sorts, as gentlemen, citizens or burgesses, yeomen, and artificers, or laborers." Harrison's description of classes reflects his loyalty to his own estate, that of the clergy, and also the fact that he was writing for the Queen's printer. His philosophy of estates, what there is of it, is distinctly conservative. Only the class of artisans, laborers, and serving-men are belabored for their shortcomings. The clergy and nobility are esteemed. The estate of gentlemen is subdivided into king, prince, dukes, marquesses, earls, viscounts, barons, knights, esquires, gentlemen. The origin of each title and its contemporary significance in England are explained. In this class the bishops are also included, for they are called lords and have the same rank in Parliament as the barons. The decline of the estate of the clergy in past years is deplored: "whose countenances in time past were much more glorious than at this present it is,—because those lustie prelats sought after earthlie estimation and authoritie with farre more diligence than after the lost sheepe of Christ." In these days "their estate remaineth no lesse reverend than before," and though many call for an alteration of their estate, namely, that they be deprived of their civil authority, such a demand is impossible. But this is a digression. Nowadays the clergy are loved for their good works and not feared for their authority, as formerly. In those times, bishops and abbots took precedence over earls and barons. Now they think it sufficient to preach the word and hold their livings. Now they are better educated than formerly, especially those appointed in the last twelve or fourteen years. Citizens and burgesses serve the commonwealth in their cities and boroughs and in the common assembly of the realm, four to represent a city and two to represent a borough. The estate of the merchants is part of that of the citizens, "although they often change estate with gentlemen, as gentlemen doo with them, by a mutuall conversion of the one into the other." At present there are too many merchants, and they are a hindrance to the realm, for maintaining them makes very high the cost of foreign wares, which were formerly plentiful and cheap when every nation was permitted to bring in her own commodities. Yeomen are free men of six pounds annual revenue. They have a certain preëminence, above the rank of laborers and common artificers. They are usually farmers, some of whom by thrift become wealthy and buy the lands of unthrifty gentlemen. They often send their sons to the schools and universities and inns of court or leave them enough land to live upon without labor, so that they thereby become gentlemen. The last estate is that of the husbandmen and artificers, who "are to be ruled, and not to rule," though they sometimes, in towns, for lack of yeomen, hold petty offices, such as those of churchwarden and constable. These husbandmen and artificers were never better as a class, but the latter sometimes hurry their work, to sell rapidly, and so bungle it. Many commodities that they produce could be more cheaply provided by other countries—the reverse of Hales' opinion. Harrison also lists the chief offices of the realm and the numbers in each rank of temporal and spiritual nobility in England. Their order of precedence in Parliament is stated carefully, in the manner of the old books of precedence. Harrison's purpose, of course, is instruction and not lament or sermon.

In the prose and verse of the last decade of the sixteenth century and the first decade of the seventeenth, there is further evidence of the adaptation of the *genre* in a variety of ways. The breaking down of the lines of distinction between the estates, which we have seen in earlier Elizabethan literature of estates, continues, and in some works the *genre* very definitely begins to show traces of merging into other forms. It is important to note those changes, wherever they occur, in the following works.

One of the most interesting adaptations of the philosophy of estates in late Elizabethan prose is found in the controversy over the abolition of the estate of bishops. Puritan opposition had grown strong enough to threaten one of the most powerful estates of the realm, the Anglican bishops. In the name of law and order, much as earlier writers of the literature of estates argued, Richard Hooker's *Of the Laws of Ecclesiastical Polity*[137] sought to show that all the estates of the realm are divinely ordained and therefore cannot be abolished. At times Hooker seems most liberal, answering Puritan arguments in the name of reason, but at heart he is conservative. The régime of the past is very dear to him. The parts of the old ritual which he knows cannot be restored he speaks of in a tone of regret, and he implies that the Church of his time is so fallen that it is no longer good enough for some of the old forms. He is apparently desirous of accepting things as they are and of opposing authority as little as possible. However, the proposed overthrow of the bishops is a step that is out of keeping with all the history of the Church. The bishops, he says, are the direct successors of the apostles and were therefore originally ordained by God.[138] Through the force of custom and expedience they still hold

---

[137] Ed. John Keble, Oxford, 1888, 3 vols.

[138] *Ibid.*, Book VII, III, 151 ff.: "they which were termed Apostles, as being sent of Christ to publish his gospel throughout the world, and were named likewise Bishops . . ." Also p. 221: "Inequality of pastors is an ordinance both divine and profitable," and p. 219: "It was by the special providence of God no doubt so disposed." Also p. 278: ". . . yea bishops through the very attire of bishops, are made blessed, that is to say, marked and manifested they are to be such as God hath poured his blessing upon, by advancing them above others, and placing them where they may do him principal good service." Also p. 305: ". . . the Holy Ghost doth make bishops, . . . the whole action of making them is God's own deed . . ." Also p. 322: "Let all states be put to their moderate pensions, let their livings and lands be taken away from them whosoever they be, in whom such ample possessions are found to have been matters of grievous abuse: were this just? would noble families think this reasonable? The title which bishops have to livings is as good as the title of any sort of men; yea in this one thing the claim of bishops hath preeminence above all secular titles of right, in that God's own interest is the tenure whereby they hold . . ."

exactly the same position in the modern Christian church as did those of olden time. Their honors, titles, ornaments, attendance, privileges are meet and proper. From them the public weal derives much good. With a good deal of pointed sarcasm, Hooker puts his arguments into the form of an anecdote of estates to prove that the bishops are as necessary to the commonwealth as are the other two classes:

I have heard that a famous kingdom in the world being solicited to reform such disorders as all men saw the Church exceedingly burdened with, when of each degree great multitudes thereunto inclined, and the number of them did every day so increase that this intended work was likely to take no other effect than all good men did wish and labour for; a principal actor herein (for zeal and boldness of spirit) thought it good to shew them betimes what it was which must be effected, or else that there could be no work or perfect reformation accomplished. To this purpose, in a solemn sermon, and in a great assembly, he described unto them the present quality of their public estate by the parable of a tree, huge and goodly to look upon, but without that fruit which it should and might bring forth; affirming that the only way of redress was a full and perfect establishment of Christ's discipline (for so their manner is to entitle a thing hammered out upon the forge of their own invention) and that to make way of entrance for it, there must be three great limbs cut off from the body of that stately tree of the kingdom: those three limbs were three sorts of men; nobles, whose high estate would make them otherwise disdain to put their necks under that yoke; lawyers, whose courts being not pulled down, the new church consistories were not like to flourish; finally, prelates, whose ancient dignity, and the simplicity of their intended church discipline could not possibly stand together. The proposition of which device being plausible to active spirits, restless through desire of innovation, whom commonly nothing doth more offend than a change which goeth fearfully on by slow and suspicious paces; the heavier and more experienced sort began presently thereat to pull back their feet again, and exceedingly to fear the stratagem of reformation for ever after. Whereupon ensued those extreme conflicts of the one part with the other, which continuing and increasing to this very day, have now made the state of that flourishing kingdom even such, as whereunto we may most fitly apply those words of the Prophet Jeremiah, 'Thy breach is great like the sea, who can heal thee?' Whether this were done in truth, according to the constant affirmation of some avouching the same, I take not upon me to examine; that which I note therein is, how with us that policy hath been corrected. For to the authors of pretended reformation with us, it hath not seemed expedient to offer the edge of the axe unto all three boughs at once, but rather to single them, and strike at the weakest first, making show that the lop of that one shall draw the more abundance of sap to the other two, that they may thereby the better prosper.[139]

Hooker's device is most effective. If there should be no bishops, he asks, why should the estates of nobility or the law survive? Why not abolish all three? To that proposal there was no rational answer but retreat. Hooker's case was won.

The king, according to Hooker, is also divinely ordained, to maintain order in the commonwealth.[140] Church and commonwealth are one, but they are governed by two different laws: civil and ecclesiastical. Both king and bishops are God's lieutenants, each administering a different law. Such heads are necessary, to maintain order and to prevent self-seeking. Bishops alone could not maintain order, "forasmuch as every estate doth desire to enlarge the bounds of their own liberties." Peace and justice are secured "by preserving unto every order their rights, and by keeping all estates as it were in a even balance." This can be done in no better way then through the king, "their common parent." The Parliament is "the body of the whole realm," for there all estates are represented.

Less calmly reasonable is the *Admonition to the People of England*[141] of Thomas Cooper, Bishop of Winchester. In this, his contribution to the Marprelate Controversy, he replies to Puritan charges of vice among the clergy with the sarcasm of Hooker exaggerated several fold. He constantly speaks of the "state" of the clergy and of the other "states." To abolish the estate of the clergy would be dangerous: "The lawes of *Eng-*

---

[139] *Ibid.*, III, 141-42.   [140] *Ibid.*, Book VIII, III, 219 ff.
[141] Ed. Edward Arber, Birmingham, 1883.

lande to this day, have stood by the authoritie of the three
Estates: which to alter now, by leaving out the one, may
happily seeme a matter of more weight, then all men doe iudge
it. If there were no more than this one thing, which hitherto
I have spoken of, that is, the alteration of the state of all the
lawes of this Realme: I thinke there is no wise man but seeth
what daunger may followe in these perillous times, not onely
by fulfilling the thing, but also by offering to doe it."[142] As his
argument progresses, with bitter irony he applies his objection
and answer method to the estate of the clergy:

Perhaps they will say, that all other States do wel, and live according to their calling. The word of God is sincerely every where im-
braced: Iustice is uprightly in all places ministered: the poore are
helped and relieved: vice is sharpely of all other men corrected:
there is no corruption, no covetousnesse, no extortion, no Simonie, no
usurie, but in the Bishops, and in the Clergie. There are no Monopolies in this Realme practised to the gaine of a fewe, and the undoing
of great multitudes, that were wont to live by those trades. All
courtes be without fault, and voyde of corruption, saving the Ec-
clesiasticall courts onely. All officers are upright and true dealers
saving theirs. None other doe so carefully and covetously provide
for their wives and children. They onely give the example of all evill
life.[143]

By such corrupt reasoning, Cooper adds, various dangerous
arguments are being framed against the clergy. Suppose such
arguments were applied to the other estates. When men say:
"Our Bishops and Ministers are evill men: they aunswere not
the perfect rule, that is prescribed unto them by the worde of
God: therefore they shoulde be deposed, their state altered, and
their Lands and livings taken into the Princes hands, or be
otherwise imploied as it shall be thought good," they might just
as well say: "Princes, Magistrates and noble men are evill, they
do not fulfill that rule of right and perfect government that the
worde of God requireth: therefore pull them downe, set other
in their places, or alter their state cleane."[144] Similarly Cooper
disposes of the arguments of covetousness and other vices. The

---

[142] *Ibid.*, p. 67.   [143] *Ibid.*, p. 116.   [144] *Ibid.*, pp. 168-69.

reason that the ideal of Christ is applied only to the clergy is that they come nearest to it. "Instead of virtue, vice and wickednesse overwhelmeth all states and conditions of men."[145]

Meanwhile, in verse, a late sixteenth-century adaptation of the theme is to be found in Spenser' ingenious satire *Mother Hubberds Tale*. It would seem that Spenser, so eminently the poet of the Renaissance, would, like Shakespeare, have little use for the medieval fashion of listing the estates of the world. Yet in his verse, where so many traditions meet, it is not altogether strange to find the influence of this *genre*, also. In a manner reminiscent of *Reynard the Fox*, his satire traces the rise of the Ape and the Fox from low estate to high, incidentally revealing all the faults of each estate. This is no mere enumeration of classes, like that of Gascoigne, but an artistic narrative, full of variety of effect and interest. The Ape and the Fox begin with the commons, proceed next to the clergy, and then to the nobility at court, finally becoming king and prime minister. At the beginning of their meteoric rise in the world, in the guise of returned soldier and his dog, they lament, first to a husbandman, that this "yron world . . . brings downe the stowtest hearts to lowest state." The husbandman has pity on them and gives them charge of his whole flock. They devour the sheep instead of caring for them and then disappear in the night. They can not beg a livelihood, for no one has pity on beggars. In Spenser's time, there were newly enacted laws against them. So the Ape secures a gown and the Fox a cassock:

> For they their occupation meant to change,
> And now in other state abroad to range:
> For since their souldiers pas no better spedd,
> They forg'd another, as for Clerkes booke-redd.[146]

Meeting a priest as ignorant as themselves, they flatter him into helping them. They seem to be knowing men; why should they not rise aloft like others?

[145] *Ibid.*, p. 175.
[146] Ed. A. B. Grosart, *Complete Works*, London, 1882, III, 111, ll. 354 ff.

How manie honest men see ye arize
Daylie thereby, and grow to goodly prize?
To Deanes, to Archdeacons, and to Commissaries,
To Lords, to Principalls, to Prebendaries;
All iolly Prelates, worthie rule to beare,
Who ever them envie: yet spite bites neare.
Why should ye doubt then, but that ye likewise
Might unto some of those in time arise?
In the meane time to live in good estate,
Loving that love, and hating those that hate;
Being some honest Curate, or some Vicker,
Content with little in condition sicker.[147]

With the help of the confidence of the priest, they learn the tricks of the clerical trade and become priest and parish clerk. They prosper until their conduct betrays them, and they flee afar. Almost starved, they meet a Mule in costly trappings from court. From him they learn the tricks of courtly life. Thither they go, and again they prosper until discovered. In the forest they find the Lion sleeping, with crown and scepter and hide beside him, doffed because of the heat. Decking himself in the symbols of power, the Ape agrees to be guided in everything by the Fox. He seizes the throne and tyrannizes at will, until "all was subverst." Then high Jove, "in whose almightie hand The care of kings and power of empires stand," wakes the Lion, and thus ends the reign of Ape and Fox. As in the French poem *Des estats du siecle*,[148] the theme of estates is here made entertaining by the simple device of narrative.

Brief references to all the estates of society in some of Spenser's other poems also reflect his knowledge of the fashion. In the *Faerie Queene,* for example, Calidore, restlessly seeking the Blatant Beast, found that he had visited all estates:

Through all estates he found that he had past,
In which he many massacres had left,
And to the clergy now was come at last.[149]

---

[147] *Ibid.,* III, 114, ll. 419 ff.   [148] See pp. 69-70.
[149] Book VI, canto XII, stanza XXIII.

After long bondage in iron chains, the Beast again broke forth, and now ranges through the world, and "rageth sore in each degree and state."[150]

4. THE LITERATURE OF ESTATES IN THE SEVENTEENTH CENTURY

Most of the other late sixteenth and early seventeenth-century poets, who, like Drayton and Daniel, were involved in imitation of Renaissance forms, wrote no pieces in the fashion of the *Steele Glas,* but frequently used the word *estate.* There were a few, however, who still persisted in putting this political theory into verse and prose and who still introduced the lists of estates.

Nicholas Breton, "a brave pathetic figure of Elizabethan days," wrote several pieces, both in verse and prose, reflecting the old fashion. By the time he wrote, the *Steele Glas* and its author had come into Breton's family, for Gascoigne was his step-father. Perhaps the *Steele Glas* was Breton's model. At any rate, like Gascoigne, Breton looks about for some unusual device and then proceeds to enumerate the classes who fail in their duties. To the old lists of estates, however, he frequently adds others until one realizes that, like some of his contemporaries, he is drawing gradually away from the earlier fashion into the newer one of character writing. Each estate is so subdivided as almost to lose its identity at times; and the various classes are sometimes treated in the manner of the seventeenth-century character writer rather than in that of the medieval philosopher about estates. Breton is a conservative, a staunch moralist, who finds little fault with the "higher powers." He centers his attention on those who attack monarchy and preach the doctrine of popular sovereignty.

In *The Toyes of an Idle Head*[151] Breton adopts an apologetic

---

[150] Book VI, canto XII, stanza XXXIX.
[151] Ed. A. B. Grosart, *Works in Verse and Prose,* Edinburgh, 1879, I, 57-59.

tone at the outset. Even his title is apologetic. His theme is
one rather foreign to former literature of estates, namely, "Little
Medling, breedes mickle rest." It was the purpose of earlier
literature of estates to meddle and to reform if possible. However, Breton, too, proceeds to meddle. Lawyer, merchant, tenant, servant, and higher powers all have their faults, he says,
and he lists them, all except those of the higher powers:

> As for the higher powers:
>   they are too high for me:
> What faults are to be found in them,
>   I list not seeke to see:
> Let finde their faults themselves,
>   so shall they best be pleasde:
> And for my silence, I am sure
>   I shall not be diseasde.

The censorship was again effective. Others, "of meaner sorte,"
are included, however: "Myller, Baker, Collyer, Maltmen,
Carles who buy up wood in large lots, Bruer, Droavers, Grasiers,
Butcher, Chaundler, Draper." All have their crafty tricks. The
poet concludes that the wisest thing for him to do is "To take
good heede and hold my peace." Gower, too, decided to hold
his peace, but for a very different reason. He abandoned his
sermons to the estates out of a sense of the futility of preaching.
Breton concludes here out of a desire not to give offence.

Apparently, however, Breton could not leave the form entirely, for in *Pasquil's Mad-cappe,* "Throwne at the Corruptions
of these Times. with His *Message* to Men of all Estates," he
again lists many classes: rich and poor, clergy and laity, lawyers, judges, justices of peace, beggars, and women. All are
wicked through avarice. The same old theme persists. The "Message to Men of all Estates" addresses each class except the king
in turn, with the poet's Muse as his messenger. As usual, Breton
exempts the king. He only is virtuous. The rest are: "Courtiers,
lawyers, schollers, country Players, Fidlers at Faires, Swaggrers
that doe use to sweare, Divines, Souldiers, Merchant, Miser,

Craftesmen, Fencer, beggar, Iailour, prisoner, Poets, Authors of high Tragedies, Scrivener, Sailer, Fisher, Iuglers, pander, parasite, traitour, farmers, Labourers." This hit and miss array of types is then sermonized, "not in order," but "as thou meetst them." At the close of the poem their duties are listed more briefly:

> Goe bid the Courtier that he be not prowde,
> The Soldier bloody, nor the Lawyer blinde;
> And bid the Merchant, that he doe not shrowde
> A subtle meaning in a simple kinde;
> Goe bid the Schollers learne, the Doctors teach,
> And have a care to live as they doe preach.
>
> Goe bid the Farmer bring abroad his graine,
> The Craftesman, that he soundly make his ware,
> The Workeman, that he labour for his gaine,
> The Beggar that he waite for pittie's share;
> Then if the Sexton come to ring the bell,
> Where Faith is fixt, there is no feare of Hell,[152]

and so forth in six more such stanzas. The exhortation to all classes to remain in their own estate also finds a place in this poem. The language is somewhat different from that of medieval and earlier sixteenth-century literature of estates, but the theme is the same:

> Then let a knave be knowne to be a knave,
> A thiefe a villaine, and a churle a hogge;
> A minkes a menion, and a rogue a slave,
> A trull a tit, an usurer a dogge,
> A lobbe a loute, a heavy loll a logge;
>   And every birde goe rowst in her owne nest,
>   And then perhaps my Muse will be at rest.
>
> But if a Iacke will be a gentleman,
> And mistris Needens lady it at least,
> And every goose be saucy with the swanne,
> While the asse thinkes he is a goodly beast,
> While so the foole doth keepe ambition's feast;
>   My Muse in conscience that cannot be quiet,
>   Will give them this good sawce unto their diet.

[152] *Ibid.*, pp. 12-13.

But I doe hope I am but in a dreame,
Fooles will be wiser then to loose their wittes;
The country wench will looke unto her creame,
And workeman see, but where their profite fits,
And learne fantastickes to their idle fits:
    Pride shall goe downe, and vertue shall encrease,
    And then my Muse be still, and hold her peace.[153]

In *I Would and Would Not* Breton's device for listing the classes is to imagine what it would be like to be king, courtier, miller, tailor, collier, tradesman, brewer, divine, and many other persons. One stanza states the wish to be one or the other of them; the next takes it back. For example:

I would I were an excellent Divine,
    That had the Bible at my fingers ends:
The world might heare out of this mouth of mine,
    How God did make his enemies his friends.
I were so follow'de, as if none but I,
    Could plainely speake of true Divinity.

And yet I would not: for then ten to one,
    I should be call'd but a Precizian:
Or Formalist, and might goe preach alone,
    Unto my holy brother Puritan.
And so be flouted for my zealous love
    In taking paines for other mens behove.[154]

He decides that he desires only to be a "Religious servant of my God," to frame a kind of faithful prayer "For all estates within the state of Grace." He would:

Pray for the King, the Queene, and Countries health,
    Their Royall issue, and Peeres of Estate:
The Counsaile, Cleargy, and the Common-wealth,
    That no misfortune may their blisse abate.[155]

Further treatment of the theme of estates in verse occurs in Breton's *The Countesse of Penbrookes Love* and *The Chesse Play*. The former begins with the bringing of all gifts to the

[153] *Ibid.*, p. 10.　　　　　　　　[154] *Ibid.*, p. 11, stanza 88.
[155] *Ibid.*, p. 14, stanza 137.

Countess of Pembroke—"souldiers, pesants, merchants, lawiers, courtiers, scholars, sailers, shepards, poets"—all in vain. She is left alone with Love—heavenly love—in "this lothsome world of ours." *The Chesse Play*, as the title indicates, describes King, Queen, Knight, Bishop, Rooks, Pawns, and their duties, in the manner of the medieval chess books.

Some of Breton's prose also mirrors the estates of the world, with further evidence, however, of the growing interest in character writing and of the combination of that new form with the old one of cataloguing all society.

His *A Dialogue Full of Pithe and Pleasure*[156] contains a peculiar inversion of the fault-finding of earlier literature of estates. It is an examination of the complaints against the various estates, in an effort to determine the best and worst in each, and to show that what may seem to be a fault is after all a virtue; for "there is no estate of man, from the Prince to the begger, but in the worst that they are, they may be better then they seeme to be."[157] It attempts to reform by praise rather than by fault-finding.

In the dialogue Antonio enumerates the faults or indignities of the different estates, and Meandro presents their virtues or dignities. There is much good in man, says Meandro. Though a king be a tyrant over the wicked, he may be a friend to the virtuous, and by clemency to the repentant, he may reclaim them. A counsellor may be avaricious, but thereby teach thrift to the prodigal, and his hauteur may breed fear in the envious. A soldier's slaughter may bring speedy victory and peace; his desire of gain may breed a desire to save, lest he lose what he has won. A lawyer's partiality may be due to pity, and his covetousness may make him studious. A merchant's poverty may breed patience, and care may recover his credit. A usurer may help the needy and punish the spendthrift. A tradesman

[156] Ed. A. B. Grosart, *Works*, Edinburgh, 1879, Vol. II.
[157] *Ibid.*, p. 11.

may be cunning and so wealthy, or honest, though not rich. A farmer learns that good husbandry is not churlishness. A grazier learns that every fat beast is not an ox. A miller's much-maligned large thumb may be only a sign of a strong hand. A laborer learns that recreation is not laziness. A beggar learns the value of charity. As for the Queen, God preserve her. There is no better in the world.

But in briefe, who could consider the maiestie of a King, the wise-dome of a Counsellour, the valour of a souldier, the learning of a Lawier, the travaile of a Marchant, the husbandry of a Farmer, the toyle of a Tradesman, and the patience of a begger, might well avow loyaltie to the Prince, love to the Counsellour, honour to the souldier, service to the Lawier, and praise to the Marchant, and wish a good harvest to the farmer, a good chapman to the Trades man, and a good almes to the begger: and in all and every of them, finde so much matter of commendation, as no other creature can come neare.[158]

Furthermore, the physician who cures diseases and saves lives, the lawyer who delivers the distressed from oppression, the merchant who sets free his debtor in prison, the prince who pardons the penitent and unwilling offender are all a kind of god on earth.

Nevertheless, in the face of abundant evidence presented by Antonio, Meandro must admit that the estates are vicious as well as virtuous. When they are vicious they are not gods on earth but devils:

But contrariwise, if a Prince upon a false information commaund his loyall subiect unto death? that hath by many good services de-served his gratious favour, is he not if he be a Tyrant, halfe a divel unto man? If a souldier for the gaine of a little mony, betray the trust of his Captaine, and make sale of his people, is he not a kinde of divel unto man? If a Lawier shall by extortion or bribery, grieve the oppressed, wrong the poore to pleasure the rich, and pleade against his owne conscience, to the undoing of a simple creature, is he not a kinde of divell unto man? If a Phisition, will in stead of a preservative, give his patient a poysoned potion, is he not a kinde

[158] *Ibid.*, p. 11.

of divell unto man? And if a Merchant, voyd of charitie cast his debtor into prison, and there beholding his misery, without remorse of conscience, lettes him perish without reliefe, is hee not a kinde of divell unto man? . . . Last, and most of all, if he, who taketh upon him the outward habit of a Divine, and within be so farre from divinitie, that he will rather leade the sinner into hell, then the repentant to grace, is he not a kinde of divell unto man? What shall I neede to runne into a world of questions in this point, is not the vertuous a kinde of God, and the vicious a kinde of divell in the world?

Breton's *A Murmurer*[159] is a long character sketch into which he introduces some philosophy of estates in the form of two analogies: first, the familiar one of the commonwealth and the human body, and, secondly, that of the order in a kingdom and the harmony in music. "Is it not strange that all the parts and the members of the bodie, can so well agree togither, and one doe service to another, and men, the parts and members of a common-wealth, should be so at variance among themselves?" he asks. Just as all parts of the body are at the service of the head, so should all subjects serve their king. God made all parts of the body for the soul, just as he made all the subjects in a kingdom to serve their king. If any member is sick, all suffer. The counsel, the eye of the commonwealth; the artificer, the hand; the laborer, the foot—all affect each other. Instead of all working together, there is much murmuring at the will of God in men. Let the murmurers perish; it is better so. For the Scriptures say, "If thine eye offend thee, pull it out; if thy hand offend thee, cut it off," and so forth. But nothing is said in the Bible of the head. That must still be kept on. If any member, therefore, offend the head, cut him off. The king and commonwealth must not be disturbed. If the king is cruel and wicked, "take him for a punishment, and pray for his amendment." If the king is good, thank God for him and obey him. But let none murmur. To all the estates some advice is given:

[159] *Ibid.*

If thou be a king, keepe thy feare; If a Courtier, know thy place; if a Scholler, plie thy booke; if a Souldier, look to thine honor; if a marchant, take thy fortune; if a farmer, follow thy plough; if a beggar, fal to prayer; but murmur not, oh king, if thou be not an Emperor; nor courtier if thou have not grace; nor Scholler if thou loose thy day; nor Marchant, if thou loose goods; nor farmer, if thou lose thy labor; nor beggar if thou get bare alms: but murmuring at Gods wil; take heede that thou loose not thine owne soule, more precious to thee, then the whole world.

The analogy of the harmony of a kingdom and that of music is next drawn, as a lesson for murmurers. Just as music has a treble and a bass, so there are high and low estates in the structure of a kingdom: "a King is the highest, and the labourer the lowest: (I leave out the Beggar as an unnecessary member, but only for the exercise of Charity)." Between the two there are: "Counsailers, Preachers, Lawyers, Souldiars, Marchants, and Artificers"—the three estates are still recognizable under different names. When all these together serve God in due allegiance to their king, how excellent is the music! If the strings of an instrument be out of tune, the music is harsh. If the people of a state be out of order, there can be no peace. If such insensible things as the strings of an instrument can produce such pleasing harmony, why should not men also? Instead, all classes murmur:

The rich man murmures at the poore man, that hee should dwell nigh him: the Usurer murmures at the Broker, that hee geteth any thing by him; the Tradesman murmures at his neighbour, that he should prosper or thrive by him: the Lawyer murmures at the Tearme that is so short a harvest for him; The Marchant murmures at the windes, that his Shippes come not home to him: the Souldiour murmures at his paymaister, that hee keepes his money from him: The Courtier murmures at his Taylor, that his clothes are not fit for him: The Minister he murmures at the Parson, because he hath the greatest profit from him: and the Parson murmures at the parishe, that they come not to Church to pay their duties to him; and the parishe murmures at the Parson, that they pay so much, for so little paines from him: the Tenant murmures at his Landlorde for racking of his rent:

the Landlord murmures at his Tenant to see him thrive by his husbandry. In summe there is almost no profession or condition wherin one doth not murmure at another.

Such a condition permits of no love among the various classes, and love is the only remedy. The names of the estates are again somewhat altered, but the old doctrine survives.

In *The Good and the Badde, or Descriptions of the Worthies, and Unworthies of This Age* Breton is strictly the character writer. He characterizes a worthy king, a worthy queen, a worthy prince, a worthy privy councillor, a nobleman, a worthy bishop, a worthy judge, a worthy knight, a worthy gentleman, a worthy lawyer, a worthy soldier, a worthy physician, a worthy merchant, and so forth—some fifty in all—and all their opposites in those unworthy. The first characterizations, down to that of the merchant, present the familiar estates of the realm, but the rest are of general types such as a good man, an atheist, a wise man, a fool.

In his analysis of "The World" in his *Fantasticks: Serving for a Perpetuall Prognostication,* Breton stresses the variety that exists, including the various estates: "A King, a great man: a Souldier, a stout man: a Courtier, a fine man: a Lawyer, a wise man: a Merchant, a rich man: a Begger, a poore man: and an honest man, an honest man." As in *The Good and the Badde* his list concludes with a general type.

Some of Samuel Rowlands' poems, like Breton's, give evidence of the merging of the old fashion of estates with the new one of character writing. His *Looke to It: For, Ile Stabbe Ye,*[160] for example, presents a variation of the dance of death theme and begins in the usual way with "Tyrant Kinges," "Wicked Magistrates," "Curious Divines," and "Covetous Lawyers." But then it branches out to include some thirty-one other types. Among them are physicians, merchants, artificers,

---

[160] *Complete Works,* pub. by the Hunterian Club, London, 1880, Vol. I, 47 pp.

husbandmen, and gentlewomen, but such types as "Cursed Swearers," "Counterfayte Captaine," "God-lesse Athists," "Swaggring Ruffian," "Odious Quarreler," "Disloyal Traytor," "Filthy Pander," "Leasemongers," and "Adulterers" constitute another haphazard list of characters, with little regard for the estates to which they belong. Nor is there any philosophy of estates except that death levels all:

> I do defie the World and all therein,
> My challenge at the Scepter doth begin:
> Downe to the Plough Swaine, come who dare in place,
> Set foote to mine, and looke me in the face.

In another of Rowlands' tracts in verse, *A Terrible Battell betweene the Two Consumers of the Whole World: Time and Death*,[161] Time and Death debate concerning their respective powers, and the different types of humanity that Death has taken are again described, but not in the manner of the literature of estates. One stanza only is suggestive of it:

> And wheresoever, or what ere he be,
> For countenance, for credit and condition,
> Dignity, calling, office, or degree,
> Peasant, or prince, patient or else Phisition:
> Even from the Crowne and scepter to the plow,
> I make all looke as I my selfe do now.

In at least two of his works, one in prose and one in verse, Thomas Dekker also revealed his interest in cataloguing the classes of society. His catalogues, like Breton's, are presented in a new framework and with a definite bent toward character writing. Though Dekker probably sprang from the people and writes in a democratic vein in some of his other works, the tone of both these pieces is that of a loyal monarchist. It is evident that Dekker is writing with a realization of approval in high places.

In *The Double PP*[162] Dekker, like Hooker, used the form for

[161] *Ibid.*, 44 pp.

[162] Ed. A. B. Grosart, *Non-Dramatic Works*, London, 1885, II, 155-91.

religious propaganda. Whereas Hooker was involved in the conflict between Anglicanism and Puritanism, Dekker wrote against
Catholicism in praise of Protestantism. *The Double PP* was
written in 1606, when the Gun-Powder Plot made hatred of
Catholicism popular in England. It describes the pope's army
(the double PP representing Papa or Pope) and the Protestant
army (represented by a single P) and the battle between them.
The battle, however, occurs at the close of the work, and all
the rest of the verse and prose tract is devoted to description
of the two armies. Instead of sermonizing the ranks of both
armies, Dekker heaps all his condemnation upon the papist
army and has only praise for the Protestants. His dedication
"To All the Nobility, Clergy, and Gentry of Great Brittaine,
True Subiects to King James" is, of course, addressed to the
Protestant ranks. It very curiously indicates the decreasing importance of the three estates by means of graduated type:

> To *you* that (like the sollid wheeles of *Fate,*)
> Give sweets or trouble *Motion* to a *State:*

addresses the nobility in ordinary-sized letters.

> To you that bath our soules in Sacred streames,
> (In which they thrive as you grow Hot or colder:)

addresses the clergy in type half as large as the first.

> And last, to you, the Kingdomes beames
> (All, strong Collumnes that uphold her.)

addresses the gentry in type one fourth as large as the first.
Then there is a pretense at concealment of theme by means of
riddles. A solution of each riddle, however, leaves no doubt of
its meaning. "The Double PP. A Riddle on the double PP"
describes the evil purposes of the pope:

> Upon the double P.P. badder fruits grow
> Thā on al the letters in the *Christ-Crosse-Row;*
> It sets (by reason of the *Badge* it weares)
> The *Christ-Crosse-Row,* together by the eares:
> The reason is, this haughtie double PP.

Would clyme above both A.B.C. and D.
And trample on the necks of E.F.G.
H.I. (Royall K.) L.M.N.O. and Q.
Threatning the fall of R.S.T. and V.

The meaning of the riddle is explained by its "resolution":

PP. = *PaPa* = the *PoPe.*
Christ-Crosse-Row, — *Christendome.*
A.B.C.D.E. &c. the States of the land: As *Archbishops,*
Bishops, Councellors, Dukes, Earles, &c.
K. the King.
Q. the Queene.
R. Religion.
S. State.
T. Truth.
V. You all.

The riddle on the Single P. is the reverse of that on the Double PP:

The *single* P. makes all the *Letters* grow
In goodly *Ranks* upon the *Christ-crosse-Row:*
And (by the reverend, holy *Badge* it weares,)
The *Christ-crosse-Row,* from giddy *Faction* cleares.
The reason is, this (*Honest single*) P.
Lowly submits to A.B.C. and D.
Yet fights in the defence of E.F.G.
H.I. (*Roial K.*) L.M.N.O. and Q.
And runnes through *Fire* for R.S.T. and V.

The resolution of the riddle is identical with that of the first riddle, except for the substitution of *Single P.*—*Protestantisme* —for the *PP.*

The ranks of the "Romish Army" are types of papists rather than estates of the realm. They include "A Papist Couchant, . . . or the Fawner," "A Papist Passant, . . . or the Plodder," "A Papist Passant-Gardant, . . . or the Spye," and seven other such types. The hosts of the Protestant army include "The Nobilitie, The Councell of Estate, the Cleargie, The Iudges of the Land, The Universities, The Martialists, The Merchants, The Mariners, The Husbandmen, The Artificers," in fact, all loyal estates of the realm. With two or three additions this is the usual list of the estates of the world. Each member of both armies is characterized in two stanzas. Naturally the stanzas on the estates of the Protestant army are flattering, to offset the ugly pictures of the Romish army. The duties of each are stressed, and their importance to the state. The nobleman, for example, is characterized as follows:

> The first goes armde from head to foot in stiles
> Of glorious *Ancestry;* hee's the *Court Iem.*
> The Princes, *Hee,* all others are his *Foiles,*
> Hee's a rich stone stuck in the Diadem:
> A graft so wrought into the *Royal Stem,*
> Alike both suffer: thunder smiting *Him,*
> (For nought else can) the *Weale* does loose a limb.

> Since the *Republick* therefore is his blood,
> His office is to save it; to have eyes
> *Quick, piercing:* not to be more *great* than *good:*
> For of that norishing flame (In whose heate lyes
> A *Kingdomes* life) *Hee's* soule: It lives or dyes
> In him: of that free light when hee's bereaven,
> ô pittie! then a Star drops out of heaven.[163]

The Councellor of Estate "best does steere a Crowne"; the Bishop preaches the gospel and thus does "Fasten the *Kings Crowne* closer to his head"; the Judge sits as umpire between right and wrong, and without him the King would be over-thrown and confusion reign everywhere; the Scholler "beats downe *Romes* usurping ignorance"; the Souldier is the court's guard, the country's bulwark, the city's wall; the Merchant "marries *Kingdome* to *Kingdome* by *Negotiation*" and thus serves the Crown; the Sea-man is a "Terror to proud Invasion"; the Plough-man, patient as the ox, feeds all with the "labour of his brow"—"*Hees Natures Iourny-man,* but workes for Kings"; the Artificer is the arm of the city, the nervous strings that fortify the heart of the realm. The battle ensues, with victory for this mighty Protestant army of all the estates of the land.

[163] *Ibid.,* p. 183.

The theme of estates was also used by Dekker in his prose work *Foure Birdes of Noah's Arke*.[164] The device is again original, and the purpose is plainly that of securing favor in high places. The writer here offers prayers for all the estates of the land. From Noah's ark he sends four birds with four messages, the Dove, the Eagle, the Pellican, and the Phoenix. The prayers of Dove, Pellican, and Phoenix, which are suited to the mouths of young and very lowly people, to those suffering from the seven deadly sins, and to those grateful for the benefits derived from the life, death, and resurrection of Christ, do not concern us here. The prayers of the Eagle, however, are for the estates of the realm, as follows: the King, Queen Anne, Prince Henry, the Council, the nobility, the Church, the clergy, the judges, the court, the city, the country, a magistrate, and a lawyer. In addition, there are a prayer for the two universities and others against treason, civil war, pestilence, famine, and persecution, such additions as are always found in late versions of the literature of estates. Dekker's list of commons is not so complete here as in *The Double PP*. The old philosophy of estates has changed little, however, in this age of Stuart monarchy and the doctrine of "divine right":

Kings are gods upō earth, yet (O Lord) they are but thy servants; they rule kingdomes, yet the chariot of their Empire turnes over & over, unlesse thou teach their hands how to holde the bridle. More then men they are amongst men, yet lesse they are then themselves, if they breake thy lawes: for sithence they are thy Stewards, and are trusted with much, it is a great reckoning to which they must answere.

The prayer for the nobility similarly balances true nobility against the possible sins of ambition, envy, and dissention. The prayer for the clergy calls them "Angels that goe and come betweene thee and us." May God guide their feet, therefore, "that sinne may lay no stumbling blockes before them to make them fall; nor that forgetting the high honour in which thou

[164] Ed. A. B. Grosart, *Non-dramatic Works*, V, 1-101.

hast placed them, they bee cast downe for their pride, into the pit of darkenesse." May judges serve both rich and poor, without bribery and partiality. May I, the magistrate, serve humbly, with "an eye that may not lust after my owne profit, but the advancement of thy glorie, and the good of the Commonwealth." The prayers are significant for their indication of Dekker's conservative adherence to the world of things as they are while tactfully suggesting the dangers of failure in duty by means of this unobjectionable religious device.

While with Breton, Rowlands, and Dekker the literature of estates in the late sixteenth and early seventeenth century gave evidence of losing itself, as a literary form, in the new form of character writing, it was also disappearing through new channels in another direction. We have seen the growth, in the sixteenth century, of a prose devoted to political, social, and economic theory, which frequently made use of the familiar form of the literatures of estates to express that theory. By the end of the sixteenth century and in the first half of the seventeenth, the theory was becoming more and more important and the form less and less so. Moreover, as government progressed farther from feudalism, even though the feudal classes remained, the old form of enumerating and advising the estates became less adaptable. Hence, in the political prose of the seventeenth century, the treatment of estates merges into a technical discussion of the problems of government, outside the scope of the present study.

Two works that show something of this change in approach to the subject of estates are Sir Thomas Smith's *De republica Anglorum. The Maner of Government or Policie of the Realme of England*[165] and Jean Bodin's *Six livres de la république.*[166] Smith wrote his treatise to serve as a textbook in comparative politics, and Bodin's was used as a text at Oxford for some time.

---

[165] Ed. L. Alston, London, 1906, from first (1583) edition.
[166] English translation by Richard Knolles, London, 1606.

Both, in purpose and tone, if not altogether in subject matter, are quite different from Dudley's *Tree of Commonwealth*, Starkey's *Dialogue*, *The Complaynte of Scotlande*, and Crowley's, Breton's, and Dekker's shorter prose pieces. Both discuss the estates that form the commonwealth, but they use no allegory or dialogue or dream-vision in which to set forth their conclusions about these estates. They do not agree on all points, but on the whole they represent late sixteenth and early seventeenth-century philosophy of estates. Smith's work was written between 1562 and 1566, but was not published until 1583. It was widely read and reached its tenth edition in 1635. Bodin's was published in Paris in 1577 and was translated into English in 1606. It, too, had considerable influence in England.

Of the two, Bodin seems the more medieval. He embodies most of the philosophy of all preceding literature of estates, the doctrine of loyal adherence of all classes to their chief estate, the king, and he writes in a dogmatic style that has a strong tinge of medieval theology and appeal to biblical authority. He refers also, to be sure, to the political philosophy of Plato, Aristotle, Xenophon, Solon, and other classical authorities; but his chief sources are still the Bible and the Church Fathers. He takes his three types of government from the ancients— aristocracy, monarchy, and democracy. He finds that every government is one of the three; mixed forms are pure fancy. To him, England is a monarchy, and monarchy is best. The "assembly of the three estates" is still a group of feudal estates, called, not to assert their rights, but to support the king. Smith's work, on the other hand, seems more modern than medieval. His style is discursive, and his purpose is to report what he sees, not to impose any particular doctrine or authority. There is none of the influence of medieval theology in his work that Bodin's hard-and-fast conclusions show. He compares the English form of government with Greek, Roman, and French forms. Like Bodin, he thinks England is a monarchy, and he usually calls it that. But in one instance at least he calls it a democracy, and he points out its democratic nature in its representation in Parliament of all people. In discussing Parliament, moreover, he seems to be getting away from the idea of an assembly of estates that Bodin still retains. Rather, to him, it is a Parliament of two houses, not representing themselves as separate estates, but each sitting for the realm and representing all the people. Smith is patriotic and so concludes that English institutions are better than those of any other land; but his patriotism does not make him a biased observer of facts. He demonstrates that England is an ordered commonwealth, in which king, nobility and gentry, burgesses and yeomen, and even laborers play a part, and where the free coöperation of these classes is necessary for the good of the whole community. This theory provides a result identical with that of feudal theory, but it provides very different motivation for the coöperation of classes. It is not hard to see why, for different reasons, Bodin's and Smith's works were both popular in the seventeenth century.

Bodin, defining the commonweal, the kinds of commonweals, the senate and its power, magistrates, orders and degrees of citizens, the rise and fall of commonweals, and the types of coinage, has much to say about the estates of society forming a commonweal. His philosophy of government, as has been said, would serve as a summary of the philosophy of all preceding literature of estates. The king is divinely ordained and is the "lively image" of God on earth. To the king all his subjects should do obeisance. The "assembly of the three estates," instead of diminishing the power of such a sovereign, serves to augment it, "for it cannot be exalted into a more high degree of honour, of power, and of glorie, than to see an infinit number of great lords and princes, and people innumerable, of men of all sorts and qualitie, to cast themselves downe at his feet, and to doe homage unto his maiestie; seeing that the honour, glorie, and power of princes, consisteth not but in the obeysance, homage, and service of their subiects." Such a monarchy Bodin finds in England. Other types of states (or estates, for Bodin constantly uses the term *estate* to mean state or government) are not to be desired. An aristocracy is not so desirable as a monarchy, because in it there is no single head to settle disputes. Many governors hinder one another. A commonwealth in which all things are had in common is "nothing worth." Though *"Thomas Moore* Chancellor of England in his Commonweale sayth, That the only way of safetie for an estate, is when as men live in common," and though other ancient lawgivers have said the same thing, such a government "cannot be whereas is any proprietie."[167] Equality of goods is dangerous to the commonwealth. If all things are held in common, there can be no recognition of private interest. Some things must be privately owned, to make the distinction. Moreover, equality breeds hatred and quarrels.

To say, That equalitie is the nurce of friendship is but to abuse the ignorant; for it is more certaine, that there is never greater hatred, nor more capitall quarrels, than betwixt equals; and the iealousie betwixt equals, is the spring and fountaine of troubles, seditions, and civill warres. Whereas contrariwise the poore and the weake yeeld and obey willingly the great, rich, and mightie, for the helpe and profit which they expect.[168]

Like Elyot and others, Bodin says that *commonwealth* signifies simply government and not a government in which things are held in common.

Bodin's philosophy of the origin and necessity of classes of society is also that of the older literature of estates. The division of society into different degrees means "a convenient and decent order." This difference of degrees is that found in nature, as we have learned from many of Bodin's predecessors.

For why, it is a most antient and received opinion of the wise, Almightie God himselfe the great and supreme workemaster and creator of this great and wonderfull Fabrick of all things, in the creating

[167] Book V, p. 569.   [168] Book V, p. 570.

thereof, to have performed nothing either greater or better, than that hee divided the mingled and confused parts of the rude *Chaos*, and so setled everie thing in his due place and order. Neither can there be any thing fairer to behold, more delightfull to the mind, or more commodious for use, than is order it selfe. But they which goe about so as to make all subiects or Citisens equall one unto another in dignitie, order, and place, as that there shall be nothing in a Citie or Commonweal first, or in the middest, but will have all degrees so mingled together and confounded, without respect of sexe, age, or condition they seeme to mee to do as they doe which thrust barly, wheat, rise, mill, and all other kind of pulse into one heape together; whereby they loose the use both of everie kind of graine in particular.[169]

These different degrees should be so knit together as to form a harmonious whole, but every man should remain in his degree, for "a man of base degree suddenly mounted unto the highest degree of honour, thinketh himself to bee a god upon earth. For as the wise Hebrew saith, There is nothing more intollerable than the slave become a lord."[170] The political philosophy of Plato, as well as that of the Bible, is evident in Bodin's—in fact, he mentions Plato, Aristotle, Xenophon, Solon, and other classical authorities as his sources.

Though his political philosophy is that of the older literature of estates, his classes of society are somewhat different, or rather they are the old classes so subdivided by the changes of the modern industrial world as to seem a wholly new alignment.[171] He recognizes the probability of different arrays of citizens in different places, due to the "unliknesse of their lawes and customes almost infinit." Yet, in a monarchy, they may very aptly be so ordered: king, clergy, senate, martial men (general of the army first, then dukes, counts, marquesses, governors of provinces, landgraves, burgraves, captains of castles, vassals, and other soldiers), gown men (composed of magistrates, judges, lawyers of all kinds, physicians, surgeons, apothecaries, school men such as professors of divinity, law, physics, natural

---

[169] Book III, p. 387.   [170] Book VI, p. 725.   [171] Book III, pp. 402 f.

philosophy, mathematics, logic, rhetoric, history, poetry, grammar), merchants, agents, farmers, bankers, money changers, brokers, cornmongers, butchers, fishmongers, fishermen, bakers, pudding-makers, cooks, husbandmen, grasiers, "all kind and sort of handy crafts men," such as carpenters, armorers, masons, smiths, weavers, then curriers, skinners, fullers, dyers, tailors, shoemakers, and printers. As for painters, image makers, carvers, makers and sellers of women's paintings, minstrels, dancers, fencers, tumblers, jesters, and bawds, they should be driven out of cities or else be placed in the lowest place of all, so that even bath keepers, barbers, sailors, hucksters, hostlers, coach men, carters, grave-makers, sergeants, and hangmen are to be placed before them. These are necessary "for the carrying out of filth, and the clensing of the citisens and cities: whereas the other with their most base trades, the ministers of foule and vaine pleasures, not onely corrupt the citisens maners, but utterly overthrow even the cities themselves." These orders of citizens should dwell, not each by itself, but together, as a protection against an uprising among any one of them. Every government should have at least three orders, so that two of them may unite against the third. Each order should have a spokesman, as in the recent Parliament of Blois, "when as the Bishops grievously complained of the Nobilitie; and againe the Nobilitie of the Bishops; and the Comminaltie of them both." In such a situation, the advantage of a monarchy is evident, for the monarch is final judge of all controversies. Bodin's classification closes, as usual, with reference to the women, and his attitude toward their degree is quite medieval: "Now as for the order and degree of women, I meddle not with it; onely I thinke it meet them to be kept far off from all magistracies, places of commaund, iudgements, publike assemblies, and councels: so to be intentive onely unto their womanly and domesticall businesse."[172]

The *De republica Anglorum* of Sir Thomas Smith, "Knight,

[172] Book III, p. 405.

Doctor of Lawes, and one of the principall Secretaries unto two most worthy Princes, King Edward, and Queene Elizabeth,"[173] also treats of the different kinds of commonwealths and of the various classes of society in those commonwealths. Obviously basing his discussion on the political theory of Greeks and Romans, the author, like Bodin, defines three kinds of commonwealths: aristocracy, monarchy, and democracy. Most commonwealths are not simply one or the other type, he observes, but a mixed type. A commonwealth is not merely a host of men, but "a society or common doing of a multitude of free-men collected together and united by common accord and covenauntes among themselves, for the conversation of themselves, aswell in peace as in warre."[174] The division of the parts and persons of the commonwealth[175] may be made in several different ways, excluding women, however, "as those whom Nature hath made to keepe home and to nourish their familie and children, and not to medle with matters abroad, nor to beare office in a citie or commonwealth no more than children and infants; except it be in such cases as the authoritie is annexed to the bloud and progenie, as the crowne, a dutchie, or an earledome for there the blood is respected, not the age nor the sexe."[176] Here Smith is as medieval as Bodin. One division of society, that based on participation in the government, recognizes magistrates and private men. The Romans made such a division. But they also had a division into *senatores, equites,* and *plebs.* The Greeks had a similar classification. The French also have "les nobles & la populaire," or "gentill homes & villaines." England commonly divides its men into four sorts:[177] gentlemen, citizens, yeomen, artificers and laborers. Gentlemen

---

[173] From title page of 1621 edition.

[174] Book I, chap. X, p. 20, ed. Alston.

[175] Book I, chap. XVI.   [176] Book I, chap. XVI, p. 30.

[177] Book I, chap. XVI, p. 31. For discussion of Smith's probably having borrowed his statements of classes from Harrison's *Description of England* see introduction by editor, pp. xvi f. See also p. 221 above.

comprise the king, the prince, dukes, marquises, earls, viscounts, barons—called lords and noblemen—and knights, esquires, and simple gentlemen. The lords and noblemen correspond to the Roman *senatores*. The other sort of gentlemen correspond to the Roman *equites*. The citizens, yeomen, artificers, and laborers constitute the *plebs*. These sorts of men are all included in the phrase "lords and commons," just as the Romans by *Senatus populusque Romanus* meant *senatores, equites,* and *plebs.* The term "lords," of course, also includes archbishops and bishops.

From these divisions of society are drawn the two houses of Parliament, the House of Lords and the House of Commons. In the House of Lords sit lords and bishops. In the House of Commons sit citizens and burgesses, four from the ancient cities and two from each borough. Though the yeomen, another group of commons, do not sit in Parliament, they are represented by those who do sit there, and they serve the commonwealth in other ways. They are to be highly praised as those who "tend their owne businesse, come not to meddle in publike matters and Judgements, but when they are called, and glad when they are delivered thereof, are obedient to the Gentlemen and Rulers, and in War can abide travaile and labour; as men used to fight for their Lords"[178] and for the glory of their country. This group admit that they are no gentlemen and yet have a certain preëminence over laborers and artificers. They usually live well, as farmers for gentlemen. By thrift and hard work they often become wealthy and sometimes buy the lands of unthrifty gentlemen. The last and humblest group of commons, the day laborers, poor husbandmen, merchants or retailers who have no free land, copyholders, all artificers such as tailors, shoemakers, carpenters, bricklayers, masons, do not rule at all. These men are "onelie to be ruled, not to rule other," though they sometimes, for default of yeomen, act as churchwardens or as constables, "which Office toucheth more the common wealth and

[178] Book I, chap. XXIII, pp. 43-44.

at the first was not imployed uppon such lowe and base persons."[179] Thus the commonwealth of England

is governed, administred, and manured by three sortes of persons, the
Prince, Monarch, and head governer, which is called the king. . . .
The gentlemen, which be devided into two partes, the Baronie or
estate of Lordes conteyning barons and all that bee above the degree of a baron . . . and those which be no Lords, as Knights, Esquires,
and simplely gentlemen. The thirde and last sort of persons is named
the yeomanrie: each of these hath his part and administration[180]
in the work of the commonwealth.

In his analysis of the English government and the classes of
society constituting that government, the author's purpose, as
has been said, is to report what he sees. Frequently, however,
his own attitude toward what he sees is evident. In the course
of his discussion on the origin of nobility, the manner of creating nobles and knights, and the possessions of each to maintain
their rank, he reveals a tolerance new to the literature of estates.
Like most of his predecessors, he first says that "Gentlemen be
those whom their bloud and race make noble and knowne." If
they have maintained themselves notable in riches and virtue,
without labor, they remain *vere nobiles*. If not, their fame and
wealth serve to cover them as long as possible, like gilded copper,
until the gilt wears off. All this is traditional. But when the
author looks at the fact that there are many newly made gentlemen in the realm, he sees nothing amiss. He has no diatribe
against the folly of those who rise in their estate. Some citizens
and yeomen, he finds, become gentlemen by creation by the
king. Others become gentlemen, without title, by reason of the
way they live. Anyone who studies in the universities and pro-
fesses the liberal sciences and can "live idly, and without manuall labour, and will beare the Port, charge and countenance
of a Gentleman," he is declared to be one. Usually the king
creates only barons or higher degrees. In all this there is no
cause for regret. In fact, the author sees definite gains. These

[179] Book I, chap. XXIV, p. 46.   [180] Book I, chap. XXIV, pp. 46-47.

newly made gentlemen may be taxed more and must act the
part of gentlemen. Nor need one fear the arrogance of a newly
made gentleman, for it is not he who has arrived who puts on
airs, but he who still hopes to rise. This new tolerance is something of a relief after all the earlier sermons against change
of estate. The old philosophy was now antiquated, and Smith
was observant enough to note the change.

In his changed attitude toward the whole organization of the
commonwealth, he also shows a new insight and tolerance.
"Never in all points one Common-wealth doth agree with another," he comments in no medieval fashion,

no nor long time any one Common-wealth with it selfe. For all
changeth continually to more or lesse, and still to divers and divers
orders, as the diversitie of times do present occasion, and the mutability of mens wits doth invent and assay new wayes, to reforme
and amend that wherein they doe find fault.

Bodin also recognizes these changes. It is a new idea with late
sixteenth and seventeenth-century political theorists, a result,
no doubt, of more intimate knowledge of the Greek and Roman
theory and a realization that government had not always been
what men found it to be at that particular time. Medieval and
early Renaissance literature of estates propagated the feudal
myth without questioning its divine origin. Late Renaissance
theorists begin to question.

While the literature of estates in the first half of the seventeenth century was thus losing itself in new themes and forms,
the estates themselves became firmly intrenched in the government as necessary parts of the political machinery. Though developed under feudalism, they survived beyond feudalism, under
the strong monarchy of Tudor and Stuart. The impetus given by
the Stuarts to the long familiar doctrine of divine ordination
of kings threatened, for a time, to make the rule of the realm
one of a single estate, that of the king, and to end the rule of
three estates. Moreover, between 1640 and 1660 the estate of

the bishops was again threatened with expulsion from the houses of Parliament, if not with extinction. In 1660, however, in the Declaration of Breda, Charles II indicated his willingness that henceforth Parliament should consist of two houses, the House of Lords and the House of Commons, and that "according to the ancient and fundamental laws of this kingdom, the Government is, and ought to be, by King, Lords, and Commons." The estate of the clergy, as before, was to be represented in the House of Lords. The latter half of the century, therefore, saw the three estates permanently restored to their old places in the government.

In the course of all this conflict, some of the prose works of the time reflect continued interest in the theme of the classes of society and their fate, but they usually treat it in an incidental or desultory manner that bears little relation to the old literature of estates. Some of the works, like Bacon's essays *For Removing Discontentments* and *Of Honour and Reputation* and Milton's *Of Tenure of Kings and Magistrates,* treat briefly of one estate or refer to all of them incidentally. Other pieces, like Thomas Hobbes' *Leviathan* and Harrington's *Oceana,* discuss classes of society at length, but they are concerned with three new orders: "the senate debating and proposing, the people resolving, and the magistracy executing." Character writers, like Hall and Overbury, analyze some of the old estates, but with a very different purpose and in a very different manner from that of the medieval moralists. Thomas Fuller in his *Worthies of England* classifies the notables of the different counties, but his classification is obviously that of an index: Princes, Saints, Martyrs, Confessors, Cardinals, Prelates, Statesmen, Soldiers, Writers, Benefactors to the Public, Memorable Persons, Lord Mayors, Commissioners, Knights, Sheriffs, and not that of all classes in a definitely formulated political organization. John Selden's *Table-talk,* in a desultory manner, discusses such matters as the presence of bishops in Parliament, lords in Parliament, the House of Commons, the origin of gentlemen, the origin of kingship, law, and the nature of the state in a way reminiscent of the philosophy of the literature of estates. But his comments, arranged alphabetically, are short notes on miscellaneous matters and not a thorough-going treatment of any one subject. Bishops, he concludes, have as much right to sit in Parliament as have earls and barons. A gentleman he finds hard to define. His theory of kingship is no longer that of divinity: "A King is a thing men have made for their own sakes, for quietness' sake." Every law he calls a contract between king and people. The estates of the realm he finds to be three: "the Lords Temporal, the Bishops or the Clergy, and the Commons." The decline of estates he decries. The making of new lords lessens the importance of all the rest. However, aside from these scattering comments on various matters, political and otherwise, and his recognition of kingship as the source of the various titles of honor, in his *Titles of Honor,* Selden adds little to the philosophy of the estates of the realm; and he nowhere enumerates all classes in the old fashion. Much of the other prose of the period becomes too technical to be considered as literature, though even such treatises as those of Malynes and Misselden on foreign exchanges were adorned with literary graces in the fashion of the day in an effort to attract the attention of literary and courtly circles.

Even the term *estate,* by this time, seldom has the old meaning in the literature of estates. Occasionally it is still used to refer to a person of rank or to the rank alone. The fallen angels of *Paradise Lost,* as has been noted,[181] are "infernal States."[182] But Dryden, in the *Religio laici* and elsewhere, uses the term in its modern sense to mean property: "That what they thought the priest's was their estate."[183] Even in the early seventeenth

---

[181] See p. 17.
[182] *Poetical Works,* Oxford ed., London, 1925, p. 210, l. 387.
[183] *Works,* Scott-Saintsbury ed., Edinburgh, 1885, X, 50, l. 391.

century Bacon, by *estate,* usually means state or government or property, and it is more and more frequently so used, and less and less frequently used to denote rank or person of rank.

The middle of the seventeenth century marks the end, approximately, of the literature of estates. By thus tracing its progress from its origin under feudalism through all the changes incident to new conditions under which it appeared and to which it had to be adapted to mean anything, we are able to get some idea of it as a definite literary form, so far almost unrecognized. The changing anatomies, philosophy, defections, and remedies of that form will be considered in more detail in the succeeding chapters.

CHAPTER VI

THE ANATOMIES OF THE LITERATURE OF THE ESTATES OF THE WORLD

1. THE VARIETY OF FORM

IN SUCH a survey of the literature of estates as we have made it is quite evident that a wide variety exists in the places where the *genre* is found. Some of the works, as we have seen, are long; some are short. Some are in verse; some, in prose. The enumeration of classes and their shortcomings sometimes fills the whole work; sometimes it forms only a part. Sometimes the title of the work suggests the presence of such discussion of the classes of society; sometimes the discussion is tucked away among miscellaneous matter, and the reader comes upon it quite unexpectedly. Part of the interest in this literary pattern lies in the unexpectedness of its occurrence.

In addition to the variety in the sources of this literature, its external form shows many different characteristics. It may consist of didactic or satiric or narrative or philosophic or argumentative verse or prose, with or without allegory. It may form sermon, morality, epigram, tract, broadside ballad, essay or character sketch. And within these general categories, it makes use of so many different devices that one is soon led to believe that the writer went out of his way to find some trick or other that his predecessors had not played before him. No end of ingenuity must have been expended to find a new excuse for listing the estates of the world and their faults. Some of these devices are very apt; some seem forced into service. The later writers especially feel the need of new devices, finding the old outworn. The earlier writers have no objections to using the familiar devices of their predecessors. Nor do all of these older medieval forms soon die out. Some of them persist with remarkable vitality and maintain their popularity for several centuries. Few writers, however, are content with a single device.

Most of them combine two or three. The nature of the material makes such combination often very desirable and necessary. The writer who begins with one device and then forgets it and introduces another, as in *L'Instruction de la vie mortelle,* is less easy to follow. Ordinarily the combinations are naturally evolved in the course of the work.

2. TYPICAL MEDIEVAL DEVICES

The oldest and most widely used device is that of the lament or complaint on the evils of the times. Whether in a short complaint, like those of Rutebeuf or the Latin *Sermones nulli parcentes* or *Viri fratres, servi Dei,* or in longer ones, like those of Guiot, Hugues de Berzé, Robert de Blois, or Matheolus, the poet adopts the same tone of regret and then of denunciation. Sometimes, as with Matheolus and in the *Sermones nulli parcentes,* the complaint is pretty general. Usually such laments begin with regret over the loss of the good old times, the former "golden world," when everything that is now wrong was right and when all estates did their duty. Such is the lament of Guiot and Hugues de Berzé, of Robert de Blois and the Recluse of Molliens, of Gervais du Bus, Gilles li Muisis, and Rutebeuf. Later Gower, Lydgate, and Caxton express the same regret. Sometimes, as in the Latin *Viri fratres, servi Dei* or in the *Mirrour of the World,* translated by Caxton, some specific complaint is expressed. The latter laments the loss of the old "clergy," and the former the loss of faith: "Ubicunque fidem quaero." Similarly some of the shorter pieces lament the presence in all estates of one of the seven deadly sins, usually avarice or pride because those sins prevail among all classes; whereas the longer laments concern themselves with several or all of the seven sins. The pride and lust of the nobility, the greed and gluttony of the clergy, and the sloth, envy, and anger or disobedience of the commons are all given extended treatment. The almost universal theme of avarice is frequently given interest by the use of personification. Sir Nummus or Herr Pfennig or Sir Peny becomes a familiar figure. Similarly "Sir Pride the Emperor," the French poem of estates in the *Reliquiae antiquae*, treats the sin as a lordly personage, ruling all from high to low degree. Étienne de Fougères' *Le Livre des manières* and Guillaume's *Le Besant de Dieu* use the theme of pride in the form of Solomon's "All is vanity." All seven of the deadly sins find a place, for example, in *L'Exemple du riche homme et du ladre*, Gower's *Mirour de l'omme*, the *Renner*, and *Des Teufels Netz*. The theme of the seven vices naturally suggested another device, that of the conflict of the vices and virtues. Guillaume's rambling *Le Besant de Dieu* dwells more on that conflict than on any other theme. Gower's *Mirour de l'omme* presents the same theme at length, as it affects each estate of the realm.

In the sixteenth century all of these forms persisted in some pieces at least. The general complaint is the form of the ballad *Now a Dayes,* some of the *Satirical Poems of the Reformation,* and the *Complaynte of Scotlande.* The conflict of vice and virtue is the chief device of Lyndsay's *Ane Pleasant Satyre of the Thrie Estaitis.* The lament over the loss of the good old times appears in the ballad *Now a Dayes,* in the *Shyp of Folys,* in the *Complaynt of Scotlande,* and in Gascoigne's *Steele Glas.* Even Selden in the seventeenth century laments the loss of the gravity and state of the good old days of Elizabeth.

The prevalence of such a title as *La Bible* or *Le Livre* or *Mirour* in the literature of estates, especially the earlier literature, is significant. Calling his sermon a "book" or a "mirror" would seem to give the writer something of a plan to begin with; but so general is such a title that almost any other device or devices may be expected within its scope. Gower's *Mirour de l'omme* adopts that of the conflict of vice and virtue. *La Bible* of Guiot and that of Hugues de Berzé and *Le Livre* of Étienne de Fougères are laments on the passing of the good old times. The "mirror" of the Middle Ages becomes the sixteenth-century *Mirrour for Magistrates* and the "steel glass" of Gascoigne.

After that, it is no longer used. Several works that bear no reference to a mirror in their titles make a point of calling themselves mirrors of the age. Lydgate calls his *Daunce of Machabree* a "mirrour" for all whom Death escorts hence, and Alexander Barclay says his *Shyp of Folys* is to serve all men as "a bright Myrrour."

The familiar medieval *débat* form is usually an effective device for enumeration of estates and their shortcomings. It presents a conflict of opinion and is therefore naturally livelier than a single point of view. In *Le Débat du laboureur, du prestre et du gendarme* each speaks in turn of the unhappiness of his estate. Plowman and priest charge the man of war with being the cause of their troubles. The man of war retorts that his lot is hardest and that the other two, because of their sins, deserve all the unhappiness they suffer. *Le Débat de Félicité* presents Dame Église, Dame Noblesse, Dame Labeur in a dispute as to which is the happiest estate. Each regards herself as the most fortunate. In Alain Chartier's *Quadrilogue invectif* he records the four-part *débat* of France and her three sons; and the *Complaynt of Scotlande*, following the *Quadrilogue*, is a four-fold discussion of Scotland's ills. *Des Teufels Netz*, as we have seen, is a dialogue between the poet-hermit and the boastful Devil. The Dutch *Jans Teesteye* is a *débat* of complaint, especially of merchants and peasants. Lydgate's *Horse, Sheep, and Goose* presents animal and fowl in dispute as to which is more valuable. The eclogues of Barclay and Googe, though they do not derive their form from the medieval *débat*, resemble it in the dispute of shepherds as to the best estate. Sir David Lyndsay calls his poem lamenting the "miserabill estait of the warld" *Ane Dialog Betwix Experience and Ane Courteour*. In the *Dialogue* of Starkey, Cardinal Pole and Thomas Lupset represent the more liberal and the conservative views of the middle sixteenth century in England. Hake and Rastell also found the form desirable in the *Newes Out of*

Powles Churchyarde and the dialogue *Of Gentleness and Nobility*. Stubbs' *Anatomie of Abuses*, Book II, presents the abuses of Temporalty and Spiritualty in dialogue form. John Hales' *Discourse of the Commonweal* is in the form of three colloquies among a knight, a merchant, a doctor, a husbandman, and a craftsman. Nicholas Breton also uses the dialogue form in *A Dialogue Full of Pithe and Pleasure*, in which three "philosophers" argue as to the worth or dignity of man in his different estates.

The presentation of the corruptions of the classes in narrative form is also more effective than the rambling, protracted enumeration of classes and abuses in some other pieces. *Des estats du siecle* is a short story in verse of the youth who tried all estates and found all undesirable. Biblical parables serve as the framework of some pieces. In *L'Exemple du riche homme et du ladre* the *états du monde* are reviewed after the parable of the rich man and Lazarus of the sixteenth chapter of Luke has served to introduce the deadly sin of avarice. Guillaume, as his title *Le Besant de Dieu* indicates, begins his sermon with reference to the parable of the talents, but his beginning is soon forgotten and has no further connection with the plan of his work. Lydgate's *Fall of Princes*, and the *Mirrour for Magistrates* after it, is a series of biographical and autobiographical narratives of change of estate. Beast epic and fable also serve to convey the doctrine of the estates of the world. Henryson's *Moral Fables* and Wyatt's "Of the Meane and Sure Estate" preach the folly of pride in estate by means of mice, fox, wolf, lamb, and lion. The epic of Reynard the Fox is recalled in the *Mother Hubberds Tale* of Spenser. The story of the unlike children of Eve serves to explain the origin of estates in their beauty and ugliness or in their goodness and badness. Though the poems of the Recluse of Molliens, the *Roman de carité* and the *Roman de miserere*, and the *Roman de Fauvel* of Gervais du Bus suggest romance, there is little narrative in them.

The *Roman de Fauvel* has no narrative at all. The *Roman de carité* is a vain search for charity, but the story element in the poem is negligible. The *Roman de miserere* has more. Something like the search for charity of the Recluse is the search for truth of *Piers Plowman*. There, however, the allegorical narrative dominates the poem, and the introduction of the estates is secondary. Other dream-visions, like those of *Les Échecs amoureux*, Lyndsay's *Dreme*, the *Quadrilogue invectif*, and the *Complaynt of Scotlande*, have the allegorical narrative common to such visions. To be sure, bits of narrative occur in many other pieces than those named, but usually the narrative is incidental.

In two different pieces dealing with the classes of society the estates are journeying. In Chaucer's Prologue they are traveling, on horseback, to a religious shrine. In the *Shyp of Folys* they are afloat, bound ostensibly for fools' paradise, Narragonia. The large descriptive element and the narrative in Chaucer's Prologue serve almost to conceal the fact that he is passing in review some of the most interesting estates of the world. In the *Shyp of Folys* all the traits of medieval literature of folly combine to overshadow the interest in estates.

The devices most frequently met with, after the lament or complaint, are those of the dance of death, the wheel of fortune, and the analogy between the body politic and the human body. All three themes derive, of course, from biblical and classical sources, but so vividly did the Middle Ages conceive of death and fortune and the body politic that the idealism of classical use became a very systematic, exaggerated realism.[1] Death danced and fortune's wheel turned on the walls of churches and burying grounds, and men experienced in their own individual microcosmos all the secrets of cosmic order and achievement, or the lack of them. It is scarcely to be wondered at, therefore, that these devices found ready matter in the theme of estates, in short pieces in which one of the devices formed

[1] See J. Huizinga's *The Waning of the Middle Ages,* p. 195.

the whole framework, or incidentally in longer pieces built up on another framework. Many such pieces found frequent occasion to caution the reader in terms of "memento mori" or to tell him of the mutability of fortune or to remind him that his rightful service to society was as necessary as that of the ear, eye, hand, foot, or any other organ is to the body.

The number of works in which the theme of death is introduced is so great as to prohibit mention here of all of them. Certain examples, however, are typical. Hélinant advises all estates to remember death in *Les Vers de la mort*. Lydgate, translating from the French, wrote his *Daunce of Machabree*. In the *Sophilogium* it is the theme of death and the brevity of life that reminds the author of the estates of the world and leads him to begin his discussion of their defections. Incidental reference occurs in *Fauvel*, the *Renner*, the *Pricke of Conscience*, Dunbar's "Lament for the Makaris."

> Pappe, trèstout prélat, tout roy, toutes roynes,
> Gent de trèstous estas, et dames et meskines,
> Nuls n'escape le mort quant il vient ses tiermines;
> Escriptures le dient et les boines doctrines.[2]

says Gilles li Muisis, also, as he proceeds to enumerate the estates and their defections. Incidental reference continues in the sixteenth century in such works as the *Mirrour for Magistrates* and Lyndsay's *Dreme,* and the *Shyp of Folys* has a long chapter "Of folys that despyse deth makynge no provysion therefore." An early seventeenth-century survival of the theme as a framework for the whole poem is Samuel Rowlands' *Looke to It: For, Ile Stabbe Ye,* in which the humor of the Elizabethan swaggerer is ascribed to Death, while he threatens kings, magistrates, divines, lawyers, physicians, merchants, artificers, husbandmen, and gentlewomen who prove unworthy.

The wheel of fortune is the chief theme of Lydgate's *Fall of Princes* and the *Mirrour for Magistrates* and is the subject of sermons in two chapters of the *Shyp of Folys,* both preceded

[2] Ed. Kervyn de Lettenhove, *Poésies,* I, 317, stanza 5.

by a woodcut of the fools with asses' heads and dunces' caps riding up and down on the wheel. Incidental reference to the theme is, like that to the dance of death, very frequent. Gower's prologue to the *Confessio amantis,* toward the close, discusses the wiles of fortune, though what we call fortune, he says, "Out of the man himself it groweth."

> And evere goth the wheel aboute,
> And evere stant a man in doute,
> Fortune stant no while stille,
> So hath their noman al his wille.
> Als fer as evere a man may knowe,
> Ther lasteth nothing bot a throwe;
> The world stant evere upon debat,
> So may be seker non astat.[3]

As a stock device, the "slipper traces"[4] of the wavering lady persisted into the sixteenth century in arguments against "rising aloft" or against even the desire to change one's estate for the better. The device was no doubt a source of comfort to the humble and an ever-present cause of concern to those of high degree.

The analogy of the body politic and the human body is also closely bound up with medieval and Renaissance philosophy of estates. Medieval philosophers found it in the works of St. Paul and of Aristotle,[5] and developed it into an elaborate theory of government. Nicholas of Cusa in the fifteenth century pro-

[3] Ed. Macaulay, p. 20, ll. 571 ff.

[4] *Mirrour for Magistrates,* ed. Haslewood, II, 184.

[5] No doubt the biblical and classical analogy had a much older source, for the Purusha-hymn of the *Rig-Veda,* Book X, Hymn 90 (Griffith trans., II, 519, 2d ed., Benares, 1897) has the following lines:

When they divided Purusha (a primeval giant) how many portions did they make?

What do they call his mouth, his arms? What do they call his thighs and feet?

The Brâhman (priest) was his mouth, of both his arms was the Râjanya (warrior) made.

His thighs became the Vaisya (merchant), from his feet the Sûdra (servile class) was produced.

duced the most elaborate comparison, but John of Salisbury, Thomas Aquinas, Aegidius Colonna, Dante, John of Paris, Gerson, and Marsilius of Padua also discussed this theory of cosmic harmony. In *belles lettres* it was propagated by Gervais du Bus in his *Roman de Fauvel,* by the unknown author of "The Descryvyng of Mannes Members," by DeGuileville and Lydgate in the *Pélerinage de la vie humaine,* by Lydgate in the *Fall of Princes,* and, in the sixteenth and early seventeenth centuries, by Sir John Cheke's *The True Subiect to the Rebell,* by Starkey's *Dialogue,* by Fenton's *Forme of Christian Pollicie,* and by Breton's *A Murmurer.* In John Heywood's *The Spider and the Fly* a peculiar adaptation of the analogy is made, in terms of spiders, flies, and ants:

> The God hath placed us all to live out of strife,
> Spiders, flies, and ants, each sort in their degree.
> Spiders, in head parts of windows, the heads be;
> Flies in the midst; the body as it were;
> Ants at the low part, the feet accounted there.
>
> And as a spider overmatcheth a fly,
> So is a fly as far too big for an ant;
> Which seemeth wrought by divine providence (think I),
> As our degrees are in order distant,
> So the degrees of our strength are discrepant;
> And where all three sorts keep quietly their place,
> All live together in quiet wealthy case.[6]

In all except "The Descryvyng of Mannes Membres" the analogy is combined with other devices, some of them equally important, or more important than the analogy.

Some devices, though used in only one or two pieces, were as familiar as these three. Extended treatment of the currying of the fallow horse by all estates is found only in the *Roman de Fauvel.* Brief reference to Fauvel occurs in the *Nouveau Renard* of Gelée of 1288,[7] in the *Poésies* of Gilles li Muisis, in

---

[6] Ed. John S. Farmer, London, 1908, p. 346.

[7] See 1908 edition of C. V. Langlois' *La Vie en France au moyen âge. D'après quelques moralistes du temps,* pp. 276-77.

the thirteenth-century verses of Raoul le Petit used as inscriptions for a collection of paintings, and in one chapter of *Das Narrenschiff*, but the mural decorations showing the estates petting Fauvel made the device well known, especially in France. It is doubtful whether Alexander Barclay knew of it, however, in his translation of Brant's description of the currying done by "herren knecht," the flatterers of great men, platter-lickers, fawners. Brant's chapter is headed "võ falbēhengst strichē." Locher changes it to "De assentatoribus & parasytis," and so the French and English versions become "Des assantateurs blandeurs flateurs licherres et escumeux de court" and "Of flatterers and glosers." All versions have the woodcut of a horse treading a prostrate fool with his two fore feet, while beside him lie others, of which one is licking a platter. The fool that the fallow horse is treading holds a plume with which he was tickling Fauvel when Fauvel turned on him. So do great men at court turn on their flatterers. Brant's chapter is full of references to Fauvel, and Locher knows the "subdolum equum," and Riviere calls him the "cheval fraudeux." Barclay, however, makes him a "horse of hye corage," and the whole analogy following becomes rather pointless:

> He that wyll flater a horse of hye corage
> Clappynge or touchynge: if that he stands to nye
> May happen to have the fote in his vysage
> To his great hurt: and who that subtylly
> Wyll flater an estate to get some good therby
> He often at the last is cast out of favour
> For flaterynge pleaseth no wyse man of honour.

At any rate, the three preceding versions plainly show familiarity with Fauvel and his flatterers. In the *Roman de Fauvel*, and its predecessors, the device is clearly and thoroughly used. Nor is the currying limited to "herren knecht." All the estates in all the world caress him:

> Entor Fauvel a si grant presse
> De gens de toutes nacions
> Et de toutes condicions

> Que c'est une trop grant merveille:
> N'i a nul qui ne s'appareille
> De torchier Fauvel doucement.[8]

The device of the game of chess also was not widely used, but the work of Jacobus de Cessolis was so well known that this device, too, is one of the most important of the anatomies of the literature of estates. The application of Jacobus is purely political. The chessmen represent the members of the commonwealth. As stated above,[9] the work went into every country in several versions and remained popular for centuries. Caxton's version is, of course, only one of many. The use of the device for other than political literature of estates is seen in *Les Échecs amoureux,* in which the chess game between the lover and the lady no doubt suggested the following catalogue of estates open to the lover if he chooses the second path, that of the active life, and thus frees himself from the service of Venus. In the *Mirrour for Magistrates* the deposed King Sigebert, later slain by a herdsman, laments his past life in terms of chess:

> If lothsome life (of this my corps) the king
> Dooth move one way, the bishope bids me backe:
> If to that poynt the queene me backe doth bring,
> On th' other side, the knight dooth woorke my wracke,
> The other poyntes with paunes be al possest,
> And here the rooke of ruth dooth reave my rest:
>   And being brought into this strange estate,
>   I do confesse my self to have a mate.[10]

In the late sixteenth century a survival of the device is seen in Nicholas Breton's *The Chess Play,* in which the chessmen and their duties are described. Fitzherbert's reference to and comments on Caxton's *Game and Playe of the Chesse* have been noted.[11]

The dream-vision device forms a part of the framework of at

[8] *Loc. cit.,* p. 4, ll. 29 ff. [9] See p. 31.
[10] Haslewood ed., II, 431, stanza 12.
[11] See p. 220.

least four pieces of literature of estates. In *Les Échecs amoureux* the poet lies half-awake, when Nature appears to bid him be up and out into the spring morning. His game of chess with the lady in the Garden of Pleasure leads to the advice of Minerva to choose some one of the estates of the world and therein live a life of achievement. Alain Chartier's *Quadrilogue invectif* presents the dream-vision of France and her three sons. The *Vox clamantis* of Gower gets under way by means of a June dawn vision of Wat Tyler's rebellion. The rest of the work, enumerating the estates of the world, consists of the poet's contrast of his own evil times with the good old times that are past, and the dream-vision device is abandoned. *Piers Plowman* describes the dream of Will in the "somere seyson," into which are introduced the various classes of society and their duties if they are to find Truth. Sir David Lyndsay in *The Dreme* has a dream, in cold January, of "lawest hell" and of the estates punished there, of heavenly paradise, of earthly paradise, and of the "realme of Scotland," where all estates are at fault. John Higgins in his induction to Part I of the *Mirrour for Magistrates* found a book of estates, he says, in a printer's shop. As he read, Somnus came, and he slept. Somnus ordered Morpheus to present to the sleeper the British peers who were "from high state brought into dismal plight." Sackville's induction presents a vision also, but without the dream device. In the induction to Part V by Robert Niccols, the poet, in the month of August, sits thinking of Elizabeth as he gazes at the palace where she lived. He falls asleep and sees her in all her "princely state," with her "grave peeres and honorable states." In *The Complaynt of Scotlande* the Monologue Recreative, following its original, describes the author's long dream-vision of Dame Scotia and her three sons, the estates of the world, as he fell asleep after wandering one midsummer night through fields of flowers and over wooded hills, full of pastoral beauty untainted by the corruptions of political life.

The device of the marriage of the Devil's daughters to the different estates of the world appears in several pieces of the literature of estates. It is the framework of the part of Matheolus' *Lamentations* where Pride was married to women, Simony to the clergy, Hypocrisy to monks and nuns and other "religious" folk, Rapine to the soldiers, Sacrilege to the greedy farmers, Fraud to the merchants, and Usury to the citizens. Lust, the seventh daughter, was given to no one, but abandoned to all. The same framework appears in Vintler's *Die Pluemen der Tugent*, adapted from the Italian *Fiori di virtú* of Tomaso Leoni. In both, the allegory of Satan and his seven daughters carries the author's rather rambling dissertations on the corruptions of the various estates. Guillaume's *Le Besant de Dieu* briefly refers to the device: three of the daughters, Envy, Lust, and Drunkenness, he says, have been wedded to the English.

Other medieval devices serve less frequently than these, and some have little connection with the catalogue of estates included. The five senses are used in the *Roman de miserere* of the Recluse of Molliens as a basis for discussion of the abuses of society. Only in the analysis of the use of taste, however, are the estates introduced. The four ages of man form the framework of Philippe de Novarre's *Les Quatre ages de l'homme,* but the enumeration of estates and their abuses occurs in a rambling postscript containing things he has neglected to put into his main work. The ordering of the estates on or toward a tree of life or of love or of battle is a characteristic of several pieces. Matfre Ermengaud's *Le Breviari d'amor* arranges the estates, except the clergy, in a symbolic Tree of Love; but the significance of the allegory becomes pretty well lost in the sermon on their abuses. Raimon del Cornet's *Gesta* is an effort to show all estates the way to the tree of life, including the clergy omitted by Ermengaud. *L'Arbre des batailles* of Honoré Bonet catalogues society in its relation to military service. The fruit of the tree of life in Hugo von Trimberg's *Renner* is mankind in all its different classes; the wind of curiosity blows them off into the deadly sins. In the sixteenth century Edmund Dudley's *Tree of Commonwealth* presents a complete arboreal picture of the organization of the government of the three estates. The analogy between the hierarchies of angels and the estates of men is another device used by Ermengaud, and it is an important argument for the existence of different degrees of nobility and gentlemen in the treatise on coat armor in the *Boke of St. Albans.* Since there are nine orders of angels in heaven, there are likewise nine orders of nobility and nine orders of gentlemen. The *Sophilogium* and *Le Livre de bonnes meurs* use the theme of the Last Judgment, and Robert Crowley finds it still good in the sixteenth century in *Pleasure and Payne, Heaven and Hell.* Crowley uses a similar device in *The Voyce of the Laste Trumpet,* in which all the estates of men are taught a lesson of right dealing in their station. Lydgate introduces enumeration of estates with the theme "Pray for all" in "A Prayer to St. Thomas of Canterbury," and the same device is that of Dekker in his early seventeenth-century *Foure Birdes of Noah's Arke.* In the former the prayers are to be said by St. Thomas; in the latter the four birds bear prayers to those to whom they are suited, and the eagle carries the prayers for estates to offer up for preservation from their abuses. Rarely does praise of the estates of the world appear in the literature of classes except as it relates to the good old times. There is too much fault to be found with them. In Dunbar's "Treatise of London," however, he finds lords, barons, knights, ladies, prelates, and merchants of London praiseworthy; and in the early seventeenth century Breton's *Dialogue Full of Pithe and Pleasure* finds excuses for the shortcomings of the various classes and praise for their virtues. Dekker, in the *Double PP,* has only praise for the estates composing the Protestant army. New values and new motives for weighing those values made praise of estates more acceptable in the sixteenth century than in the

Middle Ages. No doubt the novelty also had something to do with the change of portraiture. To one writer at least the triple constitution of society suggested an analogy with the Trinity. To Wycliff the secular lords and rulers were the Father, the clergy were the Son, and the commons were the Holy Ghost. A less devout analogy is that of the poem "God Save the Kyng, and Kepe the Crown" in *Political and Other Poems* of the fifteenth century. To this more politically-minded poet, the estates are the stones and flowers in the king's crown. Lords, commons, and clergy are all represented by the ornaments of the crown:

> þe leste lyge-man, wiþ body and rent,
> He is a parcel of þe crowne.

3. SIXTEENTH AND SEVENTEENTH-CENTURY DEVICES

In addition to these medieval devices, some of which were used again in the period of the Renaissance, new anatomies were introduced as new conditions suggested them. Dekker's *Double PP* presents the opposed estates in the battle of Papists and Protestants. More and more frequent change of estate gave rise to much philosophizing as to the best estate in which one might find one's self, and so in several pieces the theme of the most desirable degree is the framework on which the verse or prose discussion is built up. In the lively medieval narrative *Des estats du siecle,* as we have seen, the story is that of the attempt of a youth to find the best estate, and of his discovery that none is best. In the sixteenth century the conclusion is usually that of classical philosophy, namely, that the golden mean is best. In a less lofty estate, one is less likely to fall. In the *Mirrour for Magistrates* the idea is frequently stressed, as it is in the story of the death of King Humber of the Huns by drowning while trying to conquer new realms in Britain:

> Now by his fall and his ambition vewe,
> What good they get which gaze on Fortune's blisse,
> How soone their haps and hoped Joyes they misse,

Wherefore the settled minde surmountes the rest,
The meane contented state of all is best.[12]

To be sure, the fickle wheel of fortune made such a conclusion a necessary one in the Middle Ages as well as in the sixteenth century. But added weight was lent it by the authority of the classics: the golden mean is preferable always to either extreme in degree. Wyatt's poem of the town and country mice teaches the same lesson. Sir Edward Dyer also sang of his content of mind in his estate, though his song is less impressive than it might be since his estate was scarcely a mean one. In fact, most of those who praised the mean estate were far from lowly themselves. From their elevation and in the intrigue of court, the lives of the lowly no doubt looked peaceful and safe. Had these poets been of lesser rank, their verses would have been different. The eclogues of Barclay and of Googe praise the mean estate in the stock terms of pastoral verse. Nicholas Breton, like the author of *Des estats du siecle,* tries the estates in order in a game of wishing, *I Would and Would Not,* and finds no estate to his liking. No matter what estate he might wish to live in, he would surely meet carping criticism of his conduct. All one can wish for is a noble life of prayer for all estates.

The subject of appropriate dress is the cause for enumeration of estates in several sixteenth-century pieces. Sir Thomas Elyot devotes a part of his *Boke* to the discussion of the array ordained by God for "sondry astates," and Puttenham's *Arte of English Poesie* corroborates his opinions. Phillip Stubbs decries the extravagance of dress in England and similarly advises every subject "to weare attyre every one in his degree, accordinge as his calling and condition of life requireth." There was a legal basis for this insistence on the proper dress for each estate in certain acts of Parliament. In Edward III's time attempts were made to regulate the apparel of all classes from highest to lowest by law—without much success. Similar acts were passed in

[12] Haslewood ed., I, 52.

the time of Edward IV, but were repealed in the reign of Henry VIII, when another act was substituted. In the reign of Philip and Mary, an act was passed to prohibit excess in apparel.[13] The theme is not new with the sixteenth-century literature of estates, for Lydgate, following "Bochas" in the *Fall of Princes*, digresses on the subject of the proper clothes for each estate. God's choice of wardrobe for each estate is described as follows:

> God suffreth weel ther be a difference
> Touchyng array, as men been of degre:
> Hih estatis, that stonde in excellence,
> Mut be preferrid, of resoun men may see;
> As cloth of gold, stones & perre
> Was for princis with othir fressh clothynges,
> But specialli purpil was for kyngis.

> Thus was ther set, of hih discrecioun,
> Array accordyng to princis hih noblesse;
> And for othir estatis lower doun,
> Lik ther degrees tween povert & richesse,
> An ordre kept from scarsete & excesse,
> A mene provided atween hih & lowe,
> Lich to hymsilff[e] ech man may be knowe.[14]

The comparison of the estates of the realm to the strings of a musical instrument occurs in the works of two writers. Hooker briefly compares the realm to "a harp or melodious instrument," played by the king according to the laws of the state. Breton, in *A Murmurer,* makes the king the highest pitched string of the treble cleff and the laborer the lowest pitched string of the bass cleff. Between are many more strings, counsellors, preachers, lawyers, soldiers, merchants, artificers. If all sound in harmony, in due allegiance to the king, "how excellant a musique is the sound of peace in such a kingdom." If the strings are out of tune, "the musique will be harsh," and the state can know no peace.

[13] See E.E.T.S., XXXII, clxxiv, notes.
[14] *Op. cit.*, III, 746-47.

Other sixteenth-century devices are of unique occurrence. Sir Thomas Elyot compares the estates to the various pieces of household furniture. Pots and pans, representing plowman or craftsman, are seemly decoration for the kitchen, but they are scarcely desirable in the chamber. That is, potter or tinker, plowman or carter, weaver or fuller are all right in their respective crafts, but would make "but a feble answere" as ambassador, captain of an army, or any office of magistrate. Beds, covers, and pillows belong properly in the bedchamber. They, in turn, would be out of place in the hall, where carpets and cushions are proper ornaments. The carpets and cushions would be out of place in the stable. The commonwealth, like the house, must be properly furnished, each estate in his fit place. *Pasquil's Mad-cappe* of Breton is thrown at the corruption of the classes in the form of messages "to Men of all Estates." The "gratious king" needs no message, but all the rest, in no fixed order, are told their duties. Dekker sends his prayers for the different estates on the wings of four birds.

The anatomies of the utilitarian pieces of literature of estates are usually determined by the purposes they are to serve. The books of precedence, hawking, coat armor, and so forth can be little more than lists of estates according to their places at the table, the kinds of hawks they should use, and the proper coats of arms for each degree. Caxton's *Dialogues in French and English* list the estates for two purposes: to inform the English traveler of the different orders of society and to enable him to call those orders by their French names. Fitzherbert's *Boke of Husbandry* was written to instruct the reader in the maintenance and management of a farm, and so the author's prologue preaches the dignity of labor. Each estate is ordained to labor in his own way: he who does not labor shall not eat. The theme then suggests to the author a dissertation on the duties of all the estates, according to the division of society in Caxton's chess book. Harrison's *Description of England* naturally includes a description of the estates of people in England. Contemporary conditions, such as the decline of the estate of the clergy and the increase in the number of merchants, are reflected in his account. The whole treatise is, of course, informational in tone and so is fairly detailed in its enumeration and description of the classes.

4. SIXTEENTH-CENTURY PROSE WITHOUT DEVICE

Many of the devices used in the literature of estates are quite incidental, as may readily be seen, to the purpose and trend of thought of the whole work. Others form the framework of all the discussion. In the political, economic, philosophic, or religious prose treatises, the device, whatever it is, is usually incidental and serves as a brief stimulant to the reader's lagging interest. In verse and in shorter prose pieces, the device is frequently the chief concern and ornament of the work. Some prose literature of estates has no device at all, except as it falls into a familiar literary form. The character sketch serves Rowlands and Breton, and the epigram serves Crowley. Thomas Cooper's *Admonition to the People of England* takes the form of objection and answer, something like the *débat* or dialogue, though lacking the interest of having different characters speak their contrary views. Latimer's sermons discuss the duties of the classes without device. On the whole, it may be said that the writers of the earlier prose, that of the Middle Ages and early Renaissance, seem to feel the need of some device, at least in order to get under way. They may forget or ignore it later, but they dwell on it fondly in the beginning. Some, of course, carry it through and push it to extremes, as in Dudley's *Tree of Commonwealth*. Later prose writers, those of the later sixteenth and early seventeenth centuries, have less need of such support. Their discussion becomes pure argument or exposition, without allegory. Naturally they are often less interesting to the seeker after literary oddities; but from the modern reader's point of view, it is they who grapple with the problem of class distinctions to some kind of original conclusion. The discussion of classes in Sir Thomas Smith's *De republica Anglorum* is, of course, as different from Gascoigne's *Steele Glas* as it could well be. Smith looks at the question with the critical eye of an original observer and thinker, free from the traditional scholastic method and from medieval submission to authority of Church and dogma. The very tone of his work permits of none of the devices common to prose and verse before him. Gascoigne, on the other hand, adopts method, doctrine, expression almost entirely as he found it in medieval verse of estates. Such is the difference that may exist between two works treating the same theme. In fact, a primary interest in this literature of estates, as was said before, lies in the unexpectedness of its occurrence and in the wide diversity of its anatomies.

CHAPTER VII

THE PHILOSOPHY OF THE ESTATES OF THE WORLD

1. GENERAL CHARACTERISTICS

THE philosophy that pervades most of this literature of estates is a mixture, typically medieval, of political and religious theory. The political theory, no doubt suggested by and adapted from that of Plato and Aristotle, is so highly colored at times by scholastic theology and religious dogma as to make it a kind of incongruous hybrid. The writers themselves very evidently find difficulty in harmonizing their views, not knowing whether to turn to the Scriptures and the Church Fathers for authority or to accept the more dangerous but pleasantly reasonable statements of the ancients. The earliest writers, to be sure, have little time for philosophy in their laments over the abuses of the classes. Then, with increasing interest and assurance, the later writers cite Aristotle's and Plato's views as authority for this or that idea that is to be enforced. Like Dante, they seem to feel concerning Plato that "perchance his meaning is of other guise than the word soundeth, and may have a not-to-be-derided purport."[1] This other guise they proceed to give it by viewing it in the light of religious dogma. Much that the Bible has implied about the organization of society here on earth and much that it never intended to imply, plus the accretion of classical theory, becomes the medieval explanation of the estates of the world. Actual feudal society, as the writers of the literature of estates saw it all about them, naturally set certain limits to their ability to adapt the theories of Plato and Aristotle, but they did the best they could to make those theories fit. "Meistre Aristole ce nous dist"[2] is the more frequent refer-

---

[1] *Divine Comedy*, "Paradiso," Temple Classics Edition, canto IV, ll. 55 f.

[2] Gower's *Mirour de l'omme*, l. 25969.

ence in the medieval literature of estates. As the period of humanism advances, Plato's authority is equally good, or better. Somewhat later, as in the *De republica Anglorum* of Sir Thomas Smith, the Roman organization of society, rather than the Greek, is described and compared with that of England. The time and space devoted to the philosophy of estates constantly increases. From little or none at all, it grows, in the sixteenth and early seventeenth centuries, to a bulk that sometimes excludes the voluminous medieval laments and lists of abuses. More and more, of course, as men of the Renaissance were able to free themselves from scholastic theology, and to grasp the spirit of ancient culture, they looked at government and the organization of society as things apart from the Church and its dogma, as things growing naturally from the circumstances of times and nations.

Certain well-defined theories or beliefs meet the reader of the literature of estates in almost every work, of whatever time. Along with the catalogues of classes and of their abuses, they form the earmarks of the *genre*. The divine origin of the three classes of society, the importance to the state of every class, the obligation resting upon each class to do its duty, the desirability of every man's being content with his degree and the folly of trying to change his estate, the superiority of the good old times when estates did their duties and men were content with their station in life, the origin of the defections of the classes in the sin of Adam and Eve and the necessary formation thereafter of some kind of government, the excuses of the estates for their defections, and the possible consequences of those defections are some of the matters which this literature discusses.

2. The Divine Origin of Estates

The theory of the divine origin of the estates of the world persists from the earliest work to the latest. Almost every writer asserts or implies it. This belief is, of course, distinctly medieval.

Plato and Aristotle discuss the classes necessary to the commonwealth, but say nothing about the immediate intervention of the Deity in the formation of those classes. The method of Aristotle, especially, was that of observation, and it was impossible for him to observe God's ordering of society. Not so with the cataloguers of medieval estates. If society was found to consist of three classes, nobility, clergy, and commons, there could be only one origin, that of God's will.

> Quant Diex nous ot d'enfer rescous,
> S'ordena trois Ordres de nous,

says Hugues de Berzé in his *Bible*,[3] and his explanation is typical. Sometimes the theory is phrased less succinctly, but the meaning is the same.

> Quant Deus sainte yglise sacra,
> Dou(e)s bones gardes li dona.
> Ce furent cler et chevalier,[4]

so Robert de Blois expresses the idea, and then he proceeds to the origin of the commons. Apparently he is not quite so sure of God's creation of the third estate, for he explains that "by nature" it becomes them to provide food and to serve the other two orders:

> On dist et voirs est: De nature
> Suel [t] ades passer norreture.[5]

John Gower, himself probably of the merchant class, has no doubt about the divine origin of merchants to seek in other lands the needed commodities:

> Sur quoy marchant dieus ordina,
> Qui ce q'en l'une ne serra
> En l'autre terre querre doit.[6]

Poulterers, too, are so ordained to provide us with fowl. In the *Vox clamantis* Gower is very specific about God's ordination of the plowmen to provide food. They are those who, by the sweat

---

[3] Ed. Barbazan-Meon, p. 399, l. 179.   [4] Ed. Ulrich, p. 16, ll. 491 ff.
[5] *Ibid.*, p. 34, ll. 1145-46.
[6] *Mirour de l'omme,* ed. Macaulay, ll. 25195 ff.

of great labor, seek food for us as God himself has commanded them from Adam down to the present time:

> Nam post miliciam restat status unus agrestis,
> in quo rurales grana vina colunt.
> Hii sunt qui nobis magni sudore laboris
> perquirunt victus, iussit ut ipse deus:
> est et eis iure nostri primi patris Ade
> regula, quam summi cepit ab ore dei.[7]

The divine origin of the nobility and clergy is, of course, beyond all doubt or question. John Lydgate in the *Fall of Princes*, following a digression by "Bochas" on the conduct of kings, is among the earliest of the writers of the literature of estates to proclaim the divine origin of kings, the estate concerning which the theory was last to appear because of the later growth of monarchy:

> Thestat of kynges gan be permyssioun
> Of Goddis grace & of his purveyaunce.[8]

The divine ordination of the nobility is asserted in the poem "Treuth, Reste, and Pes" of 1401:

> God made lordis governoures
> To governe puple in unyte.[9]

About the same time, Alain Chartier in war-ridden France was asserting the divine origin and sustenance of the nobles who must defend France or see her fall:

Comme les haultes dignitez des seigneuries soient establies soubz la divine et infinie puissance qui les eslieve en florissant, en prosperité et en glorieuse renommee, il est a croire et tenir fermement que, ainsi que leurs commencemens et leurs accroissances sont maintenues et adrecees par la divine providence.[10]

In his tract written to prove that the clergy may not hold property, Wycliff asserts the divine origin of all estates: "Almyȝty

[7] Ed. Macaulay, p. 216, ll. 559-64.
[8] Ed. Bergen, CXXIII, Part III, 889.
[9] *Political and Other Poems*, p. 13, stanza 17.
[10] *Quadrilogue invectif*, ed. Droz, p. 1.

god þe trinyte, fadir, sonne and holy gooste, boþe in þe olde lawe
and þe newe haþ fowndid his chirche up-on þre statis";[11] and
Caxton's chess book expands on the debt of the laborer to God
(the payment of tithes) because God has made him and given
him "all his goodes temporall / wherof his lyf is susteyned." The
humble pawn inspires the sermon—a pawn holding in his right
hand a spade or shovel with which to dig in the earth and in his
left hand a rod to drive beasts to pasture.

And god that formed us of the erthe hath ordeyned that by the
laboure of men she shold gyve nourysshyng unto alle that lyveth
/ and first the labourer of yᵉ erthe ought to knowe his god that
formed and made heven & erthe of nought And ought to have loyaulte
and trouth in hymself / and despise deth for to entende to his laboure.[12]

Similarly "all craftes & occupacions ben ordeyned not only to
suffise to them only / but to the comyn /."[13] Here, too, apparently the divine origin of king and baron and bishop is beyond
all doubt.

In the year of the accession of Henry VIII, Alexander Barclay
was no less certain of God's ordination of the classes of society
to their particular duties. In an original envoy in the *Shyp of
Folys* he beseeches the rich to have pity on the poor:

> ye great estatis and men of dignyte
> To whome god in this lyfe hath sent ryches
> Have ye compassion / on paynfull povertye.[14]

Instead of oppressing the poor, they should defend them as they
were ordained to do. The divine ordination of the other estates
is similarly asserted in numerous places. Barclay's sermon to the
rich is reversed in the *Tree of Common Wealth* of Edmund Dudley. There the "good Comoners" are warned, for their own ease,
not to covet the prosperity of the "Chevalry," nor disdain the
power of the king, but with due reverence to obey it: "ffor be ye

[11] *English Tracts*, ed. Matthew, p. 362.
[12] Ed. Axon, p. 77.   [13] *Ibid.*, p. 78.
[14] Ed. of 1509, Folium XLIX; Jamieson ed., I, 102.

sure the high providence of god is, that ye should doe soe, as he declareth himself right plainly to his chosen people, when they desired a kinge." The citation of biblical authority shows the already very evident religious origin of the theory. "But let us all consider that god hath set a due order by grace . . . betwene man and man . . . wch order from the highest pointe to the lowest, god willeth us fervently to kepe, wth out any enterprise to the contrary."[15]

As the philosophic leanings of the sixteenth-century litera-ture of estates grow stronger, there is no such immediate cer-tainty as these earlier writers have shown, but rather a ques-tioning attitude at first, that ultimately arrives at the old con-clusion of God's ordination. "Hath nat he set degrees and astates in all his glorious warkes?" asks Elyot.[16] In the estates of man, as in those of all living creatures of lesser importance, "shulde be no lasse providence of god declared than in the inferiour creatures; but rather with a more perfecte ordre and dissposition." Later on he reasserts this conclusion with more assurance: ". . . . therfore god ordayned a diversitie or pre-eminence in degrees to be amonge men for the necessary direc-tion and preservation of them in conformitie of lyvinge."[17] The idea is enforced by his elaborate analogy of pots and pans and other household furniture.[18] Sir John Cheke's theme in *The Hurt of Sedition* calls forth an expression of divine origin and divine right of a king or magistrate that is as forceful as any king could wish: "But the Magistrate is the ordinance of God, ap-pointed by him with the sword of punishment, to looke straitly to all evill doers. And therefore that that is done by the Magis-trate, is done by the ordinance of God, who the Scripture often-times doth call God, because he hath the execution of God's office."[19] Similarly, "God hath made the poore, & hath made

[15] Ed. 1859, p. 52.
[16] *The Boke Named the Governour*, ed. Croft, I, 4-5.
[17] *Ibid.*, II, 209.   [18] See p. 159.   [19] Ed. of 1641, p. 4.

them to be poore, that he might shew his might, and set them aloft when he listeth, for such cause as to him seemeth; and pluck downe the rich to this state of povertie, to shew his power, as he disposeth to order them."[20] The philosophy of the *Mirrour for Magistrates* agrees exactly with that of Cheke:

> No subject may his sword nor armoure take
> Against his prince, whom God hath placed there.[21]

Or,

> God hath ordayned the power, all princes be
> His lieutenantes or deputyes in realmes.[22]

No matter how the ruler attains his rank, whether "by birth, law, succession, or universall election," God has authorized him "in his owne roume to execute his lawes and justice among any people or nation."[23] With his characteristic blunt vigor, Latimer also states the theory of the divine origin of all estates: "Well, I woulde al men woulde loke to their dutie, as God hath called them, and then we shoulde have a florishyng christian commune weale."[24] The extent to which Robert Crowley goes in preaching the doctrine of divine origin has been noted: even the beggar has been called by God to his estate and must therefore be content therein. God appointed rulers also, and He will put down rebels. Fitzherbert recommends the chess book as a treatise wherein one may learn "that everye man, from the hyest degree to the lowest, is set and ordeyned to have labour and occupation."[25] It would be well for all to read it to find out the proper occupations for their various estates. In his analogy drawn between government and the human body, Breton, too, asserts the divine origin of estates: "God made all the parts of the bodie for the Soule, and with the Soule to serve him, and all the Subiects in a Kingdome to serve their King, and with their

---

[20] *Ibid.*, p. 9.　　　　　　　[21] Ed. Haslewood, II, 439, stanza 40.
[22] *Ibid.*, II, 164, stanza 23.　　[23] *Ibid.*, II, 415.
[24] *Sermon on the Ploughers*, ed. Arber, p. 29.
[25] *The Boke of Husbandry*, ed. Skeat, "The Aucthors Prologue," p. 1.

King to serve him . . . how then growes this murmuring at the will of God in men?"[26] The *Six Bookes of a Commonweale* of Bodin, with all their flavor of ancient philosophy, similarly find in the "apt and comely order" of society the work of the Deity:

For why, it is a most antient and received opinion of the wise, Almightie God himselfe the great and supreme workemaster and creator of this great and wonderfull Fabrick of all things, in the creating thereof, to have performed nothing either greater or better, than that hee divided the mingled and confused parts of the rude *Chaos*, and so setled everie thing in his due place and order.[27]

These instances, chosen at random, show the persistence of the theory of the divine origin of estates. No revival of the literature of the ancients by the humanists could entirely remove the myth. Beginning with its application to the origin of feudal classes, writers of the literature of estates made it apply also to the growing power of monarchy. Below the king, the estates of the realm were still what they were under feudalism, and the adaptation of the theory to the king was easy enough. As an over-lord of over-lords, he held a rank consonant with that of the feudal lord, and hence this particular bit of the philosophy of estates still prevailed.

3. THE INFLUENCE OF THE CLASSICS

Meanwhile, however, ideas of government and classes of society expressed in the literature of the ancients crept into some of the literature of estates to modify the medieval theories of estates. As early as about 1218, Guiot de Provins in his *Bible* says he proposes to follow the "bible" of the ancient philosophers who were before Christ. Those sages lived according to reason. Philosophy is a beautiful name: it signifies in the Greek "loving the good and the right." Guiot then names a score or more philosophers: Plato, Seneca, Aristotle, Virgil, Socrates, Lucan, Diogenes, Priscian, Aristippus, Cleobulus, Ovid, Statius, Pythagoras, and others. All of these were incorruptible censors

[26] *A Murmurer*, ed. Grosart, p. 10. [27] Ed. of 1606, Book III, p. 387.

of the ways of bad princes, just as Guiot proposes in his work to act as censor of all people of his evil time. In 1290, in the *Lamenta* of Matheolus, in an untranslated Latin passage, the poet explains that "old philosophers" have determined the existence and duties of the three estates:

> Preterea tres janque status nostri statuerunt
> philosophi veteres; nam clerum preposuerunt,
> ut reliquos regeret, documentis. Inde locatur
> armatus miles ut rem publicam tueatur;
> istis agricole subsunt alii laicique,
> quorum nanque labor victum largitur utrique.[28]

To be sure the philosophers have not originated the classes, but they have observed that the three classes have developed and now constitute society, says Matheolus, and for the time being the theory of divine origin is forgotten. But Guiot and Matheolus were considerably freer in their thinking than most early writers of the literature of estates. Toward the end of the fourteenth century, references to the authority of the ancients become more and more frequent. Just after citing the Scriptures in a sermon on the avarice of merchants, Gower refers to the "infinite" list of crafts that existed in Master Aristotle's time as well as in his own time.[29] They are too numerous for him to name; so he puts in only those that deserve special remembrance. Trickery or fraud is found in all of them. Lydgate finds the three medieval estates in Rome, where their assent was necessary to a triumph:

> Avis was take first of estatis thre:
> Of men of armys, which that wer present . . .
> Of the clergie thei muste have eek assent,
> And of the senat and peeple most notable.[30]

Caxton, in his *Mirrour of the World,* praises the learning of the philosophers of ancient times, who gave themselves up to the study of the universe. To Caxton, their "estate" has become that of the clergy of the Middle Ages. The three estates, including

---

[28] Ed. van Hamel, ll. 5071-76.   [29] *Mirour de l'omme,* ll. 25969 f.
[30] *Fall of Princes,* ed. Bergen, Part IV, p. 487.

that of the clergy, originated in Athens, where the philosophers named them and their duties. They called them "clerkes, knyghtes, and labourers." They set the number at three, "ffor they would seche the very trouthe." From Athens, the three orders of people made their way to Rome, and from there to France, where now they flourish best. Caxton, of course, is translating from the French, and the French version comes from the Latin of about 1245. The ideas of the *Mirrour*, therefore, are much older than the English version. All through the literature of estates, however, the Greek philosophers are authorities on which the writers rely and of whom they speak with the utmost respect. No doubt knowledge of Greek literature was much more general in the thirteenth century than is usually believed. "Latin translations of several of Aristotle's works and of Plato's *Timaeus* were certainly available. Such men as Neckham and Albertus Magnus are known to have lectured on Greek philosophy and expounded texts in Paris and at other Universities."[31] In the chess book Caxton again defers to Plato, when he quotes him as authority for the statement that "the cyte is well and Iustely governid and ordeyned in the whiche no man may saye by right · by custome · ne by ordenance / this is myn /."[32] In other words, Plato teaches communism.

With the increased knowledge of and interest in the classics, especially the Greek, sixteenth-century references to the ancients often grow into long arguments based on some theory expressed by Plato or Aristotle. Sir Thomas More's frequent references to "those thinges that Plato faynethe in his weale publique" are well known. Frequently his "geere smelleth of Plato his communitie."[33] The political philosophy of Plato is to him ideal and therefore worthy of being the basis of Utopian policies. In Bale's play of *Kynge Johan*, Plato is cited as authority for a

[31] See Introduction to Caxton's *Mirrour of the World* by Oliver H. Prior, p. x.
[32] Ed. Axon, p. 88.   [33] Bohn ed., pp. 71, 89.

remedy for political ills, and Aristotle as critic of those ills, especially those of the clergy.[34] Thomas Starkey, in his *Dialogue,* makes Cardinal Pole's philosophy of the state and its classes an adaptation of Plato's ideas concerning a commonwealth. The conflict between the medieval philosophy of the necessity of all the estates and the new philosophy of the ideals of the ancients is clearly evident in all of Pole's remarks. In spite of warnings to beware of Plato's ideal of a commonwealth that can never be made a reality, Pole persists in his approval of "the wyse phylosophar Plato," who "in al hys commyn welth chefely laburyd to see gud offycerys, hedys, and rularys, the wych schold be, as hyt were, lyvely lawys,"[35] and he hopes to find in his own time such magistrates as prefer the common good to all other things. Aristotle's "first beuk of his politiques" is the authority of the author of the *Complaynt of Scotlande* for his insistence on the necessity of all estates in the commonwealth: "for that cause aristotil hes said in his politiques, that in ilk comunite ther is ane multitude, ande ilk ane of thir degreis ar ordand til help uthirs in necessite."[36] And Cicero's *Rhetoric* is the source of an example to support Aristotle's theory. All this sounds strangely new to the reader of medieval literature of estates, accustomed to assume the divine origin of classes: instead, according to these sixteenth-century theorists, nature has evolved the classes and their diverse talents, and the word of the ancients, not that of the Bible or the Church Fathers, is sufficient authority. Sir Thomas Smith in his *De republica Anglorum* is also far removed from reliance on the theories of the medieval state. Greece, Rome, France furnish him with evidence for the propriety of the English division of society into three estates. The Romans have *senatores, equites, plebs,* derived from a similar Greek division. The French have "les nobles & la populaire," or "gentill homes

---

[34] J. M. Manly, *Specimens of Pre-Shaksperean Drama,* I, 603.

[35] Ed. Cowper, Part II, chap. I, p. 163.

[36] Ed. Murray, "Prolog to the Redar," p. 11.

& villaines." The higher orders of English nobility, including archbishops and bishops, correspond to the Roman *senatores*. The lower orders correspond to the Roman *equites*. Citizens, yeomen ("they which old Cato calleth *Aratores & optimos cives in Republica*"), artisans, and day laborers constitute the *plebs*. The day laborers, poor husbandmen, merchants or retailers who have no free land, artisans such as tailors, shoemakers, carpenters, masons, and so forth, are those whom "the old Romans called *capite sensu proletarij* or *operarij*."[37] The Greeks have defined three kinds of government, democracy, monarchy, aristocracy, and the author defines them in the manner of the Greeks, without a word of divine intervention. Bodin's *Six Bookes of a Commonweale* cites several ancient authorities: Plato, Aristotle, Appolonius of Tyana, and Xenophon; and he uses as examples the "estates" of ancient and modern commonwealths.[38] In addition, however, he quotes the Scriptures to support his statements and finds in the estate of king a divinely ordained sovereignty. The other estates, too, as has already been indicated, were devised by God to produce order in the world.

Out of this conflict of ancient and medieval points of view, certain questions grew more and more insistent. Some of them were old questions that became more acute as new light was shed on them. Some of them were direct outgrowths of the conflict of old and new. Whence came estates? Whence came government and the estate of the governor? Which estate was first? What type of government was the first? What relations do estates bear to each other in government? were some of the questions most often asked and answered.

4. THE ORIGIN OF LORDSHIP

As the theory of divine origin of estates came into conflict with the philosophy of Plato and Aristotle, it had an increasingly

---

[37] Ed. Alston, Book I, chaps. XVI f.
[38] English ed. of 1606, Book I, chap. I.

hard battle to survive. The whole question of class distinctions naturally resolved itself into that of lordship: why are some set aloft and others left below? Why do some command and others obey? Why, since all come into the world in much the same fashion, should one man have all the luxuries and pleasures of life while his fellow-citizen must get along as best he can? The mention of money, of rich and poor, seldom entered into the earlier debate of these questions, since until the later Middle Ages money was practically an unknown and therefore unimportant matter. Some of the theories concerning the origin of lordship seem naïve and amusing to the modern reader; others are wholly reasonable and show the influence of the classics.

Several of the earlier writers of the literature of estates find lordship beginning in the time of Adam or, after the flood, with Noah's sons. Gower's *Vox clamantis*, for example, calls Adam the progenitor of the non-noble class because of his expulsion from Paradise. He was commanded to labor in the sweat of his brow, and all his descendants must do likewise. Hugo von Trimberg's *Renner* tells the story of how Ham uncovered his father Noah, asleep and drunk, and called his two brothers to see him. The brothers covered him. Noah, waking, cursed Ham and said that all his descendants should be servants. Thus rose noble and non-noble degrees. But the poet hastens to add that virtue makes nobility, not birth or possessions.[39] Had Ham been virtuous like his brothers, he would never have been doomed to servility. The treatise on coat armor in the *Boke of St. Albans* goes back to Cain as the progenitor of the non-noble. For killing Abel he was cursed by God and Adam, and he and all his descendants became churls. Seth, the good son, became the progenitor of gentlemen. Noah, as a descendant of Seth, was therefore a gentleman. The line of churls was drowned in the flood. It was reborn in Ham,

[39] Stuttgart ed., ll. 1462 ff. This seems to have been a philosophical and literary commonplace from the time of Socrates to that of Milton. See below, pp. 294 ff.

however, for he uncovered his father while he slept. Here the account agrees with that of the *Renner*. Caxton's chess book likewise goes back to Cain as the source of churlship. Cain was doomed to be the first laborer because he slew Abel in a dispute over whose wife was fairer.[40] In the next breath, however, the author tells us that God ordained labor because Adam sinned.

An equally surprising explanation of the origin of classes is that of the story of God's visit to Eve and her unlike children, told by Mantuan, by Hans Sachs and other sixteenth-century German writers, and also by Alexander Barclay. The divine ordination of the estates in that version, as we have seen, is based on the physical appearance of the children: the comely ones became men of rank; and the ugly ones became laborers.

This story is scoffed at by Faustus, one of the shepherds in Barclay's fifth eclogue, and he gives what he calls the true explanation of the origin of lordship. Lordship grew out of labor, he says, for shepherds and plowmen were created first, not last, and lords were no distinct and separate creation. The descendants of Cain and Abel, the first laborers, were promoted to high estate. Lydgate, also, in a "Chaptile / descryvyng how prynces beyng hedis of ther comountees sholde have noble chevalrie true iuges &c ther commounte to governe &c," reminds princes who disdain their subjects that all lordship first rose out of labor. All fame, all power still rests on the labor of the people and is non-existent without it. Where would emperors and kings be without their commons and without clerks to write histories of their glory? Even the Nine Worthies

Be low labour off comouns was first reised.[41]

The Quadrilogue invectif and the *Complaynte of Scotlande* reaffirm the idea in the lament of the third son, the commons, to the mothers, France and Dame Scotia. They have called him the youngest. He says he is not the youngest, but the oldest. He

[40] Ed. Axon, p. 76.   [41] *Fall of Princes*, ed. Bergen, Part II, p. 222.

created the state of the other two sons, nobility and clergy. Instead of being despised and oppressed by his brothers, he should be honored and aided. He was born long before them. The nobles and clergy "hed bot pure lauboraris to there predecesouris." Now, however, they profess to be gentlemen and look down on laborers as ignorant, boorish slaves. They should go back to the descendants of Adam, all of whom were laborers, when they make up their genealogies. Instead of glorying in themselves they should glory in labor, whence they sprang. They seem to think they are descended from the angels and archangels—even as the treatise on coat armor implies that they are. The third brother marvels that they can be so proud, since the "fyrst genologe of al the nobillis that hes bene sen the varld began, hes been pure lauberaris and mecanik craftis men."[42] Similarly the ploughman in Rastell's interlude *Of Gentleness and Nobility* scorns the knight's claims to gentility because of his ancestor's possessions and ascribes the origin of nobility to a churlish desire on the part of a few to gather goods:

> For when Adam delved and Eve span,
> Who was then a gentleman?
> But then came the churl and gatherèd good,
> And there began first the gentle blood;
> And I think verily ye do believe
> That we came all of Adam and Eve.[43]

These few got their wealth by extortion, the ploughman adds:

> For when people first began to increase,
> Some gave themselves all to idleness,
> And would not labour, but take by violence
> That other men gat by labour and diligence.
> Then they that laboured were fain to give
> Them part of their gettings in peace to live,
> Or else for their lands, money a portion;
> So possession begun by extortion.[44]

[42] *Complaynt of Scotlande,* ed. Murray, chap. XV, p. 125.
[43] Ed. Farmer, p. 449.
[44] *Ibid.,* p. 453.

The most frequent explanation of the origin of lordship is that of inherent gentleness. This inherent gentleness was recognized by the people, who thereupon bestowed certain properties and dignities upon those who possessed it. In other words, lordship rose through consent of the people. This is the substance of the knight's refutation of the argument of Rastell's ploughman that nobility rose out of the selfish monopoly of possessions by a few. In the beginning all things were held in common. As people increased in number, however, each man desired property, and strife arose. The wise ancestors of the knight studied to make laws to insure peace. The people recognized their virtues and rewarded them:

> The people, perceiving then their goodness,
> Their great wit, discretion, and gentleness,
> Were content to give them part of the profit
> Coming of their lands, which they did get,
> As corn, cattle and such things as they won.
> But after, when that coin of money began,
> They changed those revenues, and were content
> To give them in money an annual rent.
> So for their good and virtuous conditions
> They came first to lands and possessions;
> So possessions began, and were first found
> Upon a good and reasonable ground.[45]

To be sure, not all descendants of those who have shown themselves worthy of the estate of nobility have properly maintained that estate. They have often shown all the characteristics of the churl: ignorance, ingratitude, and stinginess; and several writers recommend that those that are no longer of gentle nature should be thrust from their estate to that of base-born commons.[46] There they might do what they are best fitted for: tending the cattle and cultivating the fields. No more com-

[45] *Ibid.*, p. 452.

[46] Étienne de Fougères' *Le Livre de manières,* ll. 577 f.; Vintler's *Die Pluemen der Tugent,* ll. 6624 ff. (ll. 6626-6931 are Vintler's own addition to his source) ; *The Complaynt of Scotlande,* pp. 149 ff.

plete account of this theory of the origin of lordship can be found than that of Sir Thomas Elyot in his *Boke Named the Governour*:[47]

Fyrst, that in the begynnyng, whan private possessions and dignitie were gyven by the consent of the people, who than had all thinge in commune, and equalitie in degree and condition, undoubtedly they gave the one and the other to him at whose vertue they mervailed, and by whose labour and industrie they received a commune benefite, as of a commune father that with equall affection loved them. And that promptitude or redinesse in employinge that benefite was than named in englisshe gentilnesse, as it was in latine *benignitas*, and in other tonges after a semblable signification, and the persones were called gentilmen, more for the remembraunce of their vertue and benefite, than for discrepance of astates. Also it fortuned by the providence of god that of those good men were ingendred good children, who beinge brought up in vertue, and perceivinge the cause of the advauncement of their progenitours, endevoured them selfes by imitation of vertue, to be equall to them in honour and autoritie; by good emulation they retained stille the favour and reverence of people. And for the goodnesse that proceded of suche generation the state of them was called in greke *Eugenia*, whiche signifiethe good kinde or lignage, but in a more briefe maner it was after called nobilitie, and the persones noble, whiche signifieth excellent, and in the analogie or signification it is more ample than gentill, for it containeth as well all that whiche is in gentilnesse, as also the honour or dignitie therefore received, whiche be so annexed the one to the other that they can nat be seperate.

Such is the proper ideal for the "governour," to whom Elyot addresses his work. Let him grow in true gentility that he may honestly maintain his estate. The *Complaynte of Scotlande* gives exactly the same explanation, more briefly: "Of this sort began the fyrst nobilnes ande gentreis in the varld, for thai that var vailȝeant, thai var reput for nobilis ande gentil men, ande thai that var vicius & couuardis, var reput for vilainis ande carlis."[48] This was the custom of the Carthaginians, Romans, Macedonians, ancient Germans, Scythians. Mordecai and Joseph were

[47] Ed. Croft, II, 26 ff.   [48] Ed. Murray, chap. XVII, pp. 146 f.

ennobled for their virtue. The degenerate son of Scipio Africanus was degraded.

This exempil of scipio makkis manifest, that na man can mereit or can be capabil of nobilnes or gentreis bot gyf tha be verteous. There for that stait of gentreis is ane accidental qualite, in sa far as it may cum til ane persoune be his vertu, and he maye be degradit fra it for his vice.

A nobleman's coat of arms represents his gentility, and he should take care, therefore, that he conduct himself as his arms describe his estate.

Later writers, like Smith and Bodin, mention the origin by creation by the king along with that of blood or birth. The beautiful theories of Elyot are, of course, not adhered to in practice, and the later works have a matter-of-fact tone that contrasts strongly with his idealism. Dukes, marquises, earls, viscounts, and barons are either created by the king, says Smith, or they come to those honors by being the eldest sons.[49] Knights are similarly created, usually, however, for some service.[50] Gentlemen are those that blood makes noble—those whose ancestors have been notable in riches or virtues. If they can, they maintain the wealth of their ancestors; if not, they do so as long as possible, "till the gilt be worne away" from the copper within. The king may create gentlemen, too, if he so desires. But ordinarily he does not, "for as for gentlemen, they be made good cheape in England." Anyone who can "live idly, and without manuall labour" is taken for a gentleman.[51] The class very obviously has not the dignity or honor or fixity of which Elyot wrote. Of the two types—the gentleman by blood and the gentleman by creation—Selden says the gentleman by blood is civilly the better, but that the gentleman by creation may be the better morally because less debauched and a person of greater worth.

[49] Ed. Alston, Book I, chap. XVII, p. 31.
[50] *Ibid.*, Book I, chap. XVIII, p. 33.
[51] *Ibid.*, Book I, chap. XX, p. 40.

5. THE CHARACTERISTICS OF TRUE NOBILITY

Along with the discussion of the origin of nobility in the world goes much speculation, especially in the later literature of estates, as to the characteristics of true nobility, aside from that of the gentility on which most writers base the phenomenon of the estate of nobility. They usually preface their remarks with the assertion that nobility is not in blood, but in virtues and the grace of God. So *Fauvel*, the *Renner*, and *Die Pluemen der Tugent* take pains to point out, as we have seen. A favorite theme with Chaucer also is "gentilesse," the "vertuous living, that made hem gentil men y-called be."[52] Though the Franklin is an unlettered man and hence unable to theorize about gentility, the Wife of Bath sets forth the familiar "school-matter" about the futility of noble birth and the dependence of gentility upon virtue.[53] Lydgate, in the *Fall of Princes*, in several places dwells on the futility of noble birth; and Elyot, Starkey, Dekker, and Bodin reassert the doctrine in the sixteenth century. In discussing what other qualities constitute nobility, the writers include every conceivable good trait. Dudley's *Tree of Common Wealth* stresses the need of learning as well as riches and noble birth:

for be ye sure *it is not honorable bloude, and greate possessions, or rich apparel, that maketh the man honorable, himself being of unhonorable condic'ons*; and the more honorable in bloode that he is, the more noble in condic'ons ought he to be, and the more shame and dishono^r it is to him to be the contrarie, Ane therefore ye noble men, for the bett^r contynuaunce of yor bloode in hono^r, set yor childrẽ in youth, and that betymes, to learninge, vertue and conninge [knowledge], and at the leaste bringe them up in hono^r and vertue.[54]

Almost all writers stress the virtues of generosity, humility, and clean living. It is giving that makes a prince great, says Robert de Blois. Otherwise he is no better than one base-born.[55] Robert

---

[52] *Wife of Bath's Tale*, D 1122-23.
[53] *Ibid.*, ll. 109 ff.   [54] Ed. of 1859, p. 19.
[55] *L'Enseignement des princes*, ed. Ulrich, p. 46, ll. 1585 f.

de Blois' assertion that a good man of base birth is to be honored, not despised, and that the upright son of a veillein is
worth fifteen bad sons of a king was a medieval commonplace,
according to Langlois.[56] Even in the sixteenth century the *Complaynt of Scotlande* says: "ane sone of ane mechanyc plebien,
beand verteous, he is ane gentil man,"[57] though the idea was
probably only a pleasant theory, having little meaning in actual
practice. Besides being generous, the nobility should be more
upright than all other estates, be merciful and clement, arm
themselves against fleshly lusts, dress fitly, seek notable com-
panions, not be covetous or idle or deceitful, says Lydgate. They
should be merciful and "debonair," love humility and chastity,
hate falsity, and keep their word, says Caxton. The *Shyp of
Folys* advises anyone who would advance himself to high estate to have "mekenes and lyberalyte." The merchant in Rastell's interlude *Of Gentleness and Nobility* says gentility is evidenced by service to one's country, and the ploughman says
it consists of self-reliance. Elyot waxes almost poetic in his
picture of the proper "majesty" of the "governour." This
majesty is "a beautie or comelynesse in his countenance, lan-
gage and gesture apt to his dignite, and accomodate to time,
place, and company; whiche, like as the sonne doth his beames,
so doth it caste on the beholders and herers a pleasaunt and
terrible reverence."[58] With this elevated conception of nobility
the matter-of-fact tone of Smith, in his explanation of how the
king creates estates for service rendered or because of a certain
yearly revenue that makes them able to maintain the rank,
contrasts strangely, as does also Bodin's remark at the conclusion of his enumeration of the estates of society: "But we
have so described the orders of citisens, not so much that the
dignitie, as the condition of everie one of them might so the
better be understood."[59]

[56] *Ibid.*, p. 37, ll. 1247 f.   [57] Ed. Murray, p. 149.   [58] Ed. Croft, II, 12.
[59] English edition of 1606, Book III, p. 403.

Later writers of the literature of estates mention a require-
ment of nobility that medieval writers probably would never
have thought of, since the condition did not exist. This is the
stipulation that a lord must not do manual labor or engage in
trade or crafts. With the rise of the merchant class and the
artisans, no doubt many an impoverished member of the nobility debated the question of engaging in some money-making
enterprise himself. Rulers must be "maynteynyd in pompe and
plesure, and in quyat lyfe, wythout al travayle and bodyly
labur," says Cardinal Pole in Starkey's *Dialogue*, so that they
may diligently see to "the admynystratyon of justyce to the
hole commynalty."[60] Even as late as 1656, James Harrington's
Oceana also says that the nobility and gentry should devote
themselves to matters of state, since

there is somthing first in the making of a commonwealth, then in
the governing of it, and last of all in the leading of its armys; which
(tho there be great divines, great lawyers, great men in all professions) seems to be peculiar only to the genius of a gentleman. For
so it is in the universal series of story, that if any man has founded
a commonwealth, he was first a gentleman.[61]

To substantiate this rather doubtful assertion, Harrington
names, among others, Moses, who "had his education by the
daughter of Pharaoh," and the Gracchi, who "were the sons
of a father adorn'd with two triumphs." The source of this
new doctrine is obviously Aristotle's *Politics*, as Bodin indicates. By becoming craftsmen, he says, men of high estate lose
their nobility because, as Aristotle said, "they beeing mercenarie
men, and to be hired for wages, had quite lost the strength and
power of a noble and heroicall minde." *Ecclesiasticus* 38 and
Lycurgus and Romulus are cited to support this theory, and
then Bodin adds, "Truly *Plato, Aristotle, Appolonius Thyaneus*,
say, The trade of marchandise to be an enemie unto vertue."[62]

[60] Ed. Cowper, Part II, chap. II, p. 55.
[61] *Oceana and Other Works*, ed. John Toland, London, 1771, p. 53.
[62] English ed. of 1606, Book III, pp. 397, 399.

Bodin cites Aristotle pretty accurately, for Aristotle does say that "the citizens must not lead the life of mechanics or tradesmen, for such a life is ignoble and inimical to virtue. Neither must they be husbandmen, since leisure is necessary both for the development of virtue and the performance of political duties."[63]

In some pieces a similar injunction is put upon members of the clergy. The *Vision of William Concerning Piers the Plowman,* for example, adds that restriction to some others:

> Clerkes þat aren crouned · of kynde understondyng
> Sholde noþer swynke ne swete · ne swere at enquestes,
> Ne fyghte in no vauntwarde · ne hus fo greve;
>
> . . .
>
> Hit by-come for clerkes · crist for to serven,
> And knaves uncrouned · to cart and to worche.[64]

The *Mirrour for Magistrates,* in the Complaynt of Cadwallader, finds the estate of clergy best because they do not labor:

> They labour not at al, they knowe no kind of payne.[65]

Bodin, after quoting Aristotle on the proper activities of the nobility, adds that holy men, too, among the Greeks were forbidden to buy and sell.

Nevertheless, all estates must serve the commonwealth in some way; in other words, all must perform the labor peculiar to their calling.

> Chascun estat, le qu'il soit,
> Est ordiné au siecle ascun labour,[66]

says Gower. Lydgate's version of *Le Pélerinage de la vie humaine,* as we have seen, makes the Net-maker by the roadside tell Pilgrim that everyone must work according to his estate. *Richard the Redeles* finds the explanation of the deposition of

---

[63] *Politica,* ed. Jowett, 1921, Book VII, Sec. 9.
[64] C-text, ed. Skeat, Passus VI, pp. 85-86.
[65] Ed. Haslewood, I, 424.
[66] *Mirour de l'omme,* ed. Macaulay, p. 260, ll. 23617-18.

Richard II in his doing nothing but enjoy himself in a world where all must labor, even rulers of realms:

> It is not unknowen . to kunnynge leodis,
> That rewlers of rewmes . around all þe erthe
> Were not yffoundid at þe ffirst tyme
> To leve al at likynge . and lust of þe world,
> But to laboure on þe lawe . as lewde men on plowes.[67]

Latimer, preaching before the king, also maintains that all must labor, even the king: "Every man must labour, yea though he be a Kynge yet he muste labour, for I knowe no man hath a greater laboure then a Kynge. What is his labour? To studye goddes boke, to see yat there be no unpreachynge prelates in his realme, nor bribing Iudges, to se to all estates, to provyde for the poore, to see vittailes good chepe. Is not this a labour trowe ye?"[68] To Cardinal Pole's objections to the "idul route" that are found among nobility, clergy, and commons, Lupset replies that all need not labor, that if a few men work, the rest may live in idleness. Such a situation may never be, says Pole, for all were born to work in some way:

For man ys borne to be as a governour, rular, and dylygent tyllar and inhabytant of thys erthe; as some, by labur of body, to procure thyngys necessary for the mayntenance of mannys lyfe; some, by wysdome and pollycy, to kepe the rest of the multytude in gud ordur and cyvylyte. So that non be borne to thys edulnes and vanyte, to the wych the most parte of our pepul ys much gyven and bent; but al to exercyse themselfe in some fascyon.[69]

The prologue of Fitzherbert's *Boke of Husbandry* goes to Job and St. Paul for authority for the statement that all must labor and that he who does not may not eat:

Sit ista questio. This is the questyon, wherunto is everye manne ordeyned? And as Job saythe, *Homo nascitur ad laborem, sicut avis ad volandum*: That is to saye, a man is ordeyned and borne to do labour, as a bird is ordeyned to flye. And the Apostle saythe, *Qui*

---

[67] Ed. Skeat, p. 495.   [68] Arber *Reprint*, No. 13, p. 181.
[69] Starkey's *Dialogue*, ed. Cowper, Part II, p. 78.

non laborat, non manducet: Debet enim in obsequio dei laborare, qui de bonis eius vult manducare: That is to saye, he that laboureth not, shulde not eate, and he ought to labour and doo goddes warke, that wyll eate of his goodes or gyftes.

This is a severe text, says Fitzherbert, if it is taken literally, for it means that king, queen, lords spiritual and temporal should not eat unless they labor. But labor, by which Fitzherbert obviously means manual labor, is "uncomely, and not convenyente for suche estates." The only solution is that of Latimer: each must do the work suited to his station. This conclusion Fitzherbert finds in the "boke of the moralytes of the chesse," where any one who reads may see that every man, from the highest degree to the lowest, is ordained to some occupation: king, queen, bishops, knights, judges, yeomen. There one may read what is the proper work of each estate. Fitzherbert proceeds to detail the work of yeomen, namely husbandry.

The theory that in the beginning all estates were equal, or rather that there were no differences of degree, and that government consisted of a kind of communism, naturally followed the idea that nobility rose by consent of the people, who conferred it for recognized gentility. Some writers assert it boldly as fact. Others raise it as a debatable question. Still others brand it as false at the start. Those who adhere to the old idea of the divine ordination of estates have nothing to say about this more or less heretical theory. Those who have open minds to non-Christian political doctrine play with the theory with no small satisfaction. In a sermon on pride, the *Renner* suggests belief in equality. All classes are by nature kin, he says, and should live like brothers.[70] Gervais du Bus and Gower expressed the same idea, as we have seen. The author of the treatise on coat armor in the *Boke of St. Albans* is one who brands the idea as false: "A bonde man or a churle wyll say all we be cummyn of adam." But what of it? It is as ridiculous for the churl to remind him-

[70] Stuttgart ed., chap. III, ll. 527 f.

self of that as for Lucifer and his cohorts to say that all angels come from heaven. From the stock of Adam came both nobles and churls. To Dudley, too, in his *Tree of Common Wealth*, the idea of original equality is meaningless. In a sermon to the commons warning them of two figurative messengers, Discontent and Arrogance, he advises them to ignore the common talk of equality: "Therefore mynde yo^u not this purpose or intent, that is the equallitie of the mouldes betwene the nobles and you, nor the cognisaunce of the petegree from Adam, nor the indifferency of their soules in theire creacions."[71] Both messengers will tell them that they are "the children and right inherito^{rs} to Adam," as well as the nobles, and why should they toil like beasts while their equals, the nobles, have great honor, castles, manors, great holdings of land, and a life of ease? God ordained all estates, says Dudley, and God wills that they all keep to them. With More and Elyot and Starkey and the *Complaynt of Scotlande*, the theory enters the realm of philosophical controversy, untinged by biblical lore. More's communism, though first attacked by Elyot, is later recognized in no uncertain terms; for he speaks of the beginning, "whan private possessions and dignitie were gyven by the consent of the people, who than had all thinge in commune, and equalitie in degree and condition."[72] Cardinal Pole, in Starkey's *Dialogue,* is again plainly speaking by the book when he says that in the beginning man had no cities, towns, or religion, but lived in forests as beasts do now, until he realized that he was born "to hyar perfectyon then he applyd hymselfe unto," and so began to form ordinances and laws and to live in communities. Only then rose differences of degrees under three forms of government, monarchy, democracy, and aristocracy.[73] Similarly Dame Scotia, addressing her eldest son, the nobility, in the

[71] Ed. of 1859, p. 52.
[72] Ed. Croft, II, 27.
[73] Ed. Cowper, Part I, chap. I, p. 52.

Complaynt of Scotlande, described the good old days as a time when there was

no defferens of staitis . . . nothir in preeminens, dignite, superiorite, nor honour, for at that tyme al men var egal, & nocht partial nor devidit, for the pepil lyvit al to gydthir in ane tranquil & lovabil communite, ande thai left no thing to there posterite bot regrettis for the alteratione of that gude varld.

In those days living was simple: they ate acorns, wild berries, fruits, roots, and herbs, and drank water. They killed animals for food and used the skins for clothing. At that time there was none of the ceremony of precedence: "quha suld pas befor or behynd, furtht or in at the dur, nor ʒit quha suld have the dignite to vasche ther handis fyrst in the bassine, nor ʒit quha suld sit doune fyrst at the tabil." It was a long time after that "nature provokit them to begyn sum litil police." Then certain members of the community oppressed their neighbors, and government was necessary. Now they that pretend to be gentlemen are only "incivile vilainis," and they "call men vilains who never did a vilain act."[74]

6. The Meaning of "Commonwealth": Communism

The whole question of the meaning of the term *commonwealth* and of the desirability of communism in government is much discussed in the literature of estates. The Stoic attitude in ancient Greece, where slavery was taken for granted, had been that all men should be equal fellow-citizens of one great republic. Plato in the *Republic* had said that "no one should possess any private property if it can possibly be avoided." Cicero in his *De republica* had defined the commonwealth as the "wealth of the people," united by social instinct.[75] The early Christian communities were organized on communistic principles and were thus a constant source of irritation to the

[74] Ed. Murray, chap. XVII, pp. 145 ff.

[75] W. A. Dunning, *A History of Political Theories Ancient and Medieval,* New York, 1916, p. 120.

Empire under which they existed. Under the Roman Republic, Cato the Younger, Cicero, and Brutus had preached the doctrine, but with small effect in the presence of Caesar. Under the Empire, Seneca, chief minister of state, Marcus Aurelius, and later the chief justices Papinian, Paul, and Ulpian preached the doctrines of equality and universal brotherhood. The Justinian Code, formulated by the imperial jurists, chief of whom was a Stoic, gave concrete form to this idea: "all men are born free and equal by natural law."[76] Through the teachings of Christ, if not always through the dogma of Christianity, the idea was passed on to modern times with far-reaching effects. In Caxton's *Game and Playe of the Chesse,* translated from an earlier French source, which in turn came from the Latin of the late thirteenth or early fourteenth century, appear the twelve good laws of Lycurgus, one of which was that all things should be held in common; and later the Trojans are cited as a people of "one herte and one sowle," interested first of all in the "comyn prouffit." Further evidence is found in the life of monks and friars:

And also hit is to be supposyd that such as have theyr goodes comune & not propre is most acceptable to god / For ellys wold not thise religious men as monkes freris chanons observantes & all other avowe hem & kepe the wilfull poverte that they ben professid too/.

To add final weight to these arguments, Plato is quoted:

And acordynge thereto we rede in plato whiche sayth y^t the cyte is well and Iustely governid and ordeyned in the whiche no man may saye by right · by custome · ne by ordenance / this is myn / but I say to the certaynly that syn this custome cam forth to say this is myn / And this is thyn / no man thought to preferre the comyn prouffit so moche as his owen/.[77]

Barclay's *Shyp of Folys* similarly commends communism: in the golden age, when poverty was a blessing and an honor to all degrees,

[76] *Ibid.,* p. 128.　　　　　[77] Ed. Axon, pp. 88-89.

Than was theyr fode scas, theyr lyvynge lyberall
Theyr labour comon, they knew no covetyse
All thynge was comon than amonge them all
The lawe of nature from them expellyd vyce.[78]

Sir Thomas More's pronouncements in favor of communism are very familiar, and it is with him that the question gets well under way in English literature of estates. In Utopia, Raphael Hythloday tells Peter Giles and the author, "all thinges be common," and as a result "everye man hath aboundaunce of every thinge." Where every man calls his own whatever he has got together, or, in other words, where private ownership exists, it will always be true that "a fewe devide among them selfes all the whole riches, be there never so muche abundaunce and stoore," and "to the residewe is lefte lacke and povertye." Usually this latter sort are more worthy to enjoy wealth than the wealthy, because they are lowly, simple, and industrious. Though private ownership may never be done away with altogether, a law should be made that no man should possess above a certain measure of ground and have in his stock above a prescribed amount of money. To these opinions of Hythloday, More opposes objections:

. . . me thinketh that men shal never there live wealthelye, where all thinges be commen. For howe can there be abundaunce of gooddes, or of any thing, where every man withdraweth his hande from labour? Whome the regard of his owne gaines driveth not to worke, but the hope that he hath in other mens travayles maketh him slowthfull.

The result would be continual sedition and bloodshed. In his ensuing discussion of how all things are managed in Utopia, Hythloday answers More's arguments. In other places, men talk of the "commonwealth," but every man seeks his own gain. "Here where nothinge is private, the commen affaires bee earnestlye loked upon." And, as a result, "thoughe no man have anye thinge, yet everye man is ryche." There they can live

[78] Ed. of 1509, Folium CLXXII; Jamieson ed., II, 103.

joyfully, without fear of poverty for themselves and their families. Those that become sick or old and unable to work also need not worry. Who would be so bold as to compare the justice of other nations with that of Utopia?

Is not this an unjust and unkynde publyque weale, whyche gyveth great fees and rewardes to gentlemen, as they call them, and to gold-smythes, and to suche other, whiche be either ydle persones, or els onlye flatterers, and devysers of vayne pleasures: And of the contrary parte maketh no gentle provision for poore plowmen, coliars, laborers, carters, yronsmythes, and carpenters: without whome no commen wealthe can continewe?[79]

A Supplication of the Poore Commons, perhaps by Brinkelow, also preaches communism as Christ's form of government: "After whose commyng, the Christian sort had all thynges commune, so that no man toke anye thynge for hys oune, Actes iiii." The rise of cities banished communism, says the writer.[80]

To Elyot, Cheke, and Bodin this talk of the virtues of communism is a target for necessary opposition. "Commonwealth" does not mean "that every thinge shulde be to all men in commune, without discrepance of any astate or condition," says Elyot,[81] and those who suppose that it does are "moved more by sensualite than by any good reason or inclination to humanite." Not all men are alike in virtues and capacities, he argues,[82] and therefore they cannot all be of one estate. In understanding, for example, one excels another and "so shulde the astate of his persone be avanced in degree or place where understandynge may profite. . . . And unto men of suche vertue by very equitie appertaineth honour, as theyr iuste rewarde and duetie, whiche by other mennes labours must also be mainteined according to their merites." Laborers, artisans, and husbandmen do not labor for their superiors only, but also for their own necessity. But those of the estate of "governour" acquire nothing for their own necessities by the exercise of their pow-

[79] Bohn ed., pp. 71, 74-75, 184-85.
[80] E.E.T.S., ext. ser., XIII, 71.
[81] Ed. Croft, I, 2.
[82] *Ibid.*, I, 5 ff.

ers, and employ all their energies only for the preservation of their inferiors. Moreover, among those inferiors differences of degree are necessary lest the idle person participate equally with him who is industrious:

wherin shulde be none equalite, but therof shulde procede discourage, and finally disolution for lacke of provision. Wherfore it can none other wyse stande with reason, but that the astate of the persone in preeminence of lyvynge shulde be esteemed with his understandyng, labour, and policie: where unto muste be added an augmentation of honour and substaunce; whiche nat onely impresseth a reverence, wherof procedethe due obedience amonge subiectes, but also inflameth men naturally inclined to idelnes or sensuall appetite to coveyte lyke fortune, and for that cause to dispose them to studie or occupation. Nowe to conclude my fyrst assertion or argument, where all thynge is commune, there lacketh ordre; and where ordre lacketh, there all thynge is odiouse and uncomly.

The arguments of Sir John Cheke[83] are likewise against all such proposed equality: equality would mean the overthrow of labor and utter decay of work in the realm, for the slothful will not labor if they need not; it would also take away from the industrious all hope of coming to better estate; those of greater abilities would be discouraged from using them by lack of reward. The same arguments are given by Bodin in his *Six Bookes of a Commonweale*, with the additional one that equality breeds, not friendship, but jealousy, hatred, quarrels, seditions, and civil wars. Though "many antient law givers did equally divide the goods and lands among the subiectes, as in our time *Thomas Moore* Chancellor of England in his Commonweale sayth, That the only way of safetie for an estate, is when as men live in common," in this theory there can be no propriety or worth. Perhaps Spenser's attitude toward the theory in his *Mother Hubberds Tale* is likewise that of disapproval, for he puts praise of it into the mouth of the crafty Fox, as he propounds his plan to his fellow-climber, the Ape. Since they are free-born, why should they allow themselves to dwell in "servile base subjection":

[83] *The Hurt of Sedition,* ed. of 1641, pp. 8 f.

And as we bee sonnes of the world so wide,
Let us our fathers heritage divide,
And chalenge to our selves our portions dew
Of all the patrimonie, which a few
Now hold in hugger mugger in their hand,
And all the rest doo rob of good and land.
For now a few have all, and all have nought,
Yet all be brethren ylike dearly bought.
There is no right in this partition,
Ne was it so by institution
Ordained first, ne by the law of Nature,
But that she gave like blessing to each creture,
As well of worldly livelode as of life,
That there might be no difference nor strife,
Nor ought cald mine or thine: thrice happie then
Was the condition of mortall men.
That was the golden age of Saturne old,
But this might better be the world of gold:
For without golde now nothing wilbe got.[84]

The Fox has picked up all the current political philosophy, even to the new authority found in the "law of Nature."

Sincere praise of communism occurs again, however, in the mid-sixteenth century. Robert Crowley, a communist like More, shows his approval of it by satirizing the opposition, as well as in his strong plea for the commons:

For Officers and al
    do seke their owne gaine,
But for the wealth of the commons
    not one taketh paine.
An hell with out order,
    I maye it well call,
Where everye man is for him selfe,
    And no manne for all.[85]

Such magistrates, wealthy themselves, find the "paisant knaves" guilty of sedition because they desire more wealth. The commons:

---

[84] *Complete Works*, ed. Grosart, Edinburgh, 1882, III, 104.
[85] *One and Thyrtye Epigrammes*, "Of Alleyes," ed. Cowper, p. 11.

wold have al men like themselves, they would have al thinges commune! Thei would not have us maisters of that which is our owne!
They wil appoint us what rent we shal take for our groundes! We
must not make the beste of oure owne! These are ioly felowes! Thei
wil caste doune our parckes, & laie our pastures open! Thei wil have
the law in their own handes! They wil play the kinges! . . . And because they wold have al comone, we wil leave them nothing.[86]

By thus quoting the opposition, Crowley shows the folly of it.
The *Complaynt of Scotlande* also briefly praises communism by
praising the "goldin varld" of the past when there was no difference in estates and "al men var egal."[87] Cardinal Pole, in
Starkey's *Dialogue,* with his usual moderation, leans to neither
side, but says that any form of government is good so long as its
aim is the "commyn wele of the hole."[88]

Justification of the inequalities of estates by analogy with
inequalities found in all nature is a common theme in sixteenth-
century English literature of estates.

But let us all consider that god hath set a due order by grace betwene
himself and aungells, and betwen angle and angell, and by reason
betwene Aungell and man, and betwene man and man, & beast &
beast, and by nature only betwene beaste and beaste, wch order from
the highest pointe to the lowest, god willeth us fervently to kepe,
w^thout any enterprise to the contrary,

says Edmund Dudley.[89] Sir Thomas Elyot, to the justification
inherent in differences of capacities in human beings, adds further evidence from nature:

Whereof nature ministreth to us examples abundauntly, as in bees,
(wherof I have before spoken in the firste boke) cranes, redde dere,
wolfes, and divers other foules and bestis, whiche herdeth or flocketh,
(to longe here to be rehersed), amonge whom is a governour or
leader, towarde whome all the other have a vigilant eye, awaytinge
his signes or tokens, and according therto preparinge them selfe moste
diligently. If we thinke that this naturall instinction of creatures
unreasonable is necessary and also commendable, howe farre out of

[86] *The Way to Wealth,* ed. Cowper, p. 143.
[87] Ed. Murray, p. 144.　　　　[88] Ed. Cowper, p. 53.
[89] *Tree of Commonwealth,* ed. of 1859, p. 52.

reason shall we iudge them to be that wolde exterminate all superiori-
tie, extincte all governaunce and lawes, and under the coloure of holy
scripture, whiche they do violently wraste to their purpose, do en-
devour a confusion inevitable, and to be in moche wars astate than
the afore named beestes?[90]

Such a state of affairs would mean anarchy, and like beasts men
would slay one another. Fulke Greville cites the example of
order and degrees in the planets:

> And to confirm this inequality
> Have not the feignèd gods in orbs above
> Gloriously plac'd that specious hierarchy
> Whose influence doth inferior spirits move;
> And in slack or swift courses, high or low,
> The divers honours of each being show?[91]

Money or property as a new basis for the estates and government of the realm is indicated by such late writers as Smith,
Bodin, Selden, and Harrington. No such basis is even suggested
in the literature of estates of the Middle Ages, though no doubt
even then landholdings or other property were the real cause
for elevation rather than the divine ordination by which most
of the writers of the time explain the phenomenon of class distinctions. The form of government will follow the distribution
of property, says Harrington: "where there is inequality of
estates there must be inequality of power; and where there
is inequality of powere there can be no commonwealth." To
keep equality in the foundation of the government, an agrarian
law should limit the amount of property which may be held by
one man. To keep equality in the superstructure of the government, Harrington recommends rotation or succession to the
magistracy secured by "the suffrage of the people given by the
ballot."[92]

7. OTHER THEORIES OF GOVERNMENT

Other theories of state besides those relating to communism
are, of course, frequently introduced into the literature of es-

[90] Ed. Croft, II, 210-11.   [91] *Works,* ed. Grosart, I, 119, stanza 324.
[92] *Oceana and Other Works,* ed. Toland, 1771, p. 53.

tates. Not much discussion of these theories appears in the Middle Ages, however, except as the controversy between Church and State is introduced. Naturally, since the literature of estates is the literature of feudalism, it reflects the organization of feudal society in its lists of classes and their abuses. Then, as feudalism develops into monarchy, and the Church opposes the claims of State, the resultant conflict is referred to occasionally in the literature of estates of the time. Gervais du Bus in *Le Roman de Fauvel,* for example, laments the fact that temporal power is in command and that spiritual power obeys. To gain favor, all ranks of the clerical world flatter temporal power. The Church, once the sun, is eclipsed now by temporal power, the moon. Fauvel has reversed the world. God established the Church with St. Peter as his vicar. St. Peter's life was holy. Now the pope is different. He is interested only in florins and so sacrifices the Church to the pleasure of the king. Alas, that the Church is now tributary to the king. With sixteenth-century English writers of the literature of estates, the question of the best form of government becomes an important and much-discussed theme, especially for those who favor monarchy. Those who do not are the idealist proponents of communism whom we have already examined. The foes of communism are agreed that monarchy is best, with sovereignty vested in a king. There is little talk of the virtues of democracy or aristocracy, probably because a subject of the Tudors saw small opportunity to prefer either, and feudalism was dead or rapidly dying. Greville, as we have seen,[93] in his praise of monarchy takes a thrust at democracy and republics and communism. To Cheke, Elyot, Hooker, Dekker, Breton, and Bodin, also, monarchy seems best. Some one must rule; not all can command. In his chapter "That one soveraigne governour ought to be in a publike weale. And what damage hath happened where a multitude hath had equal authorite without any sov-

[93] Page 209 above.

eraygne,"[94] Elyot likens the monarch to the owner of a castle or fortress. If there were more than one owner, there would be neglect and contention and finally ruin. Greece and Italy are cited as examples of such a fate. Neither a tyrant is desirable, on the one hand, nor communism on the other. For when the commons once throw down their governor,

they ordre every thynge without iustice, only with vengeance and crueltie: and with incomparable difficultie and unneth by any wysedome be pacified and brought agayne to ordre. Wherfore undoubtedly the best and most sure governance is by one kynge or prince, whiche ruleth onely for the weale of his people to hym subiecte: and that maner of governaunce is beste approved, and hath longest continued, and is most auncient.

The reader wonders on what authority he comes to his last conclusion. Richard Hooker, too, finds peace and order dependent on one monarch: "Which thing is no way better done, than if the king, their common parent, whose care is presumed to extend most indifferently over all, to bear the chiefest sway in the making of laws which all must be ordered by."[95] To aid him, the king has Parliament, but he bears chief sway. Bodin, firm supporter of monarchy, says the king must be supreme; otherwise, if he is subject to assemblies and decrees of the people, "hee should neither bee king nor soveraigne: and the Commonwealth neither realme nor monarchie, but a meere Aristocratie of many lords in power equall."[96] His chief argument for monarchy is that in case factions arise ιo oppose one another, in a monarchy, where one man is judge of all controversies, the matter is soon settled. In other kinds of states, there is no such course open, but "the matter is still in the end put to voyces."[97] A monarchy, moreover, is natural. Many governors hinder one another.[98]

[94] Ed. Croft, I, chap. II, 8.
[95] *Of the Laws of Ecclesiastical Polity*, ed. Keble, II, Book VII, 258.
[96] English ed. of 1606, Book I, p. 95.
[97] *Ibid.*, Book III, p. 404.   [98] *Ibid.*, Book VI, p. 718.

Various ideas are expressed as to the authority of the king. To Dekker, Breton, Bodin, the king is God on earth. To Lyndsay and Selden, he is only an officer. In *Ane Pleasant Satyre of the Thrie Estaitis,* Lyndsay makes Divyne Correctioun say:

> Quhat is ane king? nocht bot ane officiar,
> To cause his leiges live in equitie.[99]

And Selden, almost a century later, in a time when the divine rights theory was strongest, says practically the same thing: "A King is a thing men have made for their own sakes, for quietness sake."[100] Starkey makes Cardinal Pole insist that a king should be chosen by election, since a king who comes to the throne by succession may be unworthy and usually abuses his power.[101] Bodin is as certain that monarchy should be by succession, not by lot or choice, since, he says, elected rulers squander their power, and since "a man of base degree suddenly mounted unto the highest degree of honour, thinketh himself to bee a god upon earth."[102] The fact that a monarch may prove a tyrant is recognized by several writers with the frequent medieval conclusion that God has ordained him and that therefore he must be endured, in the hope that some day God will see fit to remove him. The fate of tyrants has usually been sad, they point out, and so there is ground for hope. Let the tyrant beware, says Greville, lest he rouse scorn and malice instead of good will. If a tyrant is evil, however, his subjects must wait for divine intervention:

> But if Pow'r will exceed, then, let mankind
> Receive oppression, as fruits of their error;
> Let them, again, live in their duties shrin'd,
> As their safe haven from the winds of terror.
> Till He that rais'd Pow'r to mow man's sin down,
> Please for Pow'rs own sin, to pluck off her crown.[103]

[99] Ed. Laing, II, 85.   [100] *Table-talk,* ed. Arber, p. 60.
[101] *Dialogue,* ed. Cowper, Part I, chap. IV, p. 101.
[102] English ed. of 1606, Book VI, p. 725.
[103] *Works,* ed. Grosart, I, 74, stanza 191.

The author of the *Complaynt of Scotlande* reveals a mild and safe form of protest practiced by the commons, instead of mere passivity: the only recourse open to them is "to gar our vyvis & bayrnis pray nycht and daye to send ane mischeif on hym, and to send hym schort lyve dais, & to send ane uthir gude prince in his place." But even this they must do in secret and they must say "God save his grace" in public.[104] Of course, by Milton's time no such theory of non-resistance suffices. In his *Tenure of Kings and Magistrates* he describes the relation between ruler and ruled as purely voluntary and cites authorities and historical instances of deposing and killing tyrants.

Some of the writers of the literature of estates, even the earlier ones, express views that foreshadow those of Milton, and one realizes that Milton's position was after all not startlingly new. Its fundamental principles were those of the more liberal political theorists of the Middle Ages and the Renaissance. The idea of popular sovereignty, namely, that the will of the people is the source of power, was current, of course, among the ancients, as is evidenced in Greek political law and philosophy, in the Romano-Canonical doctrine of Corporations, and in the Germanic fellowship idea of a community.[105] The medieval Church, however, told a far different story of the origin of the government and the sovereignty of lordship: the Church taught, as was shown above, that the fall of man produced a state of sin and inequality, in which government was divinely instituted as a necessary restraint. The conflict of theories grew stronger. Those who doubted the theory of the Church could point to the social contract between overlord and people among the Germanic tribes, to the contract made between David and the people of Israel (II Kings 3), and to the theories of the Roman jurists. The idea of popular sovereignty and of the origin

[104] Ed. Murray, chap. XV, p. 133.
[105] See von Gierke, *Political Theories of the Middle Ages,* ed. of 1900, pp. 37 ff.

of government in a social contract therefore became more and more current, first in the realm of temporal power and then in the Church, also. Monarchy, in this sense, meant that the people ruled their ruler, that he was merely their representative —an idea that left little difference between monarchy and democracy. The pope merely represented the congregation of the Church, the emperor represented the Empire, and all lesser magistrates similarly represented the group to which they were responsible. The Church gradually abandoned the idea that the State had its origin in sin and evolved the theory that the State was a natural growth, sprung from the natural need of man for social life. God was still the source of that need, to be sure, and so God was the remote cause of the State. But the actual formation of the State was an act of will on the part of man. This social contract theory, that seems so modern, was well known in the Middle Ages.[106] Some theorists went so far as to declare, like Milton, that if a ruler neglected his duties, the people might depose him.[107]

In the literature of estates appear suggestions of this theory. The poem "Love God, and Drede," of about 1400, warns those in authority to beware of "tyrauntrye," for "The puple is godes, and not ʒoures."[108] The poem "Treuth, Reste, and Pes," of 1401, also pleads for just dealing, with the assertion that the commons make the kingdom: "A kyngdom in comouns lys . . . Þe puple, ne ryches, nys not ʒoures: Al is goddis, and so be ʒe."[109] Again in "Dede is Worchyng" of 1414 the lords are reminded that "Þe puple is goddis, and noʒt ʒoures."[110] The social contract theory as explained by Elyot and the author of

---

[106] Von Gierke, p. 187, cites Cicero's definition of State as a *societas* and names Thomas Aquinas, John of Paris, and Aeneas Sylvius as some who discuss the social contract theory.

[107] See von Gierke, pp. 43 f.

[108] *Political and Other Poems,* ed. Kail, p. 1, stanza 3.

[109] *Ibid.,* p. 12, stanzas 13 and 17.

[110] *Ibid.,* p. 57, stanza 7.

the *Complaynt of Scotlande* has been indicated above.[111] It is substantially the same as that of the *Fall of Princes* and the *Shyp of Folys* that lordship rose from the consent of the commons. The *Leviathan* of Hobbes sets forth the social contract theory in no uncertain terms. Published in 1651, when the commonwealth seemed secure, it was savory doctrine. The bill against blasphemous literature which passed the House of Commons in 1667 named the *Leviathan* as one of two such books. The natural state of man is a state of war, says Hobbes, out of which he rescues himself by means of a contract with his neighbor. To secure such peace, all men must give up their rights to one man or to an assembly of men—in other words, form another contract with a ruler or ruling body, which will henceforth bind all alike.[112] In Harrington's *Oceana* of 1656 three new orders are evolved: "the senate debating and proposing, the people resolving, and the magistracy executing."[113] The day of feudal monarchy is past.

A good deal of freedom of opinion is manifest concerning the best form of government in the works of such writers as Smith and Bodin. The government must be according to the nature of the people, says Smith.[114] Government constantly changes, he says in another place:[115]

for never in all pointes one common wealth doth agree with an other, no nor long time any one common wealth with it selfe. For al chaungeth continually to more or lesse, and still to diverse and diverse orders, as the diversity of times do present occasion, and the mutabilitie of mens wittes doth invent and assay newe wayes, to reforme and amende that werein they do finde fault.

And Bodin is of somewhat the same opinion: monarchies become popular "estates," popular "estates" become monarchies, monarchies become aristocracies, aristocracies become mon-

---

[111] Pages 171-72.

[112] Ed. Henry Morley, 2d ed., London, 1886, pp. 82 f.

[113] Ed. Toland, 1771, p. 51.   [114] Ed. Alston, Book I, chap. XV.

[115] *Ibid.*, Book I, chap. XVIII, p. 33.

archies, aristocracies become popular estates, and popular estates become aristocracies. Most of these changes occur in September, as can be detected by astrology, numerology, and other means.[116] It is impossible to combine two types of commonwealths. Plato said his was a combination, but it was a "mere popular estate."[117]

The analogy frequently drawn in the literature of estates between the state and the human body is more characteristic of medieval political theory than are the ideas drawn from Plato and Aristotle. It fits the chief tenets of the philosophy of the medieval estates perfectly. No one had to cast aside his belief in the divine origin of the estates and of their separate duties if he thought of society as a body with different members serving each other. The authority of St. Paul, moreover, gave it added weight. The magnificent picture drawn by Nicholas of Cusa, of mankind so organized, was typical of the medieval desire for pictorial representation of philosophical truth as well as of the medieval philosophy itself. The difficulty that arose in the existence of two heads and two bodies, temporal and spiritual, he neatly disposed of, as did some of his predecessors, by making a distinction between body and soul. For every temporal member of the body of mankind he found a corresponding spiritual office, representing the soul of that member: the papacy represented the soul in the brain; the patriarchate, the soul in ears and eyes; the archiepiscopate, the soul in the arms; the episcopate, the soul in the fingers; and the curacy, the soul in the feet. At the same time, the emperor, kings, lords, and commons represented the corporal parts themselves. Out of this analogy rose many political theories, such as those of the dependence of members, the necessity of a head, and the necessary differences of rank. John of Salisbury, Thomas Aquinas, Aegidius Colonna, Marsilius of Padua, William of Ockham,

[116] English ed. of 1606, Book IV, pp. 409, 453.
[117] *Ibid.*, Book II, p. 194.

Dante, John of Paris, Gerson, in fact most medieval philosophers adopted the analogy and pushed it as far as it would go.[118]

8. The Duties of Each Estate

More important than all the theories of lordship and government in the literature of estates, however, are those relating to the duties of the various estates—more important because of the large amount of attention devoted to them. Like the theory of the divine origin of estates, they run through most of the literature of this type. Scarcely a writer fails to mention them, either to state them in a line or two or to discuss them at great length. When God ordained the three estates of the world, he gave them definite duties—so the theory goes in its simplest form—which must be done if society is to survive. The nobility were ordained to defend all, the clergy were ordained to pray for all, and the commons were ordained to provide food for all. Let each member of each estate be content with his degree and do his duty, lest, by vain striving to rise to higher estate and by thus failing to do the duty to which God ordained him, he disturb and help to destroy the necessary order of society. To be sure, members of all estates, all writers say, are failing to do their prescribed duties and the times are bad— not at all like the good old times when the nobility defended, the clergy prayed, and the commons labored. Various causes for the change are given, as well as the excuses of the estates themselves. The remedies are not so easy to find and so are fewer in number. The typical defections of the times and the suggested remedies will be treated in the following chapters. It remains for us here to examine the more or less static philosophy of the necessary fixity of estates that characterizes almost all the literature of estates.

The duties of the estates of the world constitute the whole theme of Étienne de Fougères in his *Le Livre des manières*. The

---

[118] See von Gierke, pp. 22 ff.

first part treats of "les devoirs des rois, des clercs, des eveques, des archeveques, des cardinaux, des chevaliers," and the second, of "les devoirs des vilains, des citoyens et des bourgeois, des dames et des demoiselles." In the opening lines of part two, the author states the duties of the classes very concisely:

> Li clerc deivent por toz orer,
> Li chevalier sanz demorer
> Deivent défendre et ennorer
> Et li païsant laborer,
>
> Terres arer, norir aumaille.[119]

So says Hugues de Berzé, also, in slightly different phraseology:

> Quant Diex nous ot d'enfer rescous,
> S'ordena trois Ordres de nous.
> La premiere fu, sanz mentir,
> De Provoire por Diex servir
> Es Chapeles et es Moustiers:
> Et l'autre fu des Chevaliers
> Por justicier les robéors:
> L'autre fu des laboréors.[120]

The Renclus de Molliens, after three lines similar to those of Hugues de Berzé, manages to sum up the duties of all estates in a single line:

> Labours de clerc est Dieu priier
> Et justiche de chevalier;
> Pain lor truevent li laborier.
> Chil paist, chil prie et chil deffent.[121]

Caxton's *Mirrour of the World* cites the authority of the old philosophers in another brief statement of the duties of the three estates:

The labourers ought to pourveye for the clerkes and knyghtes suche thinges as were nedeful for them to lyve by in the world honestly; and the knyghtes ought to defende the clerkis and the labourers,

[119] MS copy of MS 295, Library of Angers, stanzas CLXIX and CLXX, ll. 673 ff.

[120] Ed. Barbazan-Meon, p. 399, ll. 179 ff.

[121] Ed. van Hamel, p. 218, stanza CLVI, ll. 6 ff.

that ther were no wronge don to them; and the clerkis ought to enseigne and teche these ii maner of peple, and to adresse them in their werkis in suche wise that non doo thinge by whiche he sholde displese God ne lese his grace.[122]

Gascoigne's steel glass shows him the same duties for four estates, since the king's estate is now of enough importance to be listed separately.[123]

Usually, however, such concise statements of the duties of the estates only serve, in the longer pieces, to introduce the subject, and it is then expanded at some length. Gower, for example, in French, Latin, and English gives a detailed application of this philosophy of duties to the estates of his own time. Lydgate expands the theme in the *Fall of Princes* in his analogy between the organization of society and the human body. The speech of Reason in Passus VI of *Piers Plowman* is a sermon on the same theme. Caxton's chess book devotes much attention to what the various chess pieces should do if well played. In Crowley's twelve lessons in *The Voyce of the Laste Trumpet* the chief degrees in the three estates are taught their duties individually. Lyndsay, Starkey, and the author of the *Complaynt of Scotlande* all impress upon the three estates at great length the duties in which they are so miserably failing. Latimer is briefer, but more emphatic:

And as diligentelye as the husband man plougheth for the sustentacion of the bodye: so diligently muste the prelate and ministers labour for the fedinge of the soule. . . . Lette everie man do his owne busines, and folow his callying. Let the priest preache, and the noble man handle the temporal matters.

Most of the expanded discussions of the duties of the estates are, of course, too long to be quoted here. That of Étienne de Fougères is fairly typical, however, and a brief summary of it will perhaps serve to show how the rest treat the theme. What a spectacle kings make, he begins, they who are anointed with sacred oil, born protectors of so many people, but who spend

[122] Ed. Prior, chap. vi, p. 29.   [123] Ed. Cunliffe, II, 150.

their time hooting and trumpeting behind beasts in the chase!
Such exclamations over the defections of each estate prepare the
way for Étienne's sermons. A king has great responsibility, he
proceeds. He should forget his own good in that of the commonwealth; he should live for all, not for himself; he should
be generous; and above all he should protect Holy Church and
those who serve it, clergy, monks, nuns, no matter what the
garb.[124] The abuses of the clergy are notorious, but they must
be honored nevertheless. The bishops, archdeacons, and deans
who permit such abuses are more blameworthy than the priests
who commit them. The good bishop should be anxious for
the salvation of the souls of his flock, his justice should be
free, he should choose his clergy well, he should preach where-
ever he goes and then follow his own teaching, he should
gather funds for the poor.[125] The archbishop is a person of
great dignity, but he should love right, truth, peace, honor, and
charity. Even he should be humble.[126] Above all is the pope.
He should bear the sins of all, comfort the downhearted, pardon
the repentant, and exhort the rebellious.[127] Under him are the
cardinals, who are the court of last appeal. Let them not be
high-handed in their judgments and let them guard against
covetousness.[128]

But this is enough of the clergy, says Étienne, and he turns
to the laity. The knights ought to draw the sword to maintain
justice and defend the poor. Instead they oppress them in
every way. They rob them and lay waste their property and
spend their ill-gotten gains in dancing, feasting, tourneying.
They think of nothing else. They should cherish their people,
on whose labor they all live.[129]

Though Étienne pictures the sad lot of the peasant—his hard

[124] Stanzas XLI-XLIV, ll. 161-76.
[125] Stanzas LXXII, LXXVIII, LXXX, LXXXVI-VIII.
[126] Stanzas CII, CIII.   [127] Stanza CXVII.
[128] Stanzas CXXIX, CXXX, CXXXI.
[129] Stanzas CXXXV and CXLV.

work and spare living—he has a sermon for him, too. He loses his merit by rebelling against his lot and by trying to keep back the tithes he owes. He can't trick God. Let him have faith in God, giver of all good things, and God will repay him a hundred-fold. Let the peasant till the fields and provide food for knight and priest, who depend on him.[130] The citizens and burgesses should have true measures, avoid usury, go to church, and pay their tithes. Instead, trickery prevails among them.[131] All the tricks of the trades are exposed. The duties of women complete the list. There are good women and bad women. Bad women paint their faces, live in idleness, carry on amours, even make way with their husbands. There are plenty of such stories about women of all ranks.[132] But there are good women in the world, who love and serve and counsel their husbands, as is their duty, and rear their children with care. Such women are examples for all to follow.

Étienne's list of duties is typical, though in some of the later literature of estates the enumeration becomes more detailed as new defections arise to suggest new duties. In sixteenth-century English literature, discussion of remedies frequently becomes more important than enumeration of duties. Consciousness of feudal duties was gone, and so the sermonizing about what classes of society ought to do for each other was not very impressive. Nevertheless, the subject remains a part of the literature of estates to the end. Hooker and Cooper ironically assert that the estates of nobility and commons do their duties and they, of course, are not to be destroyed, whereas the estate of the bishops has failed to do theirs and must be done away with. Such false reasoning they then decry. The bishops are no more negligent than the other estates. Dekker's description of the Protestant army in *The Double PP* is a paean of praise

[130] Stanza CLXX.
[131] Stanzas CCI, CCII, CCXIX, CCXX.
[132] Stanzas CCXLIV and CCXLV.

for the king, clergy, judges, soldiers, merchants, seamen, husbandmen, and artisans, who do their separate duties voluntarily and gladly. Breton's address to all estates in *A Murmurer* is a sermon telling them to do their duties, and the duties are still remarkably like those of Étienne de Fougères, Hugues de Berzé, Gower, and Caxton. In the philosophic treatise of Smith, the duties become services rendered to the government, in the sense of Plato and Aristotle, rather than the God-ordained duties of feudalism.

If the estates of the world deliberately ignore their duties, what then? Medieval writers answer the question with lament and more sermons on the inevitable "discord" and "dyvysion" that follow such defection. For such a state of affairs sixteenth-century English writers have a new word—born of the politics of monarchy. Sedition, they call it—a state of treason punishable by death. The seditious messenger Arrogancy stirs up the commons, says Dudley, assuring them that they are as good as their lords and governors and that they can gain equality by insurrection: "He will also displaye unto you his banner of insurreccion & saie to you 'Nowe set forwarde; yor tyme is right good.' " Woe to those who follow him!

The merchant$_\rho$, the ffarmo^{rs}, the grasiers that be rich, into this m^{ar}ket will bring their bag$_\rho$ that they have kept soe long. And as for the widowes and the wyves also [they] will ransacke their forcers [chests, coffers] and their knotted cloutes to the last penny that they can finde, and rather than faile, their girdles, their bead$_\rho$, and their weddinge ringes, thus wisely they will them bestowe, And as for men he promiseth you ynnumerable. Yet ye good Comoners, for yor owne ease, deal not wth this false core, but be contented wth the fruite of tranquillity.[133]

Written in the midst of actual rebellion, Sir John Cheke's warning is not so mild as Dudley's. The rebels have risen in the name of the commonwealth and of religion, but they have disobeyed both king and God.

[133] *Tree of Common Wealth*, ed. of 1859, p. 51.

But what talke I of disobedience so quietly? have not such mad rages run in your heads, that forsaking and bursting the quietnesse of the common peace, yee have hainously & Traiterously encamped your selfe in a towne, have gathered together all the nasty vagabonds, and idle loiterers, to beare armour against him, with whom all godly and good subjects will live and dye withall?[134]

How can a commonwealth endure thus? "We live under a King to serve him at all times." The cities are the seats of merchants and craftsmen, and they should be left alone to do their duty to the king. The shires and counties are the homes of husbandmen who must labor to supply the food of the realm. Now martial law must punish the offenders. "When brethren agree not in a house, goeth not the weakest to the walls? and with whom the father taketh part withall, is not he the likest to prevaile?"[135] Sedycyon is the chief enemy of the realm in Bale's *Kynge Johan*. When he is expelled, Cyvyle Order is restored, and Commynalte, Nobylyte, Clargy promise to do their duties. Crowley's *Way to Wealth* presents a "most present Remedy for Sedicion," namely, that all estates do that which God ordained them to do. Each estate has grievances, no doubt, but they must not therefore rebel. God appointed rulers, and He will put down rebels. Moreover, every estate has faults as well and is therefore not blameless. Let the miserable commons, who ought to be defended by the nobility and taught their duty by the clergy, consider whether they have loved their neighbor as themselves and whether they have never tried to deceive him in a bargain, before they rebel. Let the clergy of every rank, "what soever ye be, that receyve any parte of the tenth of mens yerelye encrease," give up their fat livings and let their wives give up their fine frocks and French hoods. Let the nobility in their railing at the commons, who threaten them, remember their oppression and extortion, and reform. All this by way of doing away with the sedition that prevails everywhere in the

[134] *The Hurt of Sedition*, ed. of 1641, p. 15.
[135] *Ibid.*, p. 53.

land. Cardinal Pole recommends death for those who despise the order of society:

> Moreover, to al sedycyouse personys that openly despyse thys ordur, unyte, and concord, wherby the partys of thys body are, as hyt were, wyth senewys and nervys knyt togyddur, perpetual bannyschment, or rather deth, must be by law prescrybyd, as to a corrupt membyr of the body, and so to be cut of, for feare lest hyt schold infecte the rest, corruptyng the hole. And so thys compellyng of every man to dow hys offyce and duty, wyth dystrybutyng to every man, accordyng to hys vertue and dygnyte, such thyngys as to be dyvydyd among the cytyzyns wyth concord; and, I thynke, by processe of tyme, utturly take away thys pestylent dysease and dyvysyon.[136]

Like Crowley, Pole is looking for a remedy for the sedition in the realm. Dame Scotia in her sermon to her youngest son, the Commons, says that "al the insurrectionis that evyr occurrit in ony realme contrar the prince & the public veil, hes procedit of the ignorance & obstinatione of the comount pepil,"[137] and that it is therefore they who must learn their duty of submission if sedition is to be banished. There is no worse transgression than rebellion, says Breton in *A Murmurer*, and rebellion is bred of murmuring. All classes murmur. Let them cease their complaints, that the realm may be "purged of that malicious humor."

9. THE CAUSES OF THE FAILURE OF ESTATES TO DO THEIR DUTIES

Both medieval and sixteenth-century writers also philosophize about the causes of the defections of the estates. Most of the earlier writers come to the very general and therefore inoffensive conclusion that the cause is sin, which originated with Adam and Eve. They may use various ways of expressing that cause, but the different allegories do not conceal their fundamental theory. Matheolus' *Lamentations*, Vintler's *Die Pluemen*

---

[136] Starkey's *Dialogue*, ed. Cowper, Part II, chap. I, p. 158.
[137] *Complaynt of Scotlande*, ed. Murray, chap. XVI, p. 139.

des Tugent, his original, the *Fiori di virtú,* and Gower's *Mirour de l'omme,* as we have seen, tell the story of the marriage of Satan's seven daughters, the seven deadly sins, to the different degrees of the three estates. Gower goes further and gives each daughter five more daughters and shows the conflict between all these vices and the seven virtues and their offspring. The first victims of Sin are Adam and Eve, but all the classes of society, from their fall to the present, have proved just as susceptible. *Des Teufels Netz* describes the secret machinations of the Devil and his cohorts to lead the estates from the performance of their duties into pleasanter paths of pride, greed, gluttony, lust, and sloth. The *Fall of Princes* must begin its series of tragedies with the story of the fall of Adam and Eve from high estate, through the sins of pride and avarice. Pride entered the estate of the clergy, says Lydgate later, through Constantine's gift and all the wealth it brought. Just so pride and avarice attack estates of all times.

Some of the causes of defections given by writers of the sixteenth century are only one or another of these deadly sins in more modern dress; others, however, are strangely like present-day causes. Sixteenth-century writers are not satisfied with the simple explanation of religious dogma, but try to analyze the circumstances in which they find themselves, to see whether there is any way out.[138] Times have changed, and the old philosophy of the duties of the three estates will no longer fit. One cause they give is that men of all estates are no longer concerned with the public good, but only with private gain. It is simply the old sin of avarice in the garb of sixteenth-century political theory. This theme of the conflict between public and private interests constantly recurs in the literature of the time. The nobility no longer feel the necessity of defense and relief of the commons. The commons have no sense of loyalty to the

---

[138] The most complete analysis is that of Cardinal Pole in Starkey's *Dialogue,* Part I, chap. III.

nobility and clergy. The clergy have lost sight of their responsibility for the souls of all the rest. Instead, each individual is concerned only for his own material welfare. The idea that, after all, private good makes for public good seems not to have occurred to these critics of their time. Private interest, to them, could only be the foe of public interest. Commercial competition was a sure source of the decline of the commonwealth. Only the king, or the queen as it happened to be, was thought to be whole-heartedly serving the commonwealth. Such a belief, of course, added new weight to the Stuart program of the tenure of kings.[139]

New social conditions are also cited by sixteenth-century writers as causes of the defections of the estates, and they, of course, are different from the causes given by earlier writers. The country is poor, and the estates are no longer able to do what they once did. They do not cry out for lack of money without cause. The lack of corn, the exporting of cattle, corn, wool, tin, and lead in exchange for imports of wines, fine cloths, silks, beads, knives, and such trifles, the consequent lack of work for craftsmen, the excesses in dressing, eating, and building are only a few of the causes of poverty and hence of the defections of all estates. A common cause of discord and division in the realm is the lack of justice and equity: one estate has too much, another too little. Moreover, there is lack of due proportion in the numbers in each estate. There are too few plowmen, too many courtiers and idle servants, too few good artisans, too many superstitious priests, and so on of the other orders. Men look for the easiest trade and the one most gainful. The general idleness and ignorance of all estates are also given as important causes of their defections. If they were not so lazy and so self-indulgent, they would be concerned about their shortcomings and reform. This laziness is none other than the medieval deadly sin of sloth, though it is not so labeled.

[139] See the *Cambridge History of English Literature*, IV, 345 f.

10. The Excuses of Estates for Their Defections

Meanwhile, according to medieval and sixteenth-century writers alike, the estates have their excuses for their shortcomings. Their chief plea is that the times are to blame, not they. Or, if they do not unite in finding the times at fault, they accuse each other. The commons put their accusation upon the heads of nobility and clergy; the nobility, in turn, lay the blame upon the commons and clergy; and the clergy find commons and nobility at fault. Each estate thus presents itself as the innocent sufferer of the defections of the other estates.

Chils siècles est malvais, ce dient tout et toutes,[140]

says Gilles li Muisis, in the early part of his ramblings. Since such is the case, he proposes to tell all the estates what is wrong with them. Gower has the same story to tell: all estates blame "le siecle," and none blames himself:

Mais tous diont en communal,
'Le siecle est mal, le siecle est mal!'
N'est qui son propre errour confesse.[141]

He has already shown the faults of all estates, and so he proposes to demand of "le siecle" the causes of the evils: "Puisq'il ad dit del errour de tous les estatz et comment chascuns blame le siecle et excuse soy mesmes, il demandera ore le siecle de quelle partie est ce dont le mal nous vient." Alas, Siecle, everyone says you're to blame! But God made you good. All in nature is good except man. God gave him reason, and still he has failed. So say Job and Gregory's homilies, and "Mestre Aristotle ly bons clercs" called man the lesser world. Alas, man, that you have given yourself to sin! In the sixteenth century the complaints of the estates on the evil times become much more specific, as in the *Discourse* of John Hales:

Then, I perceave every man findeth himselfe greeved at this time, & no man goeth cleare, as farre as I can perceave. The Gentleman,

[140] *Poésies,* ed. Lettenhove, I, 284, stanza 2.
[141] *Mirour de l'omme,* ed. Macaulay, p. 294, ll. 26590 ff.

that hee cannot lyve on his Landes onely, as his father did before; the Artifficers cannot set so many a worke, by reason all maner of victayle is so deere; the Husbandmen, by reason his lande is deerer rented then before; then we that bee Merchaunts pay much deerer for every thing that commeth over sea; which great derth (I speake in comparison of former times) hath bene alwayes, in a maner, at a stay, ever after that basenesse of our English Coyne, which happened in the later yeares of Kyng Henry the eyght.[142]

The complaints of the estates against each other, as excuses for their own defections, are also variously described. In Robert Gaguin's *Le Débat du laboureur, du prestre et du gendarme,* the plowman and the priest complain of the evil treatment to which the men of war make them submit. The gendarme replies that it is he who suffers privations, always exposed to the severity of his commander and to death. If he sometimes oppresses the priests and peasants, he adds, they have merited the treatment by their sins. The English ballad *Now a Dayes* of a little later date describes social evils rather than those of war:

> the people lyve in variaunce
> for lack of perseveraunce;
> semple ys there governaunce,
>   and wors ys there intent.
> Every man is fayne
> On other to complayne:
> Yf thys longer Rayne,
>   We shall yt all repent!
>
> The spirituall church, their myslevyng,
> to the temporall, evell ensample gevyng;
> & thus, ether others works reprovyng,
>   thei lyve in bate and stryfe.
> The lay men say that preestes Iett,
> alle ys ffysshe that commyth to the nett;
> thei spare none that they can gett,
>   Whether she be mayd or wyfe.[143]

[142] *Discourse of the Commonweal of This Realm of England,* ed. Furnivall, p. 27.

[143] Ed. Furnivall, stanzas 9 and 10.

Each estate, says Crowley in *The Way to Wealth,* if asked the cause of sedition in the land, would point out the faults of the other estates. So he points out the faults of each estate. This accusation of each other and want of agreement constitutes one of the chief diseases of the body politic, according to Cardinal Pole:

they partys of thys body agre not togyddur; the hed agreth not to the fete, nor fete to the handys; no one parte agreth to other; the temporalty grugyth agayn the spiritualty, the commyns agayne the nobullys, and subyectys agayn they rularys; one hath envy at a nother, one beryth malyce agayn another, one complaynyth of a nother.[144]

This has been so from the beginning of the world, says Lupset, and "hathe ever byn a grete destructyon to every commyn wele"; whereupon Pole, like Crowley, proceeds to show that each estate has its faults. Another example of the "grudging" of one estate against the others is that of the third son of Dame Scotia in reply to her charge of treason. The nobles are treasonable, but not the poor. They can't be; they are crushed. Labor has both the damage and the reproach:

allace, i laubyr nycht and day vitht my handis to neureis lasche and inutil idil men, and thai recompens me vitht hungyr, and vitht the sourd . . . allace, o my natural mother, thou repreifis & accusis me of the faltis that my tua brethir committis daly, my tua brethir nobilis and clergie quhilk suld defend me, tha ar mair cruel contrar me nor is my ald enemes of ingland.[145]

With labor's complaint Dame Scotia has little sympathy, since "everye man settis his felicite to distroy his nychtbour," and labor, once possessed of wealth and power, becomes "mair ambicius ande arrogant nor ony gentil man sperutual or temporal."[146] Breton's *A Murmurer* also describes the murmuring of estates against each other in early seventeenth-century England.[147] As a result of their murmuring they are all guilty of a "malicious humor," whereof the world should be purged that

[144] Starkey's *Dialogue,* ed. Cowper, Part I, chap. III, p. 82.
[145] *Complaynt of Scotlande,* ed. Murray, chap. XIII, pp. 122-23.
[146] *Ibid.,* chap. XIII, p. 141.　　　　[147] See pp. 235-37 above.

there might be as great a heaven on earth as there now is a hell.

Such are the ways in which the estates try to cover up their defections. There are other excuses, too, says Gower in the Prologue of the *Confessio amantis* and in the second book of the *Vox clamantis*, but these are as false as the attempt to make the times responsible. Some say, for example, that Fortune, the fickle goddess, is the cause of all the trouble: no estate is secure, since Fortune sends him up one day and down the next.[148] Others say that the planets are the cause.[149] If all those who give these vain excuses would look at themselves, they would see that man, not Fortune or the planets, is to blame. In the Bible, Gower says, he has read a story of Nabuchadnezzar's dream of an image with head and neck of gold, breast and arms of silver, belly and thighs of brass, legs of steel, and feet of mixed steel and clay. In the dream this image was destroyed by a great stone which rolled down a hill upon its steel and clay feet. Daniel explained the meaning. The four metals represented the four monarchies, Babylon, Persia, Greece, and Rome. The last age, that of Rome, is the present age, Gower says—a time of dissension and division, as may be seen in the decline of the Empire and the schism in the Church. This division, he thinks, is the true cause of the evils of the times and of the defections of the estates which he has already enumerated.[150]

Though Gower thinks so little of the stars as an excuse for the evils of the times, it is interesting to note that Spenser, in the late sixteenth century, reasserts their influence in much the same way that the Middle Ages did. In the golden age of Saturn, he says, all truth reigned; now all is changed:

> For that which all men then did vertue call
> Is now cald vice; and that which vice was hight,
> Is now hight vertue, and so us'd of all:

---

[148] *Confessio amantis*, ed. Macaulay, p. 19, ll. 511-28.
[149] *Ibid.*, p. 19, ll. 529-34. Also *Vox clamantis*, Book II, ll. 199-203.
[150] *Ibid.*, p. 28, ll. 849-55.

> Right now is wrong, and wrong that was is right,
> As all things else in time are chaunged quight.
> Ne wonder; for the heavens revolution
> Is wandred farre from where it first was pight,
> And so doe make contrarie constitution
> Of all this lower world, toward his dissolution.[151]

The succeeding description of the changed aspect of the Ptolemaic heavens is further amplification of the medieval excuse of the influence of the stars that Gower scorns. Of course such an explanation of the evils of the world was a comfortably impersonal one, and not even Gloriana could be offended. Gower preferred to find the cause in every man, "the litel world":

> And whan this litel world mistorneth,
> The grete world al overtorneth.

11. THE NECESSITY OF ESTATES IN THE COMMONWEALTH

Of the necessity of the three estates in a commonwealth all the writers of this literature have no doubt. God created this threefold society, and so it must be right. He instituted the prayers of the clergy, the defense of knighthood, and the labor of commons. What would a realm do without any one of the three? Moreover, Holy Church is dependent on all of them and without any of them could not stand. Just as the Trinity would be inconceivable without Father, Son, or Holy Ghost, so the Church would be inconceivable without its three estates. Such are the implications of the earlier writers. Later writers have new reasons for this apparent necessity. Just as the old theory of the divine origin of the estates is later colored by new ideas born of new social conditions, so the reasons for the necessity of the three estates change. In the fable of the unlike children of Eve, God explains that there must be different classes if society is to endure. Caxton shows the need of all the chessmen, representing the different degrees in the three estates. Each he finds "soverainly prouffitable unto the world,"

---

[151] "Faerie Queene," *Works,* ed. Grosart, VII, 242.

for without them "the world myght not be governed." All of them "ought doo the comyn prouffit." Rulers would be of little use without clergy and commons, and commons and clergy would soon suffer without their rulers. The analogy drawn between the commonwealth and the human body emphasizes the same idea: no one member can do the work of another, all parts are therefore necessary to the body, and all must work together to maintain a healthy body. If the different members do not perform their functions properly, they must be forced to do so:

But now, to kepe thys body knyte togudur in unyte, provysyon wold be made by commyn law and authoryte, that every parte may exercyse hys offyce and duty,—that is to say, every man in hys craft and faculty to meddyl wyth such thyng as perteyneth therto, and intermeddyl not wyth other.[152]

Those writers who do not resort to the analogy of the body talk at length of the necessary "order" which the three estates maintain in society. Elyot, Cheke, Smith, Greville, Hooker, all picture, in various ways, the peace and harmony of the commonwealth when all estates work together, and the disorder and discord when they work only for their own good and contend with one another. It is into such a discussion that the author of the *Complaynt of Scotlande* introduces the added authority of Aristotle, who also said that all degrees must work together, "as nature providit fyrst in the begynnyng." When Hooker, Cooper, Selden, and Dekker argue the necessity of the three estates, they have peculiar circumstances in mind. Dekker is concerned about their need of presenting a united front to the papists; and Hooker, Cooper, and Selden urge the necessity of all estates to prove that of the clergy in particular. "The lawes of *Englande* to this day," says Cooper, "have stood by the authoritie of the three Estates: which to alter now, by leaving out the one, may happily seeme a matter of more weight,

---

[152] Starkey's *Dialogue*, Part II, chap. I, pp. 157-58.

then all men doe iudge it."[153] It is dangerous, not only to do such a thing, but even to attempt to do it. Bodin adds the practical reason for the three estates, namely, that two of them form a majority in a disagreement.

12. THE FOLLY OF CHANGING ONE'S ESTATE

A natural corollary from such a theory is, of course, that every one should be content with his degree and not seek to change it. Of the truth of this theory, also, almost all writers of the literature of estates are convinced, and it forms a constant refrain. To be sure, if every estate is shifting, there is no very fixed or stable society. No one, however, must assume from the numerous sermons on content and on the happiness of the mean estate that there was no shifting from one degree to another. Probably the large amount of such advice is due to the fact that there was much change. The estate of clergy was open to rich and poor alike; and the ranks of the nobility were constantly being replenished by commons who, somehow or other, got wealth and power enough to offset their base birth. Society, even under a flourishing feudalism, was probably not nearly so static as we imagine. In the sixteenth century the changes in estates became more and more common, and the diatribes against social-climbers increase in number and volume. Such climbers threatened the whole social order, and so furnished the moralists with an important text. With a middle-class Tudor family on the English throne and gentlemen "good cheap" in England, there was plenty to be said about the arrogance and boorish ways of those who rise aloft and about the vanity, after all, of striving for higher degree. Fortune is fickle and death levels all. Wherefore, then, all this effort for earthly glory? Let every man be content with the rank into which God saw fit to put him, and therein humbly serve both God and man.

[153] Ed. Arber, p. 67.

The instances of such sermonizing are so numerous as to make quotation of all impossible, but some of them are fairly typical. Lydgate, in his *Fall of Princes*, rehearses the fates of several wretches, "cherlissh of nature," who rose aloft and fell again through their pride or cruelty or covetousness.

> What thyng in herte mor froward mai be thouht
> Than is the sodeyn fals presumpcioun
> Off a wrechche that cam up off nouht,
> To yeve hym lordshepe and dominacioun?

This he asks concerning the rise of Saul, of Marius, consul of Rome and opponent of Sulla, of Adrian, praetor of Rome, and of others. A serf risen from low degree, says Robert de Blois, is worse than any high-born knight could ever be:

> Tant con li sers est de plus bas
> Montez en haut, tant est plus gas,
> Plus orgoillous, plus desreez,
> Plus forfait, plus desmesuré.[154]

Hugo von Trimberg's *Renner* complains of the same arrogance.[155]

Toward the end of his *Shyp of Folys* Alexander Barclay inserts a chapter "Of Folys That Ar Over Worldly," not found in his Latin original. Based on a poem of Robert Gaguin—as the marginal note in the 1509 edition indicates: "Scribitur in fatuum nimis mūdo cōfidentē: Et est carmen dñi Roberti Gaguini"—it begins with a sermon on the fickleness of fortune. This sets Barclay off on a favorite theme: that of the arrogance of churls risen to a high branch of the tree of estates:

> No erthly thynge makes more debate
> Than a vyle chorle come to a state
>
> Whan suche a vilayne rude of his mynde
> A hye is set on a myghty tre
> To gentyll blode can he nat be kynde

---

[154] *L'Enseignement des princes*, ed. Ulrich, p. 35, ll. 1181-84.
[155] B.L.V.S., CCXLVII, 44-45, ll. 1064-67, 1083-84.

> yet he forgettis his owne degre
> But thoughe the thycke levys let not se
> Howe moche myschefe suche go about
> yet at the last it wyll come out.[156]

In another chapter, "Of the Yre Immoderate / the Wrath and Great Lewdness of Wymen," Barclay finds women more full of "elevate pride" than the men, when they rise in rank:

> Thre other thynges on erth I fynde certayne
> Whiche troubleth the grounde and also the see
> The fourth nouther see nor londe may well sustayne
> The firste is a churle that hath a bonde man be
> And so by fortune come unto hye degre
> The seconde is a fole whan he is dronke and full.
> The thirde a wrathfull woman / full of cruelte
> He that hir weddyth / hath a crowe to pull
>
> yet is the fourth wors and more elevate
> That is a hande made lowe of hir lynage
> Promotyd from a begger and so come to estate
> Succedynge hir lady as heyr in herytage
> Of suche procedeth moche malyce and outrage
> Disdayne great scorne / vilany and debate
> For the frenche man / sayth in his langage
> No thynge is wors than a churle made a state.[157]

Similarly Gilles li Muisis expands the theme of the arrogance of servants, both masculine and feminine, who have not changed estate but who nevertheless ape their masters.[158] The *Mirrour for Magistrates*, like Lydgate's *Fall of Princes*, has many opportunities for showing the fates of would-be nobility. These "syr Iohn Straws" and "syr Iohn Curs," says Coridon in Barnabe Googe's *Eclogues*, are baseborn and have "churlisshe hartes" and therefore "churles they do remayne," in spite of their position and title. Cardinal Pole describes the custom of entailing land and the resulting "arrogancy, wherby . . . every

---

[156] Ed. of 1509, Folium CCLXVII; Jamieson ed., II, 319-20.
[157] Ed. of 1509, Folium CXXXIII; Jamieson ed. II, 8.
[158] *Poésies*, ed. Lettenhove, II, 83, stanzas 2, 3, 4, 5.

Jake wold be a gentylman, and every gentylman a knyght or a lord." In Scotland, mere mechanic laborers, when they reach high estate, are so haughty that they recognize neither God nor man. They refuse the genealogy of their own fathers and mothers and claim to be of the blood of nobles and gentlemen. Then they glory in their "pretendit kyn ande blude, quhilk is occasione that there arrogance & there vane gloir garris them commit mair extorsions contrar the pepil nor dois ony uthir tirran that ar discendit of the grytest nobilis of the cuntre."[159] Breton hopes that his madcap message may not be for such arrogant knaves, but he recognizes their existence, in somewhat zoölogical fashion:

> But if a Iacke will be a gentleman,
> And mistris Needens lady it at least,
> And every goose be saucy with the swanne,
> While the asse thinkes he is a goodly beast,
> While so the foole doth keepe ambition's feast;
>   My Muse in conscience that cannot be quiet,
>   Will give them this good sawce unto their diet.

> But I doe hope I am but in a dreame,
> Fooles will be wiser then to loose their wittes;
> The country wench will looke unto her creame,
> And workemen see, but where their profite fits,
> And learne fantastickes to their idle fits:
>   Pride shall goe downe, and vertue shall encrease,
>   And then my Muse be still, and hold her peace.[160]

Similarly Bodin, in his defense of monarchy, belabors the arrogant of low birth, with biblical authority:

Another point there is also well worth the consideration, which is, That a man of base degree suddenly mounted unto the highest degree of honour, thinketh himself to bee a god upon earth. For as the wise Hebrew saith, There is nothing more intollerable than the slave become a lord.[161]

---

[159] *Complaynt of Scotlande*, ed. Murray, chap. XVI, pp. 142-43.
[160] *Pasquils Mad-cappe*, ed. Grosart, p. 10.
[161] English ed. of 1606, Book VI, p. 725.

Instead of thus striving to change their degree, members of all estates should be content with the lot in which they find themselves. After all, pride in estate is mere vanity, "our pompe a pumpe, our fame a flame, our power a smouldring smoke."[162] Even Cardinal Wolsey found his state "as brittell as a glasse."[163] Fortune is fickle and "hath hir quit"[164] to every degree. Or, if fortune seems to smile, then death levels all. There is small reason, therefore, for desiring to rise aloft. The mean estate is best, and every one should be satisfied therein. In the good old times, when each estate did its duty, men were content with their lot. Now, no one is content:

> O blinde desire: oh high aspiring harts.
> The country Squire, doth covet to be a Knight,
> The Knight a Lord, the Lord an Erle or a Duke,
> The Duke a King, the King would Monarke be,
> And none content with that which is his own.[165]

In his twelve lessons to the members of all degrees of the three estates, Robert Crowley preaches as full a sermon of content as can be found anywhere:

> Whoso woulde that all thynges were well,
> And woulde hymselfe be wyth out blame,
> Let hym geve eare, for I wyll tell
> The waye how to performe the same.
> Fyrste walke in thy vocation,
> And do not seke thy lotte to chaunge;
> For through wycked ambition,
> Many mens fortune hath ben straynge.[166]

Beginning with the beggars, Crowley tells them to be content with their degree and to walk uprightly therein. God will take care of them. In heaven, doubtless, they will be crowned at God's hand. Lazarus went to heaven, whereas the rich man

---

[162] *Mirrour for Magistrates*, ed. Haslewood, II, 220, stanza 19.
[163] *Ibid.*, II, 501, stanza 67.
[164] *Fall of Princes*, ed. Bergen, Part III, p. 1011.
[165] *The Steele Glas*, ed. Cunliffe, II, 153.
[166] *The Voyce of the Laste Trumpet*, ed. Cowper, p. 57.

at whose gate he died went to eternal torment. Servants, too, are advised to turn from their "stout & stubborne mynd" to their duty. Let them obey all their masters' commands readily and be content with their vocation:

> To make an ende: have stil in minde
> Thyne estate and condition,
> And let thyne herte be styll enclynde
> To walke in thy vocation.

The yeoman is advised to till his soil and beware of the "de-syre to be alofte":

> For what doste thou, if thou desyr
> To be a lord or gentleman,
> Other then heape on the Gods ire
> And shewe thy selfe no Christian?
>
> . . .
>
> Have minde, therfore, thyselfe to holde,
> Within the bondes of thy degre.

Above all, he must be obedient to his king. Though the king may kill his body, he cannot harm his soul. The yeoman, like the beggar, is thus assured of compensation hereafter for what he misses in this life. Popish priests, "lewde or unlerned," having lost their old estate, must not try to say masses secretly, but must do good: teach the ABC, or the primer, or else Robin Hood. That will be a good pastime. The scholar and the men of church must teach and preach to the people, and not be ambitious and look aloft. If they are promoted, let them look to their new offices and not leave the people desolate. Lawyers, too, though their calling is a good one, are greedy and ambitious to rise. Merchants are constantly looking for new sources of wealth, to increase their estate. If they are content with what they have, they will still have enough:

> Thou shalt aye have inough in store
> For the and thine in thy degre;
> And what shouldst thou desire more,
> Or of hygher estate to be?

Gentlemen and magistrates are already set aloft by God to "rule the route," but they are as much bound by duty as the poor man. It is their duty to rule wisely those entrusted to them and not to covet greater rule:

> Thou must not covet imperye,
> Nor seke to rule straunge nacions;
> For it is charge inough, perdie,
> To answere for thyne owne commons.

Women, too, must live content with what they have, and not covet the place or possessions of those above them.

This static philosophy is further applied, in some of the literature of estates, to such matters as where one should seek friendship or how one should marry. Lydgate, Lyndsay, and Elyot advise all to restrict themselves in all such matters to the members of their own estate. Especially is this necessary for those of noble birth, says Lydgate:

> Lat astatis off ther berthe honurable,
> Voide al raskail & wedde ther semblable.[167]

Of the fifteen acts of Parliament proclaimed by Diligence and Scribe in Lyndsay's *Ane Pleasant Satyre of the Thrie Estaitis*, the last reform is the prohibition of marriages of different estates:

> From this day forth, our barrouns temporall
> Sall na mair mix thair nobil ancient blude,
> With bastard bairnis of stait spirituall:
> Ilk stait amang thair awin selfis marie sall.

Friendship, says Elyot, seldom lasts "betwene him which is elevate in autoritie and a nother of a very base astate or degree."[168] To this theory Bodin later opposes a contrary opinion. He recommends the marriages of nobility and commons as a means of maintaining the nobility:

The meanes to unite the nobilitie and the common people more strictly together, is to marrie the yonger children of noble houses being

---

[167] *Fall of Princes,* ed. Bergen, Part II, p. 274.
[168] *The Boke Named the Governour,* ed. Croft, II, 125.

poore (in an Aristocraticall estate) with the Plebeians that are rich, as they did in Rome after the law Canuleia; the which is practised at this day by the Venetians, and almost in every Commonweale, whereas the nobilitie hath any prerogative over the common people: the which is the surest way to maintaine the nobilitie in wealth, honour, and dignitie.[169]

The idea that change of estate is both possible and natural occurs in the later literature of estates. Smith, for example, describes the process of creation of new estates, because of service or newly acquired wealth or learning, as a common practice in his time in England; and Bodin, likewise, recognizes the shifting from low estate to high as a necessary result of new social conditions. They are recording what they have observed, however, and are not preaching the old doctrine of the fixity of estates.

To the modern reader this too systematic medieval doctrine of a rigid hierarchy of classes seems intolerable. Placid content with one's lot in any modern country is no longer a virtue. Ambition, the deadly sin of medieval estates, is no longer a vice. To understand how the Middle Ages so long tolerated, even preached, this doctrine of content, the modern reader must keep in mind a medieval conception that is now wholly lost: namely, that every individual soul is of equal value in the eyes of the Deity and that all inequalities and injustices and suffering in this world are blotted out in the next. The soul of the serf had the same value in eternity as the soul of his lord; and the differences in their degrees and in their labors and possessions were trivial after all. With one's eyes fixed on divine compensation throughout endless time, who could not endure the brief humiliation and tribulation in this vale of sorrows? Every man, in whatever degree, was not responsible for his place in the world. Since, however, he had been given a certain work to do, he must do it as well as possible. All of this doctrine was plainly a Christian elaboration of ancient

[169] *Six Bookes of a Commonweale*, English ed. of 1606, p. 578.

political theory that the good of the state is best served by diversity of classes and occupations. Christian belief in eternal recompense supplied the medieval basis for humble submission to whatever life brought. As the critical temper of the new humanism made the old theory no longer tenable, the philosophy of estates likewise suffered decline, and with it went the peace and concord of that submission. The modern world, except perhaps for the occasional lament of a Ruskin or a Carlyle, would scorn the peace and concord reared on such a foundation, but to the medieval theorist the loss of them was real tragedy.

CHAPTER VIII

THE DEFECTIONS OF THE ESTATES
OF THE WORLD

To study the defections of the estates of the world is to attempt to trace the social changes of the Middle Ages and those of the sixteenth century. No literature of those times shows so well all the shifting fortunes of feudal classes, up the wheel of fortune and down. The more or less complete domination of commons by feudal overlords, lay and spiritual; the rise of the towns and of the disturbing merchant class, that was later to upset the whole philosophy of estates; the decline of feudalism as the estate of the commons increased in power and influence; and the growth of strong monarchy, that meant transformation of an *estate* into the *state*—all of these changes are reflected in the laments of the writers of the literature of the estates of the world over the defections of society. Even the women have an important part here. Though they count for little in matters of government, though it is meet that they be "kept far off from all magistracies, places of command, iudgements, publike assemblies, and councels: so to be intentive onely unto their womanly and domesticall businesse," in the matter of defections they rival the men, or, in some pieces like the *Lamenta* of Matheolus, they easily surpass them. A list of the defections of women frequently concludes the enumeration of those of the other estates.

1. The Deadly Sins of the Early Laments

The earlier laments, as has been pointed out, are often rather general in their accusations, whereas the later medieval moralists go into a good deal of detail and sixteenth-century English writers are even more specific. Charges of pride and avarice suffice in some of the twelfth-century Latin laments. All the tricks of all the medieval trades, lay and ecclesiastical, are revealed by the moralists of the thirteenth, fourteenth, and fifteenth centuries. And sixteenth-century English critics of society analyze the social and political defections of the different estates at great length. Naturally, the length of the work, as well as the time at which it was written, affects the treatment of these defections. Poems of a few short stanzas permit of only general charges of some one of the deadly sins; and even in the late Middle Ages and in the sixteenth century such brief general laments are found. On the whole, however, it may be said that, with the development of the fashion, the tendency grew to expand and to become more and more specific.

The charge of avarice persists throughout this literature. From the "De statibus mundi," ascribed to Gautier de Châtillon and to Walter Mapes, to *Pasquils Mad-cappe* and *Pasquils Prognostication* of Breton the love of Sir Nummus, variously expressed, is named as the chief fault of all classes.

> Omnes avaritia mentibus imbutis
> in nummo constituunt spem suae salutis;
> volunt dici prodigi rebus dissolutis:
> fallit enim vitium specie virtutis,[1]

says Gautier in the midst of his enumeration of avaricious classes; and the poem *Des diverses classes d'hommes* laments the same defection:

> A primo homine venit cupiditas
> in qua plantata est omnis posteritas.[2]

All classes love money, says Matheolus, because

> Qui plus de deniers accumule
> En plus hault degré s'intitule.[3]

The clergy, who should set an example of love of matters spiritual, are more interested in the philosophy of money than in all other studies:

> Toutes sciences repudient
> Fors celle de philopecune.[4]

---

[1] Ed. Müldener, p. 9, ll. 1-4.   [2] Ed. Du Méril, p. 131.
[3] *Lamenta*, ed. van Hamel, p. 178, ll. 663-64.
[4] *Ibid.*, p. 178, ll. 676-77.

All bow to Syr Peny, says the unknown author of the poem
by that name:

> Pope, kyng, and emperoure,
> Byschope, abbot, and prioure,
> Parson, preste, and kny3t,
> Duke, erle, and baron,
> To serve syr Peny are they boen,
> Both be day and ny3th.[5]

An analysis of the evils of the times leads Gascoigne to conclude that love of gold has corrupted all:

> What causeth this, but greedy gold to get?
> Even gold, which is, the very cause of warres,
> The neast of strife, and nourice of debate,
> The barre of heaven, and open way to hel.[6]

Crowley, too, finds all guilty of avarice:

> And this is a Citye
>   in name, but, in dede,
> It is a packe of people
>   that seke after meede;
> For Officers and al
>   do seke their owne gaine,
> But for the wealth of the commons
>   not one taketh paine.
> An hell with out order,
>   I maye it well call,
> Where everye man is for him selfe,
>   And no manne for all.[7]

Breton in *Pasquils Mad-cappe*, listing rich and poor, clergy and
laity, lawyers, judges, justices of the peace, beggars, and women,
finds avarice their chief sin:

> So that by all these consequents I see,
> It is the money makes or marres the man;

. . .

[5] *Reliquiae antiquae,* ed. Wright and Halliwell, II, 108.
[6] *The Steele Glas,* ed. Cunliffe, II, 153.
[7] *One and Thyrtye Epigrammes,* ed. Cowper, p. 11.

The golden tale is ever soonest heard,
The golden suter soonest hath dispatch,
The golden servant hath the best regard,
And what such marriage as the golden match?
And who so wise as is the golden patch?
Sweet musicke soundes it in a golden vaine,
The sweetest stroke is in the golden straine.[8]

It is unnecessary to multiply examples, since all writers in all times sing this same refrain. General as it sometimes is, it takes on much meaning as it becomes such characteristic evils as the seeking for benefices by the clergy, the robbing of poor tenants by their overlords, or the trickery and fraud of lawyers, merchants, physicians, handicraftsmen, and laborers.

The sin of pride is almost as universally ascribed to all estates as is that of avarice. It, too, with varying detail, is the charge of writers from Gautier de Châtillon to Breton and Dekker. Sir Pride, like Sir Peny, rules the land. He issues his commands to all degrees, and all, from Rome down, do him honor. Finally he has quite an army:

Hore ad sire Orguyl assemblé
Soun host a sa meynné,
E va rachaunt tere a meer
Ses mestries pur moustrer.[9]

The sins of gluttony, anger, lust, envy, and sloth have incidental place in many pieces, according as the gluttony and anger of the feudal lords, the lust of the clergy, the envy and sloth of the commons affect the imagination of the different writers. As we have seen, the seven deadly sins were married off to the estates of the world by Guillaume in *Le Besant de Dieu,* by Matheolus in his *Lamenta,* by Tomaso Leoni in his *Fiori di virtú,* and by Vintler in *Die Pluemen der Tugent;* and in many other pieces they appear, without the allegory of those writers, as the characteristic sins of one estate or another.

[8] Ed. Grosart, I, 8.
[9] *Reliquiae antiquae,* ed. Wright and Halliwell, II, 248.

2. The Specific Defections of the Later Middle Ages

The writers of the literature of estates invariably become more interesting, however, when they leave off such general moralizing and turn to specific social faults. From the latter half of the twelfth century to the end of the sixteenth, they provide a kind of political and economic history of those times.

In the latter half of the twelfth century, they lament the faults of the estates of the time of Henry II, Plantagenet.[10] Beginning with emperors and kings, they find the lot of those rulers far from desirable. If kings and emperors have their troubles, however, they are only getting their dues. They rob the poor to make feasts for the wastrels about them. When they make war, their mercenaries, the Brabants, derive all the profit. In time of peace, they pay no homage to God or the Church. They should preserve justice, but instead they spend their time in hunting. Such is the example they set for their subjects, who take on only too easily the vices of their superiors.

The clergy, though they must be honored for God's sake, do the opposite of what they preach: they drink and eat to excess and commit adultery. Their concubines and mistresses they support with the patrimony of the cross; and their children, with the gifts for trentals, which have been paid for but not celebrated. The archdeacons and deans tolerate all this, provided that it pays. When the dean orders the priest from the chase, he is appeased by five sous and some good food. The bishops are even more dishonorable, for they not only ignore these abuses, but they also sell benefices, instead of giving them to the most deserving. As a result, worthy secular clerks have no hope of churches through learning; only a gift to the bishop will secure one. Nepotism and simony prevail. Moreover, bishops

[10] For fuller analysis of the works of several of the following moralists, see C. V. Langlois' *La Vie en France au moyen âge. D'après des moralistes du temps,* Paris, 1925. *Le Livre de manières* of Étienne de Fougères gives all the defections cited here concerning this early period.

even borrow money to keep up fine stables, and make other such foolish expenditures. The pope is the head of all, and the cardinals are the court of last resort. May God preserve them in the good way.

The knights, who are ordained to defend all, rob the poor and unfortunate. While the poor go hungry, the lords eat and drink what they have stolen from them and oppress them in every way. For a trivial fault the lord strikes his man with fist or club, he puts him in bonds, he lays waste his property and leaves him to die. The knighthood has surely degenerated: nowadays the knights think of nothing but dancing, hunting, feasting, and tourneying.

The poor peasant, meanwhile, has a hard lot: he sows, harrows, mows, cards the wool, builds fences, and never tastes one good morsel of food. He eats black bread and drinks milk and is glad to have them. If he has white meal, fat geese, and wine, they go to his lord. All this the peasant was ordained to do; and if he does his duty, he has merit. Too often, however, he loses merit by complaining to God and by trying to hold back the tithes he owes to God. Let him beware. God repays the faithful a hundred-fold. The merchants, whose first duty is to have weights and measures conforming to the king's ordinances, and otherwise to deal justly, sell water for wine, the skin of a hare for coney, the fur of a pole-cat for zibeline, ordinary woods for rare ones, and so forth. Or they sell at higher prices on a deferred payment plan, which involves them in what is really usury. Usury is bad business. The borrower, out of malice, makes advances to the wife or daughter of the lender in the market-place, thinking by that means to make the lender return to the original terms of payment. Though the lender often conceals his usury under a pretext of charity, he is really tricking men into paying ten livres for what he could scarcely sell for seven livres. He will sell a bushel of tares for a bushel of oats, cloth of shoddy for cloth of wool, a sow for a hog, a

cow for a steer. He calls this "reasonable selling." Let him beware. He will be excommunicated; and if he dies excommuni-
cate, his goods will be forfeit to the dean, and he will be regarded as a pagan and be buried like a dog.

Women's defections complete the picture. The woman of
the world, to please her lover, does not spare cosmetics; the
paint-box conceals her ugly wrinkles. Gall of mutton, the fat
of dog, the depilatory paste of quick lime and of yellow arsenic
serve her purpose. This coquette may also be a sorceress, who
by plasters, images of wax and clay, charms, and evil herbs
rids herself of lovers or of her daughter's unwanted offspring.
The idle rich woman, who has no interest in weaving or spinning,
concerns herself only with making herself beautiful and with
secret love affairs. If her husband seeks to prevent her, she
pretends illness, and a go-between recommends a vigil. She goes
to church, not to pray, but to meet her lover. If he does not
come, another will do as well. Of course there are good women,
those who love their husbands and rear their children honor-
ably. Children are good to have; but sometimes they hinder
good works: the peasant, for them, holds back part of his tithes;
others spend all their lives working hard, borrowing, taking
pledges and making them, to support their children.

Such are the defections of the latter twelfth century. In the
early thirteenth century changing times are reflected in the
changing faults of the different estates.[11] The defections of the
knighthood are those of stinginess and boorishness rather than
high living and lavish expenditure. In times gone by, the nobles
were of good stock and kept fine courts and counselors. Now
they are degenerates who are so niggardly that they prefer
wretched barracks and the woods to palaces. Instead of the
honored vassals of former times, who also knew how to give
generous gifts, they have cross-bowmen and engineers about

[11] See especially the *Bible* of Guiot de Provins, the *Sermones nulli
parcentes,* the *Bible* of Hugues de Berzé.

them. They protect Jews and usurers. They practice usury themselves and think of nothing but adding to their wealth. Even on the crusades they have been proud, covetous, and boastful.

Of the "Romans," the estate of the clergy, all are now dishonorable, even the pope and the court of Rome. They are all covetous and mercenary. The cardinals are full of simony. They sell God and his Mother, they betray Christ, they devour everything. The pope has his share, so they say. He is blind, like his blind counselors. Rome exploits all its subjects. Archbishops and bishops of France are no better. Though they have four or five sees each, many of them do nothing, once they have secured their honors, but drink and eat and "gabble and swear and lie." Pride and simony possess them, too. Not all prelates are bad, but the good are few in number and have no influence. Because of the bad example of most prelates, the common secular clergy, priests, and canons, despair and finally adopt the same conduct. Now the monastics also have their own peculiar shortcomings. Formerly the abbés espoused Charity, Truth, and Uprightness. For them they have substituted three loathsome sorceresses: Treason, Hypocricy, and Simony. These three destroy all the orders. The "white Order," the Benedictines of Citeaux, are rich and pitiless, even to their own members. In no order is there less fraternity; only envy and hypocrisy prevail among them. They are real business men: they have made barns and stables of churches and pig-sties of cemeteries; they ride about in carriages; they impose heavy taxes and then drive away the poor who come to beg food. The abbés reserve the good clear wines for themselves and send the poor wines to the monks, who lament their evil lot. These are the order who say that all the world will be damned but them. The Carthusians have a fairly good reputation, but theirs is a "religion without pity." They eat and sleep alone, and do not take care of the sick in their order. Such asceticism is unnecessary and cruel. The monks of the Order of Grandmont are too rich and haughty. They make a great show of their charity. Moreover, they have many Gascon and Spanish members, who are strangers to France. They have great pride in their beautiful long beards. While Rome, bribed by gifts of money, approves, they rule princes and lords, priests and priors. The black canons of Prémontré, though once of high repute, have fallen through various indiscretions. The black canons of St.-Augustin are well dressed and housed, and they talk at meals, unlike those at Cluny. But the Templars are a finer order than the black canons for the honor and fear they have inspired in the Turks. Every one knows, however, that they are covetous and haughty and provide a refuge for thieves and murderers. The Hospitalers are also very rich and proud and therefore inhospitable. The converts of St.-Antoine have a very profitable way of cheating people: they take in refugee and infirm monks and nuns, even children, who then beg alms boldly everywhere. With these alms, the order practices usury, under the very noses of the bishops, who share in the profits. The defections of women converts and nuns Guiot prefers not to dwell on. Like pigeons, they build their nests in the Church and then do not keep their nests clean. But there are some good women.

Of the professions, theology, law, and medicine, the physicians are the worst. The theologians used to know something and have schools where they taught. Nowadays these hypocrite doctors, bishops, and legates are interested only in income. They talk much of decretals and testaments and know little else. Men of law have a fine profession, but nowadays they debase it. They, too, care only for money: they will plead any way at all to secure it. They are dishonest and envious of one another. It is right that the name of physicians begins with *fie!* Though they are ignorant wretches, they make good money. To all their expensive pills, their hellebore, and so forth, fat capons, strong sauces, and clear wines are much to be preferred.

Still it is best to follow their counsel in case of need and then let them go to Salonica, namely, to the devil.

It is strange that the citizens don't stop to think of their fate in the next world. Not that all of them are bad, but they are silent concerning evils that they know exist, and among them are robbers and thieves. Many merchants, in their zeal, have little time for anything but business. They have crossed the "great sea" to India and, returning, have perhaps found sons not their own. Let them cease their vain labors and learn to love God, who can save them. Moreover, certain merchants here at home perjure themselves in selling their wares. Like Judas, they thereby sell God, in their love of "pecunia." Let the farmers and laborers be submissive and obedient in their labor, if they wish to escape the wrath of God. Some of them secretly move the boundaries of their allotted land and so cheat their neighbors. Those who are dishonest and rebellious will suffer the most cruel tortures of hell. Women should be honored, according to these early thirteenth-century writers, for two reasons: Mary bore the Savior of the world, and every man is the son of his mother.

The defections of the estates as pictured toward the middle of the thirteenth century[12] reflect the growing power and avarice of nobility and clergy and the increasing rebellion and shiftlessness of the commons. The bishops have become niggardly. They give little and spend little, and when they visit their charges, they eat with their poor priors and abbés to save money. Those under the bishops do similar things. The archdeacons and deans and their under-officers consent to adultery and fornication for a price. They build big churches, three or four in one province, and get big rents, on which they keep their families. Even priests now find in the care of their flocks a way of exploiting them. The monks wear tight shoes and short sleeves and coats, like squires. They must have their hair cut in a queue like the

---

[12] See Guillaume's *Le Besant de Dieu* and the *Roman de carité* by the Recluse of Molliens.

tail of a mallard duck. Meanwhile the cardinals, legates, and provosts of the pope are no longer peace-makers in the lands to which they are sent. Instead, they get hold of the rich churches and seek rich bishoprics for their children and their parents. They love much "la blanche moneie" and still more "icele qui rogeie." Kings, counts, dukes, who have the rule over those beneath them, love war too much and disregard the burden of the poor. Most of them are without mercy. They think they will rule here always and so are like tyrants to those under them. On the necks of their dependents they put such bailiffs as flay them alive and rob them of lands and clothes. The poor, however, are not faultless either. There are thousands of poor folk who no longer bear their suffering and poverty with good grace. They are felons, envious, evil-speaking, proud, and full of jealousy and lust as long as they have a cent left. The laborer, though able to work with his hands, has no conscience. He says it is noon at the third hour, and at noon he says it is night. He eats and drinks in tavern or brothel without clothes on his back. He lives an idle life while alms last. Guillaume can't tell all the ways of these people. Alas, that they don't endure their poverty, like Job or Tobit, in patience and good spirit. Women have sinful pride in their appearance. They buy cosmetics and paint their faces as one would paint a statue. And what trains they wear, to sweep the dirt!

Toward the close of the thirteenth century the charges against women grow in number and vehemence. Their shortcomings are as numerous as those of the men. Their dress, their cosmetics, their love affairs, their superstitions, their conduct at home and abroad receive much attention. A few of the charges will show the faults of women in the late thirteenth century. They loiter on the way to church, say the moralists,[13] or they run in undignified fashion. They permit familiarities, such as kisses and

[13] Robert de Blois in *Le Chastoiement des dames,* Matheolus in *Lamenta,* Matfre Ermengaud in *Le Breviari d'amor.*

caresses, proper only from husbands. They look at men not their husbands. They boast of conquests. Some wear bodices cut too low and skirts too short. They accept jewels when not in earnest. They scold, swear, drink, and eat too much. They have bad table manners: they smile or talk too much at the table, take the best pieces, and wipe their noses on their napkins. They sing when uninvited. They look into houses as they pass and sometimes enter without knocking. They tell lies. Married women fail to discourage lovers and, when they have them, fail to be discreet. They are like clocks that never stop. They criticize all that their husbands do. They take credit for abundance in the house and blame their husbands for any lack. If the husband wishes peas for dinner, the wife prepares leeks; or, if he wishes white bread, she has coarse gruel, full of chaff. Women are naturally quarrelsome. Instead of answering them, it is better to go away and leave them in their wrath. Women go to church for love of the clerks and priests or to hear the gossip and scandal. The libertines go, too, to catch their prey. No woman should be allowed in church, any more than a horse. The church to a woman means a rendezvous. She likes pilgrimages as pretexts for love adventures. At the same time, women want to know all that their husbands do and don't believe them on oath. Women are disobedient, envious, greedy, and lustful. Even the nuns have their pleasures. They invent excuses for permission to leave the cloister and then they secretly meet their lovers. Women are superstitious: they have numerous devices for rousing love, for telling the future, curing sickness, finding lost objects, and so forth. In short, no woman is fit to marry, for love or money or any other reason. No woman is ever satisfied; no wife can refrain from battle. Altogether, marriage is a bad institution. Better a thousand lovers than one wife.

The other estates in the late thirteenth century seem to have invented no new ways of failing in their duties, except that temporal duties in royal courts begin to usurp the place of the spiritual duties of the clergy, both high and low; that judges are selling justice like wine in a tavern; that citizens are acquiring too many rents and properties, chiefly by usury; and that journeymen and laborers are uniting to demand higher wages. These latter charges are the result of the growing importance of the towns and crafts; the former charge, that against the clergy, reflects the rising tide of monarchy.

Fourteenth-century literature of estates reflects the defections of Church and State in the time of the Babylonian Captivity. Late thirteenth-century laments over the temporal interests of the clergy, over the increasing power of the king, and over the various defections of the townsmen grow stronger.[14]

The order of the world is now reversed. The pope is interested in gold and so sacrifices the Church to the pleasure of the king. The king gives him gifts, and for the gifts he gives prebends to the king's clerks. All the Church is now tributary to the king. Holy Church is administered lay justice by the king. The pope does not bestow the cope nor teach his clergy; the king does all that. The most deserving of the clergy get no benefices; discouraged, they enter the professions of law and medicine. Gentlemen sportsmen, beggars in secret, intriguers get the appointments. Or mere youngsters are given chairs, when they have learned little clergy. They have the name of "reverent pere" and are only "enfans." Other prelates are busy counselling the king and so neglect their duty. At inquests, at court trials, in the exchequer, in Parliament, there they are, wasting the goods that should go to the poor. Because of such prelates, Holy Church is devoid of faith. Through them the king levies taxes on the Church: the congregations are pinched by taxes and all their needs are ignored. Meanwhile, these prelates wish to be honored and bowed to on all sides, until one might think they

---

[14] See Gervais du Bus' *Fauvel*, the *Poésies* of Gilles li Muisis, Gower's *Mirour de l'omme* and *Vox clamantis*.

were not born of mortal parents. The other estates in the Church are no better. Their chief intent should be to pay God his rents and honor the Church. Instead they have large prebends and serve in niggardly fashion those from whom all their goods come. The canons especially neglect their duty. They travel about in great style, like country squires. Parish priests are an ignorant lot. No wonder people live foolishly under their foolish government. Even the mendicant sons of St. Dominic and St. Francis have grown rich and learned and proud. They no longer know how to dig, delve, build, or follow any trade, but they know only too well how to trouble the people. They have houses and churches and pay no taxes as do the orders with rents. The chief concerns of the other orders, those that have rents and lordships to render divine service, both the black and the white monks, are still good wines, good food, beautiful robes, and leaves of absence. They need more air, they say, and a visit to their parents. Or they like to sleep, or scheme for Church dignities, or boast of their lineage, or quarrel with their fellows. Besides colored robes, that can be washed and that shall belong to the wearer, they demand jewel boxes and chests of drawers. They will no longer receive their robes from the chamberlain, but insist on money to buy their own. They no longer take orders from their superiors unless it pleases them. They are too elegant for menial work in the bake-house. The pompous abbés and priors are to blame. They work hard for novices, and once they are in, they are left to their own devices, while the abbés or priors go off on temporal missions. The elections of abbés are scandalous. They are contested, whereupon appeals to Rheims and Rome follow, and then discord and ruin. The monks sing lazily and fail to stop at the response. They should leave that to the other side and not spoil their song. The nuns are no longer the coy cloistered ladies of the good old days. Entrance to their houses is too easy, especially for young men. They live like ladies and think only of how to adorn themselves. They easily obtain permission to leave the cloister, and they give people plenty of cause to talk. Even the Beguines sing and dance and make merry with the young men who visit them.

The defections of fourteenth-century laity are no less evil. The conflict that rose between King Philippe of France and Count Guy of Flanders meant wars, truces, respites for more than fifty years, and still they were not ended. As a result, the moralists have much to say of the exactions of the king and lords. Taxes, they say, have never been so heavy. Princes are robbers and impoverish their subjects. When they levy tribute, there is no escape. Moreover, these lords are unjust: if a gentleman poacher is caught on their grounds, he may make recompense; if a poor man poaches, he is hanged. The lords wish to be obeyed at once. At all times they expect to hear: "Bien dit, misire." They despoil even the churches. Their whole intent is to acquire without paying anything. They are so proud of their nobility that they despise all other people. In spite of their pride, however, many English knights engage in merchandising. Civil law says that no good knight will endanger his honor through bargaining. Those who do make the commons hate them. The counselors of lords nowadays are mercenary upstarts. Once raised aloft, they maintain themselves like great "estates." These changes from low to high estate, and from high to low, are a strange phenomenon to all the moralists.

Concerning the other members of the lay estates, fourteenth-century charges remain much like those of the thirteenth century. Bailiffs and judges are pitiless. Merchants are cruel and grasping (or hard-working and deserving of praise, according to the mood or experience of the writer). Laborers on farms and in towns are lazy and insolent. Women wear unheard-of fashions: horns, like cows, for festivals and their sleeves buttoned up, not sewed as they should be. The men's clothes are no better: they are too short and tight. Servants spend their time gossiping.

New defections appear in some of the fourteenth-century

literature of estates, particularly that of Gower, concerning the
rising citizen classes of merchants, professions, and craftsmen.
The name of the merchant guilty of these defections is Fraud or
Trickery; and he buys and sells everywhere: Bourdeaux, Seville,
Paris, Florence, Venice, Brussels, Ghent, London. Sometimes
he is a wholesale dealer (a grossour); then he sells short weight
and keeps the surplus. Also, under pretense of courtesy, he
jests and fools to deceive the people and to get their money.
The merchant who is a mercer shouts his wares louder than a
sparrow-hawk and fairly drags people into his shop. Or, if he
is a draper, he promises true measure, but beware, once he has
your money. His shop is dark, so that it is difficult there to
tell green from blue. While you pay twice the value of his
wares, he will tell you that he is giving them to you out of his
liking for you. Handicraftsmen are, of course, necessary to the
common good, but if they practice fraud, they have a vice quite
contrary to the common good. The goldsmith is most often tricky.
His fraud is substituting alloys of metal for the gold and silver
that is brought to him. Whoever delivers silver vessels to him to
be made into money will find that the vessels and the coins have
not the same qualities. If he promises to finish the work in a
week, he will do well if he has it ready in a month. And perhaps, in the end, he won't deliver it at all, for if the law doesn't
bind him, honesty won't. Similarly jewels are counterfeited. The
rich druggist is also fraudulent. Most often he defiles his conscience by having his scales register double weight. And he
makes sinful profit by selling cosmetics to the women, so that
beauty, foreign to an old face, is induced by drugs to attract
the lustful. When associated with a physician he deceives people: the one will order the prescription, the other will fill it,
and the value of a button will be sold for a florin. They always
agree; all their tricks can't be told. Among the furriers trickery
is also rife. Vanity makes it possible among them: when "ma
dame la Contesse" puts on fur, "la vaine Escuieresse" follows

suit. The furrier is joyful when he can stretch the fur in length and width, but when the mantle has been trimmed and has been worn for four days, then one can see that the furrier was stingier than the draper. The saddler is the craftsman of whom all the laborers complain. But why try to name all the devices for fraud? Formerly merchants talked of scores or hundreds and thought they were rich. Now they talk of many thousands, and without doubt there are some who do not pay their debts. In the halls of their houses are tapestries, both for winter and for summer, and curtained chambers and vessels on their tables, as if they were dukes. When they die, one finds that poverty is their excuse for not paying their debts. Every craft is good if well governed, but few crafts are. The providers of food are also full of trickery. The taverner mixes new wine with year-old wine. Sometimes such mixtures cause infirmity and death. Or he mixes red wine with white, and, if the mixture becomes yellow, he puts in enough red dye to color it. Complaints follow. If the wine be too red, he puts in white wine until it is straw color. He mixes different wines of Spain, Guyenne, France, and the Rhine, to make more money. If the mixture is too strong, he adds water. In the morning the women come and taste every kind of wine, all drawn from the same tap. The taverner bids them enjoy themselves, since they have plenty of time. The women know well how to fool their husbands, and the taverner profits. The poor complain of their beer seller: he sells poor beer; or he gives false measure and price; or, if the beer is good twice, the third time it is bad. God ordained bread, meat, beer, and wine for man: bread is the staff of life. But the bakers and butchers and poulterers are also full of trickery and avarice. They charge too much. The butcher doesn't even know that there is such a coin as a half-penny; and so one must pay twice as much for the meat as it is worth. So all estates are full of guile.

Fifteenth-century literature of estates is either general again or a reproduction of earlier pieces. *The Game and Playe of the Chesse* reproduces late thirteenth or early fourteenth-century defections, and the *Fall of Princes* reproduces those of the latter fourteenth century. Moreover, both are very general, as are the shorter works of the period. Pride, avarice, lust, tyranny suffice as descriptions of the defections of the different estates.

Many sixteenth-century works are also pretty general, or they enumerate the faults of the classes of earlier times or give in detail the defections of a single estate: that of the clergy. The *Mirrour for Magistrates,* for example, is no more specific than its fifteenth-century model. Gascoigne's *Steele Glas,* though it names specific faults, might have been written in the time of Langland and Gower. It reflects a society still unruffled by changing social and economic conditions. The king covets wealth and lands, the knights follow the king's example, the clergy are weaklings without reverence, judges and advocates think only of fees, merchants make monopolies, shoemakers make poorly sewed shoes, tailors steal the cloth of gentlemen, tanners dress their hides so hastily that they are not water-proof, colliers put dust in their sacks, the delver dallies at his work, blacksmiths shoe horses as they should not be shod, millers toll grain with a golden thumb, bakers make yeast bear the price of wheat, brewers adulterate their beer, butchers blow all over the meat, horse-dealers sell jades, weavers give housewives short measure, and so forth. Only Piers Plowman is without fault.

3. EARLY SIXTEENTH-CENTURY DEFECTIONS

A fairly complete picture of the defections peculiar to the early sixteenth century can be found in some of the literature of estates of the reign of Henry VIII.[15] Though these writers, too, charge all estates with the general sins of covetousness and

[15] See Alexander Barclay's *Shyp of Folys,* Lyndsay's *Satyre of the Thrie Estaitis,* Edmund Dudley's *Tree of Common Wealth,* More's *Utopia,* the ballad *Now a Dayes.*

pride and the desire to rise aloft to ever higher estates, at times they become very specific. Kings and emperors despise good counsel, listen only to flatterers, and with "blynde slouth and ferefull neglygence" allow the power of the Holy See to fall before that of the Turks. Even the pope, chief pilot of the ship, sleeps at his post. Much has been lost to the Turks. More will be. All Christendom fears them, but Christian princes do nothing. Would that the "Englysshe Lyon" would join his wisdom and riches with the "Scottis unycornes myght and hardynes" against them. Then, without doubt, all Christendom would live in peace. Knights, squires, gentlemen are ignorant and ill-bred: they think only of new fashions, gay apparel, and the pleasures of the senses; they increase their estate by oppressing the poor. The clergy, too, are an ignorant lot; they deck themselves out in newfangled fashions; they still study logic when they might better read Plato and Aristotle; they take on many benefices, for the rents they bring; young boys who have become masters at the universities in less than a year are promoted to the clergy; even courtiers become priests, though they know nothing but the dice; all ranks of the clergy connive for promotion; they join in the dances with children, maids, and wives; they beg gifts and then drink up all they get; they chatter in the choir-loft; if they preach, they say what the people wish to hear and dare not utter the truth; they love high-sounding titles, such as judge or doctor. Physicians practice without knowing anything of medicine: they prescribe the same herb for every disease. Surgeons heal all diseases with one salve or plaster. They are all greedy for money. Judges and lawyers know nought of civil or canon law, and "aungels worke wonders in westmynster hall." A lawyer will do nothing "without a prevy brybe." His pleading is always most effective "whan of thy purse he hath had experyence." Bailiffs live by beating and robbing the poor. Executors of estates keep what they have no right to. Merchants are usurers: they buy in great quantities and then sell at a higher price when the commodity is scarce. They let their children parade in furred coats and think them too tender to work. Such commoners should remember how hardly they won their fortunes. They should have pity on the poor. Craftsmen are full of fraud: millers and bakers hate weights and measures; tailors steal the cloth; shopkeepers make their wares "uniust and disceyvable," and each sells at a lower price than his competitor, to do him "displeasour and damage." Laborers loiter at their work and drink up their wages; they all want to be masters, and yet they know nothing about their craft; some show their hatred and envy of each other by working for little or nothing, and thus both starve. Plowmen in the country covet the life of courtiers: they want to dress and act like courtiers; they are not satisfied with one farm but must have many; so they become rich and arrogant and finally seek to be made lords. Servants of the household, such as cooks and butlers, waste their masters' goods, eat and drink their masters poor, loaf on the job, and then complain of their wages. Women dress in outlandish new fashions, indulge in secret love affairs, gossip in church, and are full of wrath; though they are supposed to have little to say, they are as coy and still as "the horle wynde or clapper of a mylle."

4. LATER SIXTEENTH-CENTURY DEFECTIONS

Many of the economic and social disorders that became notorious in the middle and latter half of the sixteenth century are barely mentioned, however, in these earlier works. Sir Thomas More's *Utopia* and the ballad *Now a Dayes* are the earliest to name those evils. The transition from tillage to sheep-farming and the consequent misery of the poor are reflected in both. The king was concerned with maintaining his authority over a none too loyal nobility and with the prestige of foreign wars. The nobility, instead of defending the poor, were busy buying up more land for sheep-grazing. The commons, thus deprived of their homes, were driven to the cities and entered the already large class of craftsmen or became vagrants or thieves, who were punished by death if they were caught, or who starved to death. The scarcity of grain and meat meant shortage of food, and "engrossing" monopolies meant prohibitive prices for what there was. The debasing of the coinage lowered its purchasing power. Idle serving-men and returned soldiers increased the rout of the poor who were driven from the farms. The clergy, meanwhile, those who should care for the poor, were busy only with their own pleasures and promotions. Priors and abbots were said to be engaged in buying and selling openly, like great grossers. Benefices were also bought and sold like merchandise. As a result, handicraftsmen were become curates. Meanwhile, because of the evil of enclosing,

> Gret men makithe now a dayes
> A shepcott in the churche.

It is by such writers as Hales and Stubbs, Hake and Crowley, Starkey and the author of the *Complaynt of Scotlande* that these new defections are described in full detail. The fullest account is that of Starkey in his *Dialogue between Cardinal Pole and Thomas Lupset*. Since the others all corroborate Starkey's list of defections it will probably suffice here to examine his charges alone.

Full of the problems of a new social era as it is, the *Dialogue* contrasts strangely with the moralizings of Gower and his predecessors. All the force of the impact of a waning feudalism and a modern industrial society is felt in the thoughtful searching of Pole and Lupset for a way out of the new difficulties. It is no longer a matter of preaching to the divinely ordained classes their separate duties; it has become necessary to recognize inevitable economic and social forces that have upset the old order and have made way for the new.

From his "lyttill experyence," Starkey says, he has gathered together "the most commyn and notabull abusis, both in manerys custummys and all commyn lawys"; and along with the abuses he tells "the maner and mean how thes abusys both in custum and law may be reformyd and the treu commyn wele a-mong us restoryd."[16] This, then, is no simple imitation of medieval literature of estates: it aims to set forth what Starkey himself has observed. His observations are put into the mouth of Cardinal Pole, who was no doubt in complete sympathy with all he is made to say.[17] The body politic is sick. The three chief diseases are: the idleness of a large number of all estates, the decline in population and the inequality of numbers in each estate, and the lack of good laws that would secure "gud ordur and pollycy" and the abundance of all things necessary.

For some of these abuses, all of the estates are to blame; for others, one estate is more to blame than the others. Idleness is found among all estates, insomuch that "you schal fynd, as I thynke, the thryd parte of our pepul lyvyng in idulnes, as personys to the commyn wele utturly unprofytabul." The nobility are brought up to hunt, hawk, gamble, eat, drink, and think nothing else is fit for a gentleman. Each, like a prince, must keep a court of idle retainers, who think they were born for nothing else. If they are not clothed in silks and velvets and have not twenty different dishes at meals, they think they lack honor. The bishops, abbots, priors, and all the other "idul abbey-lubbarys" also have their idle subordinates. Priests, monks, friars, canons form an idle train that are nothing but a burden to the earth. Great numbers of plowmen and laborers and craftsmen are also idle. The cause is simple enough: the land is not being tilled.[18] Rich graziers have bought up land for sheep-raising, and they ship the wool away. English lead, tin, iron, gold, silver are also shipped away for manufacture. As a

---

[16] Introductory letter, pp. lxxiv-lxxv.

[17] See Preface by J. M. Cowper, p. cxx.

[18] Some 300,000 persons were deprived of means of support by enclosures. See Preface by J. M. Cowper, p. cvi.

result, farmers, butchers, weavers, and other artisans have nothing to do. Nevertheless, Cardinal Pole is inclined to defend enclosures as a new source of wealth for the nation.

The second disorder, the decline in population and the inequality of numbers in each estate, is charged to the celibacy of the clergy; to the great multitude of gay but poor serving men, who never have the means to marry; to idle craftsmen and laborers, who likewise are too poor to maintain a family. Here the shift from defections in the medieval sense to the hardships of new social conditions is most evident. The decline in population is traceable in part to poor craftsmen and farmers, but they can scarcely be said to be guilty of any defection, since circumstances are against them. Moreover, since farmers, laborers, craftsmen are forced out of their trades, and since every commoner wants to be a gentleman and every gentleman wants to be a knight or a lord, the numbers of those who serve in the various ways necessary to a true commonwealth are unequal.

The third disease, the lack of good order and abundance of commodities necessary to a commonwealth, is a direct outgrowth of the second disease. Every estate is looking only for his own gain. No one considers the common good. The king himself cannot or does not cope with the disorders of the time. He should not succeed to the throne by birth, but should be elected. No country can prosper under a king not chosen by election. A like fault is primogeniture among the nobility. Even among the commons a practice similar to primogeniture has arisen, that of entailing the land upon the oldest son. This practice has sprung from arrogance and the desire of every Jack to be a gentleman. The clergy do not live in their parishes, but go off to enjoy themselves at court or in houses of the nobility, and if they do perform the service, it is all in Latin. Cardinal Pole is not a Lutheran, but the service, he thinks, should be in the vulgar tongue. The clergy, moreover, have some evil privileges: they may not be cited before a secular judge; religious houses are exempt from the jurisdiction of their bishops as well as from civil law; the privilege of sanctuary protects murderers, thieves, and fraudulent debtors. The election of prelates, by the prince or some other great man's authority, is an evil practice. As a result, the clergy are ignorant and vicious. Meanwhile, the pope takes it upon himself to dispense with the laws of God and man for money. Since the *Dialogue* was written about 1536, the pope was still to be reckoned with. The pope usurps all authorities. The power of dispensation was given by man, not to the pope alone, but to him and his college of cardinals. Only the power of absolution of sin was given by God. In abusing his power, the pope destroys the whole order of the Church. Appeals to Rome for every trifling cause, payment of annates, appeals to the Court of Arches and Probate in the archbishop's court, admission of mere youths to the clergy, the celibacy of the clergy are all sources of dishonor to the country. Judges and ministers of the law, both temporal and spiritual, have little regard for true administration of justice: "Lucur and affectyon rulyth al therin." A friend or a generous giver of fees always wins his case; the merits of the case have nothing to do with the decision. Meanwhile, plowmen and artificers have no more regard for the commonwealth than have their superiors:

Plowmen dow not dylygently labur and tyl they ground for the bryngyng forth of frutys necessary for the fode and sustenance of man; craftys men also, and al artyfycerys, schow no les neclygence in the use of theyr craftys: by reson wherof here ys in our cuntrey much darth therof and penury.

In England, one of the wealthiest countries of the world with its wool, lead, tin, iron, silver, gold, and all things necessary to the life of man, all estates complain of the lack of money. Here, again, the old charge of avarice is translated into the lack of a real commodity—money. The cities, castles, and towns are dirty and dilapidated. The country exports cattle, corn, wool, tin, lead, the necessities of life, and imports wines, fine cloths, silks, beads, knives, and such trifles. The demand for fine wines and clothes and the excess in eating and extravagant building help to impoverish rich and poor alike. Lupset concludes that the realm is probably not so poor as it seems: that no matter how fortunate they are, men will complain of poverty. Pole insists, however, that the country is poorer than it was, "for lake of gud ordur and polytyke rule."

The poverty of Scotland, much like that of England, is described in the *Complaynt of Scotlande,* and the same reasons for it are given there. The lack of agreement among estates is at the bottom of all their troubles, with one added cause: their lack of patriotism in Scotland's conflicts with England.

Toward the close of the sixteenth century and in the early seventeenth century, the abuses listed by Breton, Dekker, and Rowlands are pretty general again, or, if more specific abuses are recorded, they are those already analyzed by Starkey. The chief charge is avarice in all estates and complete disregard of the common welfare. Breton's hypothetical defections in the *Dialogue Full of Pithe and Pleasure,* of 1603, are, after all, not real shortcomings. Aside from these imaginary faults, he finds all estates guilty of disloyal murmuring against each other and of avarice. The estates in Dekker's Protestant army in *The Double PP,* of 1606, have no faults; the defections are all to be found among the Papists. These "badder fruits" consist of efforts to "clyme above" the estates of the realm and to "trample on the necks of" the king, the queen, religion, state, truth, and all the subjects of the king. The defections of the estates in Rowlands' *Looke to It: For, Ile Stabbe Ye,* of 1604, are as general as those of medieval treatments of the dance of death theme, except for the charge to the "Curious Divines" that they are "seedesmen of dissention," making the Scriptures mean what they please and stirring up their congregations about trivial matters that have no bearing on salvation.

In the political philosophizing of Smith, Bodin, Bacon, Selden, Hobbes, and Fuller the fashion of listing the defections of the estates is lost completely. No longer is it worth while to charge the different classes of society with their shortcomings. Instead the writers are interested in trying to determine the origins of institutions, the causes of their rise and fall, the best kinds of government, the classes of society in different kinds of commonwealths, and the nature of the changes in those classes. Most of the old defections are recognized as social phenomena that are as inevitable as changes in the world of nature.

CHAPTER IX

THE REMEDIES

Not all of the writers of the literature of estates feel obliged to find a remedy or remedies for the abuses that they so generously proclaim. They lament the evil days into which the world has fallen and let their lamentations suffice. Perhaps reform was expected to follow automatically, once the defections were pointed out. After all, devising remedies is a process requiring no small amount of ingenuity. In the whole range of the literature of estates about four kinds of remedies stand out as most characteristic, in four successive periods of time.

1. MEDIEVAL EXHORTATIONS TO "TURN TO GOD"

The earliest is so simple as to be scarcely recognized as a remedy. No modern political scientist, needless to say, would call it that, but to the early medieval moralist it was the only remedy. It was a religious one, as might be expected, and consisted simply of the exhortation to "turn again to God"—to cease evil-doing and do the duty ordained by God. It was also a very personal kind of remedy: a very close relation between individual sin and social disorder was always strongly felt. No social disorder could ever be removed unless every member of that society felt a personal conviction of sin and made his peace with God. The avenue of approach to God might differ slightly with the various writers, but the ultimate goal was the same. Let all classes return to God through Christ, says the author of the Latin poem *Viri fratres, servi Dei*. Only through Mary can the estates of the world approach God, says Gower. The "celestiall court" of "thre in one without begynnyng, the father & sonne & holy goost," are appealed to for "some Remedy" by the author of the ballad *Now a Dayes*. The all-important matter for every one was to seek some "remede de la court celestre."

Since sin comes solely from man, these writers show, sometimes at great length, "comment l'omme se refourmera et priera a dieu." Dudley's *Tree of Common Wealth*, Barclay's *Shyp of Folys*, and the *Mirrour for Magistrates* continue the exhortation in the sixteenth century. The author of the ballad *Now a Dayes* likewise advises individual reform:

> He that made this treatise
> Which ys called "now a dayes,"
> sheweth how the Realm decayes
>   By them that be unkynd:
> though yt be Rudely exprest,
> Desiryng to take the best,
> uppon no man to rayle ne gest
>   for that was not his mynd.
>
> But for them who doth hit Rede,
> to ther own fawtes shold take hede,
> & them reform, for hit ys nede;
>   thus he did entend;
> That people shold amend ther lyvyng
> and love God above all thyng
> beyng true and faythfull to the kyng
>   then shuld thys world amend.

Gascoigne, in the *Steele Glas*, urges all degrees of all estates to do their duties and priests especially to pray to God for amendment of all estates. It is in a kind of outburst against this constant advice that John Bale makes Cyvyle Order say: "Have ye nothyng elles but this? than God be with ye!" Even Crowley and Starkey, whose attention is usually fixed on specific disorders and remedies, take time to appeal to God for aid in determining the remedies. Cardinal Pole in Starkey's *Dialogue* asks God to "yllumynate and lyght our hartys and myndys (wych wythout hym can no truthe perceyve) that we may see the convenyent mean of restoryng to our polytyke body his perfayt state and commyn welth." Crowley advises all to pray to God for mercy and then to be content with their estate. Breton, also, urges all classes to "doe true service unto God" by performing their divinely ordained duties. With Rowlands, as with all those who used the dance of death theme before him, the advice becomes a kind of threat: do your duty, for death takes all estates in the end. Dekker, in the *Foure Birdes of Noah's Arke,* offers up prayers for all estates.

2. THE DOCTRINE OF LOVE

Out of this first remedy another grows quite naturally, that of the renewal of love among the estates of the world. If the estates fall short in their divinely appointed duties, they not only disobey God, but they also fail all mankind. They evidence a lack of love—a very necessary element in human society. The nobility must love the clergy and the commons; the clergy must love the nobility and the commons; and the commons must love their superiors, the nobility and the clergy. This remedy, like the first, would probably not be regarded by a modern political philosopher as a very important remedy; but it, too, is an earmark of much of the literature of estates and is an important medieval remedy. When a present-day president of the United States tells Brazil that peace through "affection" is the bond of the two nations, one wonders whether even now this medieval remedy is outgrown or can be superseded by laws or leagues or military manœuvres. At any rate, to the Middle Ages and to the sixteenth century love was a very practical remedy for social evils. The sources of it are not hard to find. They are biblical, classical, and medieval. The commandments of Christ bade man love God with all his heart and soul and mind and his neighbor as himself. This love of man for man was the same thing as the friendship that Plato described in *The Laws.* If one must have authority for his remedy, he could turn, then, to both the Bible and to his master Plato. The necessity of love between estates was further stressed by the medieval political doctrine that the body politic bore an analogy to the human body. In the human body, each member serves all the others in its own peculiar capacity; nor does it complain of its function or try to hinder the other members in their functions. All work together for the good of the whole. If one member should offend the rest, it should be plucked out or cut off. This doctrine, biblical in its origin, with Nicholas of Cusa and others became definite political dogma, as has been pointed out. With this three-fold authority behind it, the doctrine of love as a remedy for the defections of the medieval estates became a very important one.

The inclusion of the class satire in Ermengaud's *Le Breviari d'amor* was perhaps suggested in part by its theme of love. The love of God, the love of the sexes, the love of parents for children would be incomplete without the love of man for his neighbor. God is the source of all love, and so he is placed in the first circle of Ermengaud's symbolic Tree of Love. Nature occupies the second circle, into which the loves of mankind, both good and bad, are introduced. The vices of the various classes of society can be reformed only by love, love of God and of mankind—though the remedy is almost lost sight of in the long satire on the evils of the day.

Late medieval critics of the classes of society also preach this doctrine of love. Gilles li Muisis addresses it to each class. The prelates, for example, should love much, both great and small; all was established by reason and all should be sustained in their rights:

> Tout estoit par raison et fait et maintenut;
> Les prélas moult amoient li grant et li menut,
> Car adont tout estoient en leurs drois soustenut:
> Or pleust à Dieu k'ensi fust ore revenut!

The Game and Playe of the Chesse similarly tells all magistrates that they should love the people of their city or town and should charge no man with any villainy without cause or through envy or hate. They should be sorry and heavy-hearted to see any man complained of for any cause. The efficacy of the remedy of love is most thoroughly preached by John Gower, in the

Prologue and in the opening lines of Book I of his *Confessio amantis*. After two long works on the defections of the estates of the world, which changed no one, he proposes to treat a more hopeful theme, namely that of love:

> Forthi the stile of my writinges
> Fro this day forth I thenke change
> And speke of thing is noght so strange,
> Which every kinde hath upon honde,
> And whereupon the world mot stonde,
> And hath don sithen it began,
> And schal whil ther is any man;
> And that is love, of which I mene
> To trete, as after schal be sene.[1]

To further enforce his theme, Gower prefaces his change of program with eight Latin lines pronouncing love the ruler of the world. To be sure, his book is to be one of love stories, but he cannot resist a prologue of sermonizing once more about the corrupt estates of the world and their lack of love. In the good old days, he begins, all was as it should be. Then the estate of royalty was safe, the nobility were duly worshipped, the clergy were good examples to all the rest, and the people were obedient to the rule of government. Then love reigned:

> Tho was ther unenvied love,
> Tho was the vertu sett above
> And vice was put under fote.[2]

Now all is changed, for love is lost:

> Now stant the crop under the rote,
> The world is changed overal,
> And therof most in special
> That love is falle into discord.[3]

In the past, God has guided them with the good counsel

> That hate breke noght thassise
> Of love, which is al the chief
> To kepe a regne out of meschief.[4]

---

[1] Ed. Macaulay, Book, I, ll. 8-16.   [2] *Ibid.*, Prologue, ll. 115-17
[3] *Ibid.*, Prologue, ll. 118-21.   [4] *Ibid.*, Prologue, ll. 148-50.

But now the war of estates breaks out anew each day:

> But now men tellen natheles
> That love is fro the world departed,
> So stant the pes unevene parted
> With hem that liven now adaies.[5]

The only remedy is to restore love: May God

> Amende that wherof men pleigne
> With trewe hertes and with pleine,
> And reconcile love ayeyn,
> As he which is king sovereign
> Of al the worldes governaunce.[6]

Temporal lords, clergy, commons have all sinned through lack of love. Four empires of the world have been overthrown. Now we live in the last age, that of dissension and division between empire and papacy. The end of the world is near; so it is best to be at peace with others and to love them as one's own brother:

> Forthi good is, whil a man may,
> Echon to sette pes with other
> And loven as his oghne brother.[7]

Would that there were harmony such as "Arion" made from his harp. He brought all into accord:

> So that the comun with the lord,
> And lord with the comun also,
> He sette in love bothe tuo
> And putte away malencolie.[8]

But no more of this matter, which "only god may stiere." So Gower turns to a pleasanter kind of love theme.

The government of Utopia is founded on love. "They lyve together lovinglye," More tells us. "For no magistrate is eyther hawte or fearfull. Fathers they be called, and lyke fathers they use themselves. The citezens (as it is their dewtie) willynglye exhibite unto them dew honour without any compulsion."[9] One

---

[5] *Ibid.*, Prologue, ll. 168-71.   [6] *Ibid.*, Prologue, ll. 183-87.
[7] *Ibid.*, Prologue, ll. 1048-50.   [8] *Ibid.*, Prologue, ll. 1065-68.
[9] Bohn ed., p. 148.

of the reasons why Raphael Hythloday regards his services at
court as undesirable is that his doctrine of love would never
be heard there. He would advise the king "to endevoure him
selfe to love his subjectes, and againe to be beloved of them,
willingly to live with them, peacably to governe them, and with
other kyngdomes not to medle." He asks More, "How thinke
you it would be harde and taken?" and More replies, "So God
helpe me not very thankefully."[10] Leagues of nations are never
entered into by the Utopians. Why should they be? If love does
not suffice, will a league serve the purpose? "As touching leagues,
which in other places betwene countrey and countrey be so ofte
concluded, broken and renewed, they never make none with anie
nation. For to what purpose serve leagues? say they. As thoughe
nature had not set sufficient love betwene man and man. And
who so regardeth not nature, thinke you that he will passe for
wordes?"[11]

This doctrine of love as the solution of all corruptions continues in sixteenth-century literature of estates. The ballad *Now
a Dayes* and Barclay's *Shyp of Folys* lament the loss of "godly
charyte" and the fact that "where love was before," now mortal
hate exists, "with the comonty, and many great estate." The
avowed purpose of the *Mirrour for Magistrates* is to teach all
estates "which way to love." The writer[12] has gone to the
printer's shop to buy a book to read. There he finds this *Mirrour*,
full of the tragedies of great men. Let every reader draw his
lesson:

> Examples there, for all estates you finde,
> For iudge (I say) what justice hee shoulde use:
> The noble man, to beare a noble mynde,
> And not him selfe ambitiously abuse.
> The gentleman ungentlenes refuse,
>   The rich and poore, and ev'ry one may see,
>   Which way to love, and live in due degree.

[10] *Ibid.*, p. 62.   [11] *Ibid.*, pp. 150-51.
[12] Of Part I, Thomas Higgins. Haslewood ed., Induction, I, 17, stanza 8.

Cheke's *Hurt of Sedition* closes with the admonition to the commons that love is the strength of the commonwealth: "For love is not the knot onely of the Commonwealth, whereby divers parts be perfectly joyned together in one politique bodie, but also the strength and might of the same, gathering together into a small room with order, which scattered would else breed confusion and debate."[13] The *Complaynt of Scotlande* laments the loss of the good old days when there was no difference in estates and when the "pepil lyvit al to gydthir in ane tranquil & lovabil communite."[14] Brinkelow's *Complaynt of Roderyck Mors* laments the oppression of the poor by the rich through lack of love: the "rich covetous carl, which hath to moch already," puts off his land the poor man, who must then become a beggar and a thief, "so lytle is the lawe of love regarded, oh cruel tyrannys!"[15] Fenton's *Forme of Christian Pollicie,* in a discussion "Of Christian amitie, and how many sorts of friendships there be," preaches the doctrine of love as a remedy for the ills of the commonweal.[16] To Nicholas Breton, love is the cure for the murmuring of all estates against each other: "In summe there is almost no profession or condition wherin one doth not murmure at another; which murmuring while it continueth in the hearts of the people, it will suffer love to have no life among them: but were the worlde purged of that malicious humor, then would there bee as great a heaven, as there is now a hell in the world; wher love should establish such a Law as should never bee broken."[17]

Evidence of the biblical origin of this law of love is found in Lyndsay's *Pleasant Satyre of the Thrie Estaitis.* When Correctioun and Diligence begin to reform the realm of Rex Humanitas, they bring in three famous clerks of great intelligence, who preach the doctrine of love:

[13] Ed. of 1641, pp. 52-53.   [14] Ed. Murray, p. 144.
[15] Ed. J. M. Cowper, E.E.T.S., London, 1874, ext. ser., XXII, 9.
[16] Book VI, chap. 3.   [17] *A Murmurer,* ed. Grosart, p. 14.

Luife bene the ledder, quhilk hes bot steppis twa . . .
The first step, suithlie of this ledder is,
  To luife they God, as the fontaine and well
Of luife, and grace; and the secund, I wis,
  To luife thy nichtbour as thou luiffis thy sell.[18]

Crowley's remedy for sedition, which, like Sir John Cheke's, is
love, is drawn from the same source: "Consider, firste, if thou
have loved thy neighboure as they self; consider if thou have
done nothing unto him that thou wouldeste not that he shoulde
do unto the."[19]

Evidence of Plato's influence on this doctrine of love is found
in abundance in the *Utopia*. In Bale's *Kynge Johan* also Plato
is cited as authority:

Plato thowght alwayes that no hygher love coulde be
Than a man to peyne hymself for hys own countreye.[20]

Examples of the influence of the analogy drawn between the
human body and the body politic on the doctrine of love are
found in Starkey's *Dialogue*. A commonwealth, to be healthy,
must have "every one also dowyng hys duty to other wyth
brotherly love, one lovyng one a nother as membrys and partys
of one body."[21] Perfect harmony can exist only "where as al
the partys, as membrys of one body, be knyt togyddur in perfayt love and unyte; every one dowyng hys offyce and duty."[22]
Such love and harmony are a foreshadowing of that to be experienced in the hereafter: "And so thus, when every parte,
aftur thys maner, dothe hys offyce and duty requyred therto,
wyth perfayt love and amyte one to a nother, one glad to succur
and ayd another as membrys and partys of one body; to the
intent that, aftur thys worldly and cyvyle lyfe here paysybly
passyd and vertusely spent, they may at the last al togydur
attayne such end and felycyte as, by the gudness of God and

[18] *Poetical Works,* ed. Laing, II, 173, ll. 3506, 3509-12.
[19] *The Way to Wealth,* ed. Cowper, p. 135.
[20] Ed. Manly, p. 603.   [21] Ed. Cowper, p. 50.   [22] *Ibid.,* p. 55.

ordynance of nature, ys determyd to the excellent dygnyte and nature of man."[23]

3. THE NEW DEPENDENCE ON LAW

Such a Utopian remedy does not satisfy all the writers of the literature of estates, however, for many of the English writers of the sixteenth century enumerate more or less specific solutions, somewhat in the manner of modern sociological or economic treatises. The same writers who detected the new social problems of the time are those who try to find remedies: Hales, Stubbs, Crowley, Starkey, and the author of the *Complaynt of Scotlande*. Starkey's *Dialogue*[24] is again most complete, and the rest agree or disagree with his solutions. Here, as in modern times, not all the theorists have the same remedy; in some cases their conclusions are quite opposed to each other. The first abuse, that of idleness, Cardinal Pole would remove by proper training of the youth of the realm and by law. Every man should be compelled to put his children in school or at some craft at seven years of age. Every one who excels in his calling should be rewarded by the king. Those busy about useless occupations—merchants importing wines and trifles and exporting necessities—should be regarded as idlers and, like all idlers, should be banished. Officers should be appointed in every town to see that people are properly employed. Idleness among the nobility must also be removed, by education. They must be constrained, "by lawful punnyschement," to exercise themselves in all such things as are necessary to the defense of the commonwealth: they must learn the discipline of the commonwealth and must practice feats of arms, to be worthy of their name. All this they should do with the same diligence that plowmen labor and till the ground for the common food. Concerning idleness among the clergy, Pole is less explicit. There are a great many unprofitable religious persons, but he wouldn't

[23] *Ibid.*, pp. 55-56.
[24] *Ibid.*, pp. 143 ff.

banish them and their monasteries. Rather some reform should be made in them. Youths should not be allowed to enter: only men with a fervent love of religion. This is not the place, he says, to discuss the matter.

The second abuse, that of a declining population and inequality of numbers in the different estates, is to be remedied by natural procreation, brought about by marriage. The celibacy of the church should be done away with, at least for secular priests. For monks, canons, friars, and nuns, Cardinal Pole thinks there should be abbeys, to which, after lawful proof of chastity, they might retire. Also, an ordinance should be passed that no gentleman may be allowed to keep more serving-men than he can "promote and set forward to some honest fascyon of lyvyng and lawful matrymony." Those who marry should be given a house and a portion of waste land, for a nominal rent. Privileges should be given to those having five children: "they schold pay nother talage" (labor tax or money tax), "except he were worth a hundred markys in guddys; nor he schold not be constraynyd to go forth to warre, except he wold of hys owne voluntary wyl, wyth such other lyke immunytes and pryvylegys, as may easely be founde." Those who do not marry should not have the honor of married men, nor hold office in their city or town. Every bachelor should pay a tax, a shilling to a pound, yearly. This money should be given to those who have many children and to virgins. When these bachelors die, half of their goods should be distributed, if they are not priests, and all of them, if they are priests. The cause of the inequality in numbers in the different estates is that everyone takes the easiest trade and the one in which there is hope of most gain. There are too few plowmen, too many courtiers and idle servants, too few good artisans, too many superstitious priests, and so on. A "chief mean" should exist in every craft, to determine who and how many can enter. Then every man should be compelled by law to apply himself to his work. Death should be the punishment for those who despise the order of society.

The third abuse, the general disorder, is due to the lack of good rulers and good laws. Good rulers are necessary, as Plato also said. It is not too much to expect to find such a ruler as prefers the common good to all other things; but he should be elected by Parliament and not succeed to the throne. Since "we are barbarous," however, "it is convenient to take him by succession." If he must succeed, then he must rule jointly with a council, not of his choosing, but chosen by a majority in Parliament. The Great Parliament should assemble only to elect a king, or for some other urgent cause. But the authority of Parliament, vested in a council of fourteen, should always remain in London, to see that the king does not violate the laws, to call the Great Parliament when necessary, and to pass on acts of federation, peace, or war. The king should have his council, besides, consisting of ten men: two bishops, four lords, four men learned in law. Without the consent of this council, the king should do nothing. With these checks on the authority of the king, the realm would be freed from tyranny and disorder. All inferior officers would be called to account, and the people would be cured of that negligence which allows the land to lie untilled and crafts to be "so ill occupied." If the Statute of Enclosures were enforced and pasture land were turned into arable as before, there would be abundance and prosperity. All drunkenness, gluttony, gambling, poverty would disappear. Imports and exports must be restricted by law: wool, tin, and lead must not be exported, but must be used in manufactures at home. The Statute of Apparel must be revised, taverns prohibited, unreasonable duties on imports of necessities abolished, more cattle raised, rents not increased. The law concerning the entailing of estates must be revised: younger brothers must be provided for, and fathers, after proof before a judge, should have power to disinherit heirs who have not behaved well. The faults of the spiritualty should also be corrected by law. The pope usurps authority to dispense with all laws without consulting his cardinals. This he should not do. Appeals to Rome are bad. The Peter's Pence may be paid, but not the Annates or first fruits, except in the case of archbishops. The manner of living of bishops and abbots should be changed. Every bishop's income should be divided in four parts: one to re-build churches in their dioceses, one to maintain poor youths in study, one to be given to poor maidens and others, and one to be reserved for maintenance of himself and his household. Abbots and priors should be elected every three years as in Italy. They should give an account of their office, should live among the brethren, and not "triumph in chambers" as they do now. Parsons and curates similarly should be compelled to reside upon their benefices, there to teach and preach and distribute all they can spare to the poor of their parishes. No one should be admitted to the priesthood until thirty years of age. Good schools must be founded, universities and grammar schools must be reformed, and the order of studies changed. There should be one superior officer in every great city to see that the others do their duty, like the censor in Rome. There should also be an edile to look after the health of the community.

In spite of Cardinal Pole's very evident dependence on legis-lation to reform the estates, he adds that the laws should be reduced to a small number and written in English or Latin. The civil law of Rome should be adopted as the English com-mon law, as it is in almost all Christian countries. This "most auncyent and nobyl monument of the Romaynys prudence and pollycy" should replace "the lawys gyven to us of such a bar-barouse natyon as the Normannys be."

With Starkey's remedies those of Hales and Stubbs and Crowley more or less coincide. They too would discourage ex-ports of the necessities and would manufacture cloth, clothes, paper, leather goods, glass, iron tools, and so forth at home. New trades should also be started. By these means twenty thousand people would be set to work. Skilled workmen should be encouraged to remain by free house-rent and by loans of money. Makers of goods for export should be encouraged. It is Harrison in his *Description of England,* written some twenty-five years later, who reverses this judgment by saying that there are too many trades in England and that many commodities could be more cheaply provided from other countries. Bodin, writing in the latter part of the sixteenth century, stresses, as does Starkey, the need of censors in every town. All agree that the enclosures should be reopened to tillage, that the towns and villages should be rebuilt, that the old rents should be restored, that the coinage should be put on a firm basis, and that the clergy should shun pluralities and render up all tithes in excess of their needs. To be sure, Parliament in the sixteenth century was always enacting statutes about enclosures, restoration of towns and villages, raising of rents, poor relief, monopolies, bribery, the coinage; but, as in modern times, law was disregarded and many ways were found to evade it. "The Act against pulling down farm houses was evaded by repairing one room for the use of a shepherd; a single furrow was driven across a field to prove that it was still under the plough; the cattle owners, to escape the statutes against sheep, held their flocks in the names of their sons or servants."[25]

This sixteenth-century tendency to seek relief in law is in strong contrast with the medieval religious exhortation. It is significant of a changing age, when feudal restrictions are giving way to more democratic principles, and it foreshadows the decline of a literature that was primarily a literature of feudalism.

4. New Theories of Government

The fourth kind of remedy suggested by these critics of the estates of the world is obviously an outgrowth from the third

[25] Starkey's *Dialogue,* Preface by J. M. Cowper, p. cix. See also K. L. Gregg's "Thomas Dekker: A Study in Economic and Social Backgrounds," *University of Washington Publications,* II: 68-69, 76 f., 85-86 (July, 1924).

type. Once the stamp of legislation is set, it persists; and so such political theorists as Smith, Bacon, Bodin, Hobbes, and Selden, without protesting over the faults of society, seek the means to social and political order in forms of government. To Bacon and Bodin, the beauty of order is best maintained by monarchy and a society of three estates, each consisting of fitting numbers and not overburdened. To Smith, Selden, and Hobbes, government is a kind of social contract, a "society or common doing of a multitude of free men collected together and united by common accord and covenauntes among themselves, for the conversation of themselves, aswell in peace as in warre."[26] In such a society, "A King is a thing men have made for their own sakes, for quietness sake. Just as in a Family one Man is appointed to buy Meat. . . . "[27] With little or no mention of the defections of the estates, these theories seem to have less of the nature of remedies than of political thory for its own sake. The end of the literature of estates is near, as another of its characteristic traits drops out of sight.

A nice study in contrast of early and late remedies is afforded by comparing Bacon's essay *Of Seditions and Troubles* with Cheke's *Hurt of Sedition*. Cheke's method, as we have seen, is exhortation to the commons to do their duty and to love the estates who rule over them. Bacon has no such "general preservatives," but a "just cure," that "must answer to the particular disease."[28] The remedy must be one of "counsel rather than rule." The causes and motives of seditions he analyzes as: "innovation in religion; taxes; alteration of laws and customs; breaking of privileges; general oppression; advancement of unworthy persons; strangers; dearths; disbanded soldiers; factions grown desperate; and whatsoever, in offending people,

---

[26] Thomas Smith, *De republica Anglorum,* ed. Alston, Book I, chap. 10, p. 20.

[27] John Selden, *Table-talk,* ed. Arber, p. 60.

[28] *Essays,* ed. Henry Morley, London, 1888, pp. 99 f.

joineth and knitteth them in a common cause." For this matter-of-fact array of causes and motives (not defections), Bacon suggests remedies:

The first remedy or prevention is to remove by all means possible that material cause of sedition whereof we spake: which is want and poverty in the estate. To which purpose serveth the opening and well-balancing of trade; the cherishing of manufactures; the banishing of idleness; the repressing of waste and excess by sumptuary laws; the improvement and husbanding of the soil; the regulating of prices of things vendible; the moderating of taxes and tributes; and the like. . . . Above all things, good policy is to be used that the treasure and moneys in a state be not gathered into few hands. For otherwise a state may have a great stock, and yet starve. And money is like muck, not good except it be spread. This is done chiefly by suppressing, or at the least keeping a strait hand upon the devouring trades of usury, ingrossing, great pasturages, and the like.

Bacon, like Cheke, recognizes the need of military force to suppress sedition, but, unlike Cheke, he has a warning: "But let such military persons be assured, and well reputed of, rather than factious and popular; holding also good correspondence with the other great men in the state; or else the remedy is worse than the disease." Cheke belongs to the old order; Bacon is of the new. Cheke writes in the spirit of the old literature of estates; with Bacon, the fashion is about to disappear.

CHAPTER X

THE DISAPPEARANCE OF THE TYPE
IN OTHER FORMS

THE middle of the seventeenth century, significant for
many changes in the history of literature, also marks
the disappearance, approximately, of the literature of the
estates of the world. For some five and a half centuries, in various forms, this feudal philosophy survived in a more or less distinct literary fashion. "Syllables govern the world," said John
Selden about the time that the literature of estates became a
form of the past. To be sure, syllables still govern the world, but
now they are somewhat different. Many of the syllables that
governed the feudal world are gone and with them the forms
of literature expressing that world.

1. Causes of Disappearance

The causes of the disappearance are not hard to find. With
its earmarks of lament, of enumeration of the classes of society
and their defections, of a philosophy of the divine origin of
those classes and their duties to each other, and of exhortation
to turn to God or to love one another, the literature of estates
could not long survive in a world of new conditions, new tastes,
and new literary forms. The shift in authority from estate to
state, the shift in authority from clergy to individual conscience,
and the growing importance of the commons meant the gradual
decline of a literary pattern constructed on the philosophy of
a feudal society. New tastes, seeking classical and Renaissance
matters and manners, were no longer satisfied with the dogmatic,
encyclopedic classifying of men and things that delighted an
earlier time. The highest praise that Abbé Gilles could bestow
upon the Recluse of Molliens and the *Romance of the Rose* was
that they were so all-inclusive:

Il parollent de tout et de tous et de toutes.[1]

The encyclopedic treatment of humanity was as delightful as that of science. All mankind must be put into classes. In a Renaissance world, where the individual was important, where lyrics, epics, drama, classical satire, and a new kind of prose lent new charms to literature, the wonder is that the literature of estates survived so long. Its survival in England is further evidence of the medieval woof in the Renaissance tapestry. By 1612, however, only ten years after *Hamlet* appeared, even the word *estate* had begun to lose its old significance. Bacon writes of nobility "first as a portion of an estate; then as a condition of particular persons,"[2] meaning, as his following remarks show, the nobility of a state. The particular persons prove to be the old estates. And in the middle of the century one chapter of James Harrington's *System of Politics* begins with the aphorism: "That which is the matter of government, is what we call an estate, be it in lands, goods or mony."[3] The "syllables" have taken on the new significance.

2. OTHER FORMS INTO WHICH IT MERGED

The subject matter of the literature of estates was obviously not suited to verse. It is not surprising, therefore, that it merged into certain prose forms that treated some one phase of the old combination of matters. The old interest in class defections found expression in a new prose of analysis of social and economic abuses.[4] The old interest in origins and duties of classes found expression in a new prose of political theory. The rise of formal satire, on classical models, gave opportunity for the satiric threatenings of social critics, whose predecessors used the form of the literature of estates. The new essay form gave

[1] *Poésies,* ed. Lettenhove, I, 355, stanza 6, l. 1.
[2] *Of Nobility.*
[3] *Oceana and Other Works,* ed. Toland, 1771, chap. II, p. 466.
[4] See *Cambridge History of English Literature,* "Early Writings on Politics and Economics," Vol. IV, chap. XV.

Bacon and others a short, concise medium for expression of social, political, and economic truths. The constantly increasing tendency of writers of the literature of estates to enumerate more and more degrees or types of people within each estate found vent in the new interest in character writing in the seventeenth century. As has been pointed out, with Breton and Rowlands the line between enumeration of estates and character writing becomes almost indistinguishable.

3. MODERN INSTANCES

As a literary pattern, the literature of estates disappeared, but even now one may come unexpectedly upon a modern instance suggestive of its manner. While Carlyle, probably without much knowledge of the literature of estates, was deploring the loss of the good old feudal times, the days when a kind of land aristocracy "managed the Governing of this English People, and had the reaping of the Soil of England in return," when, as a result, a " 'Splendour of God,' as in William Conqueror's rough oath, did inform, more and more, with a heavenly nobleness, all departments of their work and life,"[5] Thackeray was writing his *Book of Snobs* for *Punch*. With what zest he portrayed The Snob Royal, Great City Snobs, Some Military Snobs, Clerical Snobs, University Snobs, and others! He had no illusions about the "heavenly nobleness" of feudal society; and he saw too many of the objectionable traits of the medieval estates of the world about him to long for more. Distinctions in rank, he says, were set up as a part of "the brutal, unchristian, blundering feudal system." The modern aristocrat who boasts of being "own cousin to Charles Martel, Orlando Furioso, Philip Augustus, Peter the Cruel, and Frederick Barbarossa," and all the other types of modern snobs, are remnants of that system. Times are improved, but feudal traits survive.

More definite modern remnants of the literature of estates

[5] *Past and Present*, New York, 1898, p. 246.

may be found, however, in broadside verse and song and in woodcut, tavern signboard, and caricature.[6] In the beginning of the nineteenth century, an engraving was made for a shop in Chartres by a theatrical producer who was giving some performances there. The picture contained four figures: a soldier in the uniform of the first Empire, a priest, a lawyer seated and holding a bag, and a peasant with basket and shovel. Each figure was accompanied by some verses, which stated his service to the rest. The sense of the verses was as follows: for the soldier, "Je vous défends tous"; for the priest, "Je prie pour vous tous"; for the peasant, "Je vous nourris tous"; for the lawyer, "Je vous mange tous."[7]

Apparently at the time of the second Empire, a broadside printed in vivid reds and blues bore the same four figures. They were accompanied by the words of four songs, each lamenting his difficult "estate." The priest sang:

> Je prie pour vous.
> À l'exemple des immortels,
> Être à chaque instant en prière,
> Au culte sacré des autels
> Vouer mon existence entière;
> Tel est mon état; mais hélas!
> Pour cette fonction auguste,
> Autant qu'on peut l'être ici-bas,
> Il faudrait toujours être juste.
> Malgré mes efforts et mes soins,
> Si je ne puis, en digne prêtre,
> Être juste, être saint, du moins
> Je veux vous enseigner à l'être;
> Suivez du code chrétien
> La morale facile et pure:
> Aimez-vous; vous servirez bien
> Le créateur de la nature.

[6] See *Melusine*, VI: 49-50, 97-99 (1892-93); and VII: 147-154 (1894-95). Notes by H. Gaidoz.

[7] Reproduced in J. M. Garnier's *Histoire de l'imagerie populaire à Chartres*, Chartres, 1869, p. 113.

The soldier sang:

> Je vous défends tous.
> A moi-même toujours pareil;
> Pour moi, chaud, froid ont mêmes charmes;
> Vous vous plongez dans le sommeil
> Pendant que je suis sous les armes.
> J'y suis pour vous, pour vos parents,
> Procureurs, paysans et prêtres,
> Je défendrai vos descendants,
> Et j'ai défendu vos ancêtres.
>
> Goûtai-je un instant de loisir!
> Le tambour bat, et sans murmure,
> J'abandonne repos et plaisir,
> L'amour, l'amitié, la nature.
> Je pars sans savoir où je vais;
> Qu'importe! c'est à la victoire:
> Je pars, sous l'étendard français,
> Le seul qui conduit à la gloire.

The peasant sang:

> Je vous nourris tous.
> La bêche et le pic à la main,
> Je tourne et retourne la terre,
> Et force à sortir de son sein
> Les sucs nourriciers qu'elle enserre.
> Vous passez le temps à prier,
> A plaider, vous faites la guerre,
> Je vous apprends à m'oublier,
> En vous sauvant de la misère.
>
> Vilains, je porte en vos marchés,
> Chaque jour votre subsistance;
> Pendant que vous êtes couchés
> Je pourvois à votre abondance;
> Je la varie en vos repas:
> Mon repas est toujours le même
> Pour vous c'est toujours *mardi gras,*
> Et pour moi toujours le carême.

The lawyer's song was a defense of his profession to his client.

I am like the soldier, he said to the client. How so? asked the client. Then the lawyer sang:

> Je vais vous l'apprendre:
> Il vous défend tous par état;
> Et le mien est de vous défendre.
> Le soldat en propre n'a rien,
> Mes écus sont toujours les vôtres:
> Il sert et meurt pour votre bien,
> Je ne veux que celui des autres.

The client objected: the lawyer only devoured all the rest. And the lawyer concluded his song:

> Dans ce monde tout est mangé;
> Le ver que tel oiseau consomme,
> Un jour par l'homme en est vengé,
> Et je venge l'oiseau de l'homme.

The popularity of the design is shown by the fact that similar pictures were made in the nineteenth century in Switzerland, England, Scotland, and Germany. The Swiss picture[8] also had four figures: a king, with the inscription "Je gouverne tout"; a priest with "Je prie pour tout"; a soldier with "Je combat pour tout"; and the people, inscribed "Je paye pour tout." The English[9] apparently dates from the end of the eighteenth century and bears five figures in full regalia of office and with five inscriptions: a king, whose motto is "I govern all'; a bishop, whose motto is "I pray for all"; a lawyer, whose motto is "I plead for all"; a soldier, whose motto is "I fight for all"; and a poor farmer with scythe and rake, whose motto is "I pay for all." These Five Alls decorated a country signboard. They were adapted by the Scotch caricaturist John Kay (1742-1826) to ridicule some contemporary celebrities.[10] Two cartoons, ap-

[8] Reproduced in Blavignac's *Histoire des enseignes d'hôtelleries*, Geneva, 1878, p. 397.

[9] Reproduced in Fr. Grose's *A Classical Dictionary of the Vulgar Tongue*, 1796, under "Alls."

[10] The original caricature is in the British Museum. Reproduced in the *Magasin pittoresque*, 1871, p. 344, and in H. Paton's *A Series of Original Portraits and Caricature Etchings* by John Kay, Edinburgh, 1838, II, 46.

parently printed by a large printing house, that publishes works in different languages and leaves off its name so that they can be sold in different countries without evidence of foreign source, appeared in French, Italian, German, and Spanish. The figures were eight in number and were arranged on ascending and descending stairs. On the first step of the ascending stairs stood the sovereign or ruler, who said: "I govern all of you"; on the next step stood the nobleman, who said: "I command all of you"; on the next step stood the priest, who said: "I pray for all of you"; and on the top step was the Jew, who said: "I make money on all of you." On the first step of the descending stairs stood the soldier, who said: "I defend all of you"; the beggar stood just below him, saying: "I ask alms of all of you"; the peasant, just below the beggar, said: "I leave it to the good God, for my duty is to feed all six of you." Below all these seven figures and in the center of the whole design was a picture of the plowman, driving his plow. A Viennese adaptation appeared in the satiric journal *Kikeriki* on October 29, 1893. The engraving bore four figures, arranged with inscriptions as follows:

A peasant holding his scythe and standing near a large sack bearing the word *Corn*.	A school-master standing near a blackboard, with stick in one hand and book in the other.
NAEHRSTAND	LEHRSTAND
An Austrian soldier equipped for battle.	A man in frock coat and spectacles holding in his raised left hand an enormous pair of shears, and carrying under his right arm a portfolio with the inscription: *Minister of Finance*. In front of him, a sheep on which was written: *People*.
WEHRSTAND	
	SCHEERSTAND

Both the editor of the *Magasin pittoresque* and H. Paton, as Gaidoz points out, regarded the theme as original with John Kay.

The appearance of the Minister of Finance as the one who "shears all," like the caricature of John Kay, must have lent a startling significance to this old medieval design.

So the interest in the estates of the world survived in these popular forms, with their attention to pictorial values rather than to literary uses. Like the medieval woodcuts and mural paintings of Death leading the dance of all estates to the grave or of Fauvel enjoying the caresses of all classes of society, these modern designs render vivid the old world of nobility, clergy, and commons in a way that the printed page cannot do. It is to the literature of estates, however, that the present-day reader must turn for the most complete and most intimate revelation of that world.

BIBLIOGRAPHY

THE following list includes all books used in this study, except such general reference works as might be necessary in any work in comparative literature.

ALDEN, RAYMOND MACDONALD, The Rise of Formal Satire in England under Classical Influence, Philadelphia, 1899.

ALLEN, JOHN WILLIAM, A History of Political Thought in the Sixteenth Century, London, 1928.

ARISTOTLE, Politica, trans. by Benjamin Jowett, revised ed. W. D. Ross, Oxford, 1921.

ASHBY, GEORGE, Poems, ed. Mary Bateson, "E.E.T.S.," ext. ser., No. LXXVI, London, 1899.

BACON, SIR FRANCIS, Essays, ed. Henry Morley, London, 1888.

BARACK, KARL AUGUST, ed., Des Teufels Netz, "Bibliothek des Litterarischen Vereins in Stuttgart," Vol. LXX, Stuttgart, 1863.

BARCLAY, ALEXANDER, Certayne Egloges, reprint from 1570 ed., "Spenser Society, Pubs.," No. XXXVIII, Manchester, 1885.

——— The Mirrour of Good Maners, reprint from 1570 ed., "Spenser Society, Pubs.," No. XXXVIII, Manchester, 1885.

——— The Shyp of Folys, original ed., London, 1509.

——— The Ship of Fools, ed. T. H. Jamieson, 2 vols., Edinburgh and London, 1874.

BODIN, JEAN, Six livres de la république, trans. by Richard Knolles, London, 1606.

Boke of St. Albans, facsimile reprint, Introduction by William Blades, London, 1899.

BONET, HONORÉ, L'Arbre des batailles, Paris, 1493.

BRANT, SEBASTIAN, Das Narren Schyff, original ed., Basle, 1494.

——— Das Narrenschiff, ed. Friedrich Zarncke, Leipzig, 1854.

BRETON, NICHOLAS, The Works in Verse and Prose, ed. the Rev. A. B. Grosart (Chertsey Worthies' Library), 2 vols., Edinburgh, 1879.

BRINKELOW, HENRY, Henry Brinklow's Complaynt of Roderyck Mors, ed. J. Meadows Cowper, "E.E.T.S.," ext. ser., No. XXII, London, 1874.

BROOKE, FULKE GREVILLE, "Poems of Monarchy," The Works in Verse and Prose Complete, ed. the Rev. A. B. Grosart (Fuller Worthies' Library), 4 vols., Vol. I, Blackburn, Lancashire, 1870.

BULLEIN, WILLIAM, A Dialogue against the Fever Pestilence, ed. Mark W. and A. H. Bullen, "E.E.T.S.," ext. ser., No. LII, London, 1888.

CALLERY, ALPHONSE, Histoire de l'origine, des pouvoirs et des attributions des États Généraux et Provinciaux depuis la féodalité jusqu'aux États de 1355, Brussels, 1881.

CAMPBELL, GEORGE, The Philosophy of Rhetoric, 2 vols., London, 1776.

CARLYLE, THOMAS, Past and Present, ed. Henry Duff Traill, New York, 1898.

CAXTON, WILLIAM, Dialogues in French and English, ed. Henry Bradley, "E.E.T.S.," ext.ser., No. LXXIX, London, 1900.

―――― The Game and Playe of the Chesse, reprint of 1st (1494) ed., by William E. A. Axon, London, 1883.

―――― The Mirrour of the World, ed. Oliver H. Prior, "E.E.T.S.," ext. ser., No. CX, London, 1913.

CHARTIER, ALAIN, Le Quadrilogue invectif, ed. E. Droz, Paris, 1923.

CHAUCER, GEOFFREY, Complete Works, ed. the Rev. Walter W. Skeat, 6 vols., Oxford, 1894-1900.

CHEKE, SIR JOHN, The True Subiect to the Rebell. Or the Hurt of Sedition, How Greivous It Is to a Common-wealth, reprint from 1st (1549) ed. by L. Lichfield, Oxford, 1641.

CLAUDIN, ANATOLE, Histoire de l'imprimerie en France au XVe et XVIe siècle, 4 vols., Paris, 1900-14.

COOPER, THOMAS, An Admonition to the People of England, ed. Edward Arber (English Scholars' Library, No. XV), Birmingham, 1883.

CRANSTOUN, JAMES, ed., Satirical Poems of the Time of the Reformation, "Scottish Text Society, Pubs.," Nos. XX, XXIV, XXVIII, XXX, 2 vols., Edinburgh and London, 1891-93.

CROWLEY, ROBERT, Select Works, ed. J. Meadows Cowper, "E.E.T.S.," ext. ser., No. XV, London, 1872.

D'AUSSY, LEGRAND, "Le Doctrinal rural du temps présent," described with quotations by Legrand d'Aussy, Notices et extraits des manuscrits de la Bibliothèque Nationale et autres bibliothèques, V, 523-41, Paris, 1798.

DEKKER, THOMAS, Non-dramatic Works, ed. the Rev. A. B. Grosart (The Huth Library), 5 vols., London and Aylesbury, 1885.

DESCHAMPS, EUSTACHE, Œuvres complètes, ed. Le Marquis de Queux de Saint-Hilaire, "Société des anciens textes français, Pubs.," No. IX, 11 vols., Vol. II, Paris, 1880.

DRYDEN, JOHN, Works, ed. Sir Walter Scott and George Saintsbury, 18 vols., Vol. X, Edinburgh, 1885.

DUDLEY, EDMUND, The Tree of Common Wealth, printed for the first time by the Brotherhood of the Rosy Cross, Manchester, 1859.

DU MÉRIL, ÉDÉLESTAND, ed., Poésies inédites du moyen âge, Paris, 1854.

—— ed., Poésies populaires latines du moyen âge, Paris, 1847.

DUNBAR, WILLIAM, Poems, ed. H. Bellyse Baildon, Cambridge, 1907.

DUNNING, WILLIAM ARCHIBALD, A History of Political Theories Ancient and Medieval, New York, 1916.

ELYOT, SIR THOMAS, The Boke Named the Governour, ed. Henry Herbert Stephen Croft, 2 vols., London, 1883.

ERMENGAUD, MATFRE, Le Breviari d'amor, ed. Gabriel Azaïs, "Société archéologique, scientifique et littéraire de Béziers," 2 vols., Béziers, 1862.

ÉTIENNE CHARLES L'ABBÉ BRASSEUR DE BOURBOURG, ed., Popol Vuh, Paris, 1861.

ÉTIENNE DE FOUGÈRES, Le Livre de manières, facsimile of MS 295 in the library of Angers, France.

FEGER, GERHARD, Rutebeuf's Kritik an den Zuständen seiner Zeit, Freiburg, 1920.

FENTON, SIR GEOFFREY, A Forme of Christian Pollicie, original ed., London, 1574.

FITZHERBERT, SIR ANTHONY, The Book of Husbandry, ed. the Rev. Walter W. Skeat, "English Dialect Society," Series D, London, 1882. (Wrongly attributed to Sir Anthony.)

FLÜGEL, EWALD, "Gower's Mirour de l'omme und Chaucer's Prolog," Anglia, XXIV (Oct., 1901), 437-508.

FULLER, THOMAS, The History of the Worthies of England, original ed., London, 1662.

FURNIVALL, FREDERICK JAMES, ed., The Babees Book, "E.E.T.S.," orig. ser., No. XXXII, London, 1868.

——ed., Ballads from Manuscripts, "Ballad Society, Pubs.," Nos. I-III, X, London, 1868-73.

—— ed., Queene Elizabethes Achademy, "E.E.T.S.," ext. ser., No. VIII, London, 1869.

GAGUIN, ROBERT, Roberti Gaguini epistole et orationes, ed. Louis Thuasne, "Bibliothèque littéraire de la renaissance," Vols. II-III, Paris, 1904.

GAIDOZ, HENRY, "Un ancêtre du 'Quatrième État' dans l'imagerie populaire," Melusine, VI (1892-93), 49-50, 97-99; and VII (1894-95), 147-54.

GASCOIGNE, GEORGE, Complete Works, ed. John W. Cunliffe, 2 vols., Cambridge, 1910.

GERVAIS DU BUS, Le Roman de Fauvel, ed. Arthur Långfors, "Société des anciens textes français, Pubs.," Vol. LXXII, Paris, 1914-19.

GIERKE, OTTO VON, Political Theories of the Middle Ages, trans. by Frederic W. Maitland, Cambridge, 1913.

GOOGE, BARNABE, Eglogs, Epytaphes, & Sonettes, ed. Edward Arber, London, 1871.

GOWER, JOHN, Works in Verse and Prose, ed. G. C. Macaulay, 4 vols., Oxford, 1899.

GRABEIN, PAUL, Die altfranzösischen Gedichte über die verschieden Stände der Gesellschaft, Halle, n. d. —ca. 1894.

GREGG, KATE LEILA, Thomas Dekker: A Study in Economic and Social Backgrounds, "University of Washington Pubs. Language and Literature," Vol. II, No. 2, July, 1924.

GUILLAUME, Le Besant de Dieu, ed. Ernst Martin, Halle, 1869.

GUILLAUME DE DEGUILLEVILLE, Le Pèlerinage de la vie humaine, ed. J. J. Stürzinger, Roxburghe Club, Pubs., London, 1893.

GUIOT DE PROVINS, Les Œuvres de Guiot de Provins, ed. John Orr, "Pubs. de l'Université de Manchester, Ser. française," No. I, Manchester, 1915.

HAKE, EDWARD, Newes Out of Powles Churchyarde, ed. Charles Edmonds, London, 1872. A reprint of the amplified 1579 ed.

HARRINGTON, JAMES, Oceana and Other Works, ed. John Toland, London, 1771.

HARRISON, WILLIAM, A Description of England, ed. Frederick J. Furnivall, "New Shakespere Society," London, 1877. New ed., London, 1908.

HASLEWOOD, JOSEPH, ed., A Mirrour for Magistrates, 3 vols., London, 1815.

HÉLINANT, Les Vers de la mort, ed. Fr. Wulff and Em. Walberg, "Société des anciens textes français, Pubs.," No. LIII, Paris, 1905.

HENRYSON, ROBERT, Poems, ed. G. Gregory Smith, "Scottish Text Society," 3 vols., Edinburgh, 1906, 1908, 1914.

HEYWOOD, JOHN, The Spider and the Fly, ed. John S. Farmer, London, 1908.

―――― Of Gentleness and Nobility, printed with *The Spider and the Fly*. (Probably wrongly attributed to Heywood.)

HILDEBRAND, KARL, AND GERING, HUGO, eds., Die Lieder der älteren Edda, Paderborn, 1904. Trans. by Henry Adams Bellows, *Edda Sæmundar*, New York, 1923.

HILL, RICHARD, Songs, Carols, and Other Miscellaneous Pieces, from

Balliol MS 354, Richard Hill's Commonplace-book, ed. Roman Dyboski, "E.E.T.S.," ext. ser., No. CI, London, 1907.

HOBBES, THOMAS, Leviathan, ed. Henry Morley, 2d ed., London, 1886.

HOOKER, RICHARD, Of the Laws of Ecclesiastical Polity, ed. John Keble, 3 vols., Oxford, 1886.

HUGO VON TRIMBERG, Der Renner, ed. Gustav Ehrismann, "Bibliothek des litterarischen Vereins in Stuttgart," Vols. CCXLVII-CCXLVIII (1908-09) and CCLII (1909).

HUGUES DE BERZÉ, "La Bible au Seigneur de Berzé," *Fabliaux et contes des poètes françois des XI, XII, XIII, XIV et XVe siècles,* pub. by Barbazan-Meon, 4 vols., II, 394-420, Paris, 1808.

HUIZINGA, J., The Waning of the Middle Ages, London, 1927.

JACOBUS MAGNI, Sophilogium, printed by the R Printer, Strassburg, 1468.

JONES, HARRIE STUART VEDDER, "The Plan of the Canterbury Tales," *Modern Philology,* XIII (May, 1915), 45-48.

JUBINAL, ACHILLE, ed., "Le Doctrinal le Sauvage," *Nouveau recueil de contes, dits, fabliaux, et autres pièces inédites des XIIIe, XIVe et XVe siècles,* 2 vols., II, 150-61, Paris, 1842.

KAIL, DR. J., ed., Twenty-six Political and Other Poems, "E.E.T.S.," orig. ser., No. CXXIV, London, 1904.

KARAJAN, THEODOR VON, ed., "Sermones nulli parcentes," *Zeitschrift für deutsches Althertum,* II, 15-92, Leipzig, 1842.

KARL, LOUIS, Un moraliste bourbonnais du XIVe siècle et son œuvre. Le Roman de Mandevie et les mélancolies de Jean Dupin, "Société d'émulation du bourbonnais, lettres, sciences, et arts. Bull.," XX, 38-49, 73-80, 113-28, 159-62, 184-94, 209-18, Moulins, 1912.

KELLER, ADELBERT VON, ed., Fastnachtspiele aus dem fünfzehnten Jahrhundert, "Bibliothek des litterarischen Vereins in Stuttgart," Vols. XXVIII-XXX, Stuttgart, 1853.

KITTREDGE, GEORGE LYMAN, "Chaucer and the *Roman de carité,*" *Modern Language Notes,* XII (Feb., 1897), 113-15.

———— "Chaucer's Discussion of Marriage," *Modern Philology,* IX (April, 1912), 440-67.

LANGLOIS, CHARLES VICTOR, La Vie en France au moyen âge d'après quelques moralistes du temps, Paris, 1908.

———— La Vie en France au moyen âge de la fin du XIIe au milieu du XIVe siècle, Vol. II, *D'après des moralistes du temps,* Paris, 1925.

LATIMER, HUGH, Sermon on the Ploughers, 18 January, 1549, "English Reprint," ed. Edward Arber, No. II, London, 1869.

LATIMER, HUGH, Seven Sermons before Edward VI, on Each Friday in Lent, 1549, "English Reprint," ed. Edward Arber, No. XIII, London, 1869.

LECOMPTE, IRVILLE C., ed., Le Roman des romans, "Elliott Monographs in the Romance Languages and Literatures," No. XIV, Princeton, 1923.

LE MUISIT, GILLES, Poésies de Gilles li Muisis, ed. M. le baron Kervyn de Lettenhove, 2 vols., Louvain, 1882.

LENIENT, CHARLES, La Satire en France au moyen âge, Paris, 1893.

LOCHER, JACOB, Stultifera navis, original ed., Basle, 1497.

LORENS, FRIAR, Le Mireour du monde, ed. Felix Chavannes, Lausanne, 1845.

LYDGATE, JOHN, "The Daunce of Machabree," in Appendix to the *Fall of Princes*, ed. Dr. Henry Bergen, "E.E.T.S.," ext. ser., No. CXXIII, London, 1924.

—— Temple of Glas, "Duodecim abusiones," ed. J. Schick, Appendix II, p. 68, "E.E.T.S.," ext. ser., No. LX, London, 1891.

—— "Fabula duorum mercatorum," *Quellen und Forschungen zur Sprachgeschichte*, ed. Dr. Gustav Schleich, Vol. LXXXI-LXXXIII, Strassburg, 1897.

—— The Fall of Princes, ed. Dr. Henry Bergen, "E.E.T.S.," ext. ser., Nos. CXXI-CXXIV, London, 1924-27.

—— Horse, Sheep, and Goose, ed. Frederick J. Furnivall, "E.E.T.S.," ext. ser., No. XV, London, 1866. Reëdited 1905.

—— The Pilgrimage of the Life of Man, ed. Frederick J. Furnivall, "Roxburghe Club, Pubs.," Vol. CXLV, London, 1905.

LYNDSAY, SIR DAVID, Poetical Works, ed. David Laing, 3 vols., Edinburgh, 1879.

MACCRACKEN, HENRY NOBLE, ed., "The Lydgate Canon," *The Minor Poems of John Lydgate*, "E.E.T.S.," ext. ser., CVII, v-lviii, London, 1911.

MAGNUS, LEONARD A., ed., Respublica, "E.E.T.S.," ext. ser., No. XCIV, London, 1905.

MANLY, JOHN M., ed., Specimens of the Pre-Shaksperean Drama, 2 vols., Boston, 1897.

MATHEOLUS, Les Lamentations de Matheolus, ed. A.-G. van Hamel, "Bibliothèque de l'École des hautes études," Vol. I, Paris, 1892.

MEYER, FRITZ, Die Stände, ihr Leben und Treiben, dargestellt nach den altfranzösischen Artus- und Abenteuerromanen, Marburg, 1888.

MEYER, PAUL, ed., "L'Exemple du riche homme et du ladre," *Notices et extraits des manuscrits de la Bibliothèque Nationale et autres bibliothèques*, XXXIV, Part I, 168-69, Paris, 1841.

―――― ed., "Fragment d'un poème sur les états du monde," *Romania*, IV (April, 1875), 385-95.

―――― "L'Instruction de la vie mortelle par Jean Baudouin de Rosières-aux-Salines," *Romania*, XXXV (Oct., 1906), 531-54.

―――― "Le Mariage des neuf filles du diable," *Romania*, XXIX (April, 1900), 54-72.

―――― "Notice sur la *Bible des sept états du monde* de Geufroi de Paris," *Notices et extraits des manuscrits de la Bibliothèque Nationale et autres bibliothèques*, XXXIX, Part I, 255-322, Paris, 1909.

MILTON, JOHN, Poetical Works, ed. the Rev. H. C. Beeching, Oxford, 1925.

―――― The Prose Works, ed. J. A. St. John, 5 vols. (Bohn's Standard Library), London, 1878-87.

MONTAIGLON, ANATOLE DE, AND RAYNAUD, GASTON, eds., Des estats du siecle, *Recueil général et complet des fabliaux des XIIIe et XIVe siècles imprimés ou inédits*, 6 vols., II, 264-68, Paris, 1877.

MORE, SIR THOMAS, Utopia, trans. by Ralph Robynson, ed. George Sampson (Bohn Library), London, 1914.

MOREL-FATIO, ALFRED, ed., El Libro de Alexandre, Gesellschaft für romanische Literatur, Vol. X, Dresden, 1906.

MORRIS, RICHARD, ed., The Pricke of Conscience, Berlin, 1863.

MÜLDENER, WILHELM, ed., Die Zehn Gedichte des Walther von Lille genannt von Châtillon, Hanover, 1859.

MÜLLER, MAX, ed., The Hymns of the Rig-Veda, 2 vols., London, 1877. Trans. by Ralph T. H. Griffith, 2d ed., Benares, 1897.

MURRAY, JAMES A. H., ed., The Complaynt of Scotlande vyth ane Exortatione to the Thre Estaits to be Vigilante in the Deffens of Their Public Veil, "E.E.T.S.," ext. ser., No. XVII, London, 1872.

MUSTARD, WILFRED PIRT, Eclogues of Baptista Mantuanus, Baltimore, 1911.

NEILSON, WILLIAM ALLAN, "The Original of *The Complaynt of Scotlande*," *Journal of English and Germanic Philology*, I (Oct., 1897), 411-30.

NODIER, CHARLES, ed., Satyre menipée de la vertu du Catholicon d'Espagne et de la tenue des estats de Paris, 2 vols., Paris, 1824. Also ed. C. Labitte, Paris, 1841, and C. Reed, Paris, 1876.

PARIS, GASTON, "Le Roman de Fauvel," *Histoire littéraire de la France*, XXXII, 108-53, Paris, 1848.

PETIT DE JULLEVILLE, LOUIS, Histoire du théâtre en France. Réper- toire du théâtre comique en France au moyen âge, Paris, 1886.

PHILIPPE DE NOVARE, Les Quatre ages de l'homme, ed. Marcel de Fré- ville, "Société des anciens textes français," Paris, 1888.

PICOT, GEORGES, Histoire des États Généraux, 5 vols., 2d ed., Paris, 1888.

PLATO, The Republic, *Works*, 6 vols., Vol. II, trans. by Henry Davis, (Bohn's Classical Library), London, 1861.

POMPEN, FR. AURELIUS, The English Versions of the "Ship of Fools," London, 1925.

RAIMON DEL CORNET, "Aissi comensa la gesta de Fra Peyre Cardi- nal," ed. François Juste Marie Raynouard, *Lexique roman*, I, 464-73, Paris, 1838. (Wrongly attributed to Peire Cardinal.)

RAYNAUD, G., AND LEMAITRE, H., eds., Le Roman de Renard le con- trefait, 2 vols., Paris, 1914.

REED, A. W., Early Tudor Drama, London, 1926.

RENCLUS DE MOLLIENS, Roman de carité, ed. A.-G. van Hamel, "Bibliothèque de l'École des hautes études," Vol. LXI, Paris, 1885.

——— Roman de miserere, ed. A.-G. van Hamel, "Bibliothèque de l'École des hautes études," Vol. LXII, Paris, 1885.

RIVIERE, PIERRE, La Nef des folz du monde, photostatic reproduction of the Grenville copy in the British Museum, Paris, 1497.

ROBERT DE BLOIS, "L'Enseignement des princes," *Sämmtliche Werke*, ed. Dr. Jakob Ulrich, 3 vols. in 1, Vol. III, Berlin, 1889-95.

ROWLANDS, SAMUEL, The Complete Works, "Hunterian Club," Vols. II-IV, London, 1880.

ROY, WILLIAM, AND BARLOWE, JEROME, Rede Me and Be Not Wrothe, "English Reprint," ed. Edward Arber, No. XXVIII, London, 1871.

RUTEBEUF, Œuvres complètes, ed. Achille Jubinal, 3 vols., Paris, 1874-75.

SACHS, HANS, Dichtungen, ed. Karl Goedeke, "Deutsche Dichtungen des sechszehnten Jahrhunderts," 4 vols., Leipzig, 1870.

——— Dreizehn Fastnachtspiele aus den Jahren 1539-50 von Hans Sachs, ed. Edmund Goetze, "Neudrucke der Litteratur der XVI und XVII Jahrhunderts," No. XXXI, Halle, 1881.

SCHULTZ, JOHN RICHIE, "The Life of Alexander Barclay," *Journal of English and Germanic Philology*, XVIII (July, 1919), 360-68.

SEDGEFIELD, WALTER JOHN, ed., King Alfred's Old English Version of Boethius' "De consolatione philosophiae," Oxford, 1899.

SEIGNOBOS, CHARLES, The Feudal Régime, trans. by Earle W. Dow, New York, 1908.

SELDEN, JOHN, Table-talk, ed. Sir Frederick Pollock, London, 1927.

SHAKESPEARE, WILLIAM, Hamlet, ed. Horace Howard Furness, 20 vols., Vol. III, 5th ed., Philadelphia, 1877.

SIEPER, ERNST, Les Échecs amoureux, analyzed with quotations by Ernst Sieper in Litterarhistorische Forschungen, Vol. IX, Weimar, 1898.

SKEAT, REV. WALTER W., ed., The Vision of William Concerning Piers the Plowman, "E.E.T.S.," orig. ser., No. LIV, London, 1873.

SMITH, THOMAS, De republica Anglorum. The Maner of Government or Policie of the Realme of England, ed. L. Alston, from 1st (1583) ed., London, 1906.

SOILLOT, CHARLES, "Le Débat de félicité," described by Legrand d'Aussy, Notices et extraits des manuscrits de la Bibliothèque Nationale et autres bibliothèques, V, 542-45, Paris, 1798.

SOUTH, HELEN PENNOCK, ed., Proverbs of Alfred, New York, 1931.

SPENSER, EDMUND, The Complete Works in Verse and Prose, ed. the Rev. A. B. Grosart, 10 vols., London, 1882-84.

STAFFORD, WILLIAM, Compendious or Briefe Examination of Certayne Complaints of Divers of Our Countreymen in These Our Dayes, ed. Frederick J Furnivall, "New Shakespere Society," London, 1876. (Wrongly attributed to Stafford.)

STARKEY, THOMAS, England in the Reign of King Henry the Eighth, ed. J. Meadows Cowper, "E.E.T.S.," ext. ser., Nos. XII, XXXII, London, 1878.

STUBBS, PHILIP, Phillip Stubbes's Anatomy of the Abuses in England in Shakspere's Youth, ed. Frederick J. Furnivall, "New Shakespere Society," Series VI, No. 6, London, 1879.

THOMASSY, RAIMOND, Essai sur les écrits politiques de Christine de Pisan, Paris, 1838.

THORPE, BENJAMIN, ed., Analecta Anglo-Saxonica, 2d ed., London, 1846.

TRIGGS, OSCAR LOVELL, ed., Assembly of the Gods, "E.E.T.S." ext. ser., No. LXIX, London, 1896.

TUCKER, SAMUEL MARION, Verse-satire in England before the Renaissance, New York, 1908.

TUPPER, FREDERICK, Types of Society in Medieval Literature, New York, 1926.

VINTLER, HANS, Die Pluemen der Tugent, ed. Ignaz V. Zingerle, "Ältere tirolische Dichter," Vol. I, Innsbruck, 1874.

WRIGHT, THOMAS, ed., The Latin Poems Commonly Attributed to Walter Mapes, "Camden Society, Pubs.," No. XVI, London, 1841.

——— ed., Political Poems and Songs, Relating to English History, Composed during the Period from the Accession of Edward III to That of Richard II, "Great Britain Public Record Office. Rerum britannicarum medii aevi scriptores," No. XIV, 2 vols., London, 1859-61.

——— ed., The Political Songs of England, from the Reign of John to That of Edward II, "Camden Society, Pubs.," No. VI, London, 1839. Revised ed., Edinburgh, 1884.

——— and Halliwell, J. O., eds., Reliquiae antiquae, 2 vols., London, 1845.

WYCLIFF, JOHN, The English Works of Wyclif, Hitherto Unprinted, ed. F. D. Matthew, "E.E.T.S.," orig. ser., No. LXXIV, London, 1880.

——— Select English Works, ed. Thomas Arnold, 3 vols., Oxford, 1869-71.

INDEX